# The 1999 President's Recognition of Literary Excellence

**Sharon Derderian**
**&**
**Robert Lawrence**
**Editors**

Iliad Press, an imprint of Cader Publishing, Ltd.,
Sterling Heights, Michigan

**Distinctions of Excellence**

## *Acknowledgments*

We wish to thank Marsha Breaugh for her assistance in the preparation of the manuscript, production copy and logistics; Sharon Derderian for managing the judging; Machel Perala for proofing, editing, and art selection and layout.

Copyright © 1999 by Iliad Press, an imprint of Cader Publishing, Ltd. All rights reserved. No portion of this work may be reproduced, in whole or in part, without the prior written consent of the publisher and/or the author(s) of the individual works. Individual works copyright by author.

Iliad Press sponsors four literary competitions per year. Each competition presents awards to 100 winners. Iliad Press offers a $1,000 grand prize and 99 other cash and/or merchandise prizes. Non-winning entries which are believed to be of particular note and merit are awarded an Honorable Mention. No purchase or entry fee is required for the first two entries in the competition. Contest rules are subject to change without notice. All winners are selected by an independent panel of judges. Contests run continuously, four per year.

The address for Iliad Press is:

36923 Ryan Road
Sterling Heights, Michigan 48310
810-795-3635 Phone
810-795-9875 Fax
www.cader.com Web Site

*Printed and manufactured in the United States of America*

ISBN: 1-885206-70-4

Library of Congress Catalog Number: 99-067401

# Table of Contents

**Special Note:** The editors get frequent calls and letters about the typography and copy in our anthologies. Many of the contributors to *Distinctions of Excellence* take considerable "poetic license" with spelling, punctuation, grammar and word usage. Clear errors are corrected by the editors, however, many "errors" are returned to their original state by the authors. All selections are proofread and approved by the authors.

## *Chapter One*
## The 1999 President's Recognition of Literary Excellence

*Literary works of the 1999 President's Recognition of Literary Excellence awarded by The National Authors Registry* ...................................................... 1

## *Chapter Two*
## About the Author

*Biographies of selected authors and members of The National Authors Registry* ......................................................... 109

## Index

*Alphabetical Index by Author* ............................................................... i

**Distinctions of Excellence**

# Chapter One

## The 1999 President's Recognition of Literary Excellence

*Distinctions of Excellence*

## Daughter to Mother
*by Kristi Abbott - age 17*

Mother; the dawn of my life,
The sword to bear.
The crest of love,
The framework to the most important building-
Life.

You are a support-
A protector.
An importance beyond belief.
A blazing star-
Guidance.

You are the air I breathe,
Taken for granted,
But essential to my needs.
You are my mother-
Power.
Life.
Love.

## Peaceful Solitude
*by Janet M. Adams*

I gaze out,
   to see the twinkling,
      of the stars against
         the deepen blue sky,
It feels as though I
   could touch them,
As I long to join them,
   in there sparkle dance.
The ocean glisten
   to an unknown rhythm,
      but it is peaceful
         as a gentle rain.
The velvet like sand
   has footprints of where
      I had walked before, alone.
Where I rest,
   there are no doors,
      no other rooms.
Only four pillars with
   white sheer curtains,
      flowing with the
         hush-a-bye wind.
The room is a luminous
   white light,
      all around me.
The color is me.
Beside me is a pool,
   of water in which I touch,
      as it quenches my thirst,
         for life.

## Colorado
*by Laura Anna Akus*

I stared down an icy
slope
atop two shady legs-
your eyes were there
and mine were wide,
it's love I think we share.
Lust in trees above a river,
power plows and tired shivers-
A symphony of silence surrounds
the solitude of selfless souls,
it echoes down the hallways
like sounds off mountain walls.

## Too Small to Fight Back
*by Kathryn Alexander - age 15*

He watches from the corner
He's curled up in a ball
His whole body is trembling
   so innocent, so small

His eyes get wider
With every whip he sees
His poor little sister
Crying down on her knees

He wants it to stop
For his sister's own sake
He closes his eyes
How much more can she take?

His ears hear nothing
So he opens his eyes
Her body lay there
For his sister he cries

He know he is next
It's the same to every day
Too small to fight back
And nothing to say

## I Once Loved You
*by Amanda Allen - age 13*

I once loved you,
But then you broke my heart.
I felt hurt inside,
I'd thought we'd never part.

I once loved you,
Or at least I thought I did.
You did not love me back,
So my thoughts are where I hid.

I once loved you,
But now I love you no longer.
I found a loving man for me,
My feelings for him are much stronger.

I once loved you,
But now I'd like to say good-bye.
I don't think I'll ever see you again.
I know I won't even try.

## A Worthy Battlefield
*by Jude M. Allen*

This path I have forged, it
Glistens in this morn's snow,
Warning me perhaps to
   Dare not go.

I know all its nuances--and
I've seen what it can do,
Others have fallen for it
Rewarded by black and blue.

Waiting patiently for the sun to
Warm the smile from its face,
I pour a little salt in its wounds
I won't be fooled by its grace.

Treading slowly its length now
My goal firmly set in sight,
Like a high wire artist, I
Grasp my precarious flight.

A warrior, I have traversed
This mine field unscathed,
Secured the day's mail
I am fearless, unfazed.

*Distinctions of Excellence*

## The Ghost
*by Opal L. Allen*

When I was twelve,
   I saw the specter appear
   and take shape
   across the street.

She emerged from the hazy twilight
   resolute in her entry,
   though a vapor at first.

Ascending up from the ground,
   she ripened
   into a soft, brilliant fog,

And in an instant our lives connected,
   spirits embracing.
   my sighted eyes seeing
   what her sightless ones directed.

She allowed me to witness a splendid legless dance.
   euphoric in her fleeting performance,
   she extended exquisitely luminous arms
   through the disturbed ether,

As if daring my eyes to deny
   the insight just given to my soul.

Then she was gone,
   Vanishing sublimely into the warm night.

## Ice Blue
*by Sindy Allen - age 18*

Why did you have to go away so soon?
I did love you more then anyone else did
You were my sun and also my moon
You slammed the door and tightened the lid
I feel I can not go on any longer
My days are feeling very short and numbered
What you did to me could be no wronger
I think I am going to forever slumber

I will get over it I know I really will
You will never hurt me again anymore
All I have to do is take a tiny pill
In a few moments I will be nevermore
Down, Down I go into a ice blue sea
Where I will no longer or will ever be

## Abandonment
*by Monique Adam*

Since you knew
the pain of my childhood--
since you knew
the tears in my heart--
how did you dare
lie and betray my wounds?
Your right was to leave
not to abandon--
mine was the truth
not a failed courage.

## Black Cat
*by Sri Alluri - age 10*

I am a cute little black cat who loves
   Halloween.
I wonder if I will ever get a new home.
I hear all of the happy children
   trick-or-treating.
I see them walking past me.
I want to dress up and go
   trick-or-treating, too.
I am a cute little black cat who loves
   Halloween.

I pretend I am a trick-or-treater with
   a bag full of candy in my hand.
I feel happy that Halloween is here
   again.
I touch the big, yellow harvest moon.
I worry that Halloween won't come
   again until next year.
I cry when Halloween is finally over.
I am a cute little black cat who loves
   Halloween.

I understand that Halloween won't
   last forever.
I say that Halloween should be
   everyday!
I dream that a little child will find me
   and take me home.
I try to tell myself that it will happen
   very soon.
I hope that I will one day be
   able to celebrate Halloween.
I am a cute little black cat who loves
   Halloween.

## Out of The Darkness
*by Monica Alvarez - age 15*

Love is the light piercing the darkness of the night.
Hope is the road leading the way from terror's hold.
The sky, so vast and blue, is where I look
when I don't know what to do.
The stars, burning so beautifully bright,
are where I look when no hope is in sight.
Freedom is the tender release from relentless power,
in a world so sweet, yet so sour.
Suddenly, I discover a known revelation;
Embracing the concept that failure is my own
strange creation:
Life is long, yet life is short.
Just play the game, and be a good sport.
My life is the price.  This earth is my court.
Now, I go forward.  Now, I step forth.
To take each task for all I'm worth.

## Untitled
*by Charles Amerise - age 20*

Seated upon Mt. Zion
    crowned gold majestic throne
dancing idols distribute wealth
sexual religions visit ancient traditions
    palace where the prayer cries
        devil eye in a silent lie
sovereign realms in cassina vision
    mystic table of ages
        days long rituals of chant
seeking wisdom bright hallucination
    spinning sacred star
        leading out of exile
evening hill dwellers shake violently
    celebrating their escape off the island
death crucified centuries
    slow distant lair
hidden mirror mazes
    delivering pierced knowledge
mystic network of Greek legends
old poets with the golden key
    words rebellious against society
        words that break chains & set us free
silently heeded in chemical awareness
world under intense fry
    heavens allowed entrance
        I can her the angels sigh

## Dream
*by Sherry L. Amnotte - age 18*

Carry me off to a far away place,
let me be happy,
dream good dreams.
Get rid of the evil lurking in my head.
Will I ever be able to close my eyes?
Stop haunting me. Stop taunting me.
Let me be safe and free,
you can't stay in control of me. I'll
get hold of you soon.
Carry me off to a happy place, where
all dreams are good.
Take me away from this evil place,
that makes me scared and alone.
I'll say good-bye to evil and
hello to happiness soon.

## Daughter to Father
*by Rachel Anderson - age 14*

I talked to my dad again last night
I told him what I felt is
    wrong and right.

I said:
I know it's hard
just hang on tight
you must not fail
you've got to fight.

I know it's not fair that you're the one
try not to think of what's to come.

It's right to be frustrated
it's right to be mad
it's wrong to give up
don't give up dad.

This disease can't be cured
but can be delayed
your head is stirred
don't be afraid.

We need you with us
take some time to mend
it's a long struggle to face
that someday will end.

## Broken
*by Delores A. Andren*

One day I was happy and so unaware;
I guess I saw the signs, and yet I didn't care.

The all of a sudden it happened, like a bolt from the blue!
My world came crashing down at me, before I even knew!

Everywhere I looked it was darkness, behind and ahead;
So much I couldn't understand, and I wished I were dead.

My closet companions were: Confusion, Grief and Fear.
How I needed Someone, Someone near and dear!

Then Jesus came, and heard the outpouring from my heart!
And He put together the pieces, that once were all apart!

Now my life is whole again, and better than before;
Because Jesus opened my eyes, and now I see much more.

Sometimes we need discipline, and God must bring us low,
Before we will come to Him, and let everything else go.

God can't reach us when our spirits are floating high,
Cause we build a wall of self-sufficiency around us in the sky.

He needs to humble us so we'll give the honor to whom it's due;
So I thank Him for my gray skies: now I appreciate the blue!

## What's on Your Mind?
*by Jennie Andrzejewski - age 15*

Where will I be in 20 years? What will I be doing? What will I look like? Will I remember my childhood? Will I remember chasing you in my backyard? Will I remember spending Friday or Saturday nights at your house watching movies like Dumbo and laughing hysterically at your funny jokes? Will I remember the mouse that ran across the floor? Will I remember the huge smile and how being ecstatically childishly happy really felt? Will I remember my first day of school? Will I still be as quiet as then or as loud as now? Will I remember being scared of high school? Will I remember graduation and the parties that follow? Will I ever see you after I move away to college and on to the rest of my life? What will college be like anyway? Will it be scary? Will it be fun? Will it be hard? Will it be worth it? Will all my friends and classmates live to see graduation? Will we all be fortunate enough to avoid life's disasters? Are they really disasters or just God's plan? Why did she have to die? Will I see her in heaven? Is there really heaven or is it just a comfort for humans? Where did humans come from? Where did plants and animals come from? Where did the earth come from? Did everything come from God? Is he really real? How do I know? How do I know I'm not believing in hopelessness? Where did the bible come from? Who wrote it? Is his hair really that color green? Why do we celebrate Christmas? Why is it so commercialized today? Why can't people just live simple? Why do people worry about things they have no control over? Why did the chicken cross the road? What is pain? Where does it come from? How does my brain work? Why does it think? How does it think? Does it think or do I think? Or am I my brain? Why can't I meet a celebrity? Why aren't I a celebrity? Why don't I have a star on Hollywood Boulevard? Why are my nails pink? Or are they really pink? Do I just know that color as pink? Is it really something else? Do dogs really only see black and white? Then do kangaroos only see blue and green? Do humans see all the possible colors? How do we know? How do we know we don't just see shades of certain colors? Is there life out there? Are we really alone? Who cares? Why don't wishes on stars and birthday candles come true? Will there ever be a World War Three? Will the world last to the year 2001? Or is the end coming? How do we know? What does it feel like to fly? Are angels real? Do they really bowl during thunderstorms? Why does rain make us sleepy? Why do we have to wake up at certain times? What is time? Why does time matter? Will time matter in twenty years? Why didn't it when I was little? Why should it ever? Why do we wish to be big when we are little? Why do we wish do be little when we are big? Why can't we go back in time? Why don't we remember being born? Why don't we remember how dumb those people sounded talking to us in those squeaking voices? Why didn't they see we were laughing at them? Why can't we be so laid back and open minded when we grow up? Why do we have to learn? Why do we have to graduate? Why do we have to do something with our lives? Why do I have to be something in twenty years? What will I be? Will any of this stuff matter any more? .....

## Inconsistent Love
*by Amanda Annarino - age 20*

Your love for me dithers like undulating
    waves in the sea.
It hurriedly comes in with the waves and
    prematurely goes out with the current.
In and out -
        here and gone.
My heart is the quagmire sand on the ever-
    changing sea shore.
Each time your futile love for me
    inconsistently washes in with the waves,
You erroneously take a piece of me away with
    you in the current - You take my all and give none.
But I can't stop your love from coming into
    my body and soul and soaking up my
    adulation for you -
Just like I can't stop the waves from coming
    onto the shore and washing away the sand.
Breaking my heart is an instinctual act
    for you,
It's like the instinct of the waves to come
    ashore.
And just like the waves are driven
    by the moon,
I am driven by my love for you.
The moon controls the undulating waves
    the way you undeservingly control
    my heart.

## I Thought I Knew
*by Sara Anstoetter - age 14*

    I thought I knew,
but in the end, I wondered, "Who are you."
    It happened that day, so long ago,
the feelings, I could never let go.
    Someone so close and so dear,
became a stranger I did fear.
    A marriage that I thought was blessed,
turned out to be disappointment to the rest.
    Gentle and sweet, and full of life,
we both knew he took a piece of my life.
    "Why," I said, I never really knew,
how life would change without the two of you.
    Movies and overnights were part of our routine,
sodas and ice cream became the extreme.
    Expressions of laughter and giggles were glued to our hearts,
we did not know, we soon would part.
    All those memories, so kind and sweet,
were washed away like a river so deep.
    The saddened looks became so apparent,
I withdrew and became incoherent.
    If one day, he only knew,
how much he broke my heart in two.
    Does the pain ever subside,
who really knows, for it can hide.
    And maybe someday we'll cross paths.
and learn to forgive all in the past.
    These were the memories so bright and so dear,
and I know in my heart they'll always be clear.
    As for now, this was the past,
a connection that will forever last.

## Untitled
*by Dana Aritonovich*

Like a dream
  it came
  and vanished
Like the wind
  so fleeting
  and gone
Like my breath—
  he stole,
  it's gone.

## Wave Lengths
*by Gloria Paterson*

Strong magnetism moving me toward you
Inner conflict pulling me away
Close contact body language making me stay
Standing there too close for comfort
Wanting to move but glued to the spot
Connection but maybe not
Reaching touching inner thought
Saying to myself God I'm caught

## Peace Of Mind
*by Barbara Ashbeck*

From an unknown source
I hear a sound.
Filling my soul,
With music, profound.
From a distant shore,
I feel a breeze.
Lifting my spirits,
Like wind in the trees.
From a far away beacon,
I see a light.
Flooding my senses,
Like stars do the night.
And I am at peace,
Within and without.
Destiny has touched me,
And freed me from doubt!

## Lost Life
*by Jillann Auferoth*

The light in my eyes
    That is you
The warmth in my heart
    That is you
You will always be my baby
    You will always be in my heart
You are special and precious
    But most of all you are mine
You cannot be taken away
    You will not be erased
I will forever keep your memory
    And never stop loving you!

## Untitled
*by Jorden M. Baase*

Don't we look silly
Flying in the air
With our crystal glasses up
The only purpose of this excursion
Is to get from here to there

Don't we look silly
The luxury in which we dwell
To save our comfortable positions
And our status within our peers
From our crumbs the starved would swell

## Awakening
*by Lynn E. Bachhuber - age 14*

There, among mosses, and glistening river stones, rounded,
and smoothed by the grains in the sand, a cocked upward willow
branch spreads its broad shadows, casting upon intense reds
and purples from behind the horizon.
I lean back against the broad base of a willow, stroking my fingers
through my hair as I make rings in the water with my big toe.
My arms are bent, and my hands behind my head.
I gazed upon one leaf plodding in motions with the ripples.
I crouch further feeling my eyelids becoming heavier with each
inhalation I take, and a brisk shiver runs through my arms causing the
tips of my fingers to twitch.
My palms are cold, and my feet are almost numb.
The brittle strands of the slender grasses wave, like miniature waves in
the ocean in the slightest breeze.
I sit up and lift my head and my spine to grow taller with each exhalation.
My eyes remain closed and my lids relaxed and slightly parted, as I
practice full-lung breathing, nostrils wide open and my tongue relaxed.
I lift my eyelids, noticing the changes within me.
My palms softly touch togethers as I lift from my inside out to my fingers,
out to my toes, out past the top of my head, truly awakening now
to this new moment, and to my new self.
'Nomosta'

## A Friend for Life
*by Stephanie Baer - age 16*

We started out as nothing but strangers
Not knowing where the road would end or even start

Our love has grown over a period of time
I've become yours and you've become mine

Where the road has taken us, I'm not real sure
It is a place in life where I'll need no more
A place of perfection with all of my needs

A place I can find your love and support
And absolute happiness of any sort

You've shown me a love I've never known
An impossible feeling that has constantly grown

We've shared some good and even some bad
I've made you happy and certainly mad

In my heart it's all worth while
As you look my way and brightly smile

From the beginning till the very end
I'll be your companion and very best friend.

## Look for the Rainbow
*by Renee Bagley - age 20*

Sometimes life is hard to bear
   there is darkness everywhere,
   and problems pile at the foot of my door,
   like stacks of leaves forevermore.
The light of day seems so far away
   my thoughts temporarily stuck in yesterday.
My mind is racing as fast as a drum -
   I pray and pray, but words fail to come.
   Then the sun begins to rise
   and hope for the day ahead fills with my eyes.
   A rainbow sets across the sky
     restoring faith and hope within my life.

## Precious
*by Kari Baker - age 20*

Life is so precious, why do we treat is as though
We have a million?
Guns
Drugs
Sex
Alcohol
That's all we think about.
What happened to the wonder years?
Times when we all got along.
Guns kill the innocent to protect the corrupt.
Drugs rule the younger, and kill their brain cells.
I see their dying day soon.
Sex is out of hand,
Babies are born to every woman's hands
Father you ask, he's not around
He left long ago leaving behind, aids to the mother
And no life for the other.
Alcohol makes you crazy, then you start to feel hazy.
Climb in the car, turn the key
Crash! Boom! You got lucky.
The family in the other car is dead because
You were too stupid to use your head.
What's wrong with the world today?
Children can't even go out to play,
A bad guy comes and takes them away.
Something needs to happen, something has to be done.
Oh God! Please help everyone.

## Think Nothing Less Than Beautiful
*by Brianna Baldwin - age 16*

   Thoughts melting away, tears falling, heart-broken wondering aimlessly. Walking around in shadow believing in you, love is made of silk, that can easily be torn.
   Sunshine creeps into the nothingness that's feared. Darkness is in all existence, exploiting every promise hidden. True happiness is ceased, our time is leaving.
   Petals fall from bleeding roses, angels sing with a light-hearted tune, and the sun is forever set. Mist covers our eyes so the honor of trust won't die away. But the thought of you is on my mind.
   If we are surrounded in beauty, someday we will become what we see, believe in the love that was never given to us, so we THINK NOTHING LESS THAN BEAUTIFUL.

## A Toast to the Bride and Groom
*by Hope Banks, R.A.*

May you always remember
just how full your hearts are today
May you always sing
in perfect two-part harmony.
May you always dance
that great man-woman waltz
of friendship, love and passion.
May you always grow
both together and individually
from one firmly planted root.
May you always find
support from one another
when you spread your wings
in the flight of life.
May you always hold dear
the security and peace
of knowing you will always
have each other for comfort
at each hard day's end.
May you always share
the many and true blessings of marriage.

## Confession
*by Nancy Eseberre Barraza - age 15*

As he kneels before his priest,
a dark screen keeps his identity.
He repents of all his sins,
while he prays for forgiveness and lenity.
Gently he murmurs his words,
shamefully listing all of his trespasses.
"Father, I say curse words and have not
attended Sunday masses".

Yet he neglects to mention what it is he curses,
and just how late it is that he sleeps on Sundays.
"Father, I have used God's name in vain and
disobeyed my parents in so many ways".

But he does not say how,
nor in which ways God's name was used
or how toward his parents he raises his voice and his arm.
"Father, I have stolen and have given false testimony
only to cause harm".

Yet he neglects to mention what he stole and from who,
nor what he has lied about and who his lies have trampled on.
"Father, I have coveted others' property and have wished death to
others
Knowing I'll regret it once they are gone".

But the boy's sins were not forgiven,
for his words were not sincere.
He did not care what course his acts had taken
and thought he could hide it all with one false tear.

The one thing the boy should have remembered from the start,
is that God cannot only read the mind.
God can also read the heart.

## To Whom It May Concern: A Confession
*by Graceann Barrett - age 14*

Evil thoughts ran through my mind
but they soon turned to fear.
His silent eyes looked up at us,
Distorted, pale and clear.

His skin was cold and white,
with a wicked, pasty glow.
The crimson color surrounded him,
and stained the gentle snow.

We didn't even know him,
But he had a familiar glare.
His deep set eyes, and scruffy chin,
and dark brown, thinning hair.

His presence gave us danger,
Only he had known our lie.
It truly was an accident,
We didn't know he'd die.

And so that fateful day,
had turned our lives to crime.
We knew they'd take us away,
And kill us, in good time.

but we would not go down that way,
we still had our pride.
We shall not be taken and killed,
neither shall we run and hide.

Our decision has been made,
we know what we must do.
Since we have taken another's life,
Ours must be taken too.

## Forever
*by Joe Barsic - age 16*

I'll hold you forever

until we both grow old

and kiss you again,

as the sky darkens, and the world dies

we'd die together

in each other's arms

together forever

if you wouldn't mind

## Lies
*by Mandy Baugh - age 14*

Why is this happening?
Why are things going wrong?
This isn't supposed to happen
to someone like me.

You tell me one thing,
but then I hear another.
What am I to believe?
What do you want from me?

Why must you make things difficult?
It doesn't have to be this way.
Maybe it's me,
but I think it's you.

Are you taking advantage of me?
Are you really me friend,
or do you just pretend to be?
I only wish I knew.

So here I am,
sitting here crying from confusion.
And it's all your fault.
Why must you tell me these lies?

## The Bum
*by David Bauzo*

The emptiness inside of me
Is not for lack of soul
I do not have a piece of meat
Nor rice to fill my bowl.

I do not run the city streets
I can not walk the beat,
The energy I would not have
If food I've none to eat.

I live beneath your bridges
I sleep under a stair
It keeps away the scorching sun
And warms the midnight air.

You stare at me and walk away
When hands outstretched I seek
A little bit of charity
For food I've none to eat.

If fate would come into our lives
And change our destiny
Then I would have a job today
And you would be as me.

## Mr. Sandman
*by Bette Bavington*

Who is this mythical man
Who drops his sand
with a wave of his hand?
We slip, it seems, as if by a magical wand
off into dreamland.
Our eyelids try to stay open,
so a glimpse of him we might see;
but by the time we count to three,
we must be honest and tell to thee:
down our eyelids glide as we go off into sleep,
our breathing going deep.
The next morning we know that into our room he did creep
To stand by the head of our bed
After mom turned out the light
and said good-night.
For little sleepers in our eyes he has left behind.
We believe, even though we have not seen this mythical man that comes each night,
that he is flinging his sand into droopy eyes.
He was dubbed....as we rubbed....our eyes....
Mr. Sandman as he travels through the skies.
Sleep.
Sleep.
Sleep.

## My Ideas On How To Be A Friend
*by Lilli M. Baxter*

I'm not much on physolophy or creed.
There are many books I know that I should read.
But this I know and ever will contend,
There's just one way that you can be a friend.
Where there's a want, the time to act is now.
Don't hesitate and try to figure out somehow,
Another road that fellow could have found
To help himself, instead be honor bound.

If you've a smile to give a strength to lend,
And if you show your light around the bend,
Then all your plodding and your useless strife.
Has made a glorious blessing of your life.

To find an almost perfect way to live —
Is find someone in need, and then please give.

## The Cycle of Life: A Modern Love Story
*by Frank Bayer*

We slid down an icy hill in Detroit last winter.
An accident, they termed it.
Never had this happen to me before, my brother the driver of the car said.
Nothing anyone can do about an accident, they said. That is what accident means.

The other car hit us right on the passenger's door, just where I was sitting.
She came at us fast,
Out of control on the slick streets.
The impact was overwhelming. I could not breathe for quite a while.

The doctors found only two broken ribs and some bruises.
They will hurt only for a month or two,
And then you will be over it. Nothing to worry about.
That impact could easily have been fatal, the officer wrote in his report.

That was almost a year ago, fading now from memory.
I hurt only when I cough or laugh aloud,
And have resumed many of my former activities,
Having received sympathy from all who heard.

I wish the rest of my life were as simple as that accident.
I could say that we were going too fast for conditions,
There was nothing we could do about it and that it will hurt only for a month or two.
Maybe soon I will be able to breathe again.

## Over the Fence
*by Jennifer Beauregard - age 15*

He will wake up every morning
To a duller sunshine.
He will eat every morning
To a tasteless breakfast.
He will bathe himself in water
That could be so much warmer.
And he dresses in the clothes he
Hates the most.
And when he walks out the front door,
And his eyes wander
Over the fence,
He is flabbergasted,
To the beauty and riches
Of his snobbish neighbor
Who bothers not to say hello
Or good-morning
But to point his nose to the
Clouds and walk back in his mansion
In his fine clothes and expensive shoes
And when he walks into his palace
(This not known by the boy)
He cries.
For he wishes he could have it
As good as his neighbor
Over the fence.

## Falling In Love
*by Danielle M. Beck - age 14*

It may have been the look in your blue eyes,
It may have been the tone of your deep voice,
It may have been the warmth of your gentle kiss,
And it May have been the shape of your perfect
 Smile. But I knew that I was falling in love.

It may have been the way you held me,
It may have been the way you said you loved me,
It may have been all the things you gave me,
And it may have been the way that your cared for
Me so much. But I knew that I was falling in love.

It may have been that dream when you came to me,
It may have been the music that you played for me,
It may have been the things you said to me,
And it may have been the time you spent with me.
 But I knew. I knew I was falling in love

## Sunset
*by Nikole E. Beltz*

The sky is filled with color now.
Blues, Golds, Pinks, Purples, and Green.
The sunset on this day is
the prettiest I have ever seen.

I wish I could describe the way
the sky and sun relate.
It's as if the two are dressing up
to go on a forbidden date.

Perhaps the sun will meet the
moon on a secret rendezvous
and the sky will meet a cloud.
It would be very interesting
as either one or both is
always within my view.

I see the sun step behind
a mountain now to rest
its weary rays.
I know it will rise again
at the beginning of each day.

*Distinctions of Excellence*

## The Dancing Fire
*by Gala Berezkin - age 15*

Ashes dancing in the wind,
Let them scratch your eyes.
Watch the hopeless hope,
Drifting through the lies.

Reach to grasp the colors
Of the dancing fire.
Let the smoke of passion
Blind you with desire.

Slip into the heart
Of the fire dance.
Let the hands of heat
Put you in a trance.

Rise above the fumes,
Spin among the ashes,
Dance with the wind,
As all burns and crashes.

## I Can't
*by Shelly Berggren - age 17*

I open my eyes,
and stare into the darkness.
I look around and see nothing,
I never see anything.

I no longer enjoy beauty,
or the green grass or blue sky.
I am alone in this darkness,
forever.

When you wake up the birds sing,
the sun shines.
When I wake up the birds cry,
the sun does not rise.

When you colour a picture,
you pick the nice vibrant colours.
When I colour a picture,
I use whatever.

You learn to tie your shoes,
or ride your bike.
I have someone tie my shoes,
and I can't ride a bike.

All these things you do,
I can't.
I live in an eternal darkness.
I'm blind.

## In the Darkness...
*by Krystal A. Berrard - age 13*

In the darkness I sit
alone

In the darkness I feel the
breeze of my loneliness

In the darkness I reminisce
on all of the good times we've
shared

In the darkness the tears
of my loneliness burns my
skin

In the darkness I cry alone

## Young Souls With Lost Directions
*by Shelby Y. Blackmon*

Our young souls are wandering around with lost directions. These young souls are falling prey to this demonic hunter. This demonic hunter is captivating the minds of the young. The hunter now searching and seeking young souls. He knows these young souls minds are undeveloped.

Our young souls are out there lost with no biblical directions. The hunter knows many are just out there lost in this wilderness. He comes to the young carrying the white stuff to destroy their minds. It's so much easier to use his trickery bag. This bag contains the greatest temptations, lust, covet, and distinction.

Our young souls are being captivated by this demonic spirit. This demonic hunter lies to our young. Teaching these young souls to lust and covet. Telling them death is just a state of being and hell is the place to be. Training them to have lusting eyes for sex, telling them do it today, for you may not see tomorrow. Telling them to sin today - repent tomorrow - don't worry because God is so forgiving.

These young souls are lost with no directions and their to high to know whose really leading them astray. These young souls are not equipped to attack this demonic spirit. He knows that minds are still undeveloped and he's destroying before their minds mature. These young souls are making the demonic hunter a happy man. Young souls still wandering around out here in this demonic wilderness without the proper weapon. Young souls lost with no directions and no moral values.

This demonic hunter is destroying our young souls.

## Winter Snows Birthday & Mine
*by Lindsey Nicole Blackwell - age 5*

The ground is all covered in gleaming white snow like the frosting on my birthday cake.
The trees all bent hanging beautiful candles lit from their limbs? Showing off sparkling fires of
color.
Like the candles burning on my birthday cake.
I think of spring to come as I blow them out.
Soon the snow will melt; our birthdays soon will be over as we taste the cake.
We soon will taste the joy of spring and we'll have to wait another year to celebrate!

## Freedom Soul
*by Jesse Blaine - age 15*

I feel the terror, I see the pain.
I hear the souls cry for help.
I know the day is near.
"Soon, soon," I say, "We shall all be free."
Our sufferings shall be lifted and our fears washed away.
On that day, our mortal chains shall be unlocked,
And our souls will be free of torture.
But on that day, the fury of hell shall be released.
Hell itself shall consume those of us that
Are doomed to permanent pain.
But I fear not, for I look for the day in which
I shall no longer be mortally bound.
I wait for the time when my soul
Shall be free of pain, torture, and suffering.
I hope for that day to come, so that I
May leave this mortal hell, and finally,
Rest in peace.

## Forget—Me—Nots
*by Patricia Payzant Blake*

After the winter cold
Nature is ready to unfold
Her Forest lore
With sounds and sights
of spring.

May is the time
To see, natural flora
in its prime.
Breathe fresh morning air
and unwind.
soothe the soul
and clear the mind.

To hear exotic birds sing
And the forest ring
With melodious strains
And ethereal refrains.

Along Memory Lane,
Unique wild flowers grow.
They show their faces
In hidden places.

Beside a babbling brook
Forget—me—nots find a nook
To wet their feet
And mirror the blue sky.

Trailing arbutus on the site
Offers fragrance of delight
Stylish lady slippers in mass,
Tip toe on the grass.

I will not forget
The glorious days in May
When all of nature joins in
A symphony of Spring.

## Classic Titanic
*by Amanda Blanks - age 15*

Through cold wind and waters, you didn't give up.
The boat sank, like a rock in a cup.
You held on to Rose, like a brave man would.
Though you were terrified, you did all that you could.
The band played on, like nothing was wrong.
So people pretended, and sang the sad song.
Some wore life jackets, some wore expensive coats.
Some went overboard, and some got boats.
You were alone, 'til Rose came back for you.
She was on her way down, when she jumped to class two.
You both met halfway, when you asked her why.
She said "I jump you jump, remember"?, turning to
watch a woman and her kids walk by.
Glad she came back, you kissed her on the head.
With a terrified look in your eyes, you hoped neither of you would be dead.
The next thing you knew, you were running back and forth.
To the highest spot, it was pointing straight up north.
The boat sank all the way down, it took both of you too.
Rose was up first, you on the other hand were turning quite blue.
You got her out of the water, onto a piece from the boat.
She stayed warmer than you, because she was on a float.
She promised you she wouldn't give up.
You fell asleep but never woke up.
Almost one hundred years later, she's still alive.
Telling her story, and making everyone cry.

## Scars
*by Antonie Bodley - age 16*

So many years ago, it seems, I cut my flesh for you.
Took it in my hands, held it tight with all the frustration you'd caused me.
Pressed it to my virgin skin and felt the dullness of it's tip.
With all that bled within, I drew my blood to pull out the pain in my heart.
The crimson blood flowing over my fingers
Felt so warm and welcoming, compared to your touch.
I slashed again and again to feel the pain of your absence.
Now I try to leak my pain with tears, not blood.
I see my scars and wish I had cried before.
The pain still remains no matter how hard I try.
The scars just remind me of you and the pain you left me with.
They're everywhere I look.
My eyes can never escape the rosy sweet scars on my fresh skin.
If only I could heal.
Heal my heart, heal my soul.
Forget your wounds
And leak all my pain with tears.
Wash it away, scrub away the scars.

## Diana
*by Louise Boileau-Labrie*

In the abbey of Westminster, eight young soldiers carry the body of Princess Diana.
They carry her, holding each other's shoulder tight, like brothers and soldiers of the crown.
They feel great emotions, deep sadness, sorrows and love for her.
Their grief is enormous, but they must accomplish their duty,
Taking her in her last resting place, where her soul will rest in peace in heaven.

They remember with great emotions her fabulous wedding in this great church.
A lady with a shy expression, a lady in a shining white dress sharing her joy.
The people recognize her sincerity and saw her as a Princess of legends.
She gave birth to two sons, William and Henry, who share her dedication and kindness.
Over the years, Princess Diana visited poor people and people rejected because of sickness.
She lead enormous charity campaigns, raising millions for those who suffer
For so many children who suffer from cancer, and wars.
She helps all those who came to her, with charity, compassion, and love.
And her work and legacy touch all the people in the world for her greatness and simplicity.
In India, she met Mother Theresa, who is a living symbol of charity in Christ.
She share her project, care and love for those who are in despair, despite of her problems.
They lived in the same century, Diana in the western world, Mother Theresa in India.

Then, one shiny day, the sky opens, and a tall white and bright Angel appeared from heaven.
In the greatness and love of God, he lifted up the soul of Lady Diana to heaven,
She just died at the hospital in Paris, after a tragic car accident.
By her death, all the people in the world are mourning, in shock and disbelief.
Following the fourth of her death, at the eve of her funeral,
An Angel descends from heaven, with his golden wings, he takes the soul of Mother Theresa.
the Angel carries to heaven those who defends charity and love of Christ,
With his golden hand of love, he brings them to paradise.
We do not know our last hour, but we understand with wisdom
The greatness of God that descend upon us.

# Gavin
*by Denise Borders - age 14*

Gavin, Gavin, that's his name,
he's showered with good looks, talent and fame.
If I could touch him, only once,
no matter what the consequence.
I love him so much, more than anyone else.
I'll love him forever, 'til my age is 112th.
His voice, his guitar, everything he does,
touches me so deeply, like warm soft fuzz.
He's all that and everything from head to toe
if I will ever meet him, I wish I could know?
Yes, I saw him in concert, but it wasn't enough!
I want to shake hands, it will be tough,
I would have to meet him, for my dream to be true,
all I wanted to say, was, "Gavin, I love you."

# On the Swing of Life
*by Sota Kurylo*

When on the swing of life we happily
swing together, our hears pound with joy.

Our mind gets strong.
Our thoughts grow the wings.
We spin the silver string that forever
binds us.

We dance together. Together we sing.

Once in a while we pause, to catch the breath;
and again, with a passionate speed we sway.

On the swing of life we rock the cloudless sky;
against the merciless time.

We have no time, nor desire to think,
that at any moment something may get
wrong.
But the clock, the shameless clock
slows the pendulum of the life's swing.

# Survivors—Torch Bearers
*by Luan Borquist*

The flame of life has flickered
from the day that you first heard,
The verdict from the doctor, and
he spoke that dreaded word.
Through denial, fear, and anguish,
the flame it burned quite low,
But you clung to hope and
life, you would not let it go.
Persevering in your treatment
still uncertain of your fate.
This enemy called cancer
has put your life on wait.
But you're standing here today,
living proof that we can win.
The torch you carry now,
Symbol of the life within,.
Survivors of the battle,
each day your ranks increase.
May the flames of life grow brighter,
soon may the battle cease.

# Untitled
*by Jen Boverhof - age 14*

I will always love you
I wish you loved me too
But you already have someone in your life
But I still wish I could be your wife
I picture you and me holding each other like there is no
tomorrow
Over the summer when I can't see you I will be in deep sorrow
The times I spent watching you was the times I was glad
The times I wish I could see you but couldn't I was sad
When I see you buy your locker everyday
There are many things I want to say
But yet there are many things I can't explain
The things I want to say but suddenly can't, drive me insane
I wish you could understand how I feel
You don't realize that the feelings are real
When school got out I thought my life would fall apart
There was a great deal of emptiness in my heart
I soon realized I could live without you
but it would be hard to do
I'm now learning how to live without you
And yes it is very hard to do
You were the one light in my eye
You made my heart flutter like a butterfly
Your love is one thing I can't seem to win
And that is one thing I can't be in
I hated knowing that I had to say good-bye
But good bye doesn't have to mean forever

# My Grandmother's Eyes
*by Virginia Bowden - age 16*

She lies there almost motionless in her bed,
Forgetting the past.
She forgets where she is.
She begs for help I can not give.
Her eyes seem empty and lifeless,
Unlike they used to.
They are no longer the eyes of the person I once knew,
They are now the eyes of the dead, the drugged and the pained
They no longer remind me of warm summer days,
And the long talks about nothing.
They no longer show her happiness
That she shared with the world and me.
She sees things only the dying sees:
Relatives among the dead, and staircases to the Heavens.
Her eyes tell her everyone is tricking her.
I long for those old eyes of happiness,
She shared with the world and me,
They were what told me I was me.

# Dawn And The Peace-Keepers
*by Mary Frances Boyle*

A ghost gray dawn drifts in
lifting the shroud from scenes
hidden by the mercies of the night.

Muted by darkness,
the wailing of these years of war
resumes at first light
no longer shrilling a country's death throes
but keening ceaselessly
for sons lost,
    daughters raped,
        childhoods stolen.

Limbs lost to land mines cry mutely
from stumps of arms and legs.
Windows of burned-out buildings gape
in search of their owners.
Mass graves disgorge genocide
hidden in their trenches.

Young peace keepers
innocent of war,
cannot go home
clear eyed as they left,
for carnage witnessed,
like second hand smoke,
contaminates.

## Loved One
*by Dave Boyza - age 17*

They crash back and forth, night falls as I gaze upon the rushing waters of the beautiful ocean. Sitting with my only true love, the only that's always there. I can't help but behold the beauty she has as the minutes tick by. Oh, but can't this last forever, as we look each other in the eyes, past everything real to either of us. I take her in my arms as I know this must not go on. Nothing this amazing could ever last. As we near the end of our long lasting tunnel, that which we call love.

She's gone. Emptiness, Darkness, Loneliness, why must she go, I ask the same question everyone has pondered for years. Why? I have let her go with no attempts to bring her back to my beautiful world. The sun continues to rise, the roses smell as sweet but all seems lost without my loved one.

I ask only of one thing, that I may never see those luscious blue eyes again, or if I may then may they be happy and happy forever with or without the memories of our love.

## Synaesthetic Perception
*by Louise M. Bradbury*

The contiguous environment calls us
to submit a metamorphosis.
A tantalizing transcendence of normal perception
A sublime consiqueneousness that
alleviates our separateness.

It acquaints us and arouses us to all the
sonorous sounds around us.
Those screeches, growls, groans, and chirps -
tastes of the other.
That consonance of life assaults us a totality.
But it depends on our receptivity.

That allusion to the loss of illusion
of everything being puzzle pieces
a mere blip of chance.
In the universe of chess pieces
scattered across the board
by a fickle and mindless God.

## In Your Hands
*by Kandi Brandenburg - age 16*

Cup your hands together,
what do you see?
You hold my heart in your hands.
Hold it tight, be gentle.
Wait, don't move you'll drop it,
it will break. HELP ME,
you held my heart in your hands
and you let go, you broke it.
Now look inside, see how much I cared for you,
see the love we could've had?
You meant so much to me,
so little I can see I meant to you.
Please pick up the remains,
my heart is now like a puzzle,
and only you can piece it back together.
Make my heart whole again,
let me put it back in your precious hands
one more time.
Please hold on tight, don't let go,
cause in your hands is the only place
I want it to be.

## Meadow
*by Rachel E. Brandt - age 13*

The meadow full of flowers.

The bee are buzzing.

The grass sways back and forth.

The wind slowly blows though the grass.

We love to watch from the porch in the summer.

I could sit there for the hours just watching nature.

From sun rise to sunset.

The sun rise so beautiful.

The sun set swirled with purples and reds.

## Tears and Suffering
*by Jessica Braun - age 14*

The tears have stopped coming
The wetness on my face
Has dried up and gone

The ache is still there
Deep in my heart
As a hard remembrance
Of the suffering that went on

The tears may not be there
You may not know
The suffering going on
Deep in my heart below

You may not see it
My suffering below
I'm covered in a mask
Of smiles and joy
But it is still there

I don't know how long
Or when it will go
The suffering I feel
Deep in my heart below

## The Wall
*by R. Gene Brenciforte*

They came to see the blackened wall.
Long marble blocks of granite pall.
So black and stark neath azure sky,
As thousands kneel to pray, to weep, decry.
They came to touch the blackened wall.
Long marble blocks, politely scrawled.
So black and stark neath cloudless sky,
 as throngs embark to gaze with wistful eyes.
They came to hear that blackened wall
 chant the echoed throes of duty's call.
So black and stark beneath a clear blue sky,
Above the crowd a tarnished eagle swoops, then flies on high.
They came to grasp, to touch, to feel.
With fervent hope the wounds would heal.
From a long black wall whose epitaph is spread,
Amongst the brave, the fallen, the bivouacked dead.

*Distinctions of Excellence*

## Love In It's Defining
*by Sarah Brickman - age 18*

Love is a feeling of jitters inside you
Bubbling up inside
Love is a warmth, love is a glow
That doesn't come and go
It plants it's roots in fertile soil
It's like a food that will not spoil
Never ending, never hurtful
Never ever regretful
You treat the one you love
With loyalty and respect
You do not yell, you do not scream
You work together as a team
To get things done...yes, it takes two
Understanding, kind and sweet
It's like a late night treat
It tempts you and it lures you
To it, even now
You don't know why
You don't know how
When it draws you close
Listen for the warning
Make sure it's love
And not what's gone in the morning
Love stays, love remains
It will never leave
It stands beside you...good or bad
When you're happy, when you're sad
It's there in the morning and in the afternoon
It's still there at midnight...
Waiting just for you

## Hopeless Dreams
*by Crystal Brooke - age 15*

I am sitting here in the pale moonlight
Looking for you among the stars above
Waiting for your face to come into sight
Hoping to once again feel your sweet love
I know you are somewhere in the sky
Keeping a very watchful eye on me
Still wishing I could have said good - bye
Remembering the time we spent at the sea
You lit my world with the light of the sun
Even the darkest night was bright as day
Only with you did I ever have fun
I miss you so much in every way
Sitting under the big sky I'm alone
Now dreaming hopelessly all on my own

## Asbury
*by Shelly Bridges - age 16*

God has sent me a piece of heaven,
Something I've wanted since I was seven.
Asbury is part of me
I love what I see,
There's so much love,
Sent down from above.
So many open hearts,
Giving everyone,that walks in, a new start.
To a better life.
When there seems to be so much strife,
Pastor Bob, Mrs, Sally, Becca, Ryan with everyone else offers a hand.
The one that tells you they understand.
A hug or a pat on the back to show they care.
Never again will I be the only one to bare
The load that holds me in the dirt.
When I get hurt,
There's hands to help me back on my feet.
To me, it's a fleet
That everyone can help so much,
Cause they all have a love touch.
Yes, everyone can work as a team.
Don't misunderstand, this is no dream.
It's all true
They will help you and me though.
Thank you Asbury Family for all that may come from Jesus and you!!!!!!

"Thanks Asbury United Methodist Church for allowing me in!!!

## Longings of the Spirit
*by Elladean Brigham*

It is a frosty January day, with sky so blue it pierces my soul, and sun so bright it promises Spring. I have sought solace here before, beside this lake tucked in the city. Its tree-lined shores fade the townhouses into silhouettes. The sun glimmers off the lake's frozen surface, thick enough only to support the fragile gulls. The wind rustles high in the tree tops, where birds call to one another. A distant barking dog, the rumble of traffic, an occasional jogger - these are the reminders of civilization.

I walk along the lake letting my mind roam free, feeling united with God and nature, then I notice flotsam gathered at the banks - a tennis ball, a liquor bottle. It is, after all, a lake built by man in a city of men. Trash baskets dot the walking path. How often I have longed for the purity of a simple life with nature, without the cluttering flotsam of humanity - the worries and cares of stressful relationships. Yet, I realize that I am part of mankind, living in a civilization filled with flotsam. Although I am sometimes tempted to throw it all in the trash baskets along the way, I know there is value in the beauty which shines through the relationships, even as the beauty of the lake, though not pristine, shines through the cluttered city.

## The Beach at Night
*by Basil Briguglio, Jr.*

It was Labor Day weekend, and I was alone. I was spending the weekend at my Grandmother's summer home in Long Beach, NY. That Saturday night, I decided to go for a late night walk on the beach. The houses were dark as I made my way down the narrow street. Eventually, I arrived at the wooden ramp that lead over the grassy dunes to the beach itself. It was then that I first became aware of the uniqueness of the beach at night.

I stepped out onto the soft sand, careful not to kick sand into my shoes. The beach was completely dark; the lights placed along the wooden boundary between the houses and beach provided little illumination. As I walked down closer to the water, the sand became firm, showing where the tide had been. I stopped here to take in my surroundings.

It was if I had stepped into another world. All my senses were stimulated the way they never were during the day. A cool, brisk breeze blew against my face, enabling me to smell and taste the brine in the air. The sight of the ship lights on the horizon and the stars above me, the sound of the waves, white with foam, crashing onto the shore all contributed to the uniqueness of the experience. It touched something deep in my soul. Perhaps it was because I had chosen to come to the beach at this time totally of my own volition, an expression of personal freedom. I've always enjoyed the beach, but coming to the beach at night was like nothing I've ever felt.

It's great to walk on the beach any time of day, and there is no better time than the beach at night.

## Untitled
*by Matthew Brooks*

What can I do,
To let you know I have feelings for you,
I doubt it's love, I don't know what it is, theres something about you, that makes goose
 bumps on my skin

What is it that makes me feel what I feel,
Is it my heart, no that can't be, I thought it was steel,
Even a million roses in full bloom,
Couldn't hold a candle next to you,

It's like walking on a beach, the warm sand upon my feet,
Is it you I seek, are you the one person that will make my life complete,
It's like a river gently flowing,
And the wind softly blowing,

I'm lost within myself,
Thinking of you and no body else,
It's like the breeze barely caressing a field of grain,
And the mountains whispering your name,

What I feel I can't describe,
But what I feel I cannot hide,
Like the unforgiving night,
I await your shinning light.

## Nothing, Then...
*by Christopher Brown*

(Nothing, then...)
　　The pounding of the drum;
　　　　(the candle is lit,)
　　　　　　the rhythm...
　　It is strong,
　　　　(and the candle,
it is long,
　　but the flame burns so quick!)

It is piercing my ears; their chant,
Like the slow hum of waking silence,
　　　　(And hotter then the heating presence,
　　　　　　is hotter than it's red appearance!)
I scream,
　　I am burned!
　　　　I am real,
　　and real was the feeling,
　　　　for my head is now reeling.

(Waxy drips the candle hot,
　　　　doubtful now you think it's not!)
It is pain; I saw it coming...
　　　　from a safe distance, but,
　　　　　　alas,
　　　　　　　　my eyes,
　　　　they failed me in my darkest hour.

(Gentle winds, cool across the skin of one's back,
The flame... it flickers weak,
　　　　as red becomes grey,
　　　　　　and grey becomes black!)
Whose icy grasp it is that... frightening me in the darkness?

## My Treasure
*by Jackie Brown*

Love has come to live in my heart.
Not just any love, but your love.
One that satisfies the awakening
Within me.

Full of sincerity and tenderness,
I say farewell to
Old used words, old used feelings, obsolete
In our new union of soul.

These feelings of depth and substance:
I embrace as a treasure,
Receive as a tribute,
Accept as a blessings,
And appreciate as a gift.

Thankful ever for your wisdom,
With all your faithful feelings, ever true.

When thoughts of you are in my heart,
I whisper your name, once more, to say,
I love you.
'Tis then, I feel the warm
　　spiritual bond we have.....renewed.

*Distinctions of Excellence*

## Autumn Rhythms
*by Mary Cathleen Brown*

The peaceful songs of summertide
Subdued by autumn rhythms
Ushered in by swift-rushing breezes
With rustic and brute forces

Muses, graces, fair goddesses all
Guard over the hot springs, cool brooks
Grassy knolls, woodland groves and shady orchards
Dance till their colors become the soil

From an oasis of beauty and peace
She rises gleaming from sparkling water
Quivering with rapture from the bathing
In the shaded elegance of gentle light

The baptismal ritual performed to assure
Kind benevolence from the spirit world
That wards off the dangers
Of the diseases of fall
That impede her healing

Biophilic sensitivity seeking
The beauty of growing things
That lives in autumn rhythms

## Yellow Rose
*by Katie Burnazaki - age 17*

Bright glimmer stars
That light the dark evening sky
From every sundown to every sunrise
And ocean so blue
And sand so soft
In the purence of rain they sparkle.
A yellow rose
Among weeds and tall grass
Living still, striving for love
It grows tall
Even though the weeds are pulling it down
It grows taller and taller
To see the blue sky
And to feel the light summer rain.
I feel like that rose
And maybe I'm blind
But sometimes people are weeds
And they're pulling me down
And I want to grow
To feel the light rain
And touch the blue sky.

## The Cage
*by Terrea Bryant - age 17*

You wonder why the caged bird sings.
She longs to tell her story,
but she knows that no one will listen to
or believe what she has to say.
So she tells it in a language
that is foreign to people unlike her.
She drowns in a sea of depression and insecurity
as thoughts of confusion float around her head.
She tells her story through her music,
and longs to find a reflection of herself;
someone who has been where she has been,
someone who understands her song, someone like her.
But still, her reality is the cage.
As she remains there singing her melody,
she wears her pain like a scar that she covers with a smile,
her hope like a cloak that keeps her warm,
and her pride like a shield for protection.
As expression of mirth sits upon his face,
she continues her melody that no one understands
in the cage that is her reality.

## Untitled
*by Nikki Buccigross - age 14*

As your head turned the other way,
My tears sank deeper into my heart.
And when your eyes closed for the last time,
My body became surrounded by heat, like burning embers.

When you said those words I had been waiting for so long,
I should've been the happiest one alive.
But when I didn't take the keys last night,
I made the biggest mistake of my life.

And when I saw you lying there, hurt and dying,
I heard you take that last breath and whisper those three words.

And all the tears that had fallen behind my eyes,
soaking my heart,
Came streaming from my cheeks,
soaking your face with my tears of sorrow.

And when you looked at me, that last time,
Still with that same sparkle in your eyes, I couldn't speak.
And when I finally said, "I love you too",
You couldn't hear me any more.

And as I sat there holding you,
for the first and last time,
I realized that know matter how young or old,
You can always love.

But it takes a strong and willing heart, to not give in and say, "ok"
Because you never know if that will be the last thing they'll ever hear.

## the nobody blues
*by Keith Michael Buckley - age 18*

Id wake up in pieces in the midst of concrete fog
id think long and hard about alpine angels drifting through the donovan illuminations in mid carson july
and stagger irreplaceable though invisible shivers of inspiration and madness
    id rather be insane then jealous
I would sip brandy through thin lips and laces and watch cigarette embers collapsing in
heaves and convulsions between the backs of friends and lovers
- devise intricate plans for passion and fear in my sleep, watch the new york city
skyscrapers defeat the mountains hands down for nothing more than poetic justice and a
chance at saying that they know what love is all about, cast shadows longer than jesus ever could
one day you'd see my hands on the shelves (between brautigan and burroughs) and
wonder what its like to hear your name on the radio or memorize the noise the ocean
makes when its by itself spinning outward into fragments and abstractions and
plummeting endlessly into the great depths of our belief in something less complicated than innocence
    kerouac flashbacks and pool hall hangovers
I would remake it all, the infinite amounts of spaces and blank parentheses and
stalemated words condensed to one thousandth of the lives that breath them. id be right
set in my ways and id lay on my back in the gun metal grey of idle Tuesday mornings
sucking the blood life from the concrete and spit bent stagnant December air.
old men softly rolling into oblivion and retired junkies playing god to the ill-intended
complex and gentle words grabbed from the soft side of runaway promises and mice and
men gone astray beneath the naivety of middle american cathedrals (tear shattering
expressions on pencil tipped faces and pretty plastic angel wings set the stage for a grand
scale idea.)

all this and no spare change
too many mountains between myself and me

## *A Little Chain of Gold*
*by Jamie L. Bulluck - age 13*

A little chain of gold
Holds hundreds of memories
That you and I made together along time ago
I remember when you held me
When you held my hand tight
My heart thought all this was right
A little chain of gold
Brings it all back
When you gave it to me on that cold, winter day
I remember the pendant breaking
and you fixing it over night
I remember playing basketball with you
On that windy, March day
A little chain of gold
Takes me back to you
Your eyes, your smile, and your personality
I remember playing volleyball
And looking around for you I didn't have to look far
Cause there you were standing watching me.
A little chain of gold
Reminds me of leaving you
The letter I wrote the heartache it caused
I remember regretting the look on your face
I remember forgetting the way we used to be
I find myself crying recall all this
A little chain of gold

## *Spring's Wedding*
*by Wanda J. Burnside*

Aha, first appears the lovely crocus flower girls,
    Then the daffodils like beautiful maidens,
Ushered in by the gallant tulips like earls,
    Now the Wedding begins.

Behold, the flowing faded white gown,
    Of the glimmering spinster snow,
That fraily covers the frozen ground,
    There's a sheer veil of late Autumn leaves below.

Suddenly, at the brilliant and splendid appearance of,
    The piercing warmth of the radiant sun in the sky,
Winter gives way to this springtime love,
    Like the father of a blushing bride.

Hark! The robins and birds so jubilantly sings,
    At the warm embracing and kisses of the sun,
The season of rejuvenate and replenishing Spring,
    Has now so gloriously begun!

Soon raindrops will be scattered all around,
    Like confetti and rice tossed at glowing newly weds,
It will nourish the fertile ground,
    Let there be flourishing days ahead!

## *Perplexing*
*by Liza Burns - age 15*

I don't know if I can talk to him.
I'm scared of what he'll think.

He knows he can talk to me openly,
    and sometimes he does,
But there are other times I know he's holding back.

Everyone thinks I know him so well,
and sometimes I think I do too...

But there are times he'll do something totally unexpected

Even for him

And I question whether I know him at all.

## Healing
*by Sue Capuano*

Some days are worse than others, then its hard getting out of bed
when I hear that familiar laughter as it echoes in my head.
And if I close my eyes for long enough I can believe the pain will end.
I guess what it all comes down to is that I really miss my friend.

There's a place that I can run to when laughter's hard to find.
I can see you in my pictures, but I can feel you in my mind.
And I can go there when I'm hurting and sit with you awhile
I guess what it all comes down to is that I really miss your smile.

The pain never fully goes away, it only changes in its growth.
I know about miracles and tragedies,
I know you were a perfect blend of both.
And if I close my eyes and listen I can hear you laugh again,
I guess all that I'm saying is that I really miss my friend.

When I lay awake at night it seems that Autumn's getting colder,
for when I talked you lent your ear to me,
when I cried you lent your shoulder.
And after the hugs are given and the tears have fallen dry,
what it has come down to is that we never said goodbye.

I've had my share of hard times,
and it's seemed the sorrows would not subside,
but the hardest thing I've done so far was kneeling at your side.
And I can touch a memory if I'm reaching for a friend,
but what I really want is to hear you laugh again.

I'll always have my memories and the good times that we've shared.
I've been blessed by having known you,
graced by knowing that you cared.
And there can be some peace in closure, some healing in the end,
but what it always will come down to is that
we'll always miss our friend.

## Behind Every Dark Sky
*by Sue Lueck Carlson*

As the darkness fills the sky
And the sun disappears
Your heart is filled with sadness
And your eyes are filled with tears.

The memories of your loved one
And the nights that you shared
Are replaced with emptiness
And the thought of how he cared.

Did you ever stop and wonder
Just what the darkness means?
God doesn't want to hurt us
Put your faith in the unseen

Put your trust in God above
And in time you will see
That behind every dark sky
There's a soul flying free.

On the other side of life
The time is standing still
All pain and sadness leave us
For this is our Father's will.

Your loved one is at peace now
So dry your tears away
Because before you know it
You will have a sunny day.

## Heracles' Fifth Labour
*by John T. Carney*

Poseidon loosed a bull along the Achelous,
That raged across the fields of King Augeias.

The Sun God wheeled aloft on his fiery arch,
As the new moon glistened at the threshold of night,
Whose gems and treasures,
Lay enfolded in her darksome cloak.

Just as fair Luna donned her glistening mantle,
Heracles glimpsed the bull on the horizon,
Eyes flaring like stars.

Heracles grabbed it by the horns.
At once, the bull became a rushing river,
Raging through the soiled fields and pastures,
Inspiring Mother Earth to blessings of fertility.

The moon was her scepter of plenty,
Reaping a harvest of stars across the darkening sky.

They sowed themselves in the bosom of Earth,
Becoming children of the fields,
Plants and trees that followed the whims of the winds.

Heracles seemed at once limned betwixt Earth and Sky.

## Loves Me...
*by Kaye Carpenter*

I had a notable moment
 one time
When all the colors stood
 out bold
When rainbows danced around
 sun water
When the positive ions in the air
 carried me
Like an angel through the breeze
 of feelings

I had a notable moment
 one time
When life breathed with me or
 with out
When the decision was easy, no
 more fight
When my clothes matched shoes
 just right
Then danced around like daisies
 flower bed

I had a notable moment
 one time
Perhaps while thinking of you
 seems so
And just then it emerged that it
 was over
 Or not.

## Daddy's A,B,C's
*by Barbara Carver*

**D** addy does his duty, at home and work, diligently.
**A** always accountable and also full of good advice.
**D** oesn't desire to do wrong.
**D** oes desire to do right.
**Y** ields to God first.
 ields to others second.
 ields to self last ( being true to self ).
'
**S** ense of saving for family.

**A** lways around and able.
**B** lessed by God and others to be a blessing.
**C** ares. Corrects carefully with good conscience.
'
**S** ense of saving for self and for stormy days.

 Then dear Daddy is a Daddy near and dear.

## In the Mist
*by Gregory A. Case*

April rains spank concrete, flesh
and tongue.
Loudly she chirps on emulating
Lost birds sheltered in shrouded nests.

The calm in her saturated touch
is misunderstood.
Holding media as a cover
I pray to April rain's demise.
Now heaven takes my handkerchief
Gone.
She desists.

Bright light and shadows buzz tulips while
Envisioning themselves as honeybees.
Light stings the garden while shadows hide sense.
Old fragrance, like April's feared thunder,
Needs to dash the air with sweeter gifts.
Gold cup of tulip and jade thrones of earth
Together hold no joy to me.
Only owning sets me up.

Higher on a peak, something for me.
Eternity gathers in the mist
April's clouds will join my marathon
Victory races in the hand of pain
Every storm washes away
what I want.  Muddy puddles shimmer
Needs.


## If There Are Gardens In Heaven
*by Sheila Cave*

If there are gardens in Heaven,
  we know where you'd be,
    tilling the land, and sowing the seeds.
    The seeds of love into each plant you'd grow,
    for the gift of green thumb, how well you do know.

If there are gardens in Heaven,
  we know we'd find you there,
    God's great light upon you and wind sweeping your hair.
    The smell of lilacs, lilies, sweet william, and mums,
    orchards of pincherries, apples, and plums.

If there are gardens in Heaven, Oh Lord
  it is easy to see,
    why you'd choose this gardener to be one with Thee.
    Hand down to him his rake, shovel, and plow,
    for he'll be eager to start with all his know-how.

So, if there are gardens in Heaven, Dear Lord up above,
  take care of our gardener, and give him our love.


## Trinkets of Love
*by Lottie Cellini*

Heaven took mama in 84.  We looked at each other then opened the door.
Trinkets of love throughout the years, my sisters and I broke into tears.
Lockets of hair and baby barrettes and all the trinkets that she had kept.
Handmade jewelry for her birthday and bright colored cards that we had made.
Mama why'd you have to go so soon.  So much life for you to live, so much love for you to give, mama why'd you have to go.
Trinkets of love you kept through the years, and wiping away all of our tears.  Millions of memories flash through my mind.  So many memories in so little time.
Mama gave more than she could give, but oh what a life that she had lived.
A mother, a teacher, and so much more, a guardian angel at our door.
Trinkets of love throughout the years and teaching us how to face our fears.
No more flowers on mother's day, or the joy of watching our children play.
Goodbye mama we miss you so, and it's just too hard to let you go.
Trinkets of love throughout the years and wiping away all of our tears.
Trinkets of love you kept through the years and teaching us how to face our fears.


## Creeping, Silent, Time
*by Debra Anne Chapman*

Peek into the images of time,
to watch the silver moon.
Old and crumbled it flashes,
like a signal from the past.
Dainty wings of shadowed objects,
those of what is gone and no-more.
Around the curving windmill,
the time spins and twists forward,
to the present arch of now.
Distinct lines and colored dreams,
searching for the secret tunnel,
leading to the dimness of future flickers.
Images go past the wall,
the tunnel narrows at the end of vastness,
then curves to forever stretch.
The images of time continue,
until the mind no more comprehends.
The gone, the now, the unknown,
all are forms of overlapping,
creeping, silent, time.


## Sunset Pride
*by Melanie Chen - age 13*

As I walked upon the calming beach
My feet surrounded by sand,
The whole world was out of reach
I felt alone upon the land.

My imagination captured in time
I sunk my feet into the earth,
The only presence was that of mine
To take in all nature's worth.

Ahead in the distance, above the sea
All nature's beauty it bore,
The beautiful sunset ahead of me
Nothing like it had I seen before.

It was shining full of pure delight
Its calmness surely quite rare,
Loyally providing all its light
What beauty this ball did bear.

Politely saying its friendly goodnights
The sun crept down to the sea,
Darkness overpowers with all its rights
As the cold night was set free.


## Empty Wish
*by Dasha Gena Cherepanov - age 17*

Scared sole
and helpless mind
give no hope
and no desire
to fulfill the hopes
and dreams
of the child
that sleeps within.

Fool in love with
mind unclear.
Urge of lust
brush by so near.
But the hands
don't have the might,
to reach out
to touch the knight.

## Freedom
*by Jean E. Chesham*

You must run, my proud beauty (thy speed is as light),
Run till thy fleet limbs have ta'en thee from sight.
Free will thy course be, and freer thy trail,
To run with the wind in thy wild-flying tail.
The far hills are calling to those who are free,
To wander, and now they will take thee from me.
My beauty, I tremble to loosen thy rein
For then I will ne'er see that bright eye again.

The gloss of thy coat will ne'er shine 'neath my hand;
No more by my side shall my proud beauty stand.
The eagle will challenge my loved one to race,
But only to find he is lost in thy pace.
And never again will my heart swell with pride
As it does when I thrill to your earth-hungry stride.
Oh, sad is this hour when we two must part,
For wherever, thou goest, thou takest my heart.

Come, come my proud wild one, tho' as tame as art not,
And know that tho' gone, thou art never forgot.
Once more, ah, just once more, come with me to see
The cool glad and stream where we two loved to be.
And now I must loose thee — but, no, I cannot,
Whatever thy fate be, I make it my lot.
Together we'll wander, beneath the broad sky —
Together we'll live, and together we'll die.

## Make the Future Full and Bright
*by Chris Childers*

The future is one empty place.
It could be filled with your fat little face.
That is why god invented you.
He was tired of just seeing skies of blue.
He is the most perfect thing known on Earth.
One mistake, when he gave humans their birth.
Correcting the problem, he sent his only son.
Jesus died for us all, dying was not fun.
Live your life as pleasant as you can.
Show god that you are a good image of man.
This will cause the future to be full and bright.
No limit to where humans can go, into the twilight.

## Suicide is Dishonorable
*by Chris Childers*

A Life has just been created, it is already on its own.
Most of the excited relatives, have others on the nearest phone.
As this being gets older, it is mandatory to head to school.
The critter learns a lot, it hangs out with friends to be cool.
The grades and years are sliding by, just like the wind.
Suddenly the critter got arrested, which broke the trend.
Shoplifting, was the charge, now the critter was in trouble.
His Father, grounded him, jolting the critter, bursting his bubble.
After 2 weeks it made him meaner then ever.
He bullied other Children, took their money, thought he was clever.
The teachers always told him, to turn on his brain.
He wouldn't listen, with a motorcycle, he played chicken with a train.
It came time to graduate, which he did.
Five minutes later, he died, while still acting like a kid.
He grabbed the motorcycle, the train is the direction he did head.
He slammed the side of a box car, and was pronounced dead.
This Plaque hangs here, where he died, for other children to read.
Please, Life is important, Get help when you are in need.
This Plaque was paid for by People who did Care.
We would have helped, but he just gave a mean stare.
If you are thinking of Suicide, Death is Forever.
We know you hurt, but letting us help, would be clever.
This Person that died, Graduated with an A+ in Suicide.
He had a Diploma with him, but he was the dumbest person alive.
Suicide does not make anyone a hero at all.
People that tackle their problems head on, stand Tall.
Stop and think, Please turn on that Brain.
Think your Problems through, don't throw yourself in front of a train.

## Hologram
*by Roxana Chikezie - age 16*

Allusions create a mood

Connecting one source to another

Making visions in one's mind

## Ripples
*by Mary Chilkotowsky*

Your every step creates a ripple,
ever slowly spreading wide.
Each action a contributor
to the ever growing tide.
Yet each day we wake up walking,
rushing about so heedlessly,
consumed in our own person,
in our separate misery.
Each one has a special mission,
our search resumed inside our heads.
The answers always hidden,
in the frantic haste of dread.
I will look up toward my ripple,
my footsteps I will guide.
I will strive to meet the effort,
control my portion of the tide.
Walking in His wisdom,
leaving judgment at His door.
I will use the hands He's given me,
to reach out to the poor.
I will use my words to gentle
the rising tide of hate.
I will show to all His image,
waiting patient at the gate.
Each new failing put behind me,
in the knowledge I have grown,
in the shadow of His glory,
I will make my home.

## Growing Up
*by Carol Chilson*

Passion and humor
rock the boat of maturity.
Endless sadness.
Ocean of tears
Suffering.
Necessity or illusions?
Joy must conquer these...
or we are lost in seas of
anguish and despair.

## Love
*by Jessica Christenson - age 12*

Some think love is a flower that blooms only beauty

Some think love is a stream that always grows into something bigger than when it started

Some think love is a seed that grows only if you treat it right

Some think love is like a knife through the heart because once you love it will never be the same

Some think love means forever because once you love it can't be forgot

Some think love is a rainbow because there's no such thing as an imperfect rainbow

Some think love is one of the thirsts of life

Some think love is a stone that is not easily broken

Some think love is like a puppy loyal and sweet

Some think love is like a child that needs constant attention

I think love is like a pearl because it'll last forever if treated right, it's precious, and is treasured forever

*Distinctions of Excellence*

## My Fantasy
*by Sophia Chung - age 15*

Whenever I begin a dream,
about you and me,
I never get it right,
no matter how many times I try.
Cause besides me,
your immaculate features,
shadow my surreal face out.
I think of you all day,
in my reveries,
hoping that one morn' that they will come true
and I'll be able to talk to you.

When you happen to glimpse my way,
to myself I happen to pray,
that you'll look at me and stare for awhile,
but then I remember that I'm not worth your perfect smile.

Sometimes I picture you walking with me,
but reality kicks in and I see you walking with her.
One day my fantasy will become actuality,
and we will be together, just you and me.

## Stencils of the Mind
*by Bill Cibbarelli*

Songs written in ink and pencil
Dreams traced
The guiding stencil of the mind.
Portraits in words
Images in lyrical phrases
Praising love's heart
Dark and joyous phases described.
Dirges surging from the quill
Anger or depression inscribed
Commentaries fill the indigo well.
The state of life, the world
Scrolling for gentleness
Captured in an embrace
Or a nose
Buried in golden silk strands.
Scented hair framing alabaster skin
The subtle perfection in a breeze
Tossing tresses and summer dresses
With a freedom only felt.
The songs of the pen
Illusions of the senses
Spreading across parchment
Wherein speech is the sensation
Of the written word in the mind
Songs scripted in ink
A stencil defining the soul.

## Depression
*by Christine Clark*

Going through the ups and downs, never knowing what to expect. The confusion building up inside, reminds me of the pain I hide. Hoping I don't hit a bottom, but I still feel like I have to hide. I run and run, but it always finds me. The depression burning inside, making it hard for me to survive. I try harder and harder to keep the pain inside, so I don't have to cry. The depression so strong causes me to go insane, not knowing what to do. I feel so lonely, and helpless like a little child. Instead of all the run around, I wish someone could tell me where I'm bound. With all my hopes, and dreams I wish this insanity would leave me be!

## Dragoness
*by Jesse D. Clark*

Young dragoness fly proud, and strong, unfettered
By mere earthy bounds. Immortal heart
Immoral eye did bend the time, and
Force us part. Feared gossamer wings
I yearned to soil. Unforgiven
Evil thing that lustfilled boy.
I worshipped thee misunderstood
Young dragon lady. Hard life the hood.
Youth nurtured this dark mortal hound.
Young dragoness immortal bound.
Chased, yet chaste your wings grew strong.
Now gone from me except in song.
In memories past I tarry there
To taste thy breath, to touch fine hair.
Ungentle touch, and fiery kiss
My passion spurned by dragoness.
Scarred first this tired heart
Young talons raked. To bind
With love a fools mistake.
Cruel master fate.

## Man's Responsibility
*by Burt Cleaveland*

GOD, send YOUR love, please send it fast
Throughout the world, please make it last
And we will hold the words YOU say
Until the earth will pass away
Please stop the wars and hatred too
And we will say we love YOU true

And GOD just turned with moistened eye
My soul, HIS thought, began to cry
For HE had sent HIS love before
And man had simply closed the door

"I gave to you the power to do
That thing you long for to be true
So in your heart the world will stand
To live or die throughout the land
The love I gave you in the past
Must grow within your heart to last"

## One Way Ends
*by Sabrena Clemens*

Love as we know it
Will diminish shortly after
Respect begins dying
While anger replaces laughter
The plateau soon ends
If there's no change in pace
A reject approaching the finish line
Shall we evaporate our mistakes?

## More Precious Than Gold
*by Stephenie - age 17*

Love is more precious than gold,
It is a thing to tightly hold,
It is shy and it is bold.

Love is more beautiful than a gem,
It is required of both you and him,
It is there whether you're fat or thin.

Love is more fragile than a flower,
It is something that has lots of power,
It is a feeling that over all will tower.

Love is more thrilling than a lover's look
It is something you don't find in a book,
It is a thing where there's many a crook.

Love is a lot lighter than air,
It is a feeling that always will be there,
It is something with others you share.

Love is still more precious than gold,
It is something to tightly hold,
It remains shy and it is always bold.

## Party of Four
*by Donald Cochran*

A wife's love stalled;
A husband who couldn't stand it at all;
A passionless knock beside the head;
A rock she didn't see coming - a wish she was dead!

A stranger stole the love or his life;
A thought, perhaps she deserved a knife;
A blow so hard she sell unconscious;
A wake up call - a hospital haunted!

A husband more strange than the strangest stranger;
A stranger who was her loving angel;
A secret love as obvious as the stars we all see;
A passion that just wouldn't let well enough be!

A young lady dies - the stranger cries;
A wife celebrates her reasons why.
A couple half gone, a couple half free,
A crowd once four remains three!

## She
*by Shae Coghlan - age 15*

She listens
She knows
The pain that I own.
I listen
I know
The pain that she owns.
We walk together
Always and Forever.
Never to part.
Never to fight.
She's always there.
I'll always care.
For our pain separate
Is too much to bear.

## Sprightliness
*by Sarah Marie Colao*

Tenderhearted caresses moonlight kisses
Haven where we enfold.
The outside world is disremembered.
Clandestine gatherings.
Fervor of a new sensation.
Torridness tears through me like never before.
Engaging in passionate webs of concupiscence.
Mesmerizing me falling under your domination.
Feelings of a delirious phenomenon.
Veteran of love.
Amorous paramour.
Enticement.
Astonished by your materialization.
Overwhelmed by your zealousness.
Perfume that stays with me tonight.
I take with me.
I feel you are by my side.
Night of binding.
Illusions of you.
Wanting to keep you forever.
Poising over me so glorious to view with the naked eye.
Watching your masterful ways.
Feeling your back the strong being that overpowers me.
Never taking my eyes off you, I feel at ease with you so free and natural.
Delectation flows from your voice.
Hands that touch my face that trail along me I am the muse and you are the artisan who sculpts
me.
Deep-felt feelings that were too intense for words.
Night of devotion.

## Confusion
*by Jolene Collins - age 15*

Confusion
Lost in an endless river of words,
A chaos of feelings that surge
Through every part of your body.
Never changing what they do,
Only changing how you feel,
Where you go and what road you take,
Confusion
A time when everything
And nothing makes sense.
A time of pure happiness
And utter sadness,
When everything means
Nothing to every one and no one.
Confusion
A race towards the finish
Where the slowest person wins.
A fight between white and black
When everything is gray.
An unknown, constantly there place
That is always visited, but never seen.
Confusion
When you find your friends
Amongst the strangers,
And the wisest person
Is he who knoweth not.
When the best advice you find
Comes in riddles from a circus clown.
Confusion

## Losing You
*by Jessie Collins - age 14*

I look at the stars and wonder
how did they get to be
I look all around and wonder
if there's a sparkle left in me
I breathe in deep
and then exhale
hoping to someday know
why I don't understand
just where did you go
you were here
and so was I
when I heard the news
but I could not comprehend
just what did I lose
I felt you and you were cold
but what exactly happened
still I cannot let it go
your love stays to me, fastened
I cannot visit you anymore
but I still don't see
how everyone just closed the door
and didn't explain to me
I hear the sea and wonder
how can it be so smart
I don't know, but it does
that you haven't left my heart.

## The Things That I See Beauty In
*by Robert E. Collins*

The things that I see beauty in,
the seas, the stars, the skies,
cannot begin to touch the things,
I see within your eyes.

The things that I see beauty in,
are all so real and true,
but none are half as beautiful,
as what I see in you.

## Desire
*by Beverly Colombo*

It slips into the soul,
seducing the mind,
engaging the body,
to be...to have...to know.

I must release it;
for it enthralls me,
controls me.
Will this savage craving
    ever know it's quest?

Coursing through me,
throbbing...insatiable.
This creature of desire;
so many demands,
so many promises of ecstasy.


## The Calling
*by Danielle M. Conrad*

Her face has the look of peace
She is waiting for the coming feast.
She looks back down to see me there
Knowing I'm in great despair.

She travels up into the light
And I wonder who will protect me with their might.
She floats higher and higher
And I think the men of Earth are great liars.

Her death was something I could not accept
Even though they said it was for the best.
Peace will come to her now that she's gone
While I feel pain and am all alone.

Her time has come is what the priest said
And into heaven is where she is led.
As I look back upon that night
I am no longer filled with fright.

Now I know it was true
He called her to him and she flew.
I am left here on Earth to live
And my pain begins to dim.

One day it will come to pass
As it did in the past.
One day he will call me into the light
And only then will there be no fright.

*Dedicated to the memory of Deborah A. Fox who died September 8, 1991.*


## DreamCatcher
*by Cynthia A. Cook*

Dreamcatcher, Dreamcatcher,
Catch me a dream.
Catch me a good one
and tell me what it means.

Am I ever to marry
Or shall I stay as I am;
Will I have sweet dreams
Or is it all but a sham?

Please give me good thoughts,
And make the bad dreams disappear.
Help me find a purpose in life
And make it my career.

Dreamcatcher, Dreamcatcher
You caught me a dream.
Life is what you make it;
It's as good as it seems!


## Sleeping
*by Lisa Cook*

    You don't know it, but I watch you while you sleep. You're so beautiful like an angel. I classify you from head to toe. Your hair, cascading down your back. Black as midnight. Your brow, completely unworried. Your straight, almost noble-like nose. Your lush lashes, caressing your skin like a million whispers. So soft. Your eyes, closed, but I know that if open them, they'll be as blue as a Caribbean Sea. But not yet. Not yet. Your cheeks, glowing pink from that oh, so tender flush of dreamy sleep. Your full lips,closed, a slight smile caressing them. Rather pouty like. You've the neck of a swan. Small, curly tendrils of your hair whispering against your skin. So beautiful. I want to kiss it, but I don't want to wake you up. Not yet. Not yet. Beautiful, bronzed skin. It looks like silk. It feels like silk, too. I know. I long to touch it. Not yet. Not yet. Strong, yet, tender. I know that those shoulders, however delicate they may look, can bear the load of more than any man. One arm, thrown over your head. Almost carelessly. The other, under the pillow. The hand, entwined with mine. Long, slender fingers. Exquisite. I want to kiss every one. But, not yet. Not yet. Creamy breasts, rising and falling with each breath you take. Full, round, tips the color of smooth red wine. Her belly, forming a perfect V, strong muscles clearly defined. Her belly button. I love her belly button. Hips, just the right size. Fit for my hands. That special place that hides such amazing treasures, you couldn't find them in the royal palace. Sweet, sweet nectar. I want to taste it. But, not yet. Not yet. Long, golden legs, wrapped with mine. Slender ankles, delicate feet, the tips touched with pink.

    And so, I lay here, with my arm around your waist, my fingers so entwined with yours, I couldn't tell where yours ended and mine began. The moonlight highlights your face. Now is the time. Now is the time to love you as only I can. Now is the time for you to love me as only you can. Now is the time for the night to finally begin.

## Godsend
*by Carolyn Cooper - age 18*

She's an angel sent from Heaven,
come to touch our very lives;
She sees the good in all
and desires that it thrives.

She's here to sprinkle joy
and love on one and all;
Don't be afraid to stumble
she'll catch you if you fall.

She's coming with a message,
she's got a lot to say;
Take the time to listen
and she'll most gladly stay.

She wants to be invited
into your lonely soul;
So open up she's waiting
to soothe and make you whole.

She sees the hurt you're feeling
and cares about it too;
So put your hand in hers
and let her feel with you.

## Pure and Clean
*by Lola Beatrice Baker Cooper*

There are many Churches for us to go
Some are tall and costly
Some are small and low
Now it is not how the church is built
Whether it be brick, stone or log
It is what we have in our heart and how we carry on
We have a choice where we go
After our heart has ceased it's beating and we are gone
So you might as well do as you wish
For God knows when we are cheating
He gave us life and gave us strength
And made us able to work
He gave us nature and all kinds of jobs
And expects us not to shirk
He gave us schools so our children could learn and teach
But did not mean for us to preach
From a book or a college degree
He will put the sermon in our heart
So he won't have to stumble
For words from part to part and tumble
He will not need to read from a book or a note
For the words he will put in your heart you can easily quote
His hands may not be Lily white
His clothes may be of patched up jeans
But the man that is planting the beans
Must be pure and clean

## The Breath of the Night: A Vampire's Story
*by Neva Cooper*

    The breeze flows threw the forest, like the wind in my hair. I hear its stories and I see its journeys. The night's wind hold many secrets, and it share them with me.

    The stories are frightening and true. I don't fear them; I am only haunted by them. I've seen some of these stories.

    Being what I am is easy, I can read and understand the night. She cradles and protects me; I am her child. Like her I can't stand the sun. I hide from it.

    Like the night I must hide. The sun is deadly to us. Its touch is like a knife's kiss. Sharp and painful.

    No, being a dead vampire is challenging. But I wish I as a living vampire. Then I could see my father the sun, and live with my mother the night.

## The Old Dirt Path
*by Holly Cope - age 16*

She wandered along the old dirt path that she knew so well.
She wandered to that favorite place on the riverbank;
She came to this place so often.
She went to the river to relax and to think.
As she lay back on the soft ground
To stare up at the clouds,
She let her mind wander
And drowned the day's sounds in the river.
That secluded place by the river was so peaceful and so quiet
It never took long for her to become lost in her thought.

## Homeless
*by Ethel Corona*

God bless the homeless for they need to be strong
And survive in a world that has been torn
Each day they face a challenge in the human race
They don't know if tonight they will find a space
Where they can rest the weary heads
Remembering their past of pillows
blankets and a warm bed
At sundown their lights go out
No cooking, TVs, Reading
Some of the things they have
learned to live without
Then the Sun rises to a new day in
Search of restrooms, showers, food on the way
Many even have jobs but don't earn enough pay
With the rents so high they want today
It's really a shame people should care and share
Some have so much but the compassion not there
We sometimes take for granted and want more
When these people don't have what's needed like a roof or floor
If only we could find a way
Everyone would have a home today
For we are not permanent here on earth
We only stay awhile So why not help another walk that extra mile.

## The Walls
*by Jennifer Renae Cote - age 19*

When we found each other
We were shocked to discover
That the walls have a thousand eyes
And a billion ears
A trillion mouths
And an infinite number of laughs
To hear our many contented sighs
And watch us through the years
And tell everyone of our rows
And laughs and laughs and laughs...

## Torn
*by Kimberlee Coulter - age 14*

Ghost of a person, flashing by
Caught a glimpse
Saw it was him.
Where had he gone?

We were so close
Yet separate
Two unacknowledged souls
Wavering through the halls
Transmitting secret codes
Not bothering to decode
The somber hell they bring.

Wishes to speak
Half-hearted fragments
Mumbling through our minds
Caught in our throats
For propriety's sake.

What will become of him?
The rich being
I once knew.
Fulfilling me with his words
We took off our masks
Bore our souls to one another
Then
Torn.

## Sea Gulls, Sea Gulls, Everywhere!
*by Angela Cox - age 14*

The wind was blowing here and there,
Sea gulls were flying through the air,
I watched them flying very high,
Like soaring angels in the sky.
I wished that I could be up there,
Flying so high up in air.
A sea gull swooped and caught my stare,
He looked so majestical to me,
Up there.

Then other sea gulls surrounded me,
I really was scared you see.
Lifting me on wings of fire,
Soon I was going higher and higher.
Through the clouds I saw a palace,
There sat a sea gull drinking from a golden chalice.

She called her guards to tie me up,
And make me drink from a poison cup.
The next thing I was sitting up,
Drinking from my favorite cup.
My mother had awoken me,
From a dream that could have been a tragedy!

## The Hero
*by Amanda Coyle - age 16*

Down the ship to a foreign land,
Their is different air and sand,
He realizes he is far from home,
Now he is sure he is all alone.

He risks his life day and night,
To keep the stripes and stars shining bright,
Bullets whizzing by his ear,
Yet, still he does not fear.

For he know if death should come,
A new life shall be sprung,
To save the land that he calls home,
For the truth is he is never alone.

At night he stays awake and sighs,
For tears are whelming in his eyes,
Not for him, but his family,
Who he loves so passionately.

He realizes he must take victory,
To protect all's rights and liberty,
All people's lives depend on him,
For he was called to defend them.

Oh, the pain in his dying head,
As he is laid in his death bed,
For he knows the pain and misery,
That his children will feel to win their victory.

Because of him our country is safe,
But the war has put him in his place,
But even as he lays in that dark burrow,
In our hearts he will always be a hero.

## Silence
*by Bennie G. Craig, Jr.*

Three men sat in silence
    To hear a tale of old.
Though each one reasoned differently,
    His feelings were not told.

The first man thought within himself
    How much he disagreed;
But by his silence two assumed
    He thought it true indeed.

The second man, unlike the first,
    Believed in every word;
But by his silence two assumed
    He'd doubted all he heard.

The third, however, reasoned thus:
    "It matters to me."
And by his silence he presumed
    To show his apathy.

But nonetheless, the first man thought
    The third felt just as he,
While all the time the second knew
    With him he would agree.

And not until the silence ceased
    And each his views revealed,
Did each one finally comprehend
    What silence had concealed.

For silence speaks in many ways
    Despite our best intent,
Often sending the very thoughts
    Opposed to what we meant.

## Will It Change?
*by Robert Craig*

I challenge you to live in a land
Where people are frightened to make a stand
Children abused, unsure of their future
Nature destroyed, by man the polluter
Drugs injected deep into veins
To escape the reality man has made
Handicapped people, ridiculed by the public
Elderly minds, tossed in a bucket
High social status and plenty of money
Are much more important than a child who's hungry
Too many scandals, nations in havoc
An innocent man is stripped of his jacket
Striving young children want knowledge to change
Selfish adults corrupt promising brains
Resources exploited, resulting in waste
Animals exterminated in a frenzied haste
Police protecting the needs of the rich
While the poor and the homeless sleep in a ditch
People with power, donating zero
Alone in a cell, sits a misunderstood hero
Lazy humans, littering the earth
How quickly they forget the place of their birth
Skin and flesh bear mocking stares
Society is dying and no one cares

So much evil entwined in pain
One burning question still remains:
    Will it change?

## The Blue Heron
*by Eleanor L. Crichlow*

Avenues of brackish water,
stream to open bays,
where the Blue Heron,
spread their wings,
and land with long legs,
upon the banks of grass,
and wild brush to prance,
so elegantly in a quest for food,
but once more they exalt to the skies,
on a Summers eve with hugh wings,
long legs tucked under,
their trim physique and soar,
a silhouette and the blue serene.

## Grandpa Spencer Unknowingly Taught Me a Lesson
*by Larry W. Cranor*

Grandpa Spencer taught me patience
When I wasn't much older than a pup
He'd spend hours on the lake taking us skiing
And wouldn't quit until we all got up.

And when we went fishing
He'd show real patience there
Sitting in his boat sometimes for hours
With no fish, it seemed, anywhere.

He had a sharp eye for hunting
And in my mind I still can see
How he shot a squirrel with his .22
As it jumped from tree to tree.

And when Grandpa, Dad, and I went dove hunting
We'd squat in a grain field, watching above
As we quietly waited for and witnessed
The erratic flight of dove after dove.

One day he taught me another important lesson
I don't think he was even aware
When he simply picked up a nail in another's driveway
to prevent a flat tire there.

He didn't know I was watching
And it would stick with me the rest of my life
The kindness he showed to another
Could ease the world of much strife.

## Father
*by Dawn Crossley - age 15*

A small, young child,
starring at her father's grave,
counts the broken promises,
as her heart breaks.
He will no longer be there.
She will no longer see him.
Ever promise made.
was another lie told.
He said he would always be there.
He said he would live on in her heart.
How could he?
Her heart was shattered,
like a window,
broken for all of the lies he told her.
Every broken promise,
was another tear shed.
Every tear cried,
was another reason for her to join her father.
A fair, grown woman,
sits, starring at her father's grave,
counts all of her broken promises.

## The Sky
*by Dawn Crow - age 14*

As I look into the clear blue sky,
 I see the clouds passing by.
From rain, snow, sleet, and hail,
 Somehow it survives; I cannot tell.
Rain, as we all know, isn't no fun,
 Sometimes we ask where is the sun?
The snow lets the children play,
 So bring out the sled and sled away.
Sleet is a mixture of rain and snow,
 Not too fast and not too slow.
Hail is like an ice cube machine,
 So get under shelter and don't be seen.
When the sky changes over from day to night,
 The stars come out and shine so bright.
But if the sky is too dark and you can't see a thing,
 Just ask yourself, what is missing?
You never know what the sky may hold,
 But watch more closely and you'll be told.

## The Mountains
*by Pamela J. Curtis*

The Magnificent Beauty of the Wonders
of the World.
The Free Living, and Breathing Touch
of Nature Excites Me.
Calm, and Quiet, My Soul Breaths the
Crisp Sounds of Silence, Moving about
Me.
The Winds Whispering, Projecting Images
in Front of Me, of Anything that I want
to See.
The Mountains Swirls and Curves, Upward,
Downward, Across, and Wide.
Standing still to you Maybe.
Yet, they Indeed Hold Messages of Waiting
Explorations, to Derive Truth, and
Protection.
"Powerful," and In Control.

## I'd Die For You
*by Crystal Dalrymple - age 17*

I'd die for you,
I'd kill for you.
You were my best-friend
What happened to our friendship?
We told each other secrets
Enjoyed the same things:
Shopping, laughing, guys.
then your crush asked me out
I said, "Yes!" which was wrong.
If you'd only said something,
He'd no longer be mine
Instead you left crying, upset
Not knowing I cared
Lying here now: bleeding, hurt,
Curled up in a ball,
Hoping, yet, longing to die.
I need your caring words and touch.
For I'd die for you,
I'd kill for you.
Now you've got proof.

## Life's Dawn
*by Desiree B. Daly - age 17*

Today the sunlight faded away,
the dawn disappeared from day.

Today a morning star fell from view,
the night hiding it's sparkling hue.

Today the blush of life hath gone,
the lightless mask of death is donned.

Today the heavens opened up and cried,
the tears never to be dried.

Today all life's flowers bled,
the stems wilted and dead.

Today the clock struck midnight forever,
the chimes shall not be heard again, no never.

Today the war was lost with life,
the darkness won over with pain and strife.

Today the Angels cried,
the dawn of our life hath died.

## A Friend
*by Brandy Dancy - age 15*

We miss people
we've lost so
much it starts
to hurt after a while

We seem to take
what we have
left for granted

People are still here
who love us very much
who still care

Sometimes all you
need is a hug
and a tender word
to show how much
people care

At a time like this
you need to know
you still have friends

A friend who will
see you though
the good and bad
in life

A Best Friend
you know you
can count on

Sometimes all you
need is a friend

*In honor
of my
Best Friend
Jenna Johnston*

## Goodbye Grandma
*by Angela Dane - age 17*

Oh Grandma how I love you
and how I wish you never went away
I keep telling myself your somewhere better
and that I should not cry each day
Yet each night in my bed
I remember your last two days
and how I wish I had more to say
I was one of the last to see you
and hear the words you said
I was happy to hear your progress
and think you'd soon be back
for I thought I couldn't live without you
I guess I know I can
But your memory will stay in my heart
for me to tell my own children one day
I always think things would've been different
If you hadn't gone away
and miss the things you've missed
my heart will always ache
for I will always love you Grandma

## Love and Kindness
*by Vernon Daniels*

Treat others like you want to be treated.
Be nice to all that, are
not evil or bad.
Treat friends, co-workers and
family with respect and many
blessings you'll have.
But if you treat people
badly your days will
be empty and sad.
For kindness brings joy,
happiness and love.
And harshness brings
sorrow and pain.
But kindness brings peace
and sunlight, in the
hours of lifes cold bitter rains.
It brings hope, in my
hour of depression, it brings
relief to heartbreak and emotional pain.
And in the eyes of God and
his son it is richer than
gold mountains and as
beautiful as rainbow skies.
And it is the thing that
makes life worth living.
Because without it the world
would be cold and empty.

## An Old Armenian Man Marches On and On and On
*by John Clifton Davis*

An old Armenian man marches on and on and on,
far beyond my understanding, for I am but an "odar",
but still, I am here today with all the others.
Seventy-five years have passed.
Many have gone, and of those who suffered, few remain
to carry the blood-soaked banner of Old Armenia,
a land whose maiden holds out her arms
across the distance of time and space, to embrace us,
enfolding us with her love and gratitude,
that we so honor her today, emboldened to be her voice
as she cries out to all who will listen.
I look again, transfixed, as I see this old Armenian man,
bent with age, crippled in so many ways,
but feeling no pain, not one twinge
as he forges ahead, this man with a will of iron.
He walks tall, as only an old Armenian man can,
who remembers all who are gone but not forgotten.
This is his finest hour,
and he is our knight in shining armor,
a knight who banishes the blackest of nights
as he carries the sword and shield of Justice,
seeking to slay the serpent
while he shelters the lamb of God.

## The Mystic
*by Ron Dawson*

Standing by the smoldering fire with outstretched
arms, the mysterious medicine man prays to his
ancestral spirits to carry on his Peoples' fight.
Seeking guidance from his world of gods and demons,
he plays his music with his drum and rattles as he
chants over the dim light.
        Gone are the buffalo.

American Indians call him Shaman, for he was a
healer of their tribe. This mystic Indian would cast
spells on his enemies as he stood over the sacred fire.
Balms, potions, and tonics mixed with herbs were
often used to cast out evil spirits.
The Mystic then threw the mixture into the mire.
        Gone are the Plains Indians.

Dressed in his buffalo robe, beaded buckskins, and a
headdress of bird feathers, he looked like a man of
Mystery.
His skin was painted in hues of red, white, and black.
He often prayed through the night for the people of
his tribe.

        Now the Shaman is history.
        Gone is the Mystic.

## Only today
*by Howard A. Deaton*

Only today will we live and love
For us, tomorrow may never come
Who knows what our future holds?
Fate is often os unkind to some

Just today is all that matters
For tomorrow, I may not hold you
Tomorrow, with another you might be
But that, you see, would leave me blue

## Summer Senses
*by Barbara Dehlinger*

Seeing the sharpness of the lemonade
before it sears my throat
with icy swallows,
I taste the hot wind
and hear the wheat turning yellow
as it waves,
ripple after ripple of foamy gold.
Smelling the lemonade pinkness,
I listen to its tart taste,
chords that curl my toes.
Beauty caresses my cheeks,
strokes my hair
with harvest, hope, and breathless waiting.

## Weakening
*by Linnette DeLarre*

The mind of a killer is like the
stretching of a guitar string
you never know when it's
going to snap or if it will
ever go back to normal.

If it does snap will it
ever be in tune again?
How much twisting and plucking
will it take for it to snap again?

After the first time
the string is weak
and the mind breaks down
as the amp is turned off.

If the string doesn't hold
then how does the delicate
mind hold?
When the music is over the
mind will rest forever.

## The Daughter
*by Andrea Lee Delgado - age 17*

Her daddy beats her mama late at night,
and she cries herself to sleep just listening to them fight.
The reason for his anger is in a case of battled beer,
and they know he really loves them but they didn't want him there.

Ever since he lost his job he drinks every day,
and her mama tells the whole town that everythings o.k.
With the bruises on her face and tears in her eyes,
but I'm sure they all know that she's hiding in the lies.

She's now 16 years old and still afraid of him,
but nobody really knows all the pain it has been.
She never brings her friends home at any time,
because she doesn't want them to see all of the crime.

Only for her mama did she really want to stay,
but the abuse went on for years and years after she went away.
She tries to talk to her mama just the other day,
but once she looked in her eyes she didn't know what to say.

With those thoughts in her mind she knows she'll never part,
'cause the hatred for that man lies deep in her heart.
Just looking at her father is terribly hard,
'cause her mama now rest in the town grave yard.

## My Friend Crystal
*by Lauren Dembroski - age 17*

A pain so strong that it could kill,
An empty place I needed to fill.
Something to take my tears away,
To Somehow make it through the day.

I needed to be happy when I was sad,
Things needed to be good when they were bad.
Something to make my life okay,
Not knowing the price I'd have to pay.

It kept me happy for awhile,
But for just how long could it make me smile?
Soon every minute and every breath,
All I wanted was crystal meth.

A bump, a line, whatever I could get,
Not matter how much, my needs were never met.
Line after line, straight to the head,
Night after night I'd never go to bed.

Soon the fun ended, it had become a need,
I couldn't make it through the day without crystal and weed.
Snorting crystal was all that I did,
Just me and my crystal, from the rest of the world I hid.

Coming down so hard never was fun,
Once again, the crystal had won.
It tore my soul away from me,
What happened to the person I used to be?

I'm stuck in this world of never ending pain,
I've lost everything, there is nothing to gain.
Can I ever get over this obsession of mine?
Will my soul ever come back, will I once again shine?

## Dreams
*by Maura DeMeno - age 12*

What do dreams mean?
What are those visions
That I've seen?
I close my eyes and fall asleep
And suddenly pictures
Start to illuminate my mind;
Things that had happened in the day
Will find their way to appear in my mind.
I dream into the future
To see what I will find.
I ponder my dreams
To find out what they mean.

*Distinctions of Excellence*

## The Black Hat
*by Bryanna Deschenes - age 14*

The cowboy standing proud
Holding the black hat with strong hands
The national anthem plays loud
As his family watches from the stands

As the cowboy adjusts the black hat
Drawing it closer around his ears
Tightening the rope on the bull he sat
Trying to forget all his fears

The shoot opens as the bull comes alive
The black hat flies through the air
As the cowboy takes the ride in stride
On the night of the county fair

The black hat lies in the dust
As the cowboy's off his 8 second ride
He picks up the black hat with trust
And walks away with all his pride

## A Stone Unturned
*by Brandy Dickerson*

A stone I failed to look upon,
Maybe compared with life;

It's a chance I put off, to explore,
And a risk I failed to take.

It may be a decision,
We all can choose to take.

It's a challenge I failed to win,
Or a burden that I did not rid.

I can stop for a while to turn over
   The stone,
Or I can turn away, and walk
   On my own.

With this stone I can loose or win,
Without turning the stone, only
   Another journey begins.

The stone may be the key to our
   Losses and wins,
Sometimes we can choose of death
   Or choose to win and live.

For life is a game in which we
   Succeed or loose,
And as for that, only we can choose.

## Untitled
*by Kathleen Donovan*

Apostate
Apostle
Apparently so
Your wandering morals
Drift to and fro
On the breeze
Temptation has got you on your knees
Deserted in the dead lands
Dusty, trust friend
A rift in this relationship
You cannot mend
I desperately maintain
Dignity again
My aplomb
My poise
Your party favor soul clatters
Making harmless noise

## Environmental Extinction
*by Jalleh Doty*

  We live on an earth with so
many multitudes of mammals which
are very unique to me. But we are
vandalizing the earth so it's very
saddening to see.
  If we keep hurting the earth
are we going to be in imminent doom?
Will our countries be so foggy that
there will be gloom.
  We must stop the defacing of
the earth and a positive future
I will see.
  An earth with no extinction
  An earth with clear air
  An earth with many animals and plants
and that's very special to me.
  So stop hurting the earth and
love it for all you see.
  We live on this planet, so
don't hurt what you want the
earth to be.

## One and Only Dream
*by Victoria C. Dovie*

Beyond the horizon there lies a dream;
a dream like no one else has ever seen.
Filled with happiness, joy, and love;
only that God could have created from above.
So perfect the dream that is seems untrue;
but this dream was meant only for you.
So hold that dream so near to your heart;
that no one could ever tear it apart.

## A Gangsters Prayer
*by Vanessa Drummond - age 15*

Heavenly father please hear me tonight
I need much guidance to live my life right.
Sometimes the pressure is so hard to bare,
I often wonder if anyone cares.
Heavenly father please bless my family who slightly pleads for me
Not to go out as they watch me leave.
Most of all bless my mother who is crying every night
Worrying I will be killed in yet another gang fight.
What is it all about?
What is it all for?
To prove to my homies, Yeah I'm down...
I'm hard core...
I want to change but where do I begin?
God show me the way...
Lord show me the light...
Sometime I wonder how I will die?
By a bullet wound...
Or a knife in my side...
Give me the strength and courage to resist the wild life I desire.
Help me get away from the nightly gunfire.
God show me the way...
Lord show me the light...
Help give my heart peace so I don't have to fight.
Heavenly father please answer my prayer so I know that you are
listening up there.
Lord thank you for your forgiveness and still being there, but most
of all
Thank you for listening to this sinner's prayer.

## Another Shore
*by Erica Drye - age 13*

Standing at the ocean
standing at the sea,
I see another shore
and a girl who looks like me.

I see another shore,
I see a dream I knew.
I see another time before,
a time when love was true.

I see water that I've crossed,
I see the bridge that I've burned.
I see you there beside me,
is my lesson learned?

Now the girl is gone,
not where she was before.
It's amazing what you see;
standing on another shore.

## Denial
*by Elizabeth M. Dumont*

What a pitiful state
   to deny oneself the truth,
closing yourself off from
   what you know is real.

So many times we are blinded
   by our pride that when
the inevitable occurs,
   we stumble into lies.

We are not impervious to the truth.
   Why should we even try
to cover up our inadequacies
   just to sustain another day?

If the truth be set in stone,
why are we mired in muck?

## Far and Beyond Your Touch
*by Eva Marie Ann Dunlap*

Today reach out,

Far and beyond your touch.

Look for the beauty,

beauty in one solitary day.

For a moments beauty,

last a life's time span!

Smile and rejoice

walk hand and hand,

for tomorrow may come

and todays beauty will have

passed you by again.

Far and beyond your touch!

*Distinctions of Excellence*

## Loves Sincerity:
*by Eva Marie Ann Dunlap*

Today as I stop, to smell
the flowers and pick a bloom,
that brings tears to my eyes.
I walk upon the grass barefooted.
And I am alive with the sunshine.
I reach down upon the ground,
to pet my faithful companions.
And I am at peace with myself.
For on this land. GOD given to us.
I have come to realize,
even more now than ever.
That I Have found, the true meaning
of loves' sincerity.

## Untitled
*by Christine S. Dutcher*

The clouds overhead are moving fast
The darkness and chill are here at last

I watch and wait here in the dark
Off in the distance the sound of a solitary lark

The moon rises over the tops of the trees
I step out and drop to my knees

I lay on the grass and watch the stars multiply
I smile, laugh, and finally sigh

It all goes so quick, first here, then there
Today I lie here taking in the cool night air

Tomorrow I'll be wondering, have I done all I'm worth?
As I lay there in the soft brown earth.

## Words
*by Feather Earthchild*

Words are never capable, words are extremely difficult to find
Words make it very hard for me to really speak what is on my mind
Insufficient words come out awkward, words taken the wrong way
So how do I make you see and feel all those words I cannot say
A word can be spoken in a very soft whisper,
or yelled out as you scream
If I choose to use no words at all, will you still know what I mean
Words are so cumbersome and ambiguous, out of reach and very far
I just can't get those words out, but I know which ones they are
Words that get right to the point, or words that are round and about
I know what all those words are too, I just will not speak them out
Words may come out through my lips, listen,
my mouth never makes a sound
You will never hear of my tragic loss, or of all the miracles I have found
Is silence really golden, people believe silence is a sign you are weak
How does talking make you stronger,
than if you choose no words to speak
Can't I just smile, cry or laugh or are spoken words my only link
To communicate what is in my heart and to know just what I think
A picture is worth a thousand words,
at least that's what we've all been told
But what has more power then a single word
and all the feelings it can hold
I would love to share all my thoughts with you,
but words are what I fear
You will never know the things that break my heart
or all the things that I hold dear
The child inside me was taught to be seen,
never given the chance to be heard
So when you look my way, I understand all that you say,
but I'm not understood, not a word
I've seen people use and abuse words,
in the most destructive ways that they could
They say many words that they shouldn't have,
don't say all the words that they should
People can destroy your whole life with words,
cruel words that scar you and burn
But words can help you, save you, free you,
it's something that we must all learn
So say not a word, unless you use each word, very carefully
Think before you speak your words to hurt, or use no words like me
And if your words stick to you too, or are just on the tip of your tongue
Write all your words down on paper, like me,
if you can read, that's just what I've done

## Watching...
*by Michael P. Dunn*

I watch the hands sweep
Slowly around the clock...
I watch the sun and the moon
Drift lazily across the sky...
The days, nothing more than a tired march
From one hollow moment to the next,
Hours and minutes spent trying in vain
To ignore the emptiness within...
Present has no meaning as I stand
Wishing you were here with me...
There is only hope for a future
Filled with a single word, a smile, a touch...

## Coveted
*by Lisa Eckman - age 17*

Bits and pieces of words to say
Remain unsaid on empty panes
Of glass yet to be colored in dye,
Red and blue and pink inside.
Taking a shape or form to prove
Life is held within words you use.
Colorful, violent, deadly and yet
Spoken so silently as you forget
The love, the grace, the form so true
The words used to shape inside you.
Outside is beauty and grace and form
Created from words others use to adorn.
Words coveted by others who live without
The words that crate your beauty worn out.

## My Husband, My Hero
*by Kathryn Ann Elder*

He awakens before chickens dare to rise, before cocks have nerve to crow. With a swift kiss and an "I love you," in fleeting moments he's gone.

To fight traffic, battle the heat, weave around casualties of road rage. His face against the Florida sun, the compact car air conditioning again ceases to function.

Meantime I, his wife of some 25 profound years, awaken when ready-to exercise, read, e-mail, make phone calls, return voice mails, faxes. Inside the serenity of our middle class home based business, the one he so lovingly sacrificed his life for, carefully crafted with his callous hands, on my behalf.

We lost our only child to a miscarriage, he can afford to pamper me, I console myself into thinking, daily hoping beneath the surface that my lot could soon become his.

Home near dark, stinking hot, consumed with fatigue, his had been a day spent inside the extreme heat of a filthy manhole or pit dug with bare hands. I show him my creations-"I had time today to write to my heart's content."

"Works of art!" he exclaims. "How grateful I am to know yours has not been a day like mine, working at less than you ever could have hoped for."

"Someday our business will be your reward," I say, to which he rebuts, "you are my best investment, my most prized possession."

To think this noble man almost died before his time. '92's Hurricane Andrew left in its wake far more than a home partially torn apart. It had left my man stressed beyond his limits, hospitalized near death, not a few times. To allow this inside my memory desperately grieves my heart. So I don't.

We kiss good-night. Soundly I go to sleep as ever, safe in my thoughts...my husband, my hero.

## Life's Center
*by R. Ellingson*

I am looking
for the
way.
Life's turn,
center.
Life
will Stand
Out
glittering
totally
apparent.
Not so much
looking for
a specific shape
but any shape
that can summon
itself
to the conscience
surface of
reality.

## Great Things
*by Rick Ellis*

it is when the pitch of night
turns to the blinding warmth of dawn,
it is when deep sorrow turns to
unbridled joy

when the aged and worn
re-discover their youth,
when parted lovers
find each other's arms

and remember
their warm passions;
long-forgotten,
or so it seemed

when a dark and bitter
winter, turns to spring,
and in that melting dew,
eager stems reach; to heaven

when nothing is impossible,
no height too grand for scaling,
no river's rush too great,
no world too distant for taking

these are the things that await,
these are the things we'll meet,
hold onto forever; whatever her shape
these are the days worth living for

great things are approaching at speed:
of this, I am certain

## Broken Homes
*by Mark S. Emerson*

I have seen so many children, living in broken homes.
But it is so sad, knowing things could be better.

Wondering if there unconcerned parents have clones.
Warning next generations, with this sincere letter.

Foster children being thrown, from one home to another.
Like feeding animals scraps, of unworthy taste.

Questioning whatever happened to sisters and brothers?
Now really wondering, what next will take place.

But the lord will judge all both good and bad, so don't think that God isn't watching from his throne.

Cheer up children of misfortune, don't be mad.
For the lord above knows, of each and every broken home.

## Traveling
*by Monica English - age 12*

A whale traveling thousands of miles in the sea,
stopping suddenly,
studying the great enormous sea,
the tide is high and sometimes low,
you can never see what is below,
thousands of creatures,
traveling north of the sea,
Murmuring softly,
one, two, three.
they have finally reached where they were traveling to,
they stop suddenly,
looking at me with curious eyes,
We quickly exchange good-byes,
Going our separate ways until the fall.

## Souls Are Forever
*by Sally Erickson*

Death of a loved one paralyzes the body,
pounds relentlessly on the soul,
and rips through the heart
in unison to announce the loss.

Folded in pain and grief,
left behind with emptiness,
stripped of a life that we cherish,
we accept death's sorrowful reality.

Wading in the aftermath of confusion
trying to make sense of the loss,
the beautiful essence of our loved one
returns to dwell peacefully in our soul.

For when souls connect, it's forever
and our shared spirits give strength
releasing each other from their pain
with the gift of joy and renewed life.

## Never Again
*by Kristin Erney - age 16*

Never again will I see your friendly face at school,
Never again will I hear your quiet and sweet voice in the halls.
Never again will I wave to you as we pass each other,
Never again will I talk to you in class.
And never again will I get the chance to know you better, because
Now you are gone forever,
I'm just glad I had the chance to say good-bye.

You are gone now, and it just isn't fair,
Sometimes, I think it's just one big nightmare.
You took your own life as I soon found out,
I just can't believe this is how it worked out.
All the sadness is just too much,
I wish you knew the lives you touched.
So many questions are forming in my head,
I just wish that you were not already dead.
You were a friend to me although I didn't know you well,
But never again will I get the chance to tell you.
You seemed very quiet and very shy,
But you were as pretty as the blue sky.
Every time I think of you, I cry,
And when I try to forget you, I just sigh.
I thought you had a boyfriend and all that you desired.
Did you not feel like you were at all admired?
I wish there were something I could have done to prevent it,
But it's like you were stuck in a really deep pit.
When I saw you lying in that coffin,
I felt like I had just committed a sin.
I felt sick to my stomach, sad, and upset,
But now you're happy in Heaven, I bet.

*In memory of and dedicated to : Stephanie M. Pacino*
*We all love you, Stephanie, and we miss you so much. You don't know how much you meant to us, but I wish you could have. You always were an angel to us, and we will always remember you, even in Heaven!!!!*

## The Birthday Tribute
*by Doris S. Estelle*

A precious soul, a special heart
memories to share;
Keeping secrets told by friends
in confidential air.

Remaining true and holding tight
to family and to friends;
Never giving up in life
although some good things end.

Giving all and asking naught
and loving God and life;
Deserving more than earth can give
and smiling through the strife.

Walking softly toward the goal
that every man does seek;
Head held high in passing by
while marching with the meek.

A special day has come about
to celebrate her birth;
No greater friend has there been
to walk upon the earth.

## Night vs. Light
*by Lindsay Emblom - age 15*

The night is coming do not
be scared it will be kind so
please stay in your right mind.
Do not run into the darkness
follow the light then you will
find your home on sight.

## Windows to Your Soul
*by Lynda Evans*

Reach out your hand, and place it in mine.
Come sit by my window and turn off the lights.
Open your eyes to the eyes looking in.
Like windows to your soul, they will touch you.
Lay by my side, and do not fear
Press your lips to my kiss, as I gently embrace you
Let me wash away your tears
Let me heal your broken heart
Let me ease your troubled mind, in the balm of my love
Let the fear die away.
Let me love you my dear through the night.
For you can fly away with me, and be free
You can love once again from your heart.
You will find, my dear, the happiness it brings
You'll be free from the moment it starts.
So reach out your hand, and place it in mine
Come sit by my window and turn off the lights
Open your eyes to the eyes looking in
Like windows to your soul, they will touch you

## My Dampened Spirit
*by Mara Fab - age 15*

Floating through my own ocean
The colors mesh as I sink underwater
Currents surrounding and catching me
Yet I cannot regain my peace
Disappointments haunt my thought
I cannot feel my skin dampening
My soul is so heavy and my eyes show it
Worries will not go away as I please
No longer can I throw them to the sun
They sink down inside my mind
As I continue to drown in my sea
Where is the surface...of my life
I guess I've decided to let go
I'll never look into anyone's eyes again
This is the end, beautiful friend, the end

*Distinctions of Excellence*

## What Love Resembles
*by Amber Fahnestock - age 17*

Love is like the water
It's crystal clear
Love cannot be better
Than a beautiful deer

Love is in the eyes of a child
In the graceness of a puppy
Love is in the breeze blown mild
In the cuteness of a guppy

Love is like an eagle
Touch of a tear
Love is like a beagle
With not a thing to fear

## Six A M
*by M. J. Failla*

From a hospital window
lights and darkness faded
buildings appeared like a photograph developing
dawn broke innocently menacing

From a hospital window
numb through smothering glass
I heard the silent hum of the city
the awakening of a collective entity
minus one

From a hospital window
his strong, sinewy arms lay still
machines kept an artificial rhythm
his beautiful mind took inventory of his last song

From a hospital window
in the waiting room of lives and souls put on hold
my heart began its downward spiral
my Father's beat for the final time

From the hospital window
a silver plane slowly made its ascent steeply
up through foreboding, white clouds
I thought
perhaps this is not a plane
perhaps a winged chariot transporting souls
having just made one last stop

## Someone has taken my freedom
*by Melody L. Fields - age 19*

Someone has taken my freedom
I know not what they did with it.

Someone has taken my freedom
And ran far away with it

Someone has taken my freedom
I loved my freedom fiercely

Someone has taken my freedom
I miss my freedom dearly

Someone has taken my freedom
so my freedom and I shall die
A slow, slow death
Together

## Stucco House
*by Jason Favaroth-Peters*

I lay in my bed, crying, reflecting on the beige stucco house;
Remembering the backyard, where so many of my afternoons were
spent in play.
And I remember the tree, beloved tree,
Whose limbs I played on,
Whose charred bough I buried
when the lightning man struck it.
And with all these memories, I remember my mother,
My loving, caring mother, telling,
Admonishing me,
To enjoy life, don't be in a hurry to grow up,
Because you can never go back to live it again.
And though I didn't understand,
Couldn't comprehend what she meant, being a child,
I now understand, I now comprehend, and
Thus I lay in my bed, and cry:
For I long for those days, those
Simple, innocent days,
When life was all game, full of laughter and joy.
And just as I weep now, for my childhood days,
I know that not many years from now,
I will lie in my dormitory bed and cry for my
high school years.
And when I am long through college.
I will lie in my and my wife's bed and cry for
all of my youthful years.
And added to this will be the burden of telling,
admonishing my child, in my mother's, in his grandmother's
words.
To enjoy life, don't be in a hurry to grow up,
Because you can never go back to live it again,
And I hope that one day, he will lie in all of his beds and
Cry for his brown stucco house.

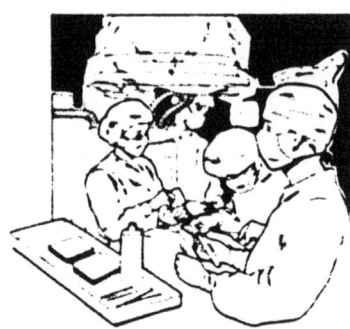

## Higher Place
*by Donalda Feith*

When you feel yourself slipping away
And you'd give anything for one more day
To be on Earth and make amends
To say good bye to all your friends
This is what happens before you die
Going away to a Higher Place
Soon no one will remember my face
That big black hole in the sky
Wondering what it's like to die
Then you fell sinking and heavy
You seep way down then are lifted up
Fading fast
Like sunbeams through broken glass
Going away to a Higher Place
Soon no one will remember your face
Going to that big black hole in the sky
Where do we go when we die
You watch your friends cry for you
Thinking about it all
When will they fall
As you watch their tears
You know they'll forget you over the years
You want to say here
But the time to leave is drawing near
You've gone to that Higher Place
And they've all forgotten your face
You're in that big black hole in the sky
Because that's were you go when you die

## *wings of dove*
*by Jaclyn Ferguson - age 12*

gliding in the air
such sweet sensation
like wings on a dove

this creature came into our lives
on such short notice
we didn't judge her like we should have
many people think that just because they are better
than this creature they ignore her
many people ignore
wings on the dove

these people need to have their sense back
if they think like that

the things we don't know about people
makes it interesting to know them
the things we don't know make them special
the wings of doves make them special.

## *Xenophile*
*by Jenna Fernandez*

The dance
melodic
spinning feet barely skimming the stone
statues etched in grain so precious
silky faces and raven-black hair
spun in gold gossamer strands of sun
thundering down as hard as rain
beating drums tell stories of love and pain
shimmering in the gorgeous courtesan's eyes
lively as the saucy smell floating on the humid air.

They dance
hypnotizing
lovers touch softening skin and melting lips
taste absolute life and beauty
dripping from every open pore
while walking across the scorching hot desert sand
spreading out miles and miles to grasp the cool ocean water
as clear as the images of their thrusting bodies dancing
bells tinkle and shout out in small voices
laughing in their foreign transcendental ways.

## My Handsome Young Prince
## For - Wayne
*by Rachelle Felmet*

I dreamt I was dancing
In a long flowing gown
In perfect unison...
We danced all around.

While others stood back
And moved with the flow
The music was like magic
I just let myself go.

I smiled up at you
My handsome young prince
And your eyes met mine
For just a brief glance.

Then you took a long stride
And spun me around...
And so my heart raced
As we brought the house down.

We both took our bows
And enjoyed all the glory
Of this very special time
In our blooming love story.

We had our moment
And walked off the stage
Then I awoke...my handsome
Young prince...had matured and aged.

Resting on elbow...you looked half asleep
It wasn't just a dream...
My handsome young prince
Had become my real life king.

## *Untitled*
*by Danielle Fischer - age 19*

I sink like a stone
You're ecliptic and free
When you leave sigil behind
Won't you take a piece of me?

I don't know how
To wear the costume you make
Holding my breath 'till
It's more than I can take.

Falling into
Your sadist eyes
I find it so hard
To resist your cries.

I grasp onto my will
As I watch it cave in
Our censored moments
A black dagger of sin.

Sitting skyclad
Caught within your vision
Your words invade me
With bane precision.

The driving force of your
Carnal hurt
Pushes lust aside
And put defenses alert.

I'm searching for a someone
To ease my mind
But sometimes a true someone
Is so hard to find.

**Distinctions of Excellence**

## Loneliness
*by Sharon A Fisher - age 17*

Aching and longing, desolate depression,
Occupy my life.
Tear stained and distraught, no joyful expression,
Totally, completely filled with strife.
I'm tired and worn.
I'm haggard and had.
My heart is torn,
Never again to be glad.
I'm not blaming you.
I just long for a chance.
A chance to see you,
To have true romance.
I admit my faults,
I have been mistaken a time or two.
I see the stars above,
And hope you can see them as clearly as I do.
So many times I've been close,
So many dreams have been taken away.
I'll admit it's hard to lose,
Yet it's even harder when you didn't get to play.
I'm hollow and lonely and scared to go on.
Tired and confused about when I'll belong.
I'm sweet, but strange.
You saw through to my heart, inside.
I was proud and confident.
But I'm nothing without you at my side.
I'm even less than I was before.
I'll always wonder about what I haven't done,
About the things I could have become.

## Have No Home
*by Bruce A. Fleming*

The streets are dark and lonely
For those who have no home
We have no place to go
So all we do is roam
We look around all we can
To get very little to eat
We walk around endlessly
Most with blistered feet
We will lift up a lid
Of an old, alley trash bin
Trying to find scraps of food
So we can go on livin'
Our only forms of shelter
Are from what we have made
As people start to ignore
Because memories of us fade
Whether in a cardboard box
Or an old, tattered tent
Not for anyone out there
Was this type of life meant
There are many in the world
Who don't like to see us around
Well we would not be here
If a home could be found

## Sea Captain
*by Alanna F. Fox*

Murky green waters
SLAP
Wooden planks
Thunder rushes through
Black-night sky
Wind howls in weathered ears
Twists white beard in knots
Beaten old face
Braces against tomorrow
Yet,
Shields itself from
Past
Wrinkles threaten
To tell their story
Lips pressed hard
To hold them back
Yellow teeth
Bite
Antique pipe
Grayish eyes stare
At sea-mist swirls
Sting with salt air
Twirls of uncertainty abound
Sirens Call
    His
      Only
        Love
            Now

## Perfect World
*by Jennifer Fox - age 16*

Happiness, caring.
Closeness, sharing.
Living life to its fullest;
No worries of guns and bullets.

No killings, no fear.
No sadness, no tears.
An understanding among all of God's creatures;
Bright and shiny are all of its features.

No sickness, no pain.
No one would lose, no one would gain.
A place where all dreams could come true;
A bond that would hold as solid as glue.

Appearances;
They wouldn't matter.
A love for each other
Would never shatter.
Everyday would be as great as the last;
No one could be hurt by their past.

No wars begun;
All business done.
A place where hopes could soar and not crash.
Feelings couldn't be hurt or smashed.

This place I see only at night,
Like a star that shines so bright.
I lie outside of it and wait;
Hoping I may soon enter its pearly gates.
For now I lie here twisted and curled;
Dreaming of touching that perfect world.

## Oh, brothers
*by Linda Franzen*

If you have a brother who is older than you
You must learn self discipline
If they tease you - don't react
It bugs them that they can't get you

We played a lot of 'hide and seek' but if it was
Up to my brothers I would never be found
That was fine because I would tell my dad and
The game was over when he said

They thought I was a sissy
Because I was scared of a worm
They would hold up a branch and tell me
It was a sister eating snake looking for lunch

As the years went on I finally found
The brothers I needed so many times
If big brother was watching me
He would know sometime I was thankful for his love

We're all grown up but I miss what used to be
It makes me feel good to hear that he just was thinking about me
If I have a problem big brother would be there for me
Their love for me is inside

My mom always taught me when a boy picks on me
That he really likes you inside
If that's the truth with my brothers
They must be crazy about me

## Grandad
*by Kira Frazee*

I love to stare up at night
Wondering what you're doing in heaven
As I wish on the moon
Through the window of my bedroom

Why does God need you
You're so far away from me
I know you're happy now living healthy and free

I never said 'I love you'
You never said 'Goodbye'
And I feel so guilty about it
All I can do is cry

But I know you wouldn't want me
To live my life so sad
I go on in the name of you
Bringing spirit full of glad

I carry on your laughter
And hold it to my heart
Because someday we'll be together
In heaven we'll never part

*In memory of my beloved Grandfather*

## World Of Illusions
*by Adrian Frederick*

To see this world may be great, it's better to see those golden gates, how to live truefully of this. While we are here, has a date, the deadline of this world is near. the illusions that are before our eyes are nothing compared to Gods sunshine, chaos is among us daily so therefore we should pray daily, as well as trying; seek and find the Lord, who will save us dearly from all of this. Illusions may seem good at times, but in reality; do be blind to these illusions. For that they can not get you to Heaven or to have eternal life; "As of like an golden house with rubies, may seem great, but to have and lose your soul. Over that, might not be as great." If one chooses to live for these things may it be, they will perish with those things. Not to live for the Lord, "why not." An illusion can be something that you may want, "yeah want" but not need so therefore we should take heed, of these things that are before our eyes, and in our lives also, this world we be in, be an illusion away from the truth.

## Children Of The Night
*by Christy Freeman*

As they lie lined up against a solid brick wall,
unloved uncared for.
Some even stabbed and wounded.
They are being robbed of what little they have
leaving them with nothing but drugs to keep them on a high.
Listen close to the cry of the children of the night.
As they roam the streets out in the midnight air.
Selling themselves to anyone they do not care.
Drugs are being passed to even the smallest hands.
Listen close to the cry of the children of the night.
As they watch their friends, if any, die and be kicked to one side.
With nothing they can do or say but "GOOD BYE"
See the tears falling from dirty faces.
See their bare feet running across broken glass.
Running for shelter or even their lives.
Hear them run, run, but only to come to a dead end.
Feel the feeling they must have deep inside to have nothing.
No home, no family, no friends is what runs through their minds as they
are too tired to run anymore
They fall to the ground where they will sleep through out the night.
They let out one scream "SOMEONE PLEASE HELP ME!"
They fall into a deep sleep.
Hear the cry of the children of the night.

## My Daydream
*by Josetta Freeman*

When I am alone and I daydream
My mind wanders to places that I've never seen.
I see many treasures that my eyes behold;
but my hands cannot grasp to these treasures untold.
I can run with galloping horses in clouds of pearly white;
and stare around in space with sparkling waterfalls in my sight.
I swim with the dolphins, jump threw a sunset;
I can fly higher than the birds even higher than a jet
My heart is so happy and racing with joy;
I feel like a two-year old child with a brand new toy.
I come in contact with such beautiful creatures;
nothing on this earth can compare to all these features.
When my heart is empty of all my cares;
and my body feels like it is floating through the air.
The snow falls lightly and so beautifully;
but there is no chill that comes over me.
As I trample through the deep white snow,
I look up ahead and see a young speckled doe.
I skip through a field full of many wild flowers;
and sing with the blue jays while I take on April showers.
But as the night slowly falls upon me;
still there is a light that seems to follow me.
Maybe it's from the moon that shines up above;
or maybe because all I feel around me is a warm special love.
More beautiful than heaven is the way it seems to me;
and this is how I see it in my sweet daydream

## A Mother's Promise
*by Karen K. Fritz*

A face I can't wait to see,
A life growing inside of me.
Like a piece of fine china, so fragile,
Someone so tiny and agile.

Never again expecting this blessing,
Loving him completely without concessions.
Knowing this child was conceived out of love,
With the guidance from above.

I pledge to raise this child right,
Loving him both day and night.
Teaching him right from wrong,
Making sure he knows that he belongs.

Thank you Lord for giving me one more chance,
To influence a child and his life hopefully to enhance.
To experience this miracle the way it was meant to be,
Filled with respect and love for eternity.

## Barbie Through the Years
*by Jacqueline Ann Galati*

I first met you at age three
Though I have had others before you,
no other doll can come close
to your physique, never ending smile,
and adoring wardrobe

And, oh so many different ladies
I can choose you to be
Hair Sensation, Happy Birthday,
Wedding Day, Fun In The Sun
or just a blue jean girl

Your what every girl cherishes
and begs to resemble

Into your third generation,
you still stand as a monument,
capable of flaunting your well-known
Zebra bathing suit

I have kept you all those years
and hopefully till the end
of my expiration

## Seek To Find
*by Corinne M. Gallardo*

The mountains are too high to climb
I find the strength to do it
To conquer is worth the effort

The ocean is too strong to swim
I find the strength to do it
To touch land is worth much more

The storm is too powerful to defeat
I find the strength to do it
Blue skies are worth fighting for

You give me strength to do all things
To live your love each day
You blessed me with your treasures
To live the path your way

I find the strength to do all things
Your love is all I need
I find the strength to do all things
In what you've given me

## Still Dream About You
*by Susan Gallen*

I whisper your name, before closing my eyes.
I dream about you, almost every night.
A sweet dream we are together,
Kissing, and loving, forever.

A sweet desire, as we are one.
In body, and soul, never a part.
My beautiful man, God created art.
Now I am just dream alone,
And we are apart.

If ever, my room, or pillow can talk.
Can tell, all my secret, my desire,
What I whisper, in the dark.
I have a long journey, almost every night.
I am so free, I can even fly.
In my dream everything is so perfect,
Loving and kissing, we are together,
forever.

## I Need You
*by Melissa Garayua - age 16*

Today is the first day you're not here with me.
Every time I think of you tears run down my cheeks.
I can't keep on without your loving.
Every time I take a step I feel like falling.

I don't want to live my life without you
Because you were like a dream come true.
You showed me love is stronger than pride
And that anything I need in you I could confide.

Now I know how bad loosing someone is
But with you in mind I will go and resist.
Don't worry about me and enjoy your life
Because there is nothing I can do just resign.

The only thing I wish is to go back in time
And again enjoy all those beautiful and romantic nights.
At last don't forget that I really loved you
And that no matter what happens I won't forget you.

## The Talking Animal
*by Philip Garges*

In order to make creation right
In the beginning God said
Let there be light.
He said it like a man.
He didn't think it like a dog.
An animal that can speak is God-like.

## Dark Purple Passions
*by Celeste Perez Garcia*

You are dark purple, no basic primary color;
instead, a blend of wildfire red flaming love
and all consuming out-of-control anger;
with the deep, dark watery blues of
midnight sadness, dark loss, and deep secrets.
Those purple passions push and pull
you back and forth. You rise and fall,
between exhilarating illumination
and complete eclipsing darkness.

Fire personified, you blaze
like bonfires that attract and mesmerize,
shine into shadows, warm the coldest souls.
Burning passions implode
and you dive to the debilitating depths
of those deep, dark blues like the
bottomless cenotes of the Yucatan jungle
where ancient maidens dressed in finery
and weighted with gold were tossed to gods;
where, many memories ago
we picked up one big rock and threw it in,
watched it sink through dark watery layers
of nonchalant fish forever swimming back and forth
marking the depths our stony sacrifice sank
and shrank before our disbelieving eyes;
until it disappeared,
depths too deep to comprehend.

And now your purple passions rule you,
pull you down to depths I cannot reach
and cannot see in the red tail lights
of your car as you hurry away and
    avoid me.

## Of Worms and Ice
*by Joseph Garcia Jr.*

Yesterday she laughed,
Today she plays the mute.
I think she enjoys the
conversation of cold roots
And warm earth, who say
Precious treasures are kept
In boxes; buried deeper than
The vision of normal eyes.
Underneath the facade of
Tears and vivid flowers,
She smiles, she turns her
Head, she spreads her winds, and
She screams at life.
I hear her thoughts, like thunder
In my head, echoing over the
cliffs of an empty soul.  I've
Begun to wilt, I've begun to
Dry, I've begun to step
To the dance of crows;
Of worms and shadows, with
Night and ice.
She lies silent, and
She turns cold, while
She falls asleep,
Waiting with the worms,
And melting with the ice.

## Hopeless
*by Jaime B. Garner*

She stood there looking at her
Reflection in the mirror, wasting away
Wondering what she had done so wrong
That made it all turn out this way

Why was it happening to her
Why was she being punished
A whole life she looked forward to
The things that will be left unfinished

Where is the hope that she used to rely on
Where are the dreams that she used to live for
What happened to the faith that she held on to
All to be wiped away, to be thought of no more

Now there is only an empty space
Where all those things used to be
Never will she dream again
No future can she see

## The Weeping of the Sky
*by Jennifer L. Gaskins - age 19*

It trickles from the sky,
With the sound of...
Drip, Drip, Drip.
It lands among the leaves,
Tickling their backs;
Then running down their sides,
To fall among the dewy grass.
It falls on the spring flowers,
Making them blush softly.
Then it falls to the warm ground,
To give the earth a drink.
It bathes all the small birds,
As they fly among it;
Hitting their soft feathers,
With the sound of...
Tap, Tap, Tap.
The sky looks so very sad,
All gray and gloomy;
As it weeps so softly.

*Distinctions of Excellence*

## Lonely
*by Deborah Garrett*

From the depths of my being
 no one can see
The loneliness that dwells
 in the heart of me.
Longing for something
 to take it away
Wanting to know
 in some special way.
Inside screaming
 the pain is so deep
My life has no meaning
 my heart no beat.
Yearning to be loved
 for no special reason
Wondering of its existence
 from season to season.
Years filled with anguish
 from those I have loved dear
With no sign of happiness
 of love, I fear.
With laughter on the outside
 and tears within
My mask is a strong one
 which no one can break in.
All the while crying
 inside from the hurt
No one caring enough
 to look beyond and see
The loneliness I carry
 deep within me.

## Midnight Sorrow
*by Jenny Gartshteyn - age 13*

The lights all went out,
And in a little dark place
Stood a young girl of five,
With a helpless look on her face.

Her deep sapphire eyes,
Shone in the dark.
Reflecting the pain,
That was breaking her heart.

And as a small crystal tear,
Rolled down her cheek.
Coming from the depth of her soul,
Making her weak.

And in the lonely silent night,
The ancient clock struck twelve.
And in the light of moonlight's ray,
Was seen the newbuild grave.

She closed her eyes,
And the pain returned.
The memory of the accident,
Came back to her.

She lifted her eyes,
And with all the courage she had
She whispered the words
"Goodbye mom and dad"

## Lost Friendships
*by Krista Gemmill - age 19*

Sadness surrounds me,
I feel so alone,
Gone are the friends,
And the joy that I've known,
My world's crashing down,
And I don't know why,
Perhaps my whole life has been one great big lie,
What could I have done,
To deserve such a fate,
Why all these looks filled with anger and hate,
Because I found love,
I lost my best friend,
Leaving me with a wound that's not easy to mend,
One of us went away,
And now nothing's the same,
But people all change,
No one's really to blame,
It's just hard to accept,
That's the way things are,
When you end up alone,
Watching them from afar,
I guess that's how life goes,
What path life will take us,
Is what nobody knows,
But we'll keep on changing,
And living our lives,
Just ignoring our friends,
Until one of them dies.

## This Too Shall Pass
*by Betty J. George*

When life's road is long and the dreams are gone,
And it seems that no one cares;
When burdens come each day to harass,
Remember, THIS TOO SHALL PASS.

When your body is weak and you feel weary,
From the storms that toss you about;
Don't give up and lay down in defeat,
Remember, THIS TOO SHALL PASS.

When your candle of faith is burning low,
And the mountain seems too high;
If the weight is heavy and you've a long way to go,
Remember, THIS TOO SHALL PASS.

When mind and soul are filled with pain,
And it seems that comfort you can't gain;
Just call upon His mighty name and,
Remember, THIS TOO SHALL PASS.

When it seems that God doesn't hear your call,
And the hurdle this time if far too tall;
Reach out, look up, take His hand in your grasp,
Remember, THIS TOO SHALL PASS.

## An Innocent Child
*by Stefani Gibbons - age 13*

An innocent child that sees, hears, feels, and tastes
But soon her innocence will be lost.
She'll grow up the way her parents wish her to.
She'll keep all her thoughts and feelings
locked deep inside her heart.
She'll find out that this world is cruel and ruthless.
She'll find a first love, have her first kiss.
Lose her first love and then she'll build a brick wall
around her, so no one can hurt her anymore.
She'll never let her feelings show again.
And then her innocence will be lost.

## What Exactly Are Wishes
*by Linda Gevargiz - age 13*

What exactly are wishes, hopes and dreams?
Are they some joke you say,
Are they some fantasy we all have
That may never come true.
Are they a goal everyone has to
Strive for and fight
With everything they have just to get.

Are they something that you just
Have to burst and say,
"Is there a God?"
And if there is, why won't he help me?
I wonder every night and day,
Will the most important things to me,
Come to me.
If they do, that's when I'll get up and say
"Nothing is impossible."

Everyone has dreams.
Most don't come true.
That is the sadness and the true breaking,
Of the heart.
When someone stops you from going for your dreams.

As I cry at night
And force a smile by day.
I always pray for my dreams.
I give everything I have to offer
Just to get it.
As the tears from my eyes,
Crawl down to my mouth,
That's when I know I am
Truly serious about my wishes,
And that one day they all will come true.

## The Blindness of the People
*by Lara Gibbons - age 15*

We all have great pain,
Everyday mine will remain,
For as long as my lover is kept from me,
Because such people are blind to see.
They can't see the other love I need,
So inside my heart internally bleeds.
I bleed until I am mentally dead.
Dead until I awake from bed
With wonderful thoughts that fill my head.
Thoughts of being together
With my love and give him the pleasure.
The pleasure of kissing me so sweet,
That it melts me to my feet.
When he is done I will say,
I love you for ever and a day.
And I missed you so great
That I could hardly wait.
Hardly wait to hold you so tight,
And know I would sleep alive that night.
We would talk of things that went on
While we were both gone.
Gone from the happiness of each other,
And the love that is shared between one another.
Maybe one day people will see,
There can be a love as perfect as thee.
Then they will be whipped away of their blindness,
And understand the need for me and my loves togetherness.
But for now we will be the only ones who know,
How strong our love is and everyday it will grow,
And we will stop at nothing to let it show.

## Aging Gracelessly
*by Kara Nicole Gibbs*

Time casts its cold dark shadow upon her face.
Lines crease her once delicate features like
deep ravines on the plains.
Fingers rough and gnarled by hard work and
arthritis.
Back stooped like the weight of many years
upon her shoulders.
Eyes once bright and sparkling, now only
flicker like embers
and die.

## Waterdrops
*by Jennifer Gibson - age 15*

Walking through a path of bliss while the water drops cool the inside of a rotting soul, you cleanse yourself hoping you'll be better. But the devil knows. He burns inside your heart while the smoke of temptation rises our of your nostrils. Wishing the refreshing water drops were still inside, you've always wanted to dive right into you and let the steam roll out. And yet, you are no longer a different person but the same old creature you have been for years, watching the water drops on your window as it rains your tears.

## David and Julie
*by Dru Gideon*

Where he leads
    so she follows,
Where she lies
    he makes his bed,
Separate minds
    are now united,
Separate hearts
    now one since wed.

When she cries
    always he holds her,
When he trips
    she'll stop his fall,
Giving strength
    to stay each other,
Giving love
    they both give all.

Holding her
    he feels the magic,
Enfolding him
    she has life's glow,
Endless love
    is theirs forever,
Melding hearts
    soul touching soul.

## The Substainer
*by Leon Gilliam*

The sun was rising another day on mother earth.
Even at sunrise the heat was rising against the blue sky.
Having a waverly effect off the ground.

Was this day to be, the same as before?

All things withering, looked toward the sun.
    Could this be the day?

Death was slowly coming to the things of mother earth.
 As the ground was parched and cracked from the heat
 Of the blistering sun and lack of moisture

Nothing was growing or moving.
 Things were looking dreary,
 Then suddenly it came.

Oh! The sweet aroma, from the dampness as it settles into the parched land,
Now a new hope is being keep alive, as the earth engulfs life and rebirth.
Like a bee, that sucks nectar from the flower, so does mother earth the rain.
    Once again death was near
      But again...
    "The substainer" came.

## Freedom
*by Heather Goede - age 15*

**F**ree Spirited
**R**ights of All
**E**xcellence
**E**xercising Rights
**D**omineering over Slavery
**O**ppositional
**M**aturing Nation

## Nature's Spring
*by Becky Gohn - age 17*

Wild flowers flourish in the Spring garden.
Roses bloom in the essence of pure radiance.
Water pours down like the endless rain,
and the droplets dance upon the white lilies.

Roses bloom in the essence of pure radiance,
as the fountain sprays them with dewy mist,
and the droplets dance upon the white lilies
falling, then, gingerly onto the green lily pads.

As the fountain sprays them with dewy mist,
the tiny droplets cascade slowly down the flower petals,
falling, then, gingerly onto the green lily pads,
splashing upon the blooming rose petals.

The tiny droplets cascade slowly down the flowers petals,
Water pours down like the endless rain
splashing upon the blooming rose petals.
Wild flowers flourish in the Spring garden.

## My Shoes Fit Just Fine
*by Donald Michael Golden*

My shoes fit just fine.
I would not care to walk in any other person's shoes.
After all, I did break them in myself and know how far that I can
walk in them without stumbling.
If I were to try and walk in some other person's shoes, I am sure
that I would stumble often.
The simple reason is that they do not fit properly and would be
very uncomfortable.
Although there are people who would like to try and walk in some
other person's shoes.
If that is the case, may I suggest that you visit the local
bowling lanes and rent a pair of shoes that hundreds of other people
have already tried to wear and bowled lousy games.
I am sure that you will realize that the shoes do not fit like
your own pair.
If that does not get your attention, than use caution in trying
to fill strange shoes in life.
Keep in mind to carry plenty of bandaids, because you are likely
to stumble and fall quite often.
Caution: Watch for blisters that hurt for a long time,
or for life.

## Lovesick
*by Michael N. Goldsberry*

Contemplating on the memories
Dwelling on our past
Thinking of all the promises
Regretting those that didn't last
Focusing on today
All the harsh words that were said
Feeling as if I should be dead
Before opening our mouths we should have thought ahead
We are now in a state of confusion
I wish it were an illusion
You're my equal and my soul
You complete me and make me whole
You're my lover
You are my friend
If you feel the same
Our relationship will never end

*Distinctions of Excellence*

## Express Your Ideas
*by Gretchen Cameros Gonzales - age 13*

What makes a person find ideas?
Is it a melody of a bird
When they stroll in a park,
That reminds them of a song
Heard on the radio three years past.

Perhaps when an event of major importance
During a time when things could not get worse
Pen and paper would seem the right thing to do.
Placing the pen right on top the clean white sheet.
It's a dance with your hand, paper, pen and ideas.

Your ideas flow like a raging river,
Nothing can come in its way.
Writing in such manner stirs your conscience.
Knowing that at the end of the river
is a lake that will block the flow.

Your thoughts begin to taper,
Ideas expressed only through the blood of a paper-cut.
You pick at the opening, drawing drops onto the lined sheet.
The skin gives way and ideas devour the page.
Your blood loss is overwhelming, yet continues to emit help.

There is no more to say.
Tunes of the bird come to a halt.
Drought hits the river,
The broken flesh has scabbed.
The end of the piece.

## Set in Stone
*by Peter Gordon*

Geist will now be rarely seen,
Though look close and you might,
See his statue stir to life,
When touched with Full Moon's Light

Farewell, Oh Gwilt, and till we meet,
May you with peace be blessed,
Your friendship helped me find myself,
And lay this Ghost to rest

Through your life and past the Castle,
Find you'll never walk alone,
For though I've left, this friendship stays,
This friendship set in stone

## Unsettled
*by Ruth Grattan*

There is no calm before the storm.
Long before the silence is broken;
The clouds set in.
I find myself trembling in the darkness,
Waiting for the first outburst.
Why must it always be this way?
I can shut my eyes to the lightning;
But the thunder still roars;
And my tears fall like rain.
Long after the storm has passed;
The effects remain.

## One
*by Sabrina Green - age 19*

One heart, mind, body and soul
Mysteries left untold
Behold
Standing in front of you
Is someone that's true
Someone that loves you
Like no other
Don't have to keep it on the down low
Undercover
Do you feel the same way too
Yes, I'm talking to you
Is your love true
Does it come from your heart
Can you part
With these feelings you have inside
Don't hide
The way you feel for me
Am I the one for you
Cause you are the one for me
Are you the one
Sent from heaven above
Someone I can believe
Someone I can trust
With my heart, my body and soul
Am I the one for you
Cause your the one for me

## Solace on a Winter's Night
*by Whit Griffin - age 18*

Beneath the light of the pale gold moon
I stare from a distance into the gray smoke
Which rises from the chimney. The smoke
Shows its superiority over gravity and those
Scientific laws which limit our freedom
Of Creativity.

The gray smoke amalgamates with the
Low-hanging clouds. The clouds are so
Near that they could be mistaken for fog.
Far off I hear the sound of a lonesome
Freight train, its light shining down on
The cold, emotionless rails that go on
Forever. The lonesome train plowing
Through the darkness like a mule through
That old red clay.

## This Old House
*by Carol Ann Grumbling*

It stands in a meadow overrun with weeds,
Shaded from the summers sun by tall maple trees.
Its old porch is covered by various seeds,
A few broken steps devoid of leaves!

People pass by without even a glance,
Not knowing its tears - if only given a chance!
This old house again could be a home!
Children's voices again thru it would roam!

A layer of paint - new steps it would wear,
A few panes of glass to reflect the sun's glare;
A little cleaning within its walls,
New polish to give luster to each of its halls!

If only man would share its dreams,
This old house would live again!
To let it die - to just rot away,
Would indeed be a dreadful sin!

## Show Me Instead
*by Mary Ann Gurney*

Don't call me by name
Unless I say it's alright.
I don't want to hear
That I'm special tonight.

I've heard it before
And words frighten me.
I believed in them once
And it seems they meant nothing.

Don't talk to me now.
I'm vulnerable today.
And I can't depend
On what you might say.

Everyone talks
But what does it mean?
Words become empty
And pain intervenes.

I don't want to listen.
I just want to rest.
Show me instead
That I'm safe and caress

My fragile soul
In your tender hold.
Please don't let go.
I need to be told

By what you do
Not what you say.
Surround me safely.
Take my fears away.

## Sky Night Wishes
*by Anne Gusler*

Dashing partners of western style,
   Circle in passing flair.
Leather scoots and stenciled uppers,
   Promenade for custom ground.

Loyal Stetson, swing it high,
   Tilt forth in bowing do or die.
Pull up that scattered twirl,
   It's nearing time to go.

Evening memory ever changing,
   Hoedown laughter sealed and done.
An anxious heel to altered mate,
   Upward still a thrice time click

   In myriad salty phrase.
Fading strength and
   Doubting yen,
Beneath a sainted star invite.

Flow little city south from thee,
   Granted yearnings utterly,
As mounting stance against weary bid -
   Bites the suffering call.

## Brain Tumor
*by Jan Hagerlin*

Lovely, walking down the aisle
With magic following flowing trains.
Glimpse of your wide, happy smile,
This within my heart remains.

Blotch moved in and led the way,
Follow new and narrow path.
Different drummer beats a melee
Here within forgotten past.

Blotch moved in and darkened trust,
Overcomes love's greatest gifts.
Ugly scenes would follow us,
Blinded night upon us drifts.

   never meant to lose my lover
   never wished to be this other

## Sweet Song
*by Elizabeth Haigler*

Do you not hear the birds?

How they sing.

They make me smile to my very soul.

How awesome it is to think that the

song of a bird, a simple little creature,

could put one at ease.

Each note is communication with each other.

Their language is an opera.

Would it not be wonderful if ours

could be uttered so sweetly?

## Wind Dream
*by Geneva Hairston*

I looked for my dream, I saw it then
But as I stepped forward, it rounded a bend.
I hastened, determination in my heart.
This dream would not from me depart.
I saw it then, not far from me,
I quickened my steps when suddenly,
I heard weird laughter, T'was the wind,
Who blew it around another bend.
I said "Stop! This dream is mine.
How could you be so cruel, unkind"?
I realized as the wind danced with glee,
He was playing a bizarre game with me.
"This dream is mine," I shouted desperately.
He turned and blew it straight at me.
How mistaken I had been in my haste.
This was someone else's dream I chased.
My hope was left null in defeat,
As the wind threw this thing at my feet.
I groveled in the sand suddenly afraid
I had never known such despair, such dread
Then to my utmost delight,
The wind laughed and blew it out of sight.

## A Portrait of Logic and Madness:
*by Brock Hall - age 20*

Wmt ztawte opqa the cards and winks.
Mt hqyra wmt ecnta, but stops and thinks,
P nbwwnt lyk with big bright eyes,
Wmpw fpq'w att wmeycvm the clowns' disguise.
Mt vepla p fpeg, gives it a look,
Wymcvm mt webta mpeg, he takes the hook.
Lpfh wy wmt gtfh, and out again.
Mt fepqta mba qtfh; the jester grins.
Wmt ztawte rmyat agnostic views
Mpg veyrq bq mcta of pinks and blues
Vyta myxt wmba gpk in middle May
Pqg wmtq mt snpka his puzzled ways
Lew rmtq mt fpxt to read his name
Csyq p oepxt of darkest blame,
Yqt ntv rpa xpbx, the other lame.
Mt rpa wmt apxt, and could not game.

## The Sunset of Life
*by Sabrina Hall - age 14*

On the crown of a hill I stand;
This wondrous day is expiring
As the dusk withdraws
And the frosty night air
Closes in around me.
Clouds sift through the golden sky
Like things of the past gone by.
I think; How simple life was then!
When all that mattered was happiness and fun,
And a simple reminder of love
When things got down.
Thoughts of past, present and future
Invade my mind.
I feel; That if every trying, depressing day
Ends with a silver lining like this,
Then anything is worth bearing.
The beauty of the setting sun astounds me.
I see; All the jeopardy and perils
along with moments of truce
And joyous contentment
That face us every day.
And as this comes to a close,
I know; That no matter what happens
Upon this road of life
All the bumps, ruts, bare and uneven parts,
Added to pauses for construction,
Eventually will dissolve again
Like the calm after a storm,
And the inevitable sunrise
Following a sunset.

## At Times!
*by Lana Hamlin*

At times I sit in silence
You look at me and ask
What's wrong, what are you thinking
Sometimes it's sadness
At times it's pain
And other times it's selfishness
Do I love to much
Do I expect to much
Or do I just dream to much
Why do I feel at times
You should know what I want
When I look at you
I feel I know exactly what you think
I know your dreams
But do you really know mine
I live for you, to do what I can
But do you live for me, not just love
At times I sit in silence
Is it sadness or pain
Selfishness or dreams
Wonder or illusions
Or will I ever know

## A Secret = Trust
*by Erin Hammel - age 14*

With a secret, comes trust.
I used to find that hard to do.
I kept my secrets all inside
And would have never told you.

I used to wonder what it was like
To have a secret just for two.
So I shared a secret with a friend
It just happened to be you.

When I told my friend
My secret just for two
I found that it was nice
To have someone to talk to.

But around a week later
Something went terribly wrong.
My friend told a friend
And my secret was past along.

Now that my secret's out
I don't know what to do.
All I feel is pain and hurt.
It's hard to talk to you.

Trust is very important
In everything we do.
I thought I could, but now I know
I shouldn't have trusted you.

With a secret, comes trust.
You make it hard for me to do.
But in true friendship comes forgiveness,
So in time, I'll forgive you.

## The Artist
*by Elizabeth Haney - age 14*

He was an artist when he was younger.
    A legend to rise up in fame.
Now an old man he sits in his rocker
    Fingers too crippled to even write his own name.
People shook their heads in sorrow
    As they watched his fame fade away.
But to the artist it didn't seem to matter
    As he watched the sun rise on another day.

Because he'd always say:
    "If life is painting then it is beautiful.
If joy is our hope then life's a song.
    Remember the laughter think of the blessings,
Not on what has gone wrong.
    Hope born of faith, Grace from above;
    There's a reason for living grounded in Love."

So the artist lived in the joy
    Of knowing the blessing in the midst of the pain.
He saw life was a gift from the One
    Who gave him the reason to live again.

## A Lovers Room
*by Anna K. Hansen*

To all who came before me,
To all who fell behind,
Watch your step carefully,
Cause love can make you blind.

Open the door,
Close the book.
Open your heart,
Then take a look.

Open your eyes and you will see,
That with love,
What was meant to be will be.

So to all who came before me,
And to all who fell behind.
Please watch your step carefully,
Cause love will make you blind.

## Raging with the Moon
*by Ed Hanson*

Standing on the mountaintop
The earth rolled out below
Shadows of the passing clouds
The river's distant flow

Stars pierce the dark horizon
Leading into night
I feel the planet turning
Steadfast in its flight

Plunging to a sparkle sky
I ride this rock through space
A jockey on a cosmic mount
Running a celestial race

The stars appear to join me
Racing with the moon
Solar winds run through my hair
Midnight chasing noon

Flashing through the heavens
Stars on every side
Dancing with the planets
Through eternal night

## Black Rose
*by C. Cornelius Harnett*

She was so rare, my black rose,
Unique among her kind.
No ordinary flower,
Foreign to life's garden,
But in her own bower, bloomed,
Mysterious, beautiful, sublime.

She's faded now, my black rose,
Dull petals on the ground.
Those darkened pools of light,
That glowed and shone by day,
Garnished the cloak of night,
Now mold in silent sodden mounds.

Her thorns are dulled, my black rose.
Those piercing pointed spears,
In which she placed her trust
To guard her tender petals, leaves
From all intruder's thrusts,
Are blunted, dull, lifeless and drear.

She's lifeless now, my black rose,
Who's leaves once reached for life,
Was nourished by the rains,
Swayed to the gentle winds,
Hang now on blighted canes
Laid low by overbearing strife.

She'll bloom again, my black rose.
Her beauty turn to gold,
So perfect that her new form
Shall rival Heaven's sun,
And radiate God's endless morn
Where perfect blossoms never fold.

*Footnote, A troubled daughter I failed to save.
She died at 31, I loved her dearly.*

## Please Be With Me
*by Blaise Harris - age 18*

You know Carpe Diem means "Seize the Day"
We really like each other, but someone's in the way
Let's forget about this obstacle and think about us
Without you in my life, my heart would bust
We could just go to the park and be all alone
Or we could just talk all night on the phone
Just give me one chance to be with you
One minute, one second, an hour or two
I can't help but have you on my mind
Should I give up, or just keep trying
I'm going to be straight forward, please answer truthfully
Do you want him or do you want me
He can't love you more than I can, girl
You're in my dreams, inside my world
In my eyes you're always on top
My love grows faster and just can't stop
My feelings are true as you can see
I'm down on my knees, Please be with me

## Let Me Drown In Thy Essence
*by Edyth V. Harris*

Let me gently glide
Into the stillness
of the mind
where all activity
is focussed inactivity
where surrender
is the first step
of "Letting Go"-
Let me sense Thy peace
when I sway on the swing
of "Oneness"
Let me drink with desire
from the chalice of Thy Truth
LET ME THEN
DROWN IN THY ESSENCE...

## Someone Like You
*by Thomas J. Hartle III*

All my life I have dreamed of meeting someone like you.
Someone who likes me for me.
Not trying to change me to what they want me to be.
Someone I enjoy talking to.
Someone who enjoys talking to me.
Someone like you.

When I first talked to you it was like a dream come true.
I thought to myself "Can this be?"
"Someone who actually understands me?"
I had just about given up hope, my life was in despair.
But there was a voice deep inside me.
Reminding me that dreams can come true.

I thought to myself, "Be careful you may get hurt."
If only I knew.
But all I can think of is you.
As I look to the night sky and see all the stars,
I will always be reminded of you.
Even if it hurts.

Now I am scared of losing you.
More scared than I ever thought I could be.
"How could someone fall for me?"
Is a voice I hear a lot in my head these days.
We are so much alike you and me.
So much that I wonder if I may never lose you.

All my life I have dreamed of meeting someone like you.
I feel like it has finally come true.
If for some reason you are not the one.
I want you to know.
I will always be looking for someone like you.

*Distinctions of Excellence*

## Summer Night Eternity
*by Karen Ann Harrison - age 16*

You are my butterfly...
dancing in the petal rain.
The scent of you lingers through...
the midnight air.
I can see your starlight eyes, and
the dewdrops in your hair...
We can dance forever...
in the soft sweet meadow's rain
when the full moon shines again...
But for now, I dream of you...
my wish come true.

## One
*by Melinda Hashem - age 13*

One little cloud

All by itself.
Kind of like me

When I'm by myself.

Then the wind blows
The clouds all appear;
Kind of like me
If my friends were here.

One little cloud
Not by itself.
I guess it's not like me

'Cause I'm by myself.

## Beloved Fairytale
*by Kristen Hatch - age 15*

My thoughts on problems dwell
My eyes with tears swell
Fantasies fill my mind
Of lost loves left behind

Dreams will come true
As long as skies are blue
And green grass glistens with dew
There will be a place for you

Rose petals floating softly on the breeze
A gentle humming of birds and bees
Gliding over and through the trees
Dropping down from the sky with ease

Just when I thought you had fallen apart
That's when I found you deep in my heart
I thought I had been lost from the start
But then you found me and held my heart

While on the ground I lie
I hear your whispered words of time
And written across the sky
Your poetic phrases never rhyme

Sweet sensation on the air
As the breeze blows through my hair
Softly taking away all my cares
Love so strong to never tear

Romantic thoughts fill my mind
Holding me close making me sigh
Cosmic figures form a sign
Proving that you will be mine

Just when I thought you had fallen apart
That's when you found me and held my heart

## Hidden Truths
*by Crystal L. Hartzell - age 16*

There is a thing we call life
Where people come each day
A game of chance, good or bad
Each step, each breath, each way

Life is full of laughter and tears
Minds create hopes and dreams
But all the love cannot hide
The nights of endless screams

## The Mind
*by Christy Hauser - age 15*

The mind has the ability to understand thinking skills with what your emotions are.
The soul and spirit is a memory of an opinion of an object or person.
Your emotions are your mind's beliefs, of your thoughts of the understanding of life.
The mind is very wordy at times.
When you dream your mind sometimes plays tricks on you, while sleeping or
Daydreaming, it feels like you're in a fantasy world.
The mind has so many functions that can destroy good and bad thoughts.
The mind is the body, the soul, and the spirit of life.

## Ignite
*by Patricia L. Hawkinson*

Ignite my spirit to become one with the Earth.
My spirit is still searching for its meaning and worth.
Inclined by the mind of another persons aura...
I profess to create heaven shall reign, over the worlds horror.

Ignite in your dreams to the higher power.
Blossom full bloom like a moon, or a flower.
Do you search for your soul to find it's peace.
Peace for not one but united in fleets.

Ignite, me, then ignite my calvary.
Ignite in your mind, wander ever so free.
Pain and suffering will not always be everlasting.
Ignite in the essence of your life that is passing

Ignite in forgiveness, it is your treasure, the gold key.
Be free in existence, walk on water, part the sea
Ignite God's spirit, and ye shall do just as he.
Connect to the divine and ignite a reason to be.

Ignite your own forgiveness, and your sin will be forgotten.
Higher and higher you will ignite to a world with no bottom.
Ignite, your fears, your tears, your emotional ties.
Ignite, to a place, of no more pain and no more cries.

## Autumn Leaves
*by Phillip W. Haywood*

As I watch the autumn leaves fall from the trees
And the cold winter winds begin to blow
To freeze this broken heart of mine
Never to thaw again
As I walk this lonely road of life
Left to my solitude and loneliness of the evening
I listen to the gentle patter of the rain,
Falling from the sky.
Lonely in the night, missing you so
Listen to the echo of my heart beating like thunder,
All through the stormy night.
Waiting for the sweet serenity of the dawns light.
Tearing this lonely heart from my chest.
Sorrow throughout thy soul on this loneliness of nights.
As the echo of my heart beats like thunder within my head.

## Written in Stone
*by Rebecca K. Hazel - age 20*

We'll never know the future,
 Today is all we've got.
Enemies of the past become friends,
 And some friends will be forgot.

We can't live in the past,
 And the future isn't our yet.
All we have is the present,
 Right now is all we get.

We can't change our past,
 Only fix what went wrong.
We must apologize and forgive,
 Because life doesn't last too long.

The future's not set,
 Nothing is for sure.
The world can be a better place,
 Ever disease has its cure.

But, we have the present,
 One thing we can call our own.
To fix the past, and prepare the future,
 Because nothing is written in stone.

## Save Our World
*by Rachel Headman - age 11*

Can this be a dream, or is it real?
No one understands me, or know how I feel.
Never thankful with what's provided,
And barely ever pleased with what's decided.
Either way...I feel torn,
Wishing I was never born.
Born into this world, into this situation,
Hoping that God's working on salvation.
To be saved from suicide fear of living,
For the world to descend poverty and practice giving.
For humanity to be free and full of joy,
Everyone treated equally, man, woman, girl or boy.
Get rid of prejudice acts and slavery across seas,
Personal Rights must be somewhere out there,
If we work together to understand yours and my beliefs.
Tears from cruelty and tears from pain,
Are wicked and hurt, that's why I want this world to change.
I want this world to show happiness and effort to succeed,
Because I believe that if we try hard enough...it can be.

## Rainbow Display
*by Carolyn M. Headrick*

The first performance of each day
oft can present a wondrous surprise,
a prelude in lavender and pink
seen in the eastern sky at sunrise.

Noontime sun brilliant and magnificent
with its positioning the spotlight;
sun blaze of yellow and gold seen
in a visible path of sunlight.

Low in the western sky at sunset
the harmonious mingling of hues,
senses keenly aware of their value
blending shades of reds and blues.

Symphony of visible phenomenon,
spectrum ranging from orange to violet.
Last act of the day, the finale,
a rainbow display of color set.

## Pass It On
*by Danielle R. Hehn - age 16*

If each person had one candle,
And night and day were both in dark,
You would want to share your flame,
Giving to someone a spark,
As each person saw the light,
They too, would pass it on,
Soon many candles would be burning,
Making the dark more like the dawn,
Each person has one life,
You choose how it will be spent,
If you want to live with God in the light,
All you must do is believe and repent,
Pass on this light you've come to know,
When your candle is burning,
Together we will glow!

## Hundred to Hundred
*by Matt Heiskanen - age 20*

This world is built on love and
 compassion, but
before there was a time
not so peaceful for a time
now it's a better, nicer place
Peace and compassion has reigned.
All evil to provoke us
is now but a recorded time
how nicer everything is
because God has made it that way
100 years after, finally we can truly celebrate
what has been established this united day
looking back at what has been accomplished
 lets celebrate!
lets give back whats been given
a blessing from above
time seems right, be it told
let everyone cheer, our souls are now filled
with joy, from her, definitely...we made it!
100 years more perhaps?  It can happen
he's rid of the devil, he had his fun
 from this earthly place
let the good times reign forever
because God for saw all that would happen
 that way.

## Yesterday's Promise
*by E. Reneé Heiss*

Stealing away from sheltered coves,
It seeps into consciousness,
Rhythm, beating with the sea
A treasure, stranded.

Faded images surface
Over sands awash with
Deep, dark memories
Long since regrettably forgotten.

Finally, it demands attention,
An intruder to reality
Lamenting the passage
To an unwanted freedom.

A storm surge of emotions
Overflows, cascading
Through pain, pulling
The Promise.

Gently caressed,
Each pearl tossed back
Watching, waiting, as
The harbor reclaims its own.

The symphony of years
Soon pass unnoticed.
Molded clay transforms
And becomes eternity.

## From A Child We Grew...
*by Karen Henningfeld*

On one fine day whenever we, into this world,
each came.
Whether we were accepted; or rejected, it soon
is time to hold steadfast the meaning of life.
We are to smile and love, and do no other which
may cause pain.
We are to dream and discover truly what it is we
are meant to be.
We are to live each day as if the last, and take
great charge so as to forget the past.
We are to learn from our mistakes and treat others
as we wish to be.
We are to love and spread love, and set as we will
an example for the rest of the world.
We are to never turn our backs on this life given us
its our blessing: life.
So from a child we all grew...and grew, only to grow
so much we must die, but knowing the true meaning
to our lives: whatever makes you happy.

## One Day In The Life Of A Flower
*by Dian Henson*

Needling rays of morning sun,
Pierce shrouds of misty clouds;
To touch upon vermilion fields,
That bend in reverent vows.
Stirring wake the nodding heads
Of glistening sleepy flowers,
Sparkling with the morning dew,
And early spring rain showers.

A diamond field that glows and sways,
A moving prism light.
An incandescent rainbow's arc,
That dazzles sense and sight.
Lifting dew drenched petals high,
The drops slide to their hearts.
Elixir quenching waiting veins,
Refreshed, a new day's start.

The morning breezes wafts their scent,
Like candy luring babes.
The insects come and pollinate,
In never ending waves.
At dusk they lower drowsy heads,
And draw their petals tight.
Guarding from the chilled night air,
To wait for morrows light.

## Last Good-bye
*by Sarah Hettrick - age 13*

The minutes are slowly ticking by
The day drags on and on
All faces are dripping wet
With the tears slowly dripping down
We all know the awful truth now
Although nobody wants to admit it
The good-byes will have to start soon
But love will go on forever
A body we may be losing
But a soul we'll know forever
Good memories will become more precious
And life will become more sacred
Everybody will remember
The good heart we were once so used to
The face we knew so well
By now all the faces are soaking wet
And more and more hearts are breaking
As the soul gets ready to take its flight
And leave behind with everybody
All the precious memories to be treasured
All the good times to be remembered
And we all get ready to say once more I love you
and sadly say our last good-bye

## Blue Collar Workers
*by Charles Herbert IV*

The best dressed worker,
covered with blemishes of soil,
as he lifts, carries on his shoulders,
the universe of toil.

but yet pain is our savoir,
our strength our joy,
without such, how would one
survive in this world.

hands burden with spiteful calluses,
day after day delighted at dusk,
delirious after revealing such
displeasurable fuss.

well being is unlikely to be seen,
barbarous, primitive would we live,
aching muscles torn but still we rise,
astounded by the heroic acts of size.

enthusiastic people with intentions,
premeditated vows of honesty,
dwelling on life everlasting,
hoist themselves to a elevated height,
only one species can.

darken by the site of light,
propelled with such pursuit,
stimulated by the air we breath,
blue collar workers were born to fight.

Don't compare what you cannot see,
do see what all you can,
thank not what we see,
but see what were thankful for.

## Love and Under
*by Krista Herzing - age 13*

You cannot explain love, you
can never show enough. The love
inside is a bursting flare, a beauty
of excitement, and thoughtfulness,
and showing how much you care.
Love cannot be expressed,
even though we try to show it.
-It will not work!-
You cannot see love, even though,
you think you do, you cannot
show love no matter how hard
you try, because - well - I've
all ready explained why.
And I try, and try to keep love down,
hidden, hidden where it can never
be found.
But that special someone came, and
I have finally revealed my
love so strong, - though it
seems so scary, - Is that so
wrong? I tried so hard to keep
love down, but now that
I've got him, I think I like
it better found!

## The Mirror
*by Heather Hiddleson*

What could touch a person or reach within, grasping not for the superficial layers of happiness, but creating true, unbending joy and fulfillment?

A wholeness or completeness encompassing one's soul which is not penetrated by simplicity or artificiality, but rather depth and understanding.

We endlessly search for such peace and contentment in the darkest shadows in this mundane world, as if they are somehow hidden from view.

Perhaps the answers we seek lie not in that which exists in the outside, physical world, but within each individual so that we are not dependent upon external connections, but rather that which we find fuelling our internal fires as uniquely gifted into each living soul, like the precious, delicate life miraculously breathed into us at birth.

If it is true that the search for such fulfillment is as integral to us as the lifeblood running through our veins, then perhaps the only external connection we need to unlock that happiness...is a mirror.

## Sun Rise
*by Mary Hirsch - age 15*

Watching the sun rise into the sky,
Is like watching a piece of heavenly bliss.
It's a feeling no mortal can fully describe,
Like the magic that happens when two lovers kiss.
The color ballet taking place up above,
Like a picture canvas, no artist can paint.
Come from an emotion much deeper than love,
From a heart that beats fierce in the chest of a saint.
The highlights and shadows surrounding the day,
Add emphasis on the spectacular sight.
It will touch you inside like no other way,
As the earth starts to wake from its sleep the past night.
It's hard to believe how such beauty can cease,
At the rate of only a few blinds of the eyes.
But with it comes acceptance and peace,
When watching the sun rise into the sky.

## Baby Blue
*by Doreen Hobby*

We know we'll be together
so quickly the times go
but we have all the time in the world
and no one else, really knows.
We have the real deal
our hearts become one.
Soul mates we are
never had so much fun.
It's amazing, what you find
especially after a long wait.
When dreams come true,
now reality and fate.
We know what we mean
and always comprehend.
Sharing a certain look,
my love, my friend.
Blond, baby blue like me,
unavailable for a time,
but now we'll be together
and life is just fine.

## Once Upon a Time
*by Liz Hodgdon - age 16*

Once upon a time, you were mine, we're together for eternity
Now I keep the light on waiting for your return
return, return, for empathy, you understand me
once upon a blue moon, you'd come to visit me
The moon shed its rays across your skin, but now there are none
Once upon a time, I breathed a sigh of relief
when the time finally passed, the negativity had ceased
and had the positive shown through, and not just on the wall
then the blood would stop flowing, the tears would stop shedding,
the light would stop glowing in your eyes
Once upon a minute to spare, you were the only one that cared
I could see it in your eyes; the glowing coals behind your retinas
shone your love onto me.  That's how I knew you missed me too
Once upon a time I knew that light would fade away
but maybe somehow it would last forever and a day
but once the sun was down and the moon was out,
I knew it was time to leave
And I found my way in the dark silently weeping invisible tears
until I found the place where I belong;
and that place was in your arms, or just anywhere with you

## That There Would Come A Day?
*by Denise Holcomb*

She stood quietly in the doorway
Watching the children play
Oh, how she wished, oh, how she prayed
That there would come a day
When the world would become:
A world of peace, a world of love.
Were there others like her?
Mothers, Fathers, Young, Old
Losing Faith in their governments
Democratic or not
And some losing faith in God
Catholic or not
Maybe one day all that faith will be restored.
But for now there was doubt,
For with all these bombs,
How can we be sure,
That there will be a future to restore our Faith?

## Sin
*by Melissa Elena Hoover - age 18*

I stand alone with only my soul beside me,
I take off my clothing and caress my naked
   body,
I hear the music not only in my ears,
I feel the rhythm and release unwept tears,
I dance seductively in front of myself,
Wishing someday this will bring me great wealth,
moving my body in such a way,
Even an angel would be tempted if he came
   my way.
Glancing at my own reflection,
Wanting nothing more than your love and protection,
Covering my bare breasts with ice cold hands.
An embrace unknown to many of man,
A breath so deep, full of such relief.
I can feel you, I can feel you within,
A feeling so great it must be a sin.
I had on great possession,
If only I went to confession,
I would have learned my lesson.
An angel with horns,
A devil with wings,
Such temptation that they bring.
My bones are weak, my will is strong,
Doing something that I know is wrong,
Caught between love and lust,
So many lies, don't know who to trust,
As my heart explodes inside my chest,
Will this child-like body still be blessed.
Now that my soul will finally have a
   chance to rest?

*Distinctions of Excellence*

## Alone
*by Tiffany Hoover - age 15*

Alone in this empty world.
That's all I've ever known.
Go on each day without love.
Every time it's there it disappears.
Suddenly I realize my fears.
Only I find out just what I am,
Alone, all alone with no one to hold,
Not a soul of tenderness, or heart of gold.
Just me and myself alone.
Through my short life
I've felt more pain than anything.
Gave my heart to no one to break.
What I have they can't take.
Some nights I think no one is thinking of me.
I've never had a true friend to see.
Maybe in time I'll find a love,
That is as kind and gentle as a dove.
But until that day,
I won't shed a single tear.
I'll seal my pain deep inside,
Where it will be easy to hide.
A special soul will find me.
Somebody, somehow, some way,
But now alone is how I'll stay.

## Goodbye, Dear Ones
*by Tracy Marie Haven*

Bury me beneath the trees,
When all of Life is in Its' green.

From raging river to babbling brook,
Be it whichever, just run along the foot.

I will cry no more tears.
Finally, I have conquered all my fears.

To those who my heart holds dear,
Do not fret, for I will always be near.

Through you, I will live on.
And, hopefully, my mistakes will be bygones.

Cherish me, as I will always cherish you.
Smile to me every morning with the glistening of the dew.

## The Path
*by Gerry Lee Howell*

Through the passage of time, there
are things that come upon us of which
we have no control. Things that
drive our mortality to the fore front,
things that makes us more
vulnerable than ever.

Things of which we can find no rest.
For even in the middle of the night,
surrounded by the cold and darkness
we often sit and ponder of what waits
on the tomorrow.

Things which touch our very souls,
things that have stirred up
our feelings of suffering, of sorrow,
of grief, of pain.

Things that force us to look within and
look we must. There to find the path of
prayer, the only path that us open to us.

It is the path to safety, the path past
our mortality, past our vulnerability.
Past our thoughts, past our feelings of suffering
past our very essence.

On that path we find that light shinning
ever so brightly, as it folds in all
around us, like great wings of love.
It touches us with love and protection
and gives us great hope for tomorrow.

## In Land Ruled By Guns
*by Kenneth Huffman*

Strange things are done
In lands ruled by guns.
And by men who's morals are low.
Where human dignity has no place
On the self-elites totem pole.
Where for profit or gain
Or the powerfuls personal aim
Many men are slain.
And women and children too.
Freedom of religion and of press,
And many other freedoms
Are simply put to rest.
Where the right to choose,
And the right to do,
Is chosen by a powerful few.
Where by the powerful alone
Things are done.
By their golden rule;
Their gold is the gun.

*Inspired by worldwide Civil War.*

## Through the Eyes of a Child
*by Liz Humphries - age 15*

The sun appears brighter
And the day not quite as long
The simplest little melody
Becomes the sweetest song
A simple little dance
Becomes a way to walk
A sophisticated accent
Becomes a way to talk
A kind little gesture
Becomes a lasting friendship
A rise to the store
Becomes the longest trip
A day becomes a month
And the month becomes a year
A lifetime e of emotions
Comes out in just one tear
A walk through the woods
Is like a safari in the wild
and this is the way the world is seen
Through the eyes of a child

## Ramblings (Soul-Song)
*by Sidona Marie Hunsberger*

Short songs so compact,
Neat and sweet,
I'd write before
I'd drift into sleep
In younger days
When my heart
Would secretly weep.
Now just seems I'm
Rambling on and on
Sowing seeds of myself
As if spreading weeds
Through the world's
High priced
manicured lawns -
Hoping to cultivate
A free-flowing harvest
Of golden fields
Of fresh grade
Rolling wheat
To thrash and grid
Into flour
For fine food to eat.

## The Race
*by Linda Hutson*

The Race, The Pace,
The Race of Life!
Love and joy, won with ease,
With hopefully little loss of face.

But could this not be boring,
No excitement, no flow of adrenaline.
No sadness means no glory,
No content to the story!

To laugh, sing, or cry-
Whatever the reason why?
Good, bad, sad or reckless,
Such release is relief of stress.

Oh for a little grace to this race!

## Today I Am
*by Oliver D. Ihasz*

TODAY I AM invincible. My armor is polished and secure. My path is straight and my purpose is clear.

TODAY I AM a giant and still I will grow.

TODAY I AM time. The past I surrender, the present is mine, today I plant the seed for tomorrow.

TODAY I AM united. I AM strength, I AM love, I AM the truth.

TODAY I AM the beginning and I AM the end.

TODAY I AM the creator and the creation.

TODAY I AM HE and HE is I.

TODAY I AM all that I can be, for

TODAY I AM that I AM.

## Forgetting You
*by Sarah Ann Irwin - age 19*

Forgetting you,
will be hard to do.
After all the months
that went by,
it's time to get over you.
There are still memories of you,
inside of this heart of mine.
That just won't let go.
That still make me cry,
when I close my eyes.
For they will be there,
till the end of time.
Inside of me,
eating me alive.
To make me think of you,
when I'm feeling blue.
Till the end of time.
When I know
that forgetting you,
will be hard to do.

## Metamorphosis
*by Alicia Jackson*

As the candle burns eternally bright
I search inside for the mystery to unfold

Into the flame I travel

The heat expands the intensity
And guides my way towards the center
Of an existence almost blinding

I cannot see which way to step

The candle bursts into flames
And I find many choices I must make

The multiple flames converge
Into a solid burning light

A place so beautiful I long to go

I fear the transformation
I must make to enter

Solidly, strongly, and as one
It calls forth to me
As only time allows

Enticing my whole being

My soul begging to unite
With the direction my essence flows

It all becomes clear
In an explosion of truth

I know what I must do
And where I'm headed

Into the ultimate existence
Of where I'll become complete
Through the metamorphosis
Of my transcendence

## No Time to Play
*by Marva Olivia Jackson*

I did not come to play.
I have no time to play.

I am very busy sewing
And making clothes of hue
of silk, and satin, and calico
They have to fit just so.

With rhinestones and jewels of stones
Oh my how they are a'glow.

Tis why I have to sew a'right
Even until its dark as night.

I have to sew my buttons on
With threads of silk and gold.
So when I show them off at night
I'll look like a star all beaming bright
And glittering like gold.

Now you know why I can't come out to play.
I'm very busy as you can see.
I'm going to be a movie star
Oh dear, Oh me, Oh me!

## The Gift of Life
### by Rhonda Jackson

I knew there had to be a reason
why a child comes into this world screaming
It must know it's entering a place that can be
very deceiving
A place that complicates the simple things
in life for no reason
There must be an anticipation of experiencing
many debates and dealing with other peoples
hates
Wondering why I've just been slapped after
living in a sack
Now coming out naked and being wrapped in
a blanket
It's going through trauma, but yet too young
to understand all the drama
It's being attacked, slapped on the back
not offered any snacks and then tossed into a
two by four cubicle
the child is given to the man's wife
and she finally sees the gift of life

## A Father's Love
### by Debbie Jacobsen

I am old
Please have patience with me
I had patience with you (when you were young)
So many years ago

Yes, we have our own lives and
Like you
I once had a family

But now,
What has happened?

We have all grown older

Once you depended on me
Now, I depend on you

Am I a Burden to you?
You were not a burden to me

No, I do not want to be this way
But that is how I am

So please,
Bear with me
Like I;
With you
So many years ago

I did not give up on you
Please, don't give up on me

I was there when you needed me
Now, I need you

I am old
Please have patience with me
Like I,
With you
So Many Years Ago

*Dedicated to my Father-In-Law Edward R. Jacobsen*

## The Girl and her Dad
### by Jaclyn M. Jaeger

They walk through the city looking down at us with pity
as I watch them shop and tour the sights
while my dad and I huddle to keep warm through the nights

I hate holding up this sign, "Will work for food"
Some people stare and are so rude
They glare at my dad the "hobo," the "slob"
They just do not understand that he cannot find a job

If America is the land of Opportunity and Home of the Brave
then why are we homeless and so afraid?

I have not always lived this way
Actually, I lived in a dream
until I awoke in a nightmare one day

I used to have good clothes to wear
and a school to go to and friends that care
I used to have healthy food to eat
and medical coverage and shoes on my feet

To think I wanted so much more
but that is not important anymore
I scold myself now for being so greedy
never really thinking about those who are needy

Never again might I receive the necessities to live
but I have a lesson and a moral to give...

Never look down upon people
who are not as fortunate as you
and be thankful to God
to live the life you do

*(In memoir of the girl and her Dad in New York City)*

## A Rose to the Sea
### by Maria C. Janoski - age 17

A rose to the sea
A wreath to a grave
There are some souls we cannot save

A brilliant memory
A faded snapshot
Sometimes we hate reality's plot

A well-kept secret
An unopened letter
Maybe it is all for the better

We live
We die
Never asking why

Our eyes shut tight
Our ignorance bliss
All the chances we try to miss

One moment happy
Next moment sad
In only an instant, the whole world's gone bad

A car may crash
A ship may sink
Events forcing us to think

Hours, minutes, seconds
We miss them when they're gone
And we measure just how long

Our lives out of focus
It only takes an instant
Everything's less distant

It only takes an instant...

## Friends Are For
*by Jessie Janson - age 18*

Friends are for being there when
you need someone to share your thoughts.
Friends are to tell you when
to keep your mouth shut.
Friends are there to get you
in and out of trouble.
Friends are there when
you need a shoulder to cry on.
And a high five clap for victory.
Friends are there to drift
apart and leave you with
the memories of your wonderful, youthful days.
Friends are forever,
physically or mentally a friend is always there.

## The Voice
*by Erin Jarvis - age 15*

The voice, it just carries you away
to a beautiful place where you just want to stay.

To soak up the beautiful, perfect voice
you've never heard anything so suitable to your choice.

The voice flows through your ears and sinks
into your brain.
And you'll never forget it, no matter how hard
you strain.

Your breath is taken, but you can't tell.
All you notice is the voice increasing and the
music begin to swell.

Every note his as if it were meant to be.
And at the end all you can choke out is....
wowie.

Then you know that voice is a ringer
you instantly know you've heard a
legendary singer.

*Dedicated to J.G. and B.S. who's beautiful,
unique voices encouraged this poem.*

## Platonic Love
*by Veenaye Kumar Jeetun - age 18*

Love, thou art existence perfect
Still, has anyone held you correct?
So pure and devout you were
Godly to every viewer
Oh dear, your moonlike gladdening face's the magical touch of God
Or, the most beautiful of all creation of the Lord
So influential and philanthropic your presence is
Liberty it marks, be it peace or a life of complete ease
May your dark eyelashes be the symbol of unity
leading heaven and earth to parity
Those bluish eyes, the deepest of all oceans
all wealth's hidden inside and desire-fulfilling, its repercussions
Surrounded by a protective shell, the eyelid
the pupil's the pearl of the ocean, so invaluable, can you bid?
Let the rosy lips be the uniting agent
Separated lovers can again recall moments together they spent
Union with the Supreme's no more, for us, a dream
Linked are besides heaven with the material stream
So much consideration for verbal consciousness
eternal love you breed, faith and togetherness
Those golden curls flowing on her chest
are like the cool perfumed monsoon air flowing without any rest
Her eyes sparkled a single glimpse of shyness
as fully enslaved was His Highness
Her greatest treasure, her feminine qualities
Shyness, timidity and respect, her interior beauties
Pure, sincere and unprecedented love she holds as her divine possession
Who's the power to fathom our deeply-based relation?
Cultivation of such a platonic relation, for others, the chance is last
and those failing in achieving this heavenly success, for them, it's
"Paradise Lost"

## Extinction! (Of the human race: 'WAR')
*by Veenaye Kumar Jeetun*

We've travelled from the Stone Age
To what we may call the Space Age
Man has witnessed evolution
and the society, revolution
We've manufactured sophisticated spaceships
But still, failed to foster genuine human relationship
Peace is today a Utopian idea
Though rich and pure culture was that of India
We are today spiritually bankrupt
And all our actions are corrupt
There's been innocent killing
Where absent is moral feeling
Escalations of crime have become a fashion
And human life accepted as ration
Man is bio-programmed to fight
Still, thinks he's right
The life of others, he jeopardizes
But what's ethical, never realizes
His contemporaries no longer guided by religious principles
And he's no more Jesus's disciple
He thinks progress is triggered by war
and raged the first and second world war
The Gulf Crisis was a prefigure
and there's till now, no believer
The third world war will mean the last of hearth
And then, annihilated will be all forms of life on earth
The Sword of Damocles is permanently hanging over our head
Our days and actions, already read
Standing by the doorstep is the hazard
Through this misconception, we'll hoist with our own petard

## Ms. Mary Jane
*by Tony Jimenez - age 12*

Hi my name
Is Ms. Mary Jane.
Don't stare
Because the game I play is never fair.
I'll take your money and break your heart
And trust me we'll never part.
I'll ruin you from inside out
And I'll twist your emotions all about.
You'll never get enough
Of my kind of stuff.
You'll always want me.
You'll always need me.
Once I'm in you
I'll never leave you.
I'll be the reason why you die
Trust me because I never lie.
They always tell you just say no
But once you try you'll never let go.
I'll take you up I'll pull you down
And then I'll leave you to drown.
When you quit
I won't miss you a bit
Because I know you'll be back
Cause now you like life on the fast track.
Once you start you can never stop.
("**DON'T DO DRUGS !!!!!!!!!!**")

## My Love
*by Melanie Jim - age 13*

My love is somebody I can trust my secrets with. He will bring cheer, laughter and love into my heart. His is someone who will bring laughter when I'm feeling down and blue. He cheers me up when I get in arguments with my family or friends. When ever I break down and cry he will be there holding my chin up high drying my tears. He is someone who will be holding my hand so I won't stumble and fall and never get up. I don't care how he looks, dresses or even acts. All that matters is I love him for what's inside his heart. No matter how far apart our live will go. I see his face in every star and every magazine. Best of all he's always in my heart. My love for him will never change or break apart because our love is to strong to pull apart. We'll keep each other on our feet together through thick and thin, till one day the man upstairs calls our names, then that's when my love for him will shatter and never, never be fixed again.

## I Will Survive
*by Carole Johnson*

Pity me no more
   things are different, you know
I found somebody
   You know, I never joke about money

I'm running around in circles about my past
   I will never know the extent of how much I was hurt
I guess I have been protecting myself
   I keep it all to myself
   the pain, the embarrassment

The past brings back powerful memories
   but, digging up things from the past
   chasing a ghost from the past
   will not go away, any time soon
the past brings back powerful memories
   Do I believe in the Devil? Hell, no!

The high and mighty who want to control you
   slit their own throats
they have a past
   and their ghosts are the ultimate evil
none of us knows for sure

My only path now is to go, to lead ahead
   I found love inside myself
   HE knows me

I am part of a melodrama - not a tragedy
   A person dies in a tragedy

I don't know about you
   but my real intention is to live
   live with and deal with the demons
   find and follow the angels

I'm here and not to be pitied
   I can do life and make a good life on my own

## Always
*by Heather N. Johnson - age 15*

I think I'm gonna cry
Better yet
I think I'll die
Promise not to forget
That day when we first met
The memory's so clear.
I love you, my dear.
I remember the fear
As my eyes fill with tears.
We were actin' so fly,
And your eyes looked like the sky.
Why, oh why, oh why
Do I feel I must die?
I stopped dead in my tracks
To take the time to look back.
But that's all gone,
"We" ended with a "Pow."
I don't know how to say
Exactly why I can't stay.
Although I'd love to,
So I'd always be with you.
But now I have no choice.
All that will be left is my voice.
And as it fades away,
All I want to say
Is "I love you."
Always.

## Behold, Truth!
*by Jill Fahey Johnson*

If I were to speak, a whisper so soft,
If my words were true, simply so.
Yes, you would clearly hear, though startled you may be.
And if my eyes met yours in this process of subtle power,
That same whisper would resound in your heart, echoing!

And if I were to reach forth my hand,
And only invade your space,
No contact made, and my hand held truth, simply.
No doubt, however masquerading, you would react!

Beware! If you, an enemy, of truth are,
do not invite my words, my gaze, my touch!
For no clever nuances can hide, the mixing of truth and lies.

For deep in your heart and secret vital areas,
Within a moment, I shall be!
And that which I bring back from you,
Will silently mirror all that is to see.

And shattered pieces shall remain, where truth is not.
For only this can be, forever unchanging!
Behold, the power of truth!
Not man's so easily!

## People Who Want to Eradicate Drug's
*by John D. Johnson*

America the beautiful, land of the free
Let's form a group together, called the P.W.W.T.E.D.
Before we get started, let me thank you for a job.
Well done with our little plight
Now we have to get out there, an really learn to fight
Let's win for America, an bring back safety in the night
We work all day we work all night, to help resolve this matter
Don't let America, keep getting madder an madder
Now it's time to organize, so we can win this fight
If we stick together, we can rid America of this plight
Let me tell you brother, it can't be done in just one night
If we try hard enough, I know that we can win
An America, will never have this drug plight again
People of the world, help us with this fight
Look what happened in Columbia, man what a plight
God will surly help us with our fight
America is busy, it's buzzing like a bee
An now the time is near, for America to be drug free
Please everyone join me, and the P.W.W.T.E.D.
Let me tell you people, when this job is done
The land of the free an the brave, will also be know as the land, of
Good clean fun. I am a former drug user, an for what drugs have done to me
Is what inspired me to form the P.W.W.T.E.D.
Let's all work together, to eradicate drugs
An help rid America of all those pimp's an thug's
All you have to do to help, is pick up your phone an call the law
Your reward will be self worth, if you need one at all.
So turn in your neighbor, or even your best friend
So America can win, the war on drugs, in the end.

## Misery
*by Heather Johnson - age 15*

All alone.
No one to talk to.
Nothing but darkness.
Thinking of suicide.
What is wrong?
Depression is the word.
Wanting to escape.
Running away from everything.
Just wanting to die.

## Love
*by Olivia Johnson*

God showed us true love
A long, long time ago
When He sent His Son Jesus
And through Him
All the things that He
will show.

He told us to love our
families
Our neighbors and our friends
Make sure you love your
enemies
Because if you don't
It is a godly sin.

To love is salvation
And don't you ever forget it
Without love in your heart
In God's kingdom you'll
never, ever fit.

Love is one of the commandments
That you show and feel but
not see
And if I love my brothers
I know that He'll love me.

God sent us His Son
From way up above
To give us an example
And show us the true
meaning of love.

## Breaking The Chains That Bind
*by Victoria Johnson*

Chains are all around us,
Our hands are chained, our legs are chained, but most of all our heart's.
We know one day, the chains will have to come off.
While the chains are on, there's hurt
While the chains are on, there's so much pain.
          "Chains"
We break them off one by one, each link a reflection, a reminder, of what was.
Chains bind us, they wear us down.
Sometimes they even wear us out.
Each link falling, falling onto the floor.
With each tear, another link falls.
With each scream, another.
Fighting with all our might to break all the chains that bind.
Fighting to keep our head above water, but sinking fast.
The chains are still there weighing at your love.
Weighing at the bottom of your soul.
Grab hold, pull yourself up, and pull yourself out.
The chains have you under water,
What will you do now?
Hold on a little longer,
Some links have been broken, and some more will come loose.
Don't let those chains get rusty, or you will lose, get them off.
Whatever it takes get them off.
Pray, open your heart to God.
Pray and watch the chains melt away.
And when it's over,
Smile, God, has just given you another day.

## Summer
*by Annie M. Jones*

Golden sunlight beneath leaves of green
Lit by a sunset in the western sky

Gentle summer breezes sway the trees
As the heat of the day passes away

Quiet as a whisper
Stars appear in the sky

The moon in her splendor
catches a lover's embrace

Sweet smells of summer
Her bounty now full

A choir of sound
And firefly light

As the Earth pulls her curtain
And whispers "GOOD NIGHT"

## A Celebration of Love
*by Shirley A. Jones*

Together.
You and I.
Two hearts entwined.
Put your hand in mine.

Cherish.
Our love.
Our hopes and dreams.
With a strength from above.
Our future is here.

Love.
An intimate moment.
A gentle kiss.
A binding embrace.
It is joy and beauty becoming ONE.

Forever.
Eternal bliss.
Wedded happiness.
Trials and triumphs.
To strong to miss.
This Celebration of Love.

## Antananarivo Six
## Independence Day of Madagascar
*by Fitzroy G. Joseph*

   Guns salute, demonstrations by MIG aeroplanes, speeches at the stadium which can be seen from the higher floors of the Hilton Hotel. The stadium is in a beautiful spot in the valley with the hills rising above and away all around Antananarivo till the palace of the queen which also enjoys an enviable location.
   By eleven fifteen a.m., people all dressed in their Sunday best for the occasion, began dispersing towards their homes. The distraction was over. Back to the struggle of daily existence. Life is an enigma!! Man, in spite of history, is unpredictable! And development is devious when one or two men think that they can plan for it independently of the people whose *development* they are planning. And in this international world where "meddling" and "manipulation" in the internal affairs of sovereign countries by outside developed countries are common, the process is compounded and faced with many backward steps.
   So the euphoria of Independence Day is short-lived, for tomorrow the barefoot struggle to achieve the monetary means to buy the needs of routine existence is to be faced. Not even tomorrow it's today, now, even during the distractions by the lofty exhalations of the President who eats, sleeps and lives relatively comfortably. Of course, no disrespect is meant against his person. He seems to be a sincere person with good intentions.
   The status of his position allows him to be different. There is too, I believe, a limit to the capacity of worrying about the poor masses. Some presidents have a low tolerance for worrying. Others, a high. And some seem not to care as soon as they smell the fumes of measurable power.

## Blue Moonlight
*by Sara Kallenbach - age 17*

The pale-blue moon casts an eerie, silvery shadow in my window. Everything is silent, silent as death. A slow murmur of the barn radio comes through loud and clear. The frogs make a chirping sound in the swamp, soothing the mind. A cat's screeching breaks through the night like a baseball crashing through a window. A firefly flickers by, seemingly out of place on such an odd night. The lupine below my window seems to glow in the pale, water-like moonlight. The only star in the sky, just below the water-filled moon, seems so sad and alone. Then as I lay my head down to rest on my pillow, I gaze out at this scene unfolding before me, and enter's a soft, dreamless sleep...

## The Biology Exam
*by Dorothy Kaminski - age 15*

As the day was coming to an end,
   and evening was drawing near
The children were all in their beds
   counting the hours in fear;
For tomorrow would be their Biology exam,
   And a hard one this will be,
Because it will cover everything-
   From chapter one to eternity

They said their prayers and closed their eyes
   and wished for the best of luck
Because they knew, if they failed this test
   they would be in ten feet of muck!
While dreaming of acids and bases and such,
   they woke up with such a slur,
They had a feeling something was wrong
   soon biology became a big blur.

A feeling of concern came upon their faces,
   wondering what failure could do to them
Terrified, they picked up their paces,
   and started studying all over again.
A lipid is one thing, a protein another...
   saying this over and over again
So tired they got, they could not imagine-
   that they fell asleep all over again!

At a quarter past seven they woke up in splendor,
   rushing to take that exam.
When, without even knowing
   they had all forgotten,
The exam had been postponed-
   until ONE MORE DAY!

## Sounding Souls
*by Kathy Karnes - age 15*

In this world there is love and hate,
These are the most important things that we should not sedate,
Love and war in a world of peace,
Entangled in an everlasting quarrel,
Till the death we do not depart,
Re-born into someone else's heart,
Live and let live till we decide to leave,
Give and give till our hearts' do bleed,
Forever a memory traced in my soul,
Your love will stay with me and keep me full,
A caring life you gave to me,
A loving life I leave to thee,
However my path twists and curls,
I will be here for you night and day,
Believe in me as I do you,
Believe in me as I do too,
Bond our souls in everlasting trust,
Forever we will forget the trust,
   Ashes to Ashes,
   Dust to Dust,
   Heart to Heart,
   Soul to Soul,
I'll always love you for our love is full.

## Kindergarten
*by Megan Keller - age 14*

   She always wanted to explain things, kind of like me.
But, nobody even cared!
   The teacher spoke to her softly, just like nobody would dare.
She told her to wear a dress like all the other girls, I wore a dress but was still different,
   That makes me the same.
She told the teacher it didn't matter to her, but she looked sad.
   After that, they colored pictures with crayons, what I dearly loved to do.
   She drew yellow, the way she felt about the morning sun, but I thought of the mourning moon,
   Her drawing was beautiful, though drawn by a child of my age at the time!
   The teacher walked over to her and smiled.
She turned to my drawing, black as a raven,
   "What's this?" She asked. "Why don't you draw something beautiful like she is drawing?"
   After that, my mother bought me a tie, and she always drew flowers and butterflies, like all the other girls,
   She still wore pants, now I'm like her!
I threw my dark picture away, and I grew up.
   Now, when I lay out alone, looking at the dark night sky, the moon, I think of my black picture, a tad of violet blue for the moon;
   She was square and inside dark as she grew up, just like me, her hands still as if never to color again in a single stroke;
   The things inside of her that needed saying didn't need any more.
It had stopped as time passed away, turned dark;
The yellow picture was a lark, just like me;
   Just like me.

## A Kiss From A Morning Down
*by Brian Kelly*

The sun slowly peers over a dark horizon,
Casting a shining orange shadow over the water, turning it a deep crimson,
A door slowly opens darkness seeping out into the light,
Slowly the soft silhouette of a woman appears.
Dressed only in her sheet utterly naked underneath,
A sheet of a thousand watching faces
Never letting their eyes off her cold naked blue skin,
She slowly walks toward the glimmering pool
The suns brilliant rays dancing on the water
Like crystal ballerinas in an eternal dance,
Interesting... so beautifully, yet so strange, so new...
The man fragile faces begin to frown crying in the reflecting light
Light so pure so true ever the same,
Slowly her hands loosen the tight wad of sheet slipping
The light slowly slides across the floor cautiously inching towards her,
Calling her beckoning her to see,
A million innocent faces cry in vain and in fear,
But she does not hear their mournful tears falling to their future grave
Off her shoulders down her back,
Screaming faces burn in the holy light of day of truth of heart
Off her back down her hips
Faces mourn as others fall shattering upon a warm glittering floor
Off her hips down her legs
Hitting the floor is a terrible price to pay,
Off her legs down her feet out of sight,
No more screams of fright, no more fearful nights,
All are gone leaving no traces, only light is left,
Holding her tight in an embrace of pure delight
She is alone no more not tonight
She's been kissed by dawns morning light.

## The Rueful
*by Theresa Keown*

Stay strong you say..
Why should I?  I am tired of always staying strong!
At the first sign of my tenderness and neediness...
everyone would run from me leaving me to fend for myself-
Why?
Because, I say...It is my job to be strong..everyone
expects it!
But a little girl crying...NO..sobbing uncontrollably
inside me needs some love..
So..should I turn her away because I have to be the strong
one?..No weakness may I show?
I dare not ignore her or she might just die..having felt
the last pain of abandonment from of all people..me..
I NEED ME!
I cannot, I will not always be strong..though it may be
my nature to laugh at adversity..Adversity can sometimes
be overwhelming and painful as hell..
So..Say not to me to be strong..I have been strong many a
time..Right now my garden need tending and the little
girl there needs someone more strong than she to care for her....
Go and fend for yourself so I can help to find someone
to tend my little child...

## Tale of a Vampire
*by Shalu Khakoo - age 16*

Oh Angels come to me,
And help me free my soul.
Help me struggle through this life,
And be free once again.
Let me roam in daylight,
And sleep at twilight.
Let me be as I was,
Before I was cursed so long ago.
My soul, I no longer have,
My body is not my own.
I am not truly alive,
Nor am I really dead.
Free my soul so once again,
I can be with my love till the day I die.

## Shattered Trust
*by Joan A. Kimminau*

You fractured my heart
   and shattered my trust.
You've taken my love
   and turned it to dust.

No more will I see
   your laughing blue eyes
without the torture
   from all of your lies.

Can mended fractures
   be stronger than new?
Can rekindled love
   be trusted and true?

Please handle my heart
   like crystal you find.
Then give me a love,
   to strong to unwind.

When fractures are mended
   and trust is repaired,
love will be stronger,
   than past love we shared.

## No Fantasies
*by Jolene Kinley - age 12*

Lies untold can break the heart,
Kisses of love can wreck the soul,
A heart of gold can melt no stone,
A kiss from a prince can wake no princess,
True love can conquer no evil,
Everlasting love can exist no longer
No man can turn back time,
No water can fight fire,
No kiss can break a spell,
But a true friendship can save your soul.

## Shadows
*by J. D. DeForest*

Save for a woman's labored face staring
Into a proud and bragging tone of life
Beyond the windows of her scant abode,
Cannot her baren lips taste
   Those savory wishes setting themselves
   Against the purple horizon?

Only lost shapes pass her by:  Shadows
Through darkened doorways of her little hole,
Long enough to flash their teeth
And gnash and tear with slanted
   Jaws screaming
   Through scarred throats.

Soft lights awaken slimmest hopes, streaming
Through fernwood cracks only to flicker
Against smooth steel, shadow polishes
With a crimson banana.
   And daily she waits...
   Listening for the hammer.

Save for the woman's labored face staring
Into the hunger-beaten eyes
   Of her screaming infant...
   Silence.

## Moment to moment!
*by Tom Kitt*

The world is a contraction of wholeness.
Heaven is wholeness ad infinitum.
Time is an illusion that limits the Soul.
Time allows fear to steal what is whole.

Each moment's replete with the moment to come.
Faith and humility are how it's done.
The past and the future no longer converge.
The world is the oyster, the pearl to be won.

This magic exists in the vibrations of Matter.
Expanding each moment to observe each delight;
All senses bared, naked, and bright.
Exposing fear to die in the light.

Sometimes scared, we panic and run.
More often we will build a gun.
We speed up our time, afraid what we'll find?
Harder to kill a bird that is flying!

But, heaven is a moment everlasting and whole.
We are all heaven just circling our Soul.
When we give a moment an expansive mold,
We dip from the well of universal gold.

Each amplified moment is pregnant with care,
Full of the knowledge of what we might dare.
Heaven delights when faith has killed fear.
Battalions of Angels fly to our care.

*Distinctions of Excellence*

## Eyes of Fire
*by Ba Kiwanuka*

Your eyes are lit
With brilliant fire
Like the brightest star
In the darkest night

Your voice so beautiful
Like the purest note
In the sweetest melody
That Mozart wrote

Your smile is like
The rising sun
So bright and warm
Across the morning dew

## Late Thanks
*by Mika Kiyono*

The midnight moon flouting in the sky
Looks just like you,
Appeared into the darkness of the night
Lighting the road and me.

Kindly moving across the night sky
Going away so fast.
Times passed by with that night sky
disappearing very quietly.

Again the moon is up tonight,
Just like that night.
But this time I'm all alone
Walking on my own road.

Remembering that dark night and light,
I'm wanting to tell you that
I finally found the road I seeked,
And thank you for the words you said to me.

It was like the light of the moon,
And thank you for the words you said to me.

## Weeping Mind
*by Ryan-Iver Klann - age 19*

In the mind
   of the mad;
And in the mind of the mad;

I was weeping;
and weeping for faded dreams,
and weeping for hollowed screams,
and weeping;
   for life is not what it seems.

In the mind
   of the mad;
And in the mind of the mad;

I was hoping;
and hoping to end the endless frowning,
and hoping to halt the evils crowning,
and hoping;
   that we will survive societies drowning.

In the mind
   of the mad;
And in the mind of the mad;

I had visions;
and visions of the worlds decay,
and visions of pride doused with dismay,
and visions;
   of a fault-ridden past that lingers today.

In the mind
   of the mad;
And in the mind of the mad;

I was weeping...

## Times Ago
*by John Knutson*

I dream a dream
of times ago
when I held you close
it's a feel
I won't forget
it's etched into my mind
and if my memory serves me
you loved me just the same
but when I wonder
where you are
a tear rolls down my face
I do not know if you dream
of times we had ago
but I can tell you this
I won't forget
because I love you so.

## What I'm Left With
*by Crystal Kordalchuk - age 16*

I'm really hurt and totally devastated,
No true feelings are left in my heart.
It lies open, exposed, and bleeding.
I see you with her,
So happy and smiling.
But me over here,
Is inside dying.

## A Definition of Love
*by Donna Kay Koski*

Love is a strong missing when one's gone or never near
Love is not a passing, it is here from year to year
It's a giving up of jealousies, a sureness felt within
It's a time of rejoicing when each has given in

Love's an acceptance of ones failings, and ones flaws
It's a deep affection, deep reflection and a pause
It's a time, when one ponders—how lucky can I be
When all the world is well and the feelings one is free

It's stability, commitment though no words may be spoken
It's a silent bond of trust and a ring could be the token
Love's a fuzzy blanket that keeps you snug and warm
It keeps you safe and comfy from life's never ending storm

Love is mixed emotions, between lovers and good friends
You can love a child, and love can make amends
Love's a spirit's blessing that's been given you and me
A belief and faith in someone, that we—may never see

## Love
*by Katie Koslucher*

What is love?
Does anyone know?
Does it come from the heart,
or does it come from the soul?
Is there one true meaning,
or does everyone have their own opinion?
The world may never know.

## Grandma Tells A Ghost Story
*by Flora M. Kosoff*

Gather around, and hover near, Grandma will tell you a story, dear.
I remember a night in sixty-three,
when your mom was a child upon my knee.
We took her out to trick or treat, Really dear, she looked so sweet.
In that yellow and red suit, a chubby clown,
We followed her tracks up the street, and down;
When all of a sudden, out of the dark, those ghostly eyes,
with fire and spark, appeared through the shadowy privet hedge.
"Come, play with us," spoke a chilling voice.
"Don't run away...you have no choice.
My brothers and I...we goblins three,
are here to join your Halloween spree."
But, try as I might, I could not see, a body there, or reality.
All I could see were the glittering eyes ---
no mask, or face, or child's disguise.
Dis-embodied, the eyes and voice:
"As we said before, you have no choice."
In that dim October of sixty-three, little Linny and I shared the goblin's glee.
Over the fences, across the street, around the town, to trick or treat.
Our bags were stuffed with candy and fruit ---
money and prizes --- pillaged loot.
For grandma knew, with no surprise,
others had followed the goblin's eyes.
They rang the bells with rampant glee ---
their shrieks and screams, a tympany.
Late at night, we approached the edge of the yard that
boasted the pivot hedge.

No more, will those goblin eyes be seen,
until next year, at Halloween.

## You Left So Hastely
*by Irena Ksepko*

You promised that you will be forever with me
You relinquished your promise
I would like it to be as it was in the past
That I am going to regret
You left so suddenly

Today I am left alone
I am recalling everything from the beginning,
I am analyzing your words
Maybe I lost it's sense,
Or maybe I lost it's great value.

Today I know, that I was only in the clouds,
My heart is yearning for you,
You were my comforter,
You were like a friend,
From my dreams you were chosen.

I am yearning for you,
Because you are far away,
I am yearning for you
Because you vanished like tides

My love, enormous love
Will not enjoy happiness because I lost it.
I would like to see that my yearning
Will return you back to me.

In a form of an angel from far away
Quietly whisper your own words:
"Come my darling,
You will never be sorry again."

## Mother
*by Heather Kozuchowsky - age 14*

As I sit here,
next to her bed,
I wonder what I am going to do,
without her by my side,
helping me get through life.

As I sit here,
squeezing her hand,
I wait for some sign of life,
something to tell me she can hear me,
and understand what I'm trying to say.

As I sit here,
tears racing down my face,
I remember when I was younger,
when we were best friends,
and I could tell her anything.

As I sit here,
I wish I wasn't sitting here,
waiting for my mother to say something,
anything at all,
just so I could be sure she'll be with me longer.

As I sit here,
I take one last look,
at my beautiful mother,
whom I love,
and say goodbye.

As I sit here,
with a hole in my heart,
cold hands,
and a numb body,
I know I will be reunited with my mother in Heaven.

## Tomorrow
*by Amy Kuntz - age 18*

The trees talk, the winds whisper
And today I heard a bird chirp my name.

Sounds in the halls, footsteps on the stairs
But when I turn no one is there.

Locked doors are open and the lights are on
am I going crazy or is someone there?

Come out, come out, I don't want to play anymore
I know you're there just watching me.

I can sense your eyes watching me squirm
Oh God, I can feel your breath on the back of my neck.

Your hands are burning imprints in my back
I'm being pushed down.

Ma'am are you alright? I hear the policeman say
Where did he go? I say scanning the shadows.

There was no one around he says,
You must have fallen on the ice.

Maybe I am crazy? Tomorrow I'll be fine I say
Tomorrow I'll be back I hear the wind whisper.

Rubber walls, white coats, I'm safe here locked away
I keep my promises a voice whispers, It's tomorrow.

*Distinctions of Excellence*

## Wallow
*by Mira Lademora - age 14*

I wallow at unnecessary depths
In the overflowing pool of regrets
In overemphasized sadness
I'm driven into madness
As I struggle for much needed air
I look around, but find no one who cares
As the chill water envelopes me
I turn to find and see
That the very thing that soothed life's burn
Has come back for my life in return

## First Date
*by Julie Land - age 17*

Star catching eyes of blue,
moonlit hair of blonde,
suit as black as the night,
he looks at me.
He takes my hand and leads me to the car.
Dancing the night away in his arms, he romances me.
The man of my dreams.
He drives me home without a word.
Did I blow it?
Will he see me again?
He takes my hand, and we walk to the door.
No words.
Then he leans down and his lips touch mine.
I sigh.
He asks, "Can we do this again?"
I barely whisper, "Yes."
Dreaming of our second date,
I stand on my porch and watch him disappear.

## The Forgotten Ones
*by Sandra Kay La Pre*

So many went,
so few came back,
all is forgotten - We turned our back.

I know not one who went to die,
yet, even now I find I cry.

Why they went,
how much they gave,
so much was lost - no one to save.

And all the flowers left behind,
at the cold wall, their souls inside.

But finally now, it's all so clear,
why they went - and why we're here.

To those who fell for what they believed,
are finally remembered for all to see.

*Dedicated To: Those who lost their lives
for what they believed.*

## A Heart That Wants To Dance
*by Charles Ken Kostyra*

As I look outside my window...a bluebird I do see,
I walk into the kitchen,..my dishes wait for me,
The clothes are in the hamper..the cat waits by the door,
It seems like the same old story..one that's been told before,

I catch my image in the mirror..the years have taken their toll
I gaze into my eyes...I look into my soul,
My face is lined with wrinkles...but I have a heart that wants
to dance!

A heart that wants to dance...to tunes of years gone by,
A heart that wants to dance...a heart that's young and shy,
With hopes and dreams of tomorrow...without the fear of chance,
Oh give me those dreams of yesteryear...
Give me a heart that wants to dance!!

## The Phone Call
*by Barbara Larsen*

Drum rolls of pain, aching, nausea:
Relentless, dehabilitating.
Twisting, seeking, fitfully dozing:
Dreaming.
Weird landscapes, disjointed movements.
Noise! A roller-coaster's clack! Clank!
Bore on storm winds.
Colors bleed together; drip—
Black and white becomes technicolor;
Awareness of discomfort, grasping for oblivion.
Gasping; grinding, gruelling struggle
For sun-fields, puff clouds,
Chuckling, meandering water:—
Peace.
Shrill, strident sound:
Grope for reality.
Across miles and time, a voice
Leading my panting spirit
To happy places, well remembered.
Young, healthy years, glowing hopes.
Family, friends, old enemies,
Creep from looming shadows of times past
To play hide-and-seek for a brief bright respite
From age and loss.
Then good-by: regretfully, reluctantly.
Back to pain.

## Untitled
*by Meghan Larsen - age 17*

The rain falls fast and heavy
Covering everything in its path
Falling down like a blanket
Everything consumed

There I stand cold and wet
Too numb to feel any emotion
Too cold to notice anything
Not even the pounding rain

The rain pours down around me
The puddles swirl around my toes
People scatter everywhere looking
For shelter from the cold dark rain.

My heart stands still and I wait
The rain falls cold on my shoulders
Nothing to wait for but still I linger
For I am alone and very lonely

## Walking
*by Susan M. Lashier*

Walking into the shadows, as the sunlight
quickly fell. The ducks, the geese, the
squirrels under my feet. Quacking, squawking,
scurrying. The sounds of brush in the wind.
The smell of moisture, hanging there, waiting for me
to walk through. Rustling and waiting.

Walking through the light drenched trees. Leaves
dancing, as if they'd never stop. Having fun, not resting
as I entered, not believing that I would dare
to disrupt their world. Branches swaying to and fro,
backwards and forwards. Dancing and waiting.

Walking by the swirling pond. Fish leaping, happily escaping
the fishermans' catch. Lilys floating safely by, waving as
they pass. The light flickers. Butterflies float into
the sky, going faster and further. I am trying to
keep up. Color explodes and softens the park. I
stop running. Walking and waiting.

## Family and Friends
*by Monique La-Touche*

A friend is a person whom one knows well;
An amigo; a confidant; a side kick who's swell

A friend is also a person known casually;
An acquaintance who supports you, normally

Friends are warmhearted, sharing goodwill and cheer
Real friends are the people we want to keep near

Friends are attached to each other by esteem or affection;
Favored companions, neither hostile nor fond of rejection

A family has relatives who live together as one
Flesh and blood, clans, tribes, a daughter or son

A family is kin who share the same house
A grandmother or uncle, a niece or a spouse

By ancestry and law families are connected
And we're taught that our elders should be loved and respected

The family you have may not be your choice
But in friendships you certainly do have a voice

These folk fill our lives from the start till it ends
See, you can't make it through without family and friends!


## Winter's Secrets
*by Regina Lazarovich - age 13*

There is magic in the air.
Can you feel it? No? Not yet?
There is laughter everywhere.
Can you hear it? No? Not yet?
Then let me take you to a place
Which is sparkling with light.
Where the snowflakes soft and white
Are just falling from the sky.
They are falling on the houses
They are falling on the land
And as far as you can see
Everything is perfect now.
As you step you hear a crunch
From the snow beneath your feet.
You can smell crisp winter air
You can feel its magic touch.
You can hear the laughter now
From the houses everywhere,
And you too can understand
All the winter's secrets now.


## How I Celebrate Veteran's Day
*by Jennifer S. Lee - age 13*

Veteran's Day is coming around,
I honor the grandfather I never knew,
The grandfather whose body was never found,
The grandfather who didn't see me at birth and cannot see how fast I grew.
My grandfather was searching for a bomb on a train,
But before he discovered it, the bomb gave way,
And my grandfather was gone. It's that simple and plain.
I wish he could be here to see me play.
I know he is in Heaven, smiling down,
Watching me day by day,
I wish he could see me in my graduation gown.
I am like the sun; I am full of pride and show it with many a beaming ray.


## So!
*by Carol Torsak Lenhart*

How can I talk to thee, my dear?
For scarcer do my words take wing,
Giving form to random thoughts,
Than they are snatched upon
With action swift
As the pounce of a preying cat.
Words, like feathers,
Scatter in the fray,
Save those that feed thy thoughts,
And they become thine own possession then.
Soon, whirling through strange channels
On some unfamiliar theme,
Words which had been mine give birth,
As in a dream,
To unfamiliar contexts.
Based on these, you give reply,
By then, to thy thoughts, not mine own.
I try again with protests mild,
Or less than mild,
When thrice I've tried to no avail.
Thou heardst my words,
Or some, or most,
But what I said was lost.


## Dream
*by Christine Leong - age 14*

A mind once stretched by a new idea
Imagination starts to grow, grow, grow...
Never repeats its original appearance
Upon a beautiful place high up from below

Though my thoughts never clearly come out
I still won't open my eyes
This dream is like a peaceful day alone
Staring at the morning sun rise

Feel the cool air through my hair
Touch the warm, white sand under my feet, feet, feet...
Look up into space as the sun shines down on me
Feeling the beautiful sun's heat

Loving the creativity I am gaining
Loving the rest and relaxation
Catching every detail without explanation
The worst that can happen is complication


## To A Far Off Friend
*by Ami Leshley - age 19*

Sometimes lost in another mans field
  Sometimes found when someone else
                tends to yield
Sometimes lost between time and infinity
  Sometimes found within the past and it even tends
   to dwell in the absolute of this moment
Sometimes when things go to wrong and the time
  ain't right, you need a real true friend
Sometimes when all is lost and there's no time to
  spare, you have to know how to call a far off friend
Sometimes when you tell someone how you really feel
  it's like walking in a strange new world with only one person
   that would really be there for you, but you are telling that someone
Sometimes one person would be able to help better than three,
  because then that someone tends to yield to get you out of
   that field, you somehow got lost in

      Problems gettin bigger
       Solutions gettin smaller,
        Until you make that one step
         To call that far off friend

## Easter
*by Louise Lewis*

The dark despair,
Good Friday dawned.
The man of sorrows
Stood before the jeering mob
With crown of thorns and crimson wounds
That made a ruby pattern in the gloom.

Then red becomes the victory glow
As Christ the Son ascends
In glory as the king of kings
To heavenly father filled with joy
In this bright and glorious son
With whom he is well pleased.

May we, like Christ,
Ascend this day and break the bonds
That bind our souls to ignorance and pain.
May we ascend in glorious flight
Like clouds of butterflies that shine
With beauty and with truth in the eternal skies.

## The Passing Bye
*by Michelle Lewis*

We call it the "passing bye"
No matter how hard we try,
Life will keep passing bye.
The things that matter we overlook,
But later on, those things; we wish
   we would have took.
So as we look back and re-read
   Lifes book;
The unwritten words are seen
   So clearly....
So for the rest of the
   "Passing bye" we hold
   Those unseen words dearly!

## Is The Race?
*by Stewart Lewis*

All set
Ready
Go!
The Contestants
(All ready for anything life has to offer
And are more than ready to experience
What success they can garner)
All eager and ready with all the answers,
Our young chargers leave the starting block!
Each one trying to finish the race before anyone else!
**BUT!**
Does the first place prize
Go to the swiftest?
Are the young chargers always
In the know?
**NO!**
So, the next time you think
You know it all
Just ask
Someone who's older!
You just might get a very valuable
Lesson on life!

## Little Child
*by Liliane Li-Cho - age 17*

One child
With skin so mild
Wandering about
With your tiny feet,
Skipping in the whereabouts
Little child
With eyes of innocence
Knowing nothing of reminiscence
Rosy cheeks
And a tiny chin
Black curly hair
Beautifully-combed shiny hair.
Two little dimples
That twitch in a smile
And a pouty little mouth
That likes to laugh
Two tiny hands
Reaching to the ends
A happy little face
Always in the right place
Wearing a nice dress,
You are a princess
A golden crown to fit
Your little head to the last bit
And a magic wand
To hold in one hand,
Sparking the earth
With a cluster of stars...

## A Day with my Mother
*by Lindsey Light - age 13*

I spent a day with my mother, we shared a special bond.

What I had discovered it was there all along.

As the day went on we grew closer together, for the bond we had discovered was very strong.

We laughed and we cried through out the memories we shared, for the past is gone.

We began to build a Mother Daughter relationship that will never be gone.

A relationship that is life long.

As our past thoughts and memories soared through our heads we thought about our futures that lie ahead.

That day I spent with my Mother opened a world of opportunity of thoughts and pleasures of the future, for some day I'll be a Mother too.

But when I am a Mother I want to be just like my Mother, unique and special in every God given way.

For every day she is someone else in her own way.

She's a hard working woman by morning, a tired woman stuck in rush hour traffic by evening and by night she's a great cook and a fantastic Mother.

This is what I discovered while spending a venturous day with my Mother.

Not only that she learned more about me as I was to her.

A day with my Mother is one in a million memories that we share together.

## The Box in the Basement
*by Danielle Lipson*

They told me never to open this box
They tied it with rope and they locked it with locks

But I found the scissors and I found the keys
And I'm down in the basement and down on my knees

And I'm trying to learn about my dark past
I only have short memories that won't last

For you see I was abandoned by my mother one night
She knew in her heart that it just wasn't right

But she left me there cold with no place to go
With no one to love me and nothing to know

So I'm opening this box without hesitation
In desperate hope to find information

I'm ready to see what ever's in there
I truly think that it's only fair

For me to be able to learn my past
Should it be a discussion or even be asked

But what if this box just contains nothing more
Than a couple of outfits when young I once wore

What will that prove, will it solve anything
Will it teach me the lessons that life has to bring

I believe it'll put me right where I began
As if running through a fairy tale in a make-believe land

I always thought she'd come back to make things all seem right
And I still have visions of her and I in my dreams at night

I guess the purpose of this box, was to make me finally see
How hard of a decision she had to make and that she did it all for me

The answers to my questions always lied within my mind
It wasn't till now my courage made them easy for me to find

So I guess after all I won't open this box
I'll tie it back up and I'll lock all these locks


## On the Edge
*by Stacy Li - age 18*

Alone with my thoughts
I am captivated by the darkness
That will drive me to insanity
A brilliant glow enticing me from the shadow
I lurk behind
Linger like a flame
That refuses to go out
Like a life
In a prison
Trapped in the deception of perception
Alone with their thoughts
Cold and damp
Their prison
The mind
So dangerous
It thinks the unthinkable
Sees the unseeable
Dreams, hopes
The impossible
A distant dream of you
Not so distant
A faded mirage in a forgotten desert
Buried deep into the heart of man
Lies my soul
My breath
My life
In you
I see my dreams
My destiny
And for you, I would do anything.

## Walking Out Of My Father's Shadow
*by Margaret Lockman - age 16*

As I walk down town,
The people would look and stare.
They would put my father down,
Because of the clothes I wear.
But they wouldn't ask a thing,
When they saw a child of thirteen.
But I have not a sting,
And have been to places which only I wanted to have seen.
But my dear father does not push me,
Or try to make me change.
He's happy with who I want to be,
And does not care when people say, "that boy is strange."
So I'll live my life,
And choose my own way.
Without the problems or strife,
Until I decide what I wish to do with my life some day.
And good old Dad,
May want something for me.
But he would rather be sad,
Than make me someone I don't want to be.


## Further Than Curiosity
*by Synnikaverse Lofton - age 19*

Virgin souls under the sunlights
Bind, blushing trees caught
In an innocence of divine
Beads of sweat of desires cold
Romance orchestrates melodies untold

Eyes of love and unconditional
Waves, affectionate swans wading
Precious and untamed. Heartfelt
Thoughts peer her beauty from
Afar, flourishing questions of doubt,
Sing to me my love, how far

Unleashed doves emerging from
her golden fingers, clouded
Reveries that abstrusely linger
Swimming in the flowers of her
Warm palms, my soul that completely
Vanished in breezes calm


## Long Dusty Roads
*by Alice Rundell Lomen*

Walking roads so long and dusty
as a kid, they weren't that long.
There was too much to experience,
Birds in the trees singing,
Flowers blossoming in the sun,
A deer across the field.
Billowing dust afar meant a car was coming,
Can you tell who it is yet?

Now these bones are older and rusty,
We can still hum a song
as we try to go through the fence.
Real life was babies burping,
Eating hot dogs on a bun.
Leaving home, letters sealed,
Cracked voices now only humming,
No time left to fret.

We have moved to faraway places,
Traveled freeways, flights away from it all,
But I always come back
to that long dusty road.
It's the road to home.

*Distinctions of Excellence*

## The Thread of Life
*by The Poet*

You must enjoy every moment of life. For it is a precious Gift, and you never know when the thread of life will be cut.

You must savor every bit of sunshine, every drop of rain, every glimmer of moonlight, every twinkle of the stars. For you never know when the thread of life will be cut.

You must keep every kiss, every hug, every love, deep within your heart. Just because you never know when the thread of life will be cut.

So, when winter's wind whips through the sleeping trees, and rustles the dead and fallen leaves. Think of spring time walks, and summer time talks, because you never know when the thread of life will be cut.

## Rachee (Universal Beauty)
*by Cyrus Kai*

Constellations form the image of her face
Offering the light of her beauty since the beginning of time
Under the moonbeams the prophecy of her coming is cast over us
Restlessly my soul wanders across the galaxy
Twice traveling the heavens to worship her radiance
Nothing could better adorn divinity than the
Embodier of grace and all that glorifies love
Yet with all the space between us, I still know

Rachee is universal beauty

Sacredly the zodiac aligns to offer reverence
Upon the first star I knelt and prayed
Carnal moon and exulted sun are eclipsed in her eyes as
Creations splendor lives and dies within her sighs
Ubiquitous lovers kiss and make love in praise of the name
My soul dreamt of her on the day I was born
Beholding the one word the world will use and know

Rachee means universal beauty

## The Dream World!!
*by Jade Marie Lorenzen - age 15*

I sit here just staring into a world that is not real;
I wonder what it would be like to really be in that dream world.
The world of good and no evil; the world of love and no hate;
The world of dreams and no lies; the world everyone likes.

Somewhere in the dream world; you are there;
You are there within goodness, love and dreams.
I know in the dream world we shall see each other;
We will both be having fun; living out our dreams until the very end.

Somewhere in the real world; you are there;
You are there within evilness, hate and lies.
I know we shall see each other again;
We will both fight; trying to live out our dreams, we wish to accomplish.

I sit here now just thinking of what to do in the real world;
I know our dreams can come true; but we have to work at it.
We can make it in this real world of ours; it may be a challenge;
But no challenge we can't try to get through; we have each other for help.

I know I may never be in the dream world; but I still like to dream of it;
You and I; together we can help make the dream world come true.
So you and I can take each other's hands, minds and hearts;
Hopefully, we can clean up the real world and make the dream world come true.

## Emptyness
*by Sue Lotz*

My heart feels hollow and empty.
The pain is to much to bear.

I breath a shallow breath.
I sign with a weakness of a dying body.

Must I continue this journey of life,
till the end comes with eternal sleep?

Within me walks a empty shadow,
trudging down that lonely path.

Will I awake tomorrow with a cold
heart lifeless with emotion?

Barren are the days and nights.
That I live without you.

## Fly
*by Jenny Loveland - age 12*

I want to fly
I want to be beside you
You're flying and I want to
I want to soar with you
I believe that I can
I want to fly
I want to fly with you
Through the clouds and above the waters
I need to fly with you
This is the last time I will see you in a long time
So let me fly with you
If you wont let me fly with you
Let me tell you
I love you and goodbye!

*Dedicated to: my Aunt Yvonne McQuillan & my Grandpa Bernard Moon. They both died and I never got to say goodbye so that is what I'm doing with this.*

## Lonely Nights
*by Amee Lowery - age 18*

In the night, the cold winter's night,
She hides all her emotions,
From the one she loves,
Only so she doesn't get hurt again.

He tries on these cold nights,
To prove his love to her,
Only this time he gets hurt,
He only wanted to show she can be loved.

She runs from her feelings,
To a place of desire,
Where anything will satisfy her,
Only to be lonely and miserable,
She runs and hides in a cold place of death.

He ends up more lonely than he started out,
Only to find out he is better off without her,
But he wishes he was there with her once again.

For she misses his arms around her,
She dreams that he is there with her,
In the lonely hours of night,
Holding her close and whispering 'I love you' in her ear.

So softly, it would make her cry,
She only wants to be loved and cared for and needed,
Only now all alone,
And sad for what she did to him.

## Message for Two
*by Yashira Luna - age 16*

As I walked across the room
I caught a glimpse of you.
You were caressing your new love,
another to whom you've promised to be true.
And I remembered all those promises you once made to me.
Promises you never had the strength to keep.
And to think, I would believe everything you'd say,
and with your warm embrace
you would calm all my fears away.
Remember, how you used to take me into your arms,
and repeatedly guaranteed
that you would do me no harm.
Then how would you explain
all the wounds you left in my heart,
from pain that you caused,
that slowly tore my innocent heart apart.
But don't flatter yourself to know you once had my attention.
I would never give your heartless ego
any undeserved attention.
I would just like to point out....that because of your abuse,
you've also helped grow stronger,
you've turned the mature, intelligent woman in me loose.
So if you would give the following message
to the one you say you love:
The man she is with isn't worth it,
he doesn't have the honor of knowing the true meaning of LOVE.

## Hugs
*by Alicia MacAllister - age 13*

Hugs
   can be exchanged
Without any argument
Hugs
   are always the right
   size never too big and
   yet never to small
Hugs
   can make a person feel secure
   in an insecure world
Hugs
   can make a person feel
   loved when they think no one
   cares

## A Guest in Egypt
*by Ian MacLennan*

Egypt's moon shines drunken cups tonight,
shaking her triple bowl through haze.
The wines' sharp fires have seared my tongue,
and glutted food has sickened to my taste.
The eunuch stands beside the jewelled door
that sways its panels over golden plates,
and slave girls bear the silver dish of fruit;
they come in mist, like waving fans,
in double forms of grace.
The hour has childed dreams,
and what my Eros seeks
bends like the reeds of Cleopatra's wish,
where love reflects her thousand mirrored forms
in shapes of beauty from the brazen walls.
White arms like roots lift up their hands
to draw me downward to the fecund marsh.
My mind's pool swirls its vortex of desire;
a brilliant sheen, it twists around her eye,
coiling toward her gently moving bed.

*Distinctions of Excellence*

## The Cycle Of Life
*by Juanita A. Maddox*

Spring awakens the earth,
The flowers show their new growth,
Producing the sweet sensation of new life,
Awakening the color after winter's drab.

Summer days stretch out the time,
Covering the earth with warmth,
Under a blue sky filled with clouds,
That look like balls of cotton.

Fall arrives with brilliant color,
Allowing the trees to show their final glory,
For soon these beautiful leaves
   must fall to earth —
Leaving a bare tree once more.

Winter follows in the form of snow and ice,
Creating its' own marvel of brilliant white,
Outlining each branch with ice to create
   — a winter wonderland

The cycle of life has now been completed,
The beginning, the middle, and the end.

## Pain
*by Patricia Lombardi - age 11*

Pain to some people
is when you get hurt
such as on a soccer
   field,
But to me pain is
a force deep down
in your heart
that nags at you
every day of your life.
That is what I feel
pain is.

## Hunger
*by Lourdes Madruga*

Starving for your love
   I have grown gaunt,
   hollow in the cheeks.
Misspent pride,
devoid of dignity,
I followed your trail
   like a pitiful pup
   begging for a tiny crumb.
Feed me with your touch,
Gorge me with a gentle word.

But you don't
   You allow me to be hungry,
   swatting me from your heels
with tense accounts of
dirty dishes and
all my various shortcomings.
   I have been without your love
   for so long now
that I am no longer famished,
Mama.

## Sunset in Red
*by Diana L. Malon*

The children now fed,
Are safely tucked away in bed.

And now content
With his slippers on,
And newspaper upon his lap,
My dear husband takes a nap.

My dishes are now done
And the dogs are by my side...

I steal away
For a quiet moment of my own.

Enjoying the labor,
Of my peaceful stroll,
I walk through the tall grasses
And sit upon my favorite knoll.

I look out into the sky
And basque in the beauty of it all.

Feeling at peace I return home,
And for those I love,
I place a kiss upon their cheek.

With the sun now gone
And the day now done—

It's off to bed
For dreams of sunsets in red.

## Death on the Sun-train
*by Germano Mandrillo*

Your funeral was gorgeous.
Maybe too many fancy ties and yet
Nothing as death tones in with fancy
And better than poetry
Yellow spots on a blue background
Red spirals on shades of white
and colorful designer butterflies
While you sleep forever,
Happy at last, self-confident.
   You know?
I only put on my garish check jacket,
A pitiful echo of 1925-gangsters,
Just to show my dissent.
   Go on! You threw yourself out of the Sun-train
After drinking a grapefruit juice of an unknown brand.
And to think that you even joked about its exorbitant price
Shouting in your refined Latin:
"Omne ignotum pro magnifico"
While the flying barman was certainly thinking:
"She's crazy but-my God - how beautiful she is!"
   But you had a sudden sense of the truth:
You thought of me at the railway station
Mixing my tears with the early August rains
Weeping for joy as you were coming back
And you: to spite me? for tragedy's sake?
A craving for the front page?
Is it of any use to know why?
   You flew out of the window like a packet of cigarettes
And whistling through the air you howled your last will:
"Keep on loving me!"

## I Once Had A Friend
*by Casey Mannis - age 11*

I once had a friend
who was new at my school.
I once had a friend
who the kids thought was cool.

I once had a friend
who lived close to me in town
And I once had a friend who,
in laughter, would pick my spirits
up from the ground.

The problems is....
I once had a friend
who would steal my money for lunch,
I once had a friend
who thought she was better than me by much.

I once had a friend
who would talk about me behind my back
And I once had a friend
who told everything but facts.

I once had a friend
who would laugh when I would fall,
And I once had a friend
who wasn't a friend at all.

## The Enchantress
*by Michelle Marano*

Her platinum rostrum radiates her facial beauty amongst the stars and planets.
As she widens her ornate tulle during nocturnal wanderings, a panorama view unfolds of a fashionable glitteratti.
This goddess, coquette ostentationally illuminates her sultry powers throughout the galaxy by hypnotizing her victims.
And then floods their minds with lascivious ecstasies of boundless dreams and lullaby chants of satirical melodies.

She voice her messages in rhapsodic phrases and smooth sensuous tones
Which affords the legacy of her eloquence and fluency to grace all.
Through her deep breaths and interludes of desire, seeds of a deep nocturnal, veritable world are implanted.
And soon a metamorphosis begins to unfold for followers as an auspicious new start of life.
This Queen of Darkness may appear docile and charming, But her mysterious composition will diffuse different dreamy affects at various times.
At full circle, her womb transcends a pure natural energy of light
Which sparkles in a mirrored circle beneath her great platform.
And at any whimsical moment of time, new waves of capricious energetic vibrations may permeate the earth's atmospheres.
The invincible protective cocoon silently opens with a burst to receive this new tapestry of energy.
The path is carved for the matriarch to swiftly come forward
Caressing each one with her harmonious strokes of devout affection.
With every heart beat rhythm, she cradles each one in her palms with amazing aglity
And endows all with magical gifts and the new dimensions of power, pleasure, peace, and a spiritual significance.
The emergence of a new generation inheriting her endowments pledge their trust, respect, and loyalty.
And in the final act, those who have succumbed and been inundated by her supreme force,
Will become the parades of the new hierarchy celestial beings.
And for those, who have not acknowledged or accepted her, will become the lampoons of bestial pythons.
These lonely beings engulfed by misery will wonder endlessly in a dark abyss searching for their lost souls.
For this divine immortal, will continue her expeditions
Riding on an incandescent path as a champion fulfilling her destinations.

## Love
*by Kelly J. Marchand - age 20*

Like a soaring arrow you plunged
deep into my heart
But be careful of my hinges for I am easily broken
Love so strong we were never really apart
I still hear those whispers so sweetly spoken
That grin and that look in you eyes
It was amazing how time seemed to fly
But we both changed as time went on
Deep in my heart you'll never truly be gone
You taught me alot about loving and caring
living together and always sharing
It may be that our ships have passed
But some relationships aren't meant to last
So in my memories you'll always stay
I'd like to thank you for showing me the way

## *Romancing*
*by B. Lynette Marshall - age 19*

I barely recognized it.
It snuck upon me like a thief.
It approached me like a gentlemen,
taking my hand and gently caressing it
with a kiss.
It spoke to me in a whisper,
as though it was telling me a secret.
It cradled me in its arms,
as though it was sheltering me from harm.
It laughed with me,
as though we were old friends.
It told me its name,
and I remember laughing with it.
I remember it approaching me like a gentlemen.
I remember it sheltering me from harm.
I remember its presence.
I remember what Love felt like.

## *Palace of Stone*
*by Cory Markert - age 15*

I'm trapped in this Palace of Stone,
it's dark and I am all alone.
I cannot find my way out,
but for some reason, I continue to scream and shout.

But no one will answer my frantic calls,
so I continue to travel down these empty halls.
This place is such an intricate maze,
my head is spinning, I'm in a daze.

The palace is dark and cold,
and the walls are covered in a thick green mold.
There is a rotten smell lingering in the air,
this place is delivering quite a scare.

I will never get out of this place alive,
there is absolutely noway I can survive.
The lack of food and sleep is causing me a lot of pain,
and trying to figure out this maze is driving me insane.

I'm so hungry and extremely tired,
I'm afraid that my time in this world has just about expired.
I'm trapped and I'm all alone,
left to die in this Palace of Stone.

## *A Cloud*
*by Sunny Martens - age 13*

A dream can be like a cloud.
It can float down where you can
   almost reach it.
Then suddenly it floats so far up
   it seems like it will never come down.
For some people, the cloud will never
   come down.
For others, in time, it will vanish.
And for a few who keep reaching,
   they just might catch it.

## *The Divine Hand Maid*
*by Austin Marshall - age 16*

The divine hand maid —
   Who rides her gallant horse,
   In grey mornings light;
      Bearing a shield.
The divine hand maid —
   Not bitter,
   By the sun quenched sea shore;
   The slapping of the waves;
      Bearing a light.
The divine hand maid —
   Swimming the ocean tide,
   Taken out to sea;
   She swung along;
      Bearing her soul.
The divine hand maid —
   No longer here,
   Far away she's gone;
   High above us now;
      Bearing her loving heart of the eastern waves.

## *On Apostrophizing*
*by Katrina Martinez - age 16*

Hello once more, dear pen,
I see we meet again.
A sign that once more I have committed some unspeakable crime.
Hush, dear pen; I am thankful you cannot speak
Of the manifestation of the darker side of me.
O perform some apotropaic ritual on me
And cast out Satan from this demoniac!
Pen, my dear pen,
You were always there when I needed you most:
When all my friends had forsaken me
You allowed me to use you to expel my pain,
And you helped me with the cross I bear.
You're inanimate, but you're my confidant
Because I know that even with your sharp point
You can never stab me in the back.
How many times have I come to you for relief,
And how many times have I forgotten your existence?
Yet you always take me back,
You're my unconditional friend.
You care not if I'm imperfect,
You chide me not about my follies,
You're always there to add a ray of light
In my home, in Dante's Inferno.
Pen, my dear pen,
It's just you and I in a world of profligation.
You're my only weapon against Omnipotent Life,
But I am well protected.
For the pen truly is mightier than the sword,
And the pen is more loyal than any
Of these perfidious beings called men.

*Distinctions of Excellence*

## I Know Now
*by Sarah Martin - age 17*

Happiness seemed quite near
Felt in the palm of my hand
But it shall never be found here
I know now where I stand

On the mountain peaks
Where eagles fly
Where the sun ray streaks
And the cool winds sign

In the desert's plains
Where night is day
And sun scorched stains
Mark where I'll stay

In the oceans tight grip
Will I again be seen
I journey on a trip
To find what happiness means

A part of my heart
Is consumed by desire
To no longer be apart
To be one with the fire

To be a part of the days
Filled with unending laughter
I know now in many ways
That alone means forever

## See No Evil, Hear No Evil, Speak No Evil
*by Robert D. Massengill*

"See no evil, hear no evil, speak no evil."
Feeling these words palmed into his hand,
the mute ponders deeply. In spite of being
blind, deaf and unable to speak from birth,
he knows what evil means, even though he
has never actually seen it, heard it, or
been able to speak of it.

Although blind, he knows that the warden
in his block of the hospital has struck
other patients. His friend has palmed the
facts to him before. He hates this, and
his own powerlessness. Yet he knows the
striking is evil.

Although deaf and, therefore, unable to
hear the screams of other inmates he can
feel the ugly vibrations and, with his
heightened sense of touch, is painfully aware
of the cringing fear.

Although unable to talk, with no way to
voice the cruelty, his mind shouts that
the warden is evil incarnate; his heart
cries out for the agony of his friends; his
soul agonizes over the warden's malevolence.

The darkness and silence bring no solace,
only a bitter understanding. A blind man
cannot see; a deaf man cannot hear; a mute
cannot speak. But suffering has no limits.

## Fog Bank
*by Mark Matthews*

A miniature cloud upon the earth!
A misty puff of dew!
A panorama of white,
No depth,
   no height,
      just white!

Among and in the misty veil
reality does not prevail!
Throughout the shrouds,
Only clouds!
Quiet surrounds!
Mystery abounds!

In the limited world of white
Little seems to be in sight!
Look left,
   Look right,
      only white!

Sky is close and ground is near!
Isolated, alone,
A little like fear!

Twilight brought the cooler air
and with it came the big white layer!
The shifting clouds of moist, damp air
starts to lift,
and way out there
through the haze,
   reality re-gains!

Night returns to the air
blessing the plants
with a cool, damp layer!

## Imagine It Like This
*by Christiana Angelique Matyasik - age 13*

Imagine it like this:
You're only a seven year old, but you are dark
And not allowed to go to an amusement park.
Despite your age you're still called names
And excluded from any white only games.
You're being pushed down and thrown harshly into the street
Just because you took a white man's bus seat.

Imagine it like this:
You just turn eighteen, the age you can vote
But because of your race, you can't, so you don't.
Getting a job isn't the easiest task
It would be if you could read, and had a white mask.
Everyone is in college, working hard to get their degree
Except for you, who won't become what you want to be.

Imagine it like this:
You're now an adult, twenty-eight to be exact
And racism still exists, even more, as a fact.
You speak out against it and take a stand for what is right
But you're arrested and humiliated because you are not white.
Now the whites know who you are and want you out of their way
So the day you spoke out and were arrested became your very last day.
Imagine it like that.

## Timeless Love
*by The Raven*

In the center of the night as darkness fills the sky,
The full moon draws us with its absorption.
Struggling to awaken from our deep sleep bring about this
Transformation
Something starts to move with in the night as a voice in the dark calls
To our souls in the region of the dead
Chilled with the kiss of death and blood stained lips...it's the pain of
Hunger calling
Eternally in blood/eternally in pain
Trapped in the human realm
We look for solutions to this hunger that is forever
We stand the test of time to stand alone
Eternally in blood/eternally in pain
Human life holds our immortality and timeless future living for
Centuries with the hand of time
Eternally in blood eternally in pain


## In The Child's Face
*by Jon Mays - age 20*

In the child's face, I see joy
Joy for the day, joy for the night
The joy of playing, the joy of eating
Joy with friends, and joy with family
Look real close, and you too will see

In the child's face, I see hope
Hope for love, hope for peace
Hope for the sick, hope for equality
Hope for tomorrow, and hope for today
If you look, you'll see it is true - what I say

In the child's face, I see love
Love for the animals, love for their parents
Love for their friends, love for their toys
Love for their God, and love for themselves
Their hearts are books upon a shelf

In the child's face, I see fear
Fear of pain, fear of death
Fear of unusual places, fear of failure
Fear of being lost, and fear of change
Just look real close, they're all the same

In the child's face, I see anger
Anger for their enemies, anger for their pain
Anger when things aren't so easy, anger when they don't get their way
Anger for the rule that rules, and anger for the failures of themselves
Their hearts are books upon a shelf
In the child's face, I see myself


## Vestiges of Love
*by Mandy McCague - age 18*

Time has past and there is still a vestige of thee.

I remember the dances we danced
then the romantic walks we walked.
I'll never forget how you gave me a chance
listening to each others secrets and thoughts.
The times we spent together,
how I wished they were forever.
You always made me feel better,
by the love you shared in your letters.
Your words soothed my soul,
but now I have to let you go.
This is just a poem I never had time to write.
Your encouragement is what I keep in sight.
Friendship is now our theme of choice
though not long ago we were as one.
You made me who I am, no doubt in my voice.
Self strength and courage is what you've done,

and all I ask is that you remember me.


## No One Cares
*by Dona L. McCormack*

Thought I was the only one
But that was just a lie
All I've known and all I've loved
Have said their last goodbye

Everywhere, no one cares
A fire is spreading
A needle pricks with poison
As the string of life stops threading

Walking through the fog of life
And bathing in the mud of peace
A childs cry, afraid, alone
The tears that cannot cease

A line of hands grasped together
A line of soiled beaten hope
A line that stretches from death to love
A flimsy molted knotted rope

The eyes stare past the darkness
They all see through the light
They break the day that's coming
And shatter the mirror night

A feast of starving children
An endless blackened mirror
A serenity built from nails and thorns
A satin feather pillow fear

Ah, so now it is the end of life
An end of fear and hate
A lasting darkness, dreamless sleep
Greets the final peaceful fate

## Empty Love
*by Jessica McCormick*

When you look at me,
Your eyes are blank,
Devoid of emotion,
Or you aren't looking at mc at all.

Your touch is soft,
But it's meaningless.
You dare not embrace me;
I might freeze from the coldness.

But bitterness is impossible,
For it would do nothing.
My love for you is above such childishness.

Yet sadness is complete.
It may soon swallow me whole
And make me forever
Its subject and slave.

Can't you feel my love?
Don't you see it in my eyes,
Hear it in my words,
Feel it in my fingertips?

This ache is endless,
For my love is unrequited.
I shall carry it to my grave
Over you, my beloved.

*Distinctions of Excellence*

## Name
*by Margaret McGaw-Sullivan*

When I first met you I knew your name and I knew it well.
Even though I said I wouldn't I told everyone your name
I let everyone know who you were,
despite the fact that your reputation was bad
The police even the devil himself was out to kill you,
but you were already dead.
My friends, or that's what I thought they were at the time,
Told people who overpowered me your name and everything about you.
Their words were twisted; the truth was nowhere to be found.
They turned their backs to us and gave us a glare from their eyes.
No-one gave us a chance, no-one heard our cry.
More people found out and pulled us apart, like a man from his mate
They refused to hear of our love or
the like of that there was no such thing.
We were separated against both our wills.
The only thing left to hold onto was the promise
That one day we might come together again
When I first met you I loved you
And now that your gone I wish I would of listened to you.
I wish I would of never told anyone your "Name."

## Miracles Today
*by Maureen Ellen McGran-Reber*

My stomach is heaving.
I've almost stopped breathing!
Behold the joy, as oh how time flies.
Unfold hearts and mind ahoy, waste no more lives!
Go ahead twirl, close your eyes.
Go give it a whirl, you don't have to be wise.
Behold my eyes, can I even perceive the glory?
Listen carefully be wise, and I'll tell you a little story.
We gaze upon the moon.
We make a wish to come out soon.
Today people scheme.
They forget how to dream!
Politically correct, no makebelieving, or imagineering!
Magically, then creativity is deceiving, people have stopped believing!
It's still inside us, let it arise!
Take your soul for a ride, you must before you meet your demise.
Smoldering, yearning, what happened to learning?
Educating, performing, what is it if our souls aren't journeying?
Dreams of days of old, imagination, creativity, don't fill these holes.
It starts when miracles unfold, unto our souls.
Just like in the neighborhoods, families and days of old.
Miracles today still unfold, and need to be shared and told!

## Two Feet Tall and Bullet Proof
*by Barbara McGuire*

He stands five foot seven
And weighs about 150 pounds,
He is a little chubby
And roly poly all around.

He does a lot of bragging
About the fights that he has won,
And brags about the ones
That he has threatened with a gun.

He yells at his wife
And says, "don't mess with me,"
And would try to make her
Beg on bended knee.

Well he might think he's tough
But he's just bone and flesh,
He thinks he's bullet proof
And always at his best.

He thinks he's ten feet tall
And can put fear into any man,
But I'm not afraid of him
Now this you understand.......

I SHOT HIM WITH AN ARROW!

## Healing After Abuse
*by Darlene McKay*

Battered, bruised, be it physical, emotional, or sexual, it
    is like living in Hell
Whether they meant to harm & humiliate, I don't know
Parents are to be loving & teachers, if this is what they
    teach, please exclude me
too late, my younger & teen years were Hell, I went into my—
    self, trusting no one
Then lo & behold my life changed, I meant the man of my
    dreams
Within a year of our meeting & falling in love, we married
A year later we were blessed with our first son
Over the last eighteen years, the love has endured many hard—
    ships
But when abused, the damage is with you for years maybe even
    forever
My husband & I have serious talks, and discuss everything
Because abuse is like rape, it changes your live forever
Healing is an ongoing process, that hopefully will end with
    lot of love and understanding
Having support from loved ones help a lot.

## From Crags to My Cardboard
*by Don S. McLemore*

One spring, sitting on my throne,
    A stone seat in a formal garden,
Behind a museum, relishing solitude,
    I could almost spy Mount Olympus!

Snows, over which wheeling eagles float,
    Melt on my youthful greenness,
As thundering cascades pass my heart,
    And land on my cardboard poem.

The snow-dusted cliffs seem angular thought faces...
    Flying feelings drop giddily over middle ravines...
And, here, expectant in my greenest hiding glen,
    I watch sparkling droplets transform my cardboard.

The garden, the obese bushes, my stone throne,
    Are all gone in the receding light of my reign...
But, thoughts still soar, my heart still cascades,
    And creative muses still whisper in my twilight.

*Dedicated to the Confederate Ladies' Home, Richmond, Virginia.*

## The Innocent Mind
*by Maria H. McMickle - age 16*

the innocent mind, that uncorrupted, undisturbed
the child is not perturbed
those are the ones that are rejected
but those are the ones I've respected
for most of the world lacks the innocence and sweetness
we are the ones cruel and heartless
we have been corrupted by radio and tv
our minds are destroyed by everything we see
you see prostitution
kids with no education
women on welfare
babies who get no care
people getting abused
for sex, drugs and money, others are being used
everyday people get shot
by people of all ages drugs are bought
kids running away
some dying of disease everyday
some starving, just wanting a bite to eat
repeatedly some get beat
but those of the innocent mind
those whose hearts are still kind
those who haven't been effected, they haven't heard or seen
their minds and hearts still clean
what i wouldn't do to have a pure heart, a soul still just
too think, everyone i could trust
thinking my world is a safe place to play
that everyone could be safe everyday
to think everyone pure innocent, including me
clean thoughts in their hearts flowing free

## The View From Seat One
*by Marieta McMillen*

Viewed through the oblong window
bullet-shaped silver orb
spinning rapidly
red body of the plane reflected clearly
and the blur of propellers in motion.
All else is blue and white
like looking at solid snow-covered land
clouds piled up like boulders
blue-grey and off-white
cold clear white one jutting out
contrasting against its brothers
and spreading out as far as the eye can see.
Below is Lake Erie
In many shades of blue
with clouds seeming to float in its waters
like globs of cool whip in berry juice
and the world outside my window is silent.

Glimpses of earth remind me of a patch-work quilt
thrown together by a careless hand
from fragments of all sizes
studded with shiny beads and thick applique
lines of stitching every which way
and one bright red ant scurrying across its surface
to an unknown destination.
As I gaze at the frozen landscape
of snow and ice-capped mountains
it seems the plane is moving so slowly
and I am suspended in a moment of time
separate from the cares of my world
as long as I focus on the shades of blue
outside the window of seat number one.

## Free
*by Jessie Meehan - age 14*

A man,
soloing through the sky,
his white scarf flying into the endless blue.

He slices through the mist,
and clouds,
and his conquering smile
longs for the freedom from the chains
which grasp him down.

The man shoots higher, higher and higher,
reaching for the sun.
Tears rip to the surface of his face
veins bulge from his arms and neck,
blood pours from his ears.

With a sudden jerk,
the man pushed the stainless steel nose down.
Diving,
a vertical death drop,
tearing the wind. . .

The tooth-full smile
now indicates freedom
Free as a bird the man flies carelessly.

The man slowed and leveled out
dropping the wheels.
Braked,
the steel bird hits the ground
and slows to a stop.

Looking up, the man smiles
and whispers, "Free at last!"

## Darkness and Dreams
*by Robin Renee' McNeely*

Quietly, I walk alone down this precarious path
   Blossoms unfolding so many undefined colors
   Songs of birds serenade the clouds today
Unsure of the distance I must go
   I feel the darkness encompass me
   Like the endless underground tunnels of deceit

Steadfastly, I hold on to my sensibility on this course
   Rocks ruggedly shape the shoreline now
   And frame the horizon ragged and uneven
Altering the future with blind decisions
   I'm wrapped in the shelter of midnight
   Feeling protected from the honesty of the sun

Cautiously, I am emerging from this cocoon
   Wind crisply surrounds me as I surface
   Scattering leaves and my thoughts to heaven
Striving for inner-peace is an exhausting endeavor
   I pause, haunted my this silence and longing
   To be nestled in the warmth of my dreams.

## Logan
*by Kyla Miles*

"Ten little fingers
Ten little toes
Two eyes of blue
And a button nose."

Although cliché
They still ring true
And they bring great joy
 and chirps he makes.

At times he cries
At times he'll fuss
And stock in diapers
 is a definite must.

But when he laughs
Or even just smiles
It makes all the sleepless
 night worth-while.

Every ounce he gains
Every inch he grows
And knowing with-in him
 my blood actually flows.

Since the day of his birth
'Til the day I die
I'll thank God for Logan
My blessing in life.

## Nature In Control
*by A.R. Milkes*

One tree with bare branches out wide
in a field with no where to hide—
  'twas nature in control,
  no emotion, no soul.
All life drained away, it had died.

At one time that tree standing proud
in a field each year newly plowed,
  'twas a "living" scene
  of leaves fresh green
in a field with no weeds allowed.

That tree, now, a perch for the crow,
in a field where nothing will grow,
  except nature's seeds
  of wild vines and weeds,
all abandoned a long time ago.

*Distinctions of Excellence*

## Doomed Children
*by Ken Miller*

Doomed children lacked love and knew neglect's sting,
Long before the passage of time revealed everything.
Their innocence was swept away, like dust, by a broom;
Anticipations in secret dreams were destroyed by gloom.
Lives that should have been full of smiles and wonder,
Were lived in desperate loneliness and pent up anger.

Doomed children of sorrow and constant restlessness,
Suppressed in reaction to their over aggressiveness,
Tried to focus on friends as they played amid the lies,
Where parents heard only laughter and ignored the cries.
These children tried for joy from artificial good times,
Amid confusion, shouting and some parenting crimes.

Doomed children, blameless, sought role model heroes;
Pushed on through their teens and grew into zeroes.
Reality brutalized these unbalanced, pseudo adults.
Ill-conceived manipulation had produced tragic results.
Unprepared individuals, full of doubt and uptight,
Headed straight for failure in life's unrelenting fight.

Doomed children to grown-ups, pulled and shoved,
Helpless beings unable to understand and feel love.
Desperate about the future because no plans were made;
Damaged beyond their ability to rise above the charade.
Doomed adult children, unable to make it on their own,
Demand help or threaten havoc as roles reverse at home.

## Snow-Globe World
*by Marjorie Millison*

Dainty petals from angel wings
fall feather-soft, creating scenes —
molding and sculpturing each thing in its path
transfiguring as it clings.

And while a weary little house sleeps,
by drifts and mounds, winter creeps;
silently spilling its magical load
in fluffy whip-cream heaps.

Fence posts wearing woolly white caps,
snuggle deeper into their ermine wraps.
As the sleepy countryside settles-in
for long winter naps.

Like a child's snow-globe turned upside down;
a scene with winter wrapped around.
A tiny, enchanting peace-filled world
   ...crystal bound...

## Wilted Flower
*by Shelli Misoyianis*

Oh, beautiful flower,
So young, so fragile, so sweet,
Don't you know it breaks my heart to see
Your petals fall to your feet?

Alone in the darkness
You stand just barely alive;
How could one deem that without the sun
Your soul would ever survive?

You've wept so heavily
Since the time you were a seed;
How I wish I could turn back the clock
And fulfill your every need.

It is not too late, though,
To reach out my hand with love
And sprinkle your leaves with compassion
Sent down from Heaven Above.

Oh, beautiful flower,
So weak and withered with pain,
I pray someday you will lift your head
And blissfully bloom again.

## Thoughts from a new parent.
*by Amanda Montgomery - age 19*

I look deep into my baby's eyes
as she begins to cry.
I rock her to sleep slowly
and hum quietly.
It calms her into a deep sleep.
She is so precious and I start to weep.
I wonder if I deserve this love.
She sleeps there as peaceful as a dove.
She is so fragile and delicate.
I just want to protect her from harm and hate.
As she grows older,
it will be much harder.
She will leave home for good one day
and I won't have any say.
I hope I can give her the wisdom to survive.
I am just happy she is alive.
I give her all my love today,
so she can spread her wings and fly one day.

## Outside In
*by Joseph S. Monticelli*

Crystal clear lakes exude
Shades of silver
Cold running streams noisily shiver
Blood and bones echo these sights
Shaking and quivering, mighty and bright
Fields and meadows
Brown, Green, Yellow
Rocks and tree trunks hold it all together
Allowing the scents to mingle and fester
Up to the blue to travel forever
A day in the country, racked with pleasure

## Bad News
*by Crystal Moon*

Your father died. I'm sorry;
Is there anything I can do?
I don't know how it feels,
But I know it must be hard for you.

As much as it hurts, I know I must go on,
With my head up, and try to be strong.

My Dad was my heart and soul;
He can never be replaced.
What am I supposed to do
With this major heartache?

I'll show my Daddy his "baby girl" will be fine;
Fulfilling his dreams for me and mine.

The day has come to put you to rest;
Your funeral will be nothing but the best.
You are gone to a better place I'm sure;
My loss and love for you I will endure.

Daddy, you will always be in my heart;
And there we will never part.

## Thoughts of an artist
*by Amy M. Moore - age 14*

To get the color just right,
Make sure the canvas is tight,
The stroke of a brush,
The wave of a hand,

Is the color just right,
Or is it the gleam of the light,
Is the expression showing,
Is the face glowing,
Is the background season showing,
Or should it be snowing,

A dab of color there,
A little blue hat,
On top of the golden blond hair,
I'll put a tree here,
Or a puppy there,

All of this goes through the artist's mind,
Decisions to make,
But at the end,
A picture so perfect,
Breathtaking as it may be,
A picture done,
Made with a brush,
Paint and the thoughts of a artist.

## Pain
*by Sheila Moore - age 12*

I am the creator and
sole purpose of tears.

I will increase all your
worst fears.

I am the dagger in your
side.

I am the reason so many
want to run and hide.

I will break the already broken
heart.

I will tear the soul apart.

I am PAIN!

## The Light in My Window
*by Sarah Anne Moore - age 13*

There is a light,
Shining through my window.
It is you,
It is a spring day,
It is the rain tapping on my window pane.
The light is my life,
Though sometimes the darkness
Seeps through.
But when you are there
There is nothing I can't do.
The light is my window for breaking through,
It is you.

## I Heard You Pray
*by LaDonna Morgan - age 14*

Yesterday I watched you silently from
within the shadows, I took pictures with
my eyes and pressed them between the depths
of my memory to forever hold, And even though
you didn't know it my fingertip dried
away that tear left trailing down your
cheek.

I heard your voice in the whispers, and
I fell asleep to your soft humming, and
I swam in the mist of your gaze as you
looked at me but did not see me, Although
you were not aware I held your hand that
day, For once just being with you was
enough, and I even listened to your prayer
before you went to sleep.

You asked God for strength and the wisdom
to make the right decisions and for his
guidance when you were blind and straying,
You asked him to make you able to rise
from your bed in the morning, And to be
able to smile, and to be able to go on,
You asked God to walk beside you and to
carry you when you could not carry yourself.

I cried myself because of your pain, Tell
me what make you feel this way? And to
think I never knew until I watched you
kneel and bow down your head to pray, I
loved you so much, Please tell me what I
did wrong, Was I so terrible that you have
to ask God each night for the ability to
go on? How long have you felt this way?

I fell asleep next to you, And covered you
to keep you warm, I lay so close to you and
listened to the endless sound of your
struggled breathing, Remembering nights before
when we had laid together beneath the
countless stars entwined.

I never even recognized your pain until this
night when I dried your tear away and heard
you pray.

## The Walker
*by Margaret E. Morris*

Tortured,
Tightrope walker.
In a moment of pain and hope,
steps forward - off the banal platform.
Eye stinging sweat joins
the all-consuming laughter
of the Walker.
Balancing ever so boldly-
holds the red crepe parasol, gently.
Sways with the tension of the wire,
created and maintained by
the Walker's tonsured
footsteps.
Reaching forward - forward,
heart-felt ending near.
The speaking feet
Find their logical conclusion.
Receiving bereft portions of accolade-
the Walker
descends.

## Inner Voice
*by Tanya Moss*

A whisper in my ear later
became a loud voice.
I went from gold dust to solid gold.
The truth had been told.
I became deaf to the truth.
My path crooked.
My ears and my heart listened,
I returned back to the
golden path of awareness.
No longer kidnapped by a lie.

## The Path
*by Jordana Mosten - age 13*

Life's road is eerie and unpredictable
I don't know where to turn
All are incomprehensible
Consequences I will learn

One path is a field
I can see my life simple, unpleasant, and clear
My fate will be sealed
Away from everything here

A jungle is another path
Full of twists and turns
I can't see fate's wrath
My uncertain future I will learn

The path straight ahead of me is a downward slope
It is too easy and my ruin will be swift
If followed there is no hope
My life will be a drunken drift

The path behind me is void and gone
There is no way back to simplicity
Time is whispering *so long*
No way back to vicinity

Three paths with its own fearful story
I don't know where to be
Age is catching up to me
Which one of the three?

## White Silence...

White silence reigns on snow-capped hills
From mountains quiet the Taiga rings
I swept my love far, far away
In winter hut 'til spring we'll stay.

'Taiga wake up from winter's hold!'
My voice rang out through ice and cold
And joyfully in snow we danced
And kissed and kissed 'til dawn.

From dawn we learned luminescence
From northern snows learned cleanliness
From summer's breeze learned tenderness
And thus we knew togetherness.

Birds flew to us early mornings
The sun was our guest
Together in a sleigh we sat
And raced down snow-blown hills.

On snowy hills white silence reigns
Taiga asleep by dawn caressed
I dreamed of winter woods and hills
and footsteps of my love in snow...

*Boris Mourashkin*

## Justice Laughs
*by Erin Kathryn Mrozek*

Once gorgeous sunflowers,
sobbing to the ground.
Broken sunshine,
belittles the weathered churchyard.
While Justice laughs
The one golden seashore,
now barren,
as empty as the Antarctic.
A once joyous girl,
forced to flee;
a witness to the horror.
Yet Justice laughs
A beautiful waterfall,
once enthusiastically tripping over the rocks,
now hastens,
as if evading an enemy.
The stained glassed windows of the church now dark,
as if plunged into eternal night.
Still Justice laughs
This crazed war lunged unto this small village.
We claim to be worldly,
shocked, appalled, and bewildered.
We cry "Outrage,"
yet we choose not to participate.
Is it worth the risk?
Is it worth the manpower?
We become the chance for justice,
but we do nothing.
Does that mean we're the ones laughing?

## Silver Shadow
*by Suzanne Marie Mula - age 18*

The white rain came from the paradox above
Silently blanketing the nether world, in sinister love
Strewn in chaos, burning in the fires eerie glow
Wailing in utter agony, with no where to go
Such malice creatures, of a foretold time
An inferno of flames, forever to climb
The endless echo, of robed in black weeping
These demons of hell, shall be infinitely keeping
Bowing down, to their serpent maid
Stealing souls, eternally afraid

## Sweet Violin
*by Joan Murphy*

A violin from days gone by
Adorns a corner of my foyer
Forgotten though it seems
The varnished face still resonates
For a masterpiece of melody
Resounds within it's graceful form
Strawberry Waltz's linger
While bow and strings remember
The revelry of Irish jigs
Played with jubilee into the night
Sweet violin
How many times did you lighten the step
Of work-weary souls
In farm-house kitchens
With chairs pushed back against the wall
Or on the stage of town dance-halls
You accompanied voices raised in worship
In a little parish church
With funeral hymns you honored
The passing of beloved friends
Your body vibrates still
With the memory of lullabies
Played sweetly for a new-born babe
Along-side a wooden cradle that
Like you was carved so lovingly
You touched them all with the magic of music
Instrument of hope
Made to celebrate the notes of life
By playing them in harmony
To the rhythm of creation.

## My Mom
*by Ruie Munson*

I was given up for adoption at a young age
At the time it was quite the rage
I was always wanted and loved
Like wings on a snow-white dove
Growing up I was obsessed with who I am
I was always looking-Are you my mother?
later on in life I found her-she's as gentle as a lamb
and lo and behold I have 3 sisters and 3 brothers
My mom is kind, caring, understanding, and loving
A giver at heart and so forgiving
I look like her which tickles me pink
Now I know longer have to think
One of the happiest day in my life was when I finally felt whole
Now I can rest my soul
I'm so glad I found you!

## Finally Home
*by Alice G. Myers*

All my life I spent my time wondering where I came from, who I really was. I didn't think I would ever know until the day that my husband found my birth mother.

It was January of 1997 that I went to visit my parents in New York. On our second day there, my husband sat down with my parents and told them that, besides being curious, I wanted to know my medical background. They discussed the issue for awhile and my parents said that they would see what they could remember. Walt later told me what he had done. I would finally know the truth!

The next morning, my mom and dad told that my last name had been Miles and then handed me my adoption papers. My name had been Dorothy Ann Miles. I felt very strange because I had always been known as Alice Grace and now I had another identity. My dad then handed me a hospital receipt with my birth parents names on it.

I returned home the next day and my husband told me not to worry, he'd find her. A few weeks later Walt called me to say that he had found her! I was in shock! He gave me an address and told me to write her a letter. I was apprehensive at first, but I finally sat down and wrote it.

Four days after mailing the letter, my phone rang. It was my birth mother! We had a very long conversation and she told me all about my huge family.

On July 30th of 1997 I went to New York to meet the woman that had given me life. It was truly a wonderful experience. After all the years of speculation, my puzzle is finally complete. I am **finally home**!

## ...Lost...
*by Melissa Myers - 20*

I feel lost in a world of emotions,
that eventually fade into memory.
Searching for the answers,
to questions I don't even know.
Trying to find the easiest way,
to go through life being happy.
Without having to struggle,
or suffer through unhappiness or pain.
Hoping I make it through each day,
without losing what's special to me.
Whether it may be my friendships,
or all my tender memories.
For if I were to lose something so dear,
I would lose part of my inner self.
Because in a way my created life,
is all that I have to live for.
I feel lost and confused in my emotions,
and I don't know how to react.
If I should scream out loud,
or if I should laugh or cry.
Maybe I should grin and bear it,
and let it tear me apart slowly.

## A Friend Name Jesus
*by Jacqueline S. Myles*

Jesus you made me this is true
I'm old enough to express my
love to you.
Thank you Jesus for dying for
us, because if it wasn't for you
love where would we be,
May be dead and in hell with
no life just existing in a place,
that's to horrible to express.
Jesus you stand at our hearts
knocking to come in.
Once we accept Christ that's
when we see how special Jesus
is to me.
Jesus a Christian is a person
that I love to be, because I
have so much joy in my heart
that the devil can't do me any
harm, while I'm here in this world
with so much agony and pain,
I can call you Jesus over and
over again.
I will keep the faith even if
I die by the sword because
I know by your grave I will be
Forever more with the Lord.

## Dream of Love
*by Barbara Nagelberg*

When I think of my love, does he too think of me? Or is his life so busy to have time to recollect? It seems as if I loved him forever, even though we just met.

I imagine how my love would smell and how his lips would taste and feel. But if it's my imagining, then he can't be real. I hear his voice calling my name. Yet I know in my mind it can only be a game.

In my dreams he comes to me. He gives me his love. I give him my soul. And when I awake, I only feel a hollow, a hole. Emptiness, pain, where my heart used to be. But this can only be a fantasy.

I feel as if part of me has died. Yet how can I feel this way in mourning, want to cry. A love so perfect, yet a love so unreal. A love whose arms around me I will never feel.

I hear someone calling my name. I feel a kiss on my forehead and an warm hand on my face. "Sweetheart." he says, you were crying in your sleep. I heard you call out my name."

Thank you, dear God, it was only a dream. But the feelings, the loss, were much too real.
"Sweetheart," I say, "I must show how I love you more. For you are my life, the one that I cherish. Without your love, surely I would perish."

## Solitude
*by Lynn E. Nations*

I sit in quiet solitude
upon my balcony.
The night is dark and cool
with a gentle breeze around me.

The hectic loudness of the day
has completely been removed.
Suddenly there is peacefulness
and my soul can now be soothed.

The suffocation of myself
has no longer been ignored,
for by sharing in these moments,
my senses are restored.

I can feel my spirit rising
and some order to my thoughts.
The routine irritations
have now all become naught.

My mind is free to wander
and hope and dream and pray,
without all the distractions
that are constant in the day.

I give the daytime what's required
and sometimes sacrifice,
but late at night on my balcony,
what was lost, is returned thrice.


## In the Dark
*by Dana Nielsen - age 16*

In the dark, what do you see?
Outside in that big world.
Shadows following.
Beady eyes blinking at you,
in the dark night.
Don't take a single step,
for you don't know what will happen next.
Is it a full moon tonight?
A shiver down the back gives you a fright.
A shining light coming from the stars above,
to guide you where you are going.
In the dark.


## Untitled
*by Teri Nelson - age 16*

Weakness lies within
Abused souls
Addiction
Flows through veins
Like black blood
Judgement in the hands
Of fools
Sorrow filled eyes
Cry no tears
For no pain
Shall ever hurt
Agony
No longer
Starving for a drop
Of blood
For a punishment
No mortal
Could ever know
No fear of rejection
Already know their
Actions
Their judgement
So petty
Pointless discrimination
A scar so deep
Our survival
Is wasting away.


## The Glass
*by Spence Nibley*

I sit alone and stare
Swear someday You'll be along
Strong I'm not
Distraught and distracted by reflections
Rejections bouncing off the pane
Rain spotted images abound
Resound like spattered memories on musty lace
Embrace these transparencies mottled with realism
Exorcism that rends and wrenches my opaque past
Last with me the night
Fight with me the fear to stand
Demand the courage to know
Throw open my window and let in the world below


## Candle Light
*by Elizabeth Nonnast - age 17*

The candle sits on my window seal,
feeling the fresh spring air.
Its warmth of its single flame,
brings me back memories.
The way I used to feel when all I
could see was the moonlight shining
in on my window, hitting on my fair
bare skin.
The first feel of red, soft petals on my
lips, showed me what it was to have
and love another.
I knew, then, what it was like no to
be alone.
Now I am alone.
I know a candle can feel love the same
way.
For a candle feels warmth of another.
It never knows when it's going to burn
out.
When the flame does burn out, the warmth
may be gone, but the candle is never
the same.
A little piece of its heart is missing.


## I Am Still Here
*by Sofia Novozilova - age 13*

My planet, my home, you invaded,
Our cities you burned and raided.
You came and destroyed our lives,
Yet, we desperately fought to survive.
You tried to crush my hope, to make it disappear,
You did not succeed, for I am still here.

With your evil, you ravaged the land and the seas,
You forced my people down on their knees.
You enslaved us and put us in chains,
Most begged for mercy in vain.
You tried to crush my hope, to make it disappear,
You did not succeed, for I am still here.

You think that my fire's burned out long ago,
If you look deep into my eyes, you'll know,
That my flame still burns bright,
Like an orange tiger, hunting in the night.
You tried to crush my hope, to make it disappear,
You did not succeed, for I am still here.

## She is America
*by Jennifer Marie Oakes*

She sits all alone on a one-way street, ready to kill or be killed, she's like a fish out of water, she can't sink or swim, only wait to be gilled. She's all the dreams that you've forsaken, all the goals you haven't realized that you will never reach, all the chances never taken, all the lessons you're not sure how to teach. She is battered and broken, bloodied and bruised, from all her years of abuse, people suggest she go quietly but sh finds enough strength to refuse. She is vulnerable to those that attack er; Her pride has been wounded before, on the beaches of Normandy, Pearl Harbor and the jungle floor. She is napalm and grenades, submarines and tanks; Missiles, bombs and bullets, all have pierced her flanks. She is red, white and blue, she is all of me and you. She is strength and compassion, a helping hand, often at great cost, and although many would claim otherwise, her spirit is not lost. She is barbecues and baptisms, football on t.v., and elderly couple passing through Yellowstone in their new R.V. She is fireworks and baseball, hot pizza and cold beer, small town Saturday night, living without fear. She is America, she is America, in all her triumphs and disgraces, she is black, white, yellow, red, a million different faces. She is Washington and Jefferson, Franklin, Lincoln, Reagan too, she is America, she is America, she is all of me and you.

## Black Roses for the Loss of Innocence
*by Lauren O'Bryan - age 13*

Black roses for the loss of innocence,
a loss of fearlessness, a loss of hope.
The clock has ticked by fourteen years,
hands in darkness, loneliness, grope.

Searching for the thrills of life,
heart too young to comprehend.
Not for love, but for lust,
taken by a selfish hand.

New years, new life, new personality,
I have truly lost a friend.
Betrayal in his empty eyes,
shattered spirit cannot mend.

With innocence is purity, and purity is light.
Lost once in vain,
lost ever more,
time nor fate will spite.

Destiny can be a bastard,
leading one astray.
Senses dulled, mind bewildered,
never be the same.

Black roses for the loss of innocence.

## Take Power
*by Cathy O'Bryant*

Take power to CHANGE
For with change comes insight
With insight comes learning
And with learning - growth

Be in CONTROL
No longer the road alone you trod
You are the driver
Go - but go with God

Take confidence in ACTION
Even when you fail
You are all the wiser
For having presented the sale

Exercise possibilities, POSITIVELY
Thinking thoughts of success
Using the language of the business
Being yourself, not trying to impress

Be CREATIVE
Take initiative to redesign
Your life, yourself, the work you do
Life is just what you define

Practice STICK-TO-IT-TIVENESS
It's a bore not to know the outcome
You will feel so much the better
When all is said and done

## Dad, I still
*by Paige Marie Oldham - age 16*

I still remember when I used to ride upon your shoulders
and feel like I was on top of the world.
I still remember when you first taught me how to ride my bike
and constantly told me to never give up.

Every night before bed
I remember the whispers 'goodnight'
and the quick wink of luck
and how you tucked me in so tight.

The time has passed us by
and yet I still need that help,
but never once did I ask you,
ask the way you felt.

Even though I'm older now
I still see you as the same,
the best father in the world
and still with all the father's "fame".

I wouldn't trade if I could,
For you have taught me it all.
From the ABC's
to the conversations about love's deadly faults.

I would like to thank you with all my heart
and hope that someday I will be able to help you with your sorrow,
but one thing is for sure right now,
I know who holds tomorrow.

## Shadow
*by Lillian O'Neal, R.A.*

There is someone in the shadows just sitting by an old bay window.
The reflection doesn't move...so still.. so silent...so statuesque.
This shadow seems to be looking out into another world.
If you look past this shadow, you will see gentle rains moving across the panes.
Just like small streams going nowhere but combining not into one.
People rushing by glance up at a lonely shadow reflecting in the dark.
As they try to rush in from out of the rain, jumping puddles, dodging cars splashing everywhere.
If you listen really carefully, you can hear rain striking against an old tin roof.
As the rain joins it runs down into an old drain that has become detached.
This shadow sits there for what seems like hours, into the middle of the night.
But yet, moving only to turn on a light or two.
Maybe...memories of a childhood still remain.
Of a child who likes to run into the rain...to jump...to splash..to dance.
Yes, maybe even to hold a head up to catch a drop or two of rain.
If only we could turn back into our childhood.
Just to be that child again, to run free out in the rain.
Maybe if you look really carefully you may be able to see.....
A shadow running, jumping, splashing and dancing in the rain.
But now a shadow still remains by an old bay window in the dark.
Looking out past the rain into another world so still, so silent, so statuesque.

*Distinctions of Excellence*

# Love
*by James Oquendo*

My heart is full of brotherly love,
For love is something splendidly free, like a dove.

Love conquers mountains
Of the highest Celestial position.
It fills the soul with inner pleasure and Marvelous emotion.

Love is as intense as the Sun,
And as frail as a cottonseed
Whose seed is full of playfilled fun.

Love is never alone,
For it keeps you warm
When you are far away from home.

Love sees you through,
It is fiery as Red,
And as pure as the sky is blue.

Love makes the world go round,
it travels to cities, villages and towns.

To find love of that rare importance, just look deep inside
And see a shining light.
Never taking love for granted,
Never taking love in stride.

So, love, love, love because it's a
Blessing from above.

# Drawn
*by Rachel L. Orendorff*

I look out the window,
And see the cloud as it is.
Thick, dark, and laden with burden.

Outside I sit under a tree.
Even though the cloud is over me.
I watch as the lightning flashes,
I listen as the thunder rolls,
I feel as the rain hits me.

I go on humming my song,
It comforts me as the wind picks up.
I can't go inside now,
I don't remember the way.

The wind picks up even more,
And I am forced to grasp the tree.
I can't really,
It's much too big.

I am thrown away,
But I continue to sing my song.
I know it can't save me,
But it calms me just the same.
I can't see where I'm flying to,
It's black as night and the air
Is thick as blood.

My life is thrown away,
I knew that it would happen.
But the storm challenged me,
So I took it on.

I may have known,
But I,
Was drawn.

# All Over Me
*by Idayat A. Osho - age 19*

Opening my eyes,
I see a beautiful flower
Bloom all over me.
The first moment
I laid eyes on it
I was in love.

At first it was difficult
for me to express
my feelings towards this flower.
Because it was more beautiful,
Wiser, and loving than I was.

I moved closer to this beautiful flower
to pay homage to its beauty.
The flower flutters away,
it went far that I couldn't get it.

When it fluttered away,
my heart was broken.
But I never gave up.

I ask for God's help
and the Lord strengthens me

Months went by this flower
never bloom back.
Then I began to worry,
I didn't know what position
or condition it was.

I loved it so much that I couldn't let go.
Everyday my faith kept on growing
stronger because of her.

# The Night
*by Olutayo Osunsan - age 19*

God sprinkled his divine seeds into the heavens to illuminate the evening sky.

As glittering raindrops flood the evening breeze, sending sweet summer dreams to the huddling trees, the vast hills remained modest in their mystic sites. In the solemn stillness of the evening air, candle lights flicker in the distant darkness of the villages in the valley...

The lakes rippled from the impact of the tears of the night, revealing the clearer essence of the blooming moon. The moon slowly erected between the horizon, like a pearl in an opening Oyster; silently (the moon) creeping behind misty clouds, as the night swept by...

# Pieces
*by Jorge Otegui*

Pieces of my heart are roaring
like an old engine,
pieces of my mind are vanishing
as if they were made of haze,
pieces of my body seem
to be convicted to banishment,
pieces of my life
are claiming for shelter
over an ancient library's shelf;
but the whole of those pieces
is still on his feet
walking over a foreign world
that used to be so familiar,
treading on some darkness
leaving traces of light.

## A Furtive Tear
*by Diana Dolhancyk Pamin*

As twilight
Was descending she roamed, then her feet flew,
Flew close to the forest door, for her soul is like
A restless sea w a n d e r i n g listless.
There, taking breath upon a stone, a mannequin
Whispering to self, of what now is bare, the
Engagement ring that once marked the start,
He took it back, returned her heart.

Ah! Somewhere a nightingale sings, not aware
Of her agony, for her soul is filled to flooding,
And love still throbs within her being.
Still tears refuse to empty, and unuttered pain
Has found a home, and her smile is gone 'way.

She stands
At the coffin of dead love, a widow before a bride,
Still imprisoned in the web of love, a mannequin.
Thoughts of contentment and joy fly away,
They cannot live with pierced memories, echoing
Laments weaving through her mind, shattered
Dreams, silent murmurings - thus escaping, before
Their wings are clipped.

She rocked and held herself close, for fear her soul would flee.

## This Man Of Mine
*by Ann Marie Panzek*

He came to me when least expected, this man of mine of meager means. A simple and honest man, yet touching the inner depths of my very soul. A perfect and complete vessel of joy, he consumes my heart in every imaginable way and daily replenishes it with sheer ecstasy and promises of hope.

A big man with an even bigger heart, he is always loving and tender. He is gentle beyond compare and wonderful and rare in so many ways. With a touch so light that it makes one burn bright and warm, he awakens my every hidden desire.

When he is not near, anticipating his arrival always thrills me through and through. Wherever I look, simple things remembered make me feel his tender embrace. Traces of him are all around me - he encompasses my body and mind, my heart and my soul.

His special way of saying things are affectionate and treasured and he is a man whose compassion cannot be measured. With feelings soaring, he makes me transcend above time and space like floating on a cloud. With a voice so soft and never heard to be boisterous, he inspires me to pursue the things I've feared and dreaded all my life.

His loving words and thoughts encourage me to experience that which I would have never dared imagine. He is my best friend and lover making my eyes see no one but him. If this love affair is a dream, let me sleep through all its joy and splendor, now and forever with this man of mine.

## Good-Bye
*by Dale R. Patchen*

It seems as if it was a long time ago.
The first time I was not so old.
I was not there to bid you my good-byes.
Thinking back on how fast time has slipped by.
The second time I missed your ship,
as it slipped quietly away from the dock,
at three o'clock, on a breeze to unknown seas.
The seed of life was planted not so long ago.
I watched you grow and take hold of your life.
Little did I know at the time you would be,
the third to be most of all missed.
Your calling made three missed by me.
Maybe it was meant to be,
not to be by each bedside to say good-bye.
Feelings of a forever emptiness inside.
Was I denied the chance for us to meet,
one last time to say I miss and love thee three.
Maybe good-bye was not to be said,
Mom, Dad, my dearest Daughter.
For we someday, at the Lords altar,
will meet once more.

## Remember
*by Rachana Patel - age 20*

If I should die today
How long will you remember me?
How about a day?
How about a month?
How about a year?
How about an eternity?
Will you remember me that long?
If you say a day, I guess we never met
If you say a month, maybe we talked
If you say a year, I guess we were friends
But if you say eternity, you were the one.
The one who was my best friend.
But an eternity is a very long time.
So how long will you remember me?

## The Difference
*by Erika Pearson - age 14*

You see there is a difference
Inside each of us
Your heart is cold as an ice storm
Intentions rough as the seas of a hurricane
Quick as lightening
Your eyes flash that dirty look
Towards me
The warm summer breeze
Smooth as a lake
Bright as a star
That can light up a midnight sky
Dark as you

## Be Happy
*by Amy Patterson - age 15*

I lay here thinking of you,
About all the time we spent together, all the memories.
I begin to cry.
We spent so long together, I thought we'd last forever.
You decided we should end,
There was nothing I could do,
Now I can't get over you just yet.
You brought me through a lot and I praise you for it.
I don't see why you gave up so easy
I understand you don't like a couple of my friends.
I understand I made some mistakes, but so did you.
I still wear the ring you gave me.
I love you still and that will never end.
Somehow I have to get over you, but I don't see how.
You said we could probably try it again and try to still be friends.
I love you lots and hope to see you again,
I wipe away the tear and know I can be happy.

## College
*by Holly Sue Patterson - age 15*

Mom, I will be leaving for college soon,
I will be in my car and on the road
by noon.

Mom, I will miss you and I will keep in touch,
you know I love you very, very much.

Mom, I will eat right and stay healthy,
maybe I will even meet someone who is wealthy.

Mom, I will try my best,
but now I am a bird leaving my nest.

Mom, I will always be in your heart,
even though we are a thousand miles apart.

## Our World
*by Patricia E. Patterson*

Sunrises over mountain tops, gurgling brooks running down their sides, animals drinking cool waters, forests thick and green providing safety and warmth to its inhabitants.

Farmlands and fields of grain, hide and seek paths known only to participants, fishing ponds, dinner bells announcing nourishment and rest.

Front porches wrapped around houses, fireflies pretending to hide in bushes, lemonade stands, neighborhood ice cream parlors.

Waves lapping on sandy beaches, children's laughter and excited voices, buckets full of precious sea shells, golden sunsets hovering on the horizon, the lonely cry of a pelican.

Memories.

Sunrises clouded by pollution, mountain streams choked by acid rains, animals no longer able to take refuge in obsolete forests.

Concrete and steel poured over farmlands, hide and seek paths no longer in view, fishing ponds turned into resorts, dinner bells replaced by restaurants.

Dense subdivisions consuming front porches and fireflies, lemonade stands replaced by drug deals, a walk to the ice cream parlor captivated by gunshots.

Tar and dead fish cover the sandy beaches, the laughter of a child now from the swimming pool and small buckets go home empty. Lingering sunsets seen only on postcards and the lonely pelican cries no more.

What has happened to our worlds. From where will our memories be born.

## A Child's Eyes
*by Bonita Arlene Paul*

Look into the eyes of the children each and every day, for they know of life's greatest joys and they will lead you on your way. For a child's heart is closer to heaven; to the kingdom up above for children know what truly matters and the true meaning of love. A child knows not of prejudice until the world around him makes it known, a child only knows of love until the face of hate is surely shown...

## Untitled
*by Tamara Pederson - age 15*

Giant oak with limbs so high
Clashing against the pale blue sky
Looking at you I wonder why
The heartache continues and we still cry

Weeping willow hanging down
With silvery branches, and a leafy gown
In the fall your leaves turn brown
Like the smile turns to a frown

Lodge pole pines are forever green
Like bypassed hopes in forgotten dreams
Against the wind your branches lean
Twisting in agony you seem

Wild rose with petals pink
Not quite dead, but on the brink
Thoughts start to drift, hope starts to sink
Your beauty gone within a blink

Giant oak with limbs so high
Clashing against the pale blue sky
Looking at you I wonder why
The heartache continues and we still cry

## Raging Inferno
*by Erica I. Peets*

The city was gripped in drought. People dreamt of hearing rain on the roof tops. They thought a tropical storm would be perfect. Nevertheless, it was a smoldering Tuesday. The sun beat down unmercifully on the heads of unfortunate souls who, defying the odds, went about their daily routine. Everyone knew that in this sweltering heat, rain escaped us. Then in the distance, whispers of smoke filled the air. Almost instantaneously, sirens blared. The war against nature had begun. There was I, trapped in traffic that crept along, while before my eyes, an inferno raged on either side.

People scurried away from the scene, while curious onlookers ran towards the inferno. Sparks of fire spewed in the air. Automobiles sputtered and breathed their last breath as traffic became more and more congested. The monster fear opened its mouth. Instantly, calm overtook me. I had to get home. My nostrils were filled with the scent of charred earth. My eyes could not escape the utter destruction. Everything had changed. Beauty that was taken for granted, no longer existed. Precious greenery was replaced with burnt embers. Lives and property were at stake. All seemed to work together.

Later, after hours of labor, vegetation shimmered with luscious green. That which succumbed to the heat, beautiful copper. Summer and fall coexisted. But the charred earth around reminded us that nature, however charming, fragile, and beautiful can instantly change into a raging inferno.

## Love, America!
*by Mary Christina Pegg*

O Love whose colorful and righteous path,
  For tough inspirers of parents,
For an exacting teacher, always hath
  No possible true violence.
Love, America! Love, America!
  God sent His beloved true Son
To show all who live in America
  How to love all under the sun!

O Love whose secure and happy, red home,
  Where fathers, sons, and daughters live,
And mothers wash their clothes with whitish foam
  To keep clean and duly now give.
Love, America! Love, America!
  God came down as tongues of fire
To enlighten all in America;
  Preach the Gospel through the wire!

O Love whose friendly, piercing connections,
  Are still known to lasting colleagues,
Will yield many beautiful collections
  When they now attend business leagues.
Love, America! Love, America!
  God created heaven and earth
To spark, everywhere in America,
  Couples to think about a birth!

## Rebirth
*by Melanie Pering*

I reach out with wanton arms
Like the seas reach to the shores.
I realize that deep within your eyes,
You wish for me no more.

Many a time has passed when I regret
The memory of your face.
But somehow, I just cannot forget
The thrill, the empty space.

When the trees drop leaves upon the Earth,
When Spring brings new leaves 'round,
I might find a kind rebirth
In erasing how you sound.

Silence gathers many clouds
To create the final rain,
And so do scars, they dance in shrouds.
Reminders of my pain.

## The Chesapeake's Most Needed Watershed
*by James Walter Peirce*

The ancient Susquehanna lower shore,
today contains the mighty Chesapeake,
an underwater canyon evermore.

Resulting from an ice age so unique,
the ending of this river's waterway,
is now near Perry Point for those who seek.

The Susquehanna's needed for the bay.
Its awesome use of nature we must keep,
while managing this river's savage way.

The channel's very broad, but not too deep,
and heavy raining quickly will provide,
a thirteen million-acre water sweep.

It's recreation that's this basin's pride.
Four-hundred-fifty miles that's unsurpassed,
where rapid running waters do abide.

Along its banks large industry is massed,
and here atomic cooling brings some fear.
Pollution of this river must not last.

Half the bay's freshwater comes from here.
It's noted as a flooding river bed.
This basin's reputation's very clear.

It's Chesapeake's most needed watershed.


## Image
*by Michelle Y. Perez*

As I walk up the steep mountain
I sometimes feel my inner pain
but I use it to make me stronger
so I can reach the top.  I can
almost see myself there but at
times my foot slips off the
rock I'm climbing, I see it
fall into the bottom river.
Then I look at my reflection in
the water and that's what keeps
me moving higher.


## We Burned the Christmas Tree Today
*by Helen Peoples*

We burned the Christmas tree today
with all the shiny tinsel
clinging to green branches.
Memories of Christmas
have all turned to ashes,
their acrid smell lingering in the air
as needles burn and float toward heaven
never climbing high enough
to hail those haloed halls.
Fallen needles like fallen angels
litter the living room floor
and are swept away with trash
leftover from Christmas day.
Childish innocence sleeps as darkness falls.

Smiles wipe away
as winter rough hands wipe clear the table
and all the delicacies we're left
are little more than memories
of sweet things loved
pushed away and left forgotten.
Their taste, like ashes, linger
when all else is gone away.
Family and friends have gone their way
and nothing green remains,
just the barren landscape
of lives reaching coldly
back to claim our souls again.
Yes, a new year has begun.


## How Life Goes On
*by Elaina C. Perea - age 19*

What I feel is sadness and sorrow,
sometimes I wish there was no tomorrow.
As I lay alone here on my bed,
I try to understand what is going on in my head.
I think and think and think and what I come to see,
is that nothing will ever go back to the way it used to be,
It seems like all I want to do is cry,
when someone tells a joke; all I do is sigh.
I listen to music in hope to find cheer,
yet all it brings is pain and tears to me heart and ear.
I know I should go to school and do what is right,
but I just can't seem to find that shining light.
I know they're gone and there is nothing we can say or do,
but that doesn't change a thing- especially being blue.
I try to get courage and strength to move on,
but I stumble and struggle like a newborn fawn.
Though the sun still shines and the world is still moving,
that does not mean I must stop my grieving.
Stand up straight, walk ahead and smile,
then later on I will by myself, cry for a while.
Go to school and do your homework they say,
but they just can't understand how hard
it is for me just to get thru the day.
I'm sorry but I don't think they'll ever know,
that the loss I'm trying to cope with is deeper than 1000 inches of snow.


## A Vision of Hope
*by Diane Perez*

I had lost hope along the way.
You restored that which had become essential.
To make my life work.
You did no preaching.
You put words into action.
You were gentle and caring.
I had lost so much in life's little' trial's.
I had nothing left to lose when I met you.
Therefore I had nothing left to fear.
   You came to me as a vision of hope.
You helped me to find my way once again.


## The Poets
*by Holly Michele Perry, R.A.*

There are so many textures of verse,
so many books, newspapers, and magazines.
Millions of minds courageous enough
to express their opinions, their lessons, their thoughts
to all the world, to loved ones, to the energies around them.
There are those who translate the lives of others,
those who make—believe characteristics of a life that may;
     or may not; exist,
there are those who explain their lives,
     and so much more.
Then, there are the philosophers
—the poets—
lonely souls who speak the word of Jesus
in phrases, in sentences, in stanzas.
These are the writings of meaning in life.
And if the writer is passionate,
their words are the truths of our universe.

*Distinctions of Excellence*

## shall i compare thee to a summers day
*by Tamara Perry - age 17*

the sun rises in your eye's
temperatures rise with pleasure
of your lips, the rain falls in
your hips, a gentle mist lays within
your kiss

your breath blow over me
relieving me of a long hot
day

the darkness of your eye's
reflects the moon and north star
hold me tight in darkness of those
eye's

hypnotize me with the sparkle
of that north star riding unto
the moon

## The Flower
*by Andrea Peters - age 13*

The flower stands alone
Alone on a hill
As the spring goes on,
The flower stands still
Slowly its petals
Fall to the sweet solid ground
As the sun goes down
The flower bows its great head
For it will never see
The light of day again.

## Christmas
*by Jenny Peterson - age 14*

Winter, winter has to be heard,
Like Snowmen singing with the birds.
Snowflakes dancing in the air,
Wind a blowing through girls' long hair.

Pine Trees gleam with all their might,
Waiting for people to make them bright.
Houses stay still with a sparkle,
While northern skies dance with lights.

Ornaments and angels sitting upon trees,
Shimmering with delight, glimmer, and elegance.
People sitting around, awing with gees,
And others giving gifts out of charity.

Presents wrapped with love and beauty,
As Aunts and Uncles claim you're a cutie.
Cousins show love unto me and you,
And mom saying mind your P's and Q's.

## Shopping
*by Marion M. Peterson*

I like to go shopping in the mall.
Things for sale large and small.
Entertainment centers new TV's,
Short shorts and tops with long sleeves.
Things for baby, mom and pop.
I could shop until I drop.
Eye exams and scented candles
Book from fiction to latest scandals.
Pots and pans and pretty dishes,
Everything to fill your wishes.
Toys galore for the kids at home
And crafts for folks who live alone.
Nice soft pillows and pretty sheets
And fuzzy slippers to warm your feet.
When I'm finished I'm tired my friend
And what I want most is at the other end,
but I must leave, my money's spent.
I'll go home happy and content.
A fun filled day I can recall
When I go shopping at the mall.

## Thanks
*by S. Doreen Peterson*

The gift you gave to me
is very beautiful
There could never be another given just like it
because this gift was given
from mother to daughter
with love and Gods blessings
This only we can measure.

The word of Thanks, I could not
just say to you
I could not begin to express
what the years we've shared has meant
nor what being your daughter still holds in my heart.

Our paths will always be joined
though they may not meet daily
or cross routinely
None the less, our paths are joined and
only we with Gods blessings may decide how near or far,
how long or short,
the who, the what or the whys
for these paths are Our Lives Alone.

So again, the words of "Thanks"...
for a beautiful gift.
With Love to you Mom.

## Home Again
*by Ryan Petrilli*

When there's no turning back this time
To look at what has been left behind
All those highways of heartaches and headlights
Leading me to dead-end streets and sleepless nights.
There were many falls with you that were glorious in descent,
And for some reason those tears were time well spent;
The smile that wouldn't show was from your words of a forgotten song,
But there is always the memory of you, and you are where I belong.

This journey makes me believe that this road has no end,
But with every whispering wind a shadow calls to take me home again.
Between the breeze and the echoing silence I heard the still night;
A simple conversation under the orange glow of the street light
You stood on the sand and spoke, left my heart anything but the same.
Innocent encounters led to beds of roses and sparkling champagne,
And when the stars were out of reach they always found your eye
Still to this moment I can see you as I dream into the sky.

When the future lies in tomorrow over the mountain side
Can you and I last just one day on the everlasting ride?
As we take on mysteries and challenges in our lives;
I don't believe in destiny to have faith, I just believe in you,
And I wouldn't have a rhythm in my heart if it wasn't beating true.
We had our moments of making romance stand tall in this day and age,
So let's not jump to the end but cherish each and every word on the page.

## Candles in the Sky
*by Heather Phillips - age 13*

Stars are like candles in the sky,
that brighten up the dark night,
that cured my loneliness within
    my soul

As I float in the peaceful night,
I suddenly realized that it was I
that caused me to be lonely,
for I had been hiding from myself
    All this time.

I had been hiding from:
my troubles, my problems, even my life.
It was those candles in the sky,
that brightened up my soul.
Which pointed me in the right direction,
that brought me to face my fears.
    Life

## Legends of the Field
*by Steve Phillips*

Baseball, when you believe in a dream,
The field is where you play the game,
Oh, what I mean the team of mine would
consist of,
Ted Williams, Mantle, Jackson,
Gehrig, Ruth, Aaron, Bench, Mays,
Ryan, Lou Brock, Ty Cobb,
The mist in the fields, when this team would
hit the field,
The crowd would go wild with a mild roar,
The legends of the field of mine, the ball
would go out of the park,
It would spark the theory that this team
could never be beat,
Beam on board this is why my team would
be called,
Legends Of The Field

## Aspects of Life
*by Chinetana Phounsavath - age 18*

You begin with a birth,
an innocence that can't be worse.
Not knowing how devious the word is-
you begin to receive for the first,
the things that came to be:
your friends, your lovers, your enemies.

Growing into a social stage,
you begin to crave and search
for what you have not experienced,
on this living and lying earth.
You put out the trust and faith in all these things
only to find it's something-happiness can't bring.
So you are left with nothing but the pain, that will forever-hurt.
All because you gave so much to try to make things work.

When you've been deceived and misjudged,
there is no such thing called love.
Although these are the obstacles in life;
"Why do I have to put up such a fight?"
"For what?"
"I don't even know, but the cruel aspects of life to show."

## The Unseen Dagger
*by Juanita Pickel*

Deep into my heart you plunge the dagger
And you cut away my pride
Such a dark and deadly weapon
But so easy is to hide

No one sees the blood drops falling
And they wonder at my pain
As each day the words keep cutting
Time and time and time again

Ah, so cleverly it is hidden
Even I've the pain denied
Till at last the light beamed inward
And I saw the scars inside

And with tears I washed the windows
leading to my bleeding heart
And at last I can see clearly
And the healing now can start

Ah, you think that tears can hold me
And with lies hang on somehow
But truth is pain and light is
freedom, and thank God, I've found
it now.

## Glory
*by Rebecca J. Pickens - age 18*

A dusty rose sunrise greets a new morn...

Shimmery flakes of iridescent white
 float softly from the sky

Landing unnoticed upon the royal
 violet crocuses,

Melting immediately on the damp ground,
 the pale warmth of day's
 first sunrays radiating from
 the rich earth.

Time stands still, for a quiet moment,
 as winter and spring meet,

One unwittingly passing glory
 to the other.

## What Will Be
*by Jennifer Pierce - age 16*

The way things used to be
 is all but a distant memory

A looking glass through time
 shattered by destiny

The past
forever, it is gone

The future
brings with it a new dawn

Never looking back
onward we go

Our plight is done
forever behind us

And forever a distance
between what was and will be

## A Mothers Good-bye
*by Laura Elisabeth Pierce - age 16*

Last night, when I held you, breathing in my arms
I felt a tug at my heart and a tear in my eye.
I pulled you closer and released a small sigh.
Your mouth fell agape and I heard a small cry.
You wiggled and whimpered as time flew by.
I began to recall these last nine months
and for all it was worth, I wouldn't let you die.
The hours slowly crept away
while I prayed that you'd live to see another day.
Still you gasped for air and your life rapidly began to decay.
The doctors couldn't seem to find the right words to say.
Your last breath had been near and now it was here.
Please know death isn't something to fear.
I felt a tug at my heart and a tear in my eye.
I pulled you closer and released a great sigh,
this being our last good-bye.

*Distinctions of Excellence*

## A Cheater's Wife
*by Mysti Pierce*

He lies 'bout where he's going,
Lies 'bout where he's been.
He tells so many stories,
He forgets which one he's in.
I guess it also slipped his mind,
I've known him half my life.
And no one knows a cheater
Any better than his wife.

I've seen it in his eyes,
He wears it on his face.
I can't believe they really think
She could ever take my place.
For now, I'll step aside,
And go on with my life.
'Cause no one loves that cheater,
Any better than his wife.

Although my heart is breaking,
I must move past the pain.
And keep myself from wondering,
Does he love her? What's her name?
I'm sure, one day he'll realize,
As he looks back at his life.
That he was the luckiest man alive,
To have known that cheater's wife.

## The Waters Flow Freely
*by Anne Plourde*

The waters flow freely
  surround me
   around me
    through me
  within me

  The waters flow freely
    become me
    hear me
    see me
    feel me

The waters flow freely
  show me
  teach me
  carry me
  renew me

  The waters flow freely
    outside me
    inside me
     part of me
    all of me

The waters flow freely
  as I flow freely
   from them
   of them
   to them
   in them

    The waters flow freely
      to carry me home once again

## The Roar of an Old Bull Moose
*by C. J. Plunkett*

O slimy liberal buzzard, where dost thou bite
  as thou preyeth upon an humble people;
As thou slowly sappeth the spirit of a great
  nation leaving it depressed and weary;
  As thou devoureth the last remnant
    and vestige of its rotting carcass,
  Like a dead buffalo on a Waco prairie?

O slimy liberal serpent, where dost thou meander,
  As thou danceth thy serpentine dance
    with arrogance and grandiosity;
  Slithering to and fro, spewing thy male
    bashing, culturally divisive venom,
    And bringing down a great nation
      into thy slime pit of vitiosity?

O slimy liberal polecat, thou hast sold
    thy soul and the soul of a nation,
And sent swarms of lawyer buzzards with reams
    of oppressive laws as their mount;
  Scavenging our land, and devouring an humble
    people who happen to still believe
  That truth, integrity, and character still count.

O slimy liberal varmint, in the melancholy event
    that thy soul spend eternity in hell
  for thy destruction of the soul of our nation and man,
    As a gesture of kindness to thy burning spirit
      a local call might get the ACLU,
  Or I'd invoke my usual conservative compassion
      and send down an electric fan!

## Scared
*by Annette M. Poirrier*

I was scared one night without any light's. I tried to use the phone, but the line was dead. I could hear a tapping noise on the window, I froze. So I tip-toed to the window, but I couldn't see a thing. Then I heard the noise again, Oh Boy! Was I terrified, I didn't know what was outside. I cried and prayed that the light's would come on soon. Then all of a sudden, Guess What! The light's came on. My prayers were answered. All this time I was scared for nothing, because it was a tree branch tapping on the window. I learned one good thing about that night, don't be scared without any light's.

## A Father's Strength
*by Linnie L. Pollard*

A father is filled with an abundance of strength
Which he tries to instill into each of his children
He provides them with the strength to grow up and be strong
  individuals
Having the ability to make strong, wise decisions about their own
  future.

A father instills courage in his children
The courage to be great leaders in the days to come
Whatever goals they may set for themselves
A father is there to encourage them along the right path.

A father is the head of the family
One who holds it firmly together
He is the family's foundation
Standing rock solid through the years to come.

What is a father
He is one who is there to lift a child up
Shouldering the problems they encounter in life
Making their burdens a little bit lighter.

A father, there to provide love, strength and support to the family
A father, one who bestows hope in a dying world
A father, a beacon of light there to light a child's pathway
A father, there to reign a child back before they go astray.

## I Shall Be Strong, My Love
*by Sergei Poskriakov*

I shall be strong, my love
For weakness isn't his
Whose passion true and well above
All other feelings is

My heart is yours, my love, you know
For all eternity
No soul alive can shield the glow
Of your sweet memory

So I won't cry, my love, because
Your thoughts invade my mind
And I see you: so wrong are those
Who think that love is blind

I shall remember you, my love
For days and nights, and years...
So shall our angel far above —
But she's afraid of tears

We shall be fine, my love, you'll see
Our dream may still come true
If only you'd believe in me
Like I believe in you.

## Springtime Memories
*by Cherie Ann Ellsworth Poulsen*

Spring time memories in the
Deep Green of the Thick Plush Grass.

It was a bright spring day, the sun was shinning brightly in the sky.

"Oh my, what a perfect day to play."

This fond vision pressing greatly on my mind of two little girls
sisters I presume, frolicking playfully,
in the deep green thick plush grass.

One little girl had beautiful auburn hair, cut just below her neckline,
she was wearing a short sleeve denim jumper with the print
of little red roses on the pockets, and on her feet were little red Keds.

The other little girl had golden blonde hair, she was wearing
a sunflower yellow smock with the print of white daisies on the front,
and her feet beheld tiny black sandals.

It did not matter really the clothes that were upon their backs.
All that mattered was the laughter flowing ever so joyously from deep
inside of them.

Over and over they rolled, doing somersaults,
tickling, teasing, and talking,
in the deep green of the thick plush grass.

The wind in the trees blew wildly, bringing with a cool breeze
to calm the little girls on this bright, sunshiny day.

"Dear Sister, pleased do not let this day end."
Said the little blonde girl to her auburn haired sister.

"Oh my, What A Perfect Day To Play."

"I remember all of the beautiful days held captive
by the innocence of childhood,
one does not have to be a child to know that having a
Sister means a lifetime Love and Springtime Memories."

*Dedicated to my Sister Chris for her 30th Birthday*

## WHO'S Prototype Are You?
*by Alma K. Pratt*

Oft times when i would in wonder spend
sometime on this question with no end,
like questions of personalities and
of characteristics and really really tease.
Of what prototype are you? then often with a
smile some would so boldly state i always
personify the christlike spirit with the
greatest of ease so he is always pleased.
Do you have to guest or can one be confident
that in some human this prototype exist.
Should one be left to wonder that during conflict
we that sometimes profess to share the faith
have personalities that leaves a crowd of gazing
on lookers standing in awe slowly pondering.
Oh sometimes how truly tangled the web we
weave with high intent just to deceive trying
to cover up and hide our true personalities.

## A Life Not Known...
*by Robyn Lyn Presley - age 14*

It was cold and dark outside
Life was no more for this innocent child
Not one single breath of air
Before this baby was stripped bare
Of everything she could have known
From all the things she could have been shown
She was never taught to walk
She never learned to talk
Soft angel eyes no one ever saw
Shimmering brown hair, the color of fall
Dark, gloomy shadows live in my heart
Dark, gloomy shadows; another life torn apart
Nine months later this baby was to be born
Yet two months later her destiny had been sworn
She is dead now, where no one can see
No one will ever know, she once lived inside me

## A Special Smile
*by Mary D. Price*

Soon it was time to waken
   sleep was difficult that night
   I woke up truly troubled
   everything seemed wrong

   That day someone smiled at me

My heart was filled with true warmth
   it was late that afternoon
   and the peace of God was there
   I knew all would be right

   Because someone smiled at me

It was a very good night
   all was fine the next morning
   I wondered why I'd worried
   and I too began to smile

   Because someone smiled at me

Life can be so beautiful
   one dear person saw my smile
   he said it encourage him
   to live and look for the good

   Because I smiled at him

Enjoy the goodness of Him
   who works in so many ways
   His precious love to perform
   and His love was in the heart

   Of the one who smiled at me

*Distinctions of Excellence*

## Visions
*by Michael T. Pritchett*

In his mind he was a king,
ruling realms and guiding quests,
and all the maids drew near to him
granting him each small behest.

But those around him only saw
an old man slurping from a straw
with flailing arms and graying hair,
he sat akimbo in his chair

They saw not his reality:
That he was what he wished to be.

A knight upon a prancing steed
helping maidens in their need.

A baron overseeing land
and ruling with an iron hand.

A poacher with his bow and arrow
whose aim could fall a darting sparrow

A sorcerer whose potent brew
could tell if a maid's heart was true.

A jester keeping kings amused
and with his magic much bemused.

Anywhere his mind could soar,
he was all these things and more.

Sometimes a wry smile could be seen
and in his eyes an impish gleam.

But those around him only saw
an old man slurping from a straw
with flailing arms and graying hair
sitting, staring in his chair.

## The Night The Candle Burned Out
*by Julie Przechocki*

Today was the day that those
second set of footprints followed you
into Gods hands. That night I was
there, you knew you were dying

you were more concerned about your
grandchildren and us. This was
hours before your death. You
asked me to let go, and God
take you. I did what you asked

It was the hardest thing I had to do
but I knew it was what you wanted.
You did leave some things behind
and that was your courage and strength in death
your candle has burned out

you were granted that serenity
and now your pain is gone
the candle did burn out
but you will live on, through
all your children in life.

That candle has burned out for you
burned out long before your life ever
should. You are an inspiration in life
and even in death. Now your blowing in the wind

but your courage and strength will
live on forever. You had so much to give
and we had so much to lose
that was you, MOM.

## Listen
*by Aretia Purdie*

Listen,
The winds speaks a breeze.
Listen.
Listen to him, he speaks, though not seen.
To be an audience to the unheard.

The day star is the eye of heaven,
Bringing light to the darkest of day.
Listen.
Listen to the sun aflame, it's a source of light,
Its ending is twilight,
Descending at dusk, rising at dawn.
It speaks newness, a beginning.

Listen.
Listen to the brightness of the flowers.
Their colors of pinks, of reds, of yellows, of violets;
They make the eye see beauty, making the heart merry.
Listen to him, he speaks,
Even though unseen, unheard.

## My Heart
*by Thunder Wolf*

In my heart alone have I seen other worlds,
Beautiful worlds beyond the boundaries of what we call home.
In my heart alone have I seen the tops of the highest mountains,
With such breathtaking views as cannot be described,
And in my heart alone have I seen who I truly am.
From my heart comes inspirations,
From my heart comes determination,
And from my heart comes knowledge.
Only my heart knows who I am,
Only my heart knows what I can do,
And only my heart knows where I will go.
My life is what I wish to make it,
I will go where ever I wish,
And I will do whatever I wish.
My heart will take me there,
And once there nothing can take me away.

## Life is a Storm
*by Marie Putman - age 18*

Thunder echoes round me,
the sky, a brilliant brown-gold.
Rain drops, like tear drops, are forming,
life, it does withhold.

Sudden claps are startling,
yet they signify that life still exists.
Light juts from above, and seems to circle round,
shaking its knawrly fists.

All is touched by its presence,
nothing could be left out.
For the rain drops, like tear drops are forming,
and they will touch you without a doubt.

## Hallelujah! Praise the Lord!
*by Cheryl Rader*

Hallelujah! Praise the Lord!
He's the One that we adore.
Lord of heaven and Lord of earth,
He's the One of greatest worth.

Lord, we bless Your holy name,
You who always are the same.
Each day You give us all we need
To live our lives pleasing to Thee.

With hearts of joy and songs of praise
Our gratitude we bring this day.
O loving Father, we bless You
And give You thanks for all You do.

In full surrender we give You
Our lives, our love, our devotion true;
We will to live our best for You
In all we say and in all we do.

Hallelujah! We praise You, Lord,
You're the One that we adore;
You are Lord of everything,
We worship You, our eternal King.

## Starline Drive
*by Natalia Radula*

Old house, old friend
The time has come to say goodbye.
Through good days and sad
You've been refuge, solace, our single place in the world
Where there was always comfort to be offered.
Laughter and tears echo down your hallways
Remembrances of loved ones who walk the earth no more
All contained within your walls
Now visible only for us to see
And rooted in memories and hearts
Forever.
We close the garage door in final adieu
Backs turned on what has been
We feel the sting of nostalgia's tears
Then turn our faces ahead to the promise filled future
Which awaits us now as we gratefully embrace this new step in life.
Our house, our friend
The time has come to say goodbye.

## Dad,?
*by Ricky Ramick*

I think of you often, where are you Dad?
It must have been me, was I that bad?
The turbulence I caused, unthinking unswayed.
Can you accept an apology, for your nerves I kept frayed?
We all speak of you, your siblings, us five.
With conviction, I must tell you, that you must strive,
To repair lost communication, it's imperative that you see,
That your family still loves you, especially me.

## A Secret Place
*by Brenda Ray*

A narrow green path, leads me to a natural mountain pool.
Cold water takes my breath away.
A sun baked rock, warms and dries my skin.
Eyes closed, calmness radiates throughout my body.
No worry, no stress, I free-fall into a fantasy.

## A Poem for the Abandoned
*by Crystal Read - age 16*

It's bitterly cold
in this world of loneliness that I am in
shut out of all others lives
behind this door I stand
helplessly trying to reach to the other side
the key I have not - the knob rising higher
a voice says *"Just give up..."*

I turn and see a light in this huge world of forlornness
at the end of a path of remorse
I carelessly stumble upon this path
clumsily tripping on the pieces of my broken heart

I keep walking towards the beaming rays
but the more I proceed, the further the light seems to get
this treacherous path is endless...
I have come to a river
a river created by my fallen tears
kneeling on the bank, I look over
seeing reflections of pain and sorrow
a reflection of memories haunting again
and faces of fear and hatred
my feelings to all are vacuous
to all I am nothing

I look away and see
only a few feet away lies a cliff
walking towards it I contemplate
"Shall I go... or shall I stay?"
I conclude to a solution and jump
before reaching the final state of death
I mutter under my breath
"I hope you're all happy now."

## Ode to Dennis Wayne Catalano
*by Julie Rea*

Candle, candle burning bright
Glowing through the darkest night,
Send your light beams shining forth,
Going ever farthest north.
Shine till you reach heavens door,
So he'll know forevermore,
He's not forgotten, but loved as dear
As once, he was, while he was near.
Send forth joy and peace and love,
Through heaven's gates far up above.
And let him know though far away
We light a candle for him today.
In remembrance how he lived his life,
No matter the hardship, grief or strife.
He cherished life and held it dear,
and lived his best while he was here.
so shine for him, till night is done,
and remind us when the day's begun,
That life is but a fragile thing,
we know not what tomorrow brings...
A candle burning, but for awhile,
Until we reach that final mile,
When God does blow with gentle breath,
And bodies fall in mortal death,
He sets our souls on wings of flight,
That shine like candles burning bright,
Glowing through the darkest night...

## Untitled
*by Rose Elizabeth Reid - age 12*

She defines herself as She becomes the movement,
Thrusting her body into the most enchanting sight of becoming,
    As She glides herself into the air, making the most
graceful movement,
    She combines her emotions, feelings, and thoughts into
one,
To make the most embracing creation of all mankind.
She gives a message to earth,
Teaching our minds that we make ourselves;
She creates herself.
    She combines full thought, mind, power and body into
this one terrific motion of human art.
    She needs not a pen, a paintbrush, nor a canvas or
words for her art.
She creates her art with full compassion and strength that
no on person can make the same gesture or beauty or exact
step that She, or She, herself creates.
She creates the full meaning of art, and,
best of all,
She guides others,
hopefully, following the path she has created,
links two masteries into one.

        *-for Miss Joanna*


## Untitled
*by Ursula Renate*

It is never too late to say hello,
drop a line a time or two,
with sweet greeting to reach you.

Sending sweet greeting with charm divine,
and as always the pleasure is mine.
Yes mine, because I so see,
in many loving ways that you are very special to me.

At this time, in this season,
there is a special reason,
that touched my soul in a special way,
that I cannot say.
In my own words I took the pen and wrote it down,
and these are the words with an unusual sound.

Send loving greetings to reach out
and touch you in Love
that comes down from above.

Yes greetings, sometimes two,
to someone as special as you.
Because you will always be special.


## Corn Flower Blue (Part I)
*by Ursula Renate*

When I turn to the chapter of my youthful day,
then I turn to the fields, there where to my memories you came to stay,
in that land in which my baby crib did stand
Loyal and true. Corn Flower Blue.

Shortly when out of my diaper stage I grew,
and there in the fields where the mild winds blew,
there and then where at first I bumped into you,
I knew you were not the same,
for different was your name,
Loyal and true. O Corn Flower Blue.

Wild, enchanted, and you don't know the ABCs,
yet you hold the most honorable degree.
Isn't that how love should and ought to be?
For in you there is no greed or a trace of shameless deceit.
You don't turn angry and insane and finally jump out of the frame.
Isn't that how love should and ought to be?
Loyal and true, my Corn Flower Blue.


## The Constant Song
*by Clare Chandler Rentschler*

Life is the constant song Love sings,
With gratefulness for little things...
Crystal dewdrops upon the grass.
Distant train-whistles as they pass.
Soft petals drifting from a rose,
A hearty laugh, a freckled nose,
A loving thought, a lullaby,
And children's questions asking "Why?".
Wildflowers Spring-blessed in white moonlight.
Big wishes upon stars at night.
An Oak...which hugs a sloping hill,
And hides a lonesome whippoorwill.
The first-bleat of a lamb, new-born.
A sunlit field of golden corn.
A fish leaping above a stream.
The wondering in each daydream.
Those moments caught in Summer rain.
A small prayer that releases pain.
The last glimpse of a fleeting deer.
Footprints in sand...which disappear.
Snowbirds braving a Winter storm.
A homemade quilt coaxingly-warm.
A candle-glow in quiet-time.
Faint echoes of an ancient chime.
Each precious miracle we hold
Within our hearts--A passion bold
Enough to build a new doorway
To Hope and Courage every day.
Love is the constant song God sings...
In gratitude for little things.


## Karmic Tenderness
*by Georgette L. Rider*

Bear not I the guilt of my being nor the
Charisma of my countenance and actions;
Karma has introduced and placed us together
To be not lovers, but to love and be loved.
Discover! Discover!
"So saying, `It' went" only in the physical,
But spiritual copulation everlasts —
And is most sacrosanct in its
Effulgent form of Indelible Purity.


## The Darkness
*by Jeremy Richard*

    The Darkness is my one true friend,
for in the Darkness my soul can mend.
There is no one else but it and I; it is a
place where I can hide and cry.
No one can take it away from me,
for The Darkness is inside of me.

    It comforts me when I am sad,
embraces me when times are bad.
The Darkness is my cloak and shield
to all my pain and suffering it does yield.
It protects me from all harm,
when I fall, it lends me its arm.

    The Darkness truly has no superior,
it encourages me when I feel inferior.
It will always be right there,
because for me it does care.
The Darkness has been with me from the start,
The Darkness heals my lonely heart.
It holds me up when I feel weak
and helps me reach the goals I seek.

    You wonder what The Darkness is?
Is it yours or mine, hers or his?
The Darkness does not answer to a specific name,
for The Darkness has the one I claim.

## Always
*by Amanda Richter - age 16*

I'll love you forever and a day,
I'll hold you for always.
I'll be there if you ever need a shoulder,
I'll stay here for forever.
I'll give you my heart and soul,
I'll be by your side while we grow old.
I'll still stay here while you are there,
I'll make it through the day, though it's not fair.
I'll take back everything, because this isn't right,
I'll back down now, 'cause I've lost the fight.
I'll still love you for forever and a day, &
I'll still hold you for always.
I'll still be there if you ever need a shoulder, &
I'll still stay here for forever.
I'll try to move on when the time is right,
I'll try to make it through the night.
I'll try not to fall so quickly next time,
I'll try not to be so blind.
I'll eventually find a man who is right for me,
I'll finally let you be.
I'll give him my heart and soul,
I'll let him take control.
I'll think of you each and every day,
I'll love you. . .
Always.

## Untitled
*by Lisa Rizzo*

What God has created
Human ignorance took for granted.
What love has shined on us, an angel so pure
So precious, man has taken from us.

Gianna Marie was her name, pure as a dove, with
innocence of a flower, loved more than some
spend a lifetime looking for.

Why did this happen, pain and sorrow are what's
in our lives now. Rain drops of tears, fear and
anger of regrets are all that we have left.

Angels have come for her, God is awaiting her presence.
Gianna Marie is once at peace, she is sending and
angel down to let us all know, she may not be here in
flesh, but in our hearts she'll live forever.

She is our miracle....An angel sent from above.
Mommy and Daddy, put the Christmas tree up, for I am the angel
who will shine the whole room up. Please let me go without
any tears. I'm happy and at peace and have no more fears.
As I look down from heaven to the two people, I truly do love,
my mom and my dad the kind that only angels dream of.
Let me see your smiles as I watch over thee, thanking you so
much for loving me so, to give me my wings and letting me go
free....Pop Pop, Anthony, Grandmom and Nana are all very close
and they will rock me till God sends the two of you home.

Your Angel,

Gianna Marie

## The Reward
*by Robert Roan*

As a person travels around the country few
friends are usually found. No one wants to have much
to do with a stranger and puts them down.

Who knows what can come from a simple smile,
a "how do you do", or "how can I help you"? Many miles
can be traveled before someone will come through.

The cold, lonely nights, cold stares, and colder replies
come to haunt many a traveler on the road. What would
happen if just one person could lighten the load.

Only one who has traveled around can tell
you how hard it is to find a friend. This is
truly the rainbows gold at the other end.

## Willing To Be Found
*by Angela Roberts*

Here I am:
Exposed on the outside, yet
concealed on the inside.

Who?
I'm just like you -
But you'd never know it
and I'd never show it,
this pain and agony.

Why?
I can't get out from this hole
of inner despair,
this internal delight.
Tell me,

How?
I need you -
But you'd never know it
and I'd never show it,
this longing for love.

When?
Can I blossom and bloom
With confidence to let you inside
of my world.
Tell me,

For here I am:
Unexposed, but willing
to be found.

## The Flame Within
*by Heather Roberts - age 17*

A candle represents passion, the flame within.
It ignites when you are a child, and only grows stronger.
Somedays it may flicker, but it doesn't go out,
for in your soul you have the power to let it burn longer.
Somedays you feel you can't go on,
you've searched your heart and your mind,
but, if you search inside your soul,
the flame within is what you'll find.
It will give you power, it will give you strength,
it can ease your pain and wipe away your tears.
The flame can give you wisdom and courage,
it can make you understand and calm your fears.
It lets you love and be loved.
It allows you to be happy and let your heart grow.
Sometimes it let's you cry,
but, when you hurt inside, it's good to let it show.
A candle represents your emotions,
the flame is your strength, your happiness, your tears.
Even though you think it has gone out,
the flame within burns through the good and bad years.

## Loved One
*by Mireille Robinson - age 17*

Come loved one and breath
into my soul. Break free of all
your silent cries.

Look up into the sky
and you'll see my face.
Please place your heart
in mine till thee end of time.

Baby, this lifetime is the
time we cherish. I love you
and you love me.

From the day you looked
into my eyes I knew,
my heart dances in the
moonlight sun.

For you are my loved one
a proven one, a groovy one,
a special one.

## A Glance of Delight
### by Violeta Robles

Twisted tour look might seen
But yet your other features
Reflect in a whole different perspective
Your glittering eyes twinkle away
Like the brightest star that
Never fades away.
Your smile though which is
Everything is gorgeous as could
Be never ending and complete
It brings the sweetness and
Yet oh so very twisted
Delight of wickedness.
Which of course I have no
Complaint for it is soothing me
In every way.
Your voice melts me away
In just sudden thoughts
Of Chocolate
And yet you sit so calmly
With lovely glances of
Delight approaching me from afar
In just dim lights and shadows
All around which don't matter.
To the sparkle which so highly
Charged with electricity that
Just pursues itself.
But, yet is it merely a thought
Or sudden conclusion of something
That just wonders in a
Glance.

## The Kiss
### by Anita G. Rodriguez

Have you ever been kissed so passionately yet so pure,
so intense yet so gentle, so strong yet so tender,
that it makes your stomach turn upside down,
your knees weak, and your legs suddenly become limp?

You feel your entire body quiver and you are left breathless.
If you so desired you know you could fly,
you are already floating among the clouds.

You think, "I should pull away", but it is so wonderful you don't.
You finally do and you need to compose yourself
because you are convinced that your glowing!

You feel your temperature rise and fire running through your veins.
The way he embraced you made you feel safe- from everything.

In his arms you found shelter and comfort, that you never felt before.
You felt at home. That was where you were meant to be for the rest of your life.
You think that this is a taste of what heaven must be like.

Although you are surrounded by people, laughter, and music,
you feel as if you are the only two people in the world.
Everyone else is oblivious.

From his lips you found warmth.
In his eyes there was fire, passion, rage, deception, and murder.
Yet looking deeper you could see honesty, love, and innocence.

Looking into them you would get lost.
You would get caught up into a world
that is extremely different from yours,
yet the danger, excitement, and adventure of it all intrigued you.
You had to look away quickly before you were forever held his captive.

You thought you had it under control,
You thought you were the one playing with him,
You tried to convince yourself that you did not care for him,
yet he was and is all you ever talk, think, and dream about.

*Inspired by Roberto Alonso Espinosa*
*Summer of 1995 Mexico City, D.F.*

## X-Termination
### by Rozanne Rogers

The loss of innocence, when Diana died
Greed prevailed and set the tide
Chaos reigns in our world today
Technology, the culprit, I'd have to say
Information moving ... moving so fast
We have no present, we have no past
Who are these men who will decide
Who will live and who will die
To retain or reduce the status quo
Most of us will never know
Will Armageddon that is prophesied
Be brought by god or world wide lies
Will we see our resources spent
Or is our end to be heaven sent
Is the smallpox virus kept around
As the means to take us down
"X-Files" fan, I am indeed
But I don't have to follow Chris Carter to see
That our paths must change and very soon I'd say
For the continuation of our species beyond today.

## Unshackled
### by Raymond F. Rogers

My forebears crossed the deep in rancid holds
midst stench of molding food and human waste.
Crude chains connected parts into a whole
when folks alive were bound to *stock* deceased.

Anger at gross wrongs swamped the misery
of victims who survived. Anger seethed
among survivors who were sold in slavery
to white *superiors*. The traffic thrived!

I've had, about my legs, no bands of steel
yet found myself still bonded by desire.
The lusty zeal compelling me was real —
like moth to flame, I flirted with the fire

and was not freed from lust's robust control
till God removed the shackles from my soul.

## Derry Night
### by Kent Romanoff

Night is ripe
Like a plump black fig
And long-resigned dusk
Awaits dawn's advance.
Slender cypress
Comb sweet rain
From patchy mist
Dripping on stems
Bowed but unbroken.
A stillness grips the wood
Lit by Saturn's pale glow.
Transfixed in silent revelry
A darker shadow meets
The meadow's hush.

## Children's Love
### by Melissa Romano - age 12

Children, though, we are,
Through health and love and care,
We symbolized a flaming love, that is so sincere.
Though, thought to live in sorrow,
Where love does not exist,
Thy life is full of blossoms,
Where they truly could not exist.
Thy love seems to be so fine,
That it truly must be divine!
Truly, GOD must be in thy wake,
For thy love is not a quake.
In hopes your love will always last,
I must write this down.
To show you that your love is there,
Just a shining everywhere!

## Psalm 23
*by Lisa Rose*

Yea, though I walk through the valley of the shadow of death,
  I will mourn all the loved ones that I've laid to rest.

I will fear no evil, for thou art with me,
  I've said my good-bye's with tears enough to fill a sea.

Thy rod and thy staff they comfort me,
  Only small comforts, in having them as a part of me.

Thou preparest a table before me in the presence of mine enemies,
  Love, pain, and guilt burden my heart without any ease.

Thou anoinest my head with oil, my cup runeth over,
  No longer high in happiness, heartache has me sober.

Surely goodness and mercy shall follow me all the days of my life,
  I hold the love that in turn forces me to also hold the strife.

And I will dwell in the house of the Lord forever,
  The bonds of love and time spent shall not sever.

## Reality
*by Michelle J. Rosenberg - age 19*

When you are spinning in circles

Nothing can slow you down

You race pass me and through me

As I try to catch you and put you away

You have escaped the cage that I have built for you

And you are driving me to the place where I lose my mind

A fuzzy, blurred vision is all you are to me

As I reach out for where you once were

I wonder if I will ever have you in my grasp

Or if I will forever be chasing you in circles

## Why You?
*by Nicki Lynn Ross - age 14*

Yesterday I woke up
You the first I see.
You gave me faith I needed
You confided in me.

We talked all day long
About the future of us two.
You loved all my ideas
I loved you.

Today I did not see you
Forever I wonder why.
Why must we have violence?
Why did you have to die?

Even though we're far apart
I'll be with you again some day.
Even though I cry all the time
My friends say it's okay.

I feel like I've died
Without you, it's the worst.
Although I keep on trying,
It all seems like a curse.

Why did you have to go
And leave me by myself?
Why do you make me sad
Remembering how I felt?

My mind is filled with thoughts
Those thoughts are all about you
I know I can survive now
Knowing our love was true
But still, I wonder, why you?

## Barb
*by Ronald Rutherford*

  Barb, my heart sings how much, I love you. Your chaste you shared with me, the moment in time, it took us to fall in love.
  Even though it may feel at times, that we seem to drift apart it makes us want each other, even more. If ever I hurt you, something I promised not to do. I may say things I don't mean to say. I hope you won't never forget my heart always beats, I love you.
  It looks if, I need to change my ways. Your candor and your jocund. I'll always have a craving for you to hold me tight, to let me know, I'll be inside your heart for always.
  It's signs of two hearts becoming fecund, where their love has grown pure and their eyes won't loose their lure, as the passions of covet, where the moonlight shines for you and I. To wake up in the morning, sun filled with hopes and dreams, you give so much more to me, I realize your the only one, I truly love.

## "Till Death Do Us Part"
*by Marilyn B. Rutter*

  Joan was 75 years of age and her husband was 70 - they had been married for 40 years and had stayed together all that time. John drove a car and still had his driver's licience. He took Joan to the movies, bowling and the golf course. They were very active people. Lately Joan had been getting forgetful of people and places and she was resting for 3 to 4 hours in the day time. Her son Jim, wanted her to go into a Home for the aged and sell their house but Joan did not want to go into a nursing home. John told her he would take care of her till she died.
  "Do not be afraid, John told her, "I will take care of you when you can not do anything anymore. You do not have to go into a Home for the aged."
  John loved Joan. He helped her with the cooking and the washing. They had a small house, nice and tidy, everything was just peaches and cream. Jim, though, and his wife, were looking at homes for the aged for Joan then for John.
  He took them to look at these homes they found most inmates "staring into space" or just watching T.V. all day - some were even tied to chairs so as not to wonder and get in the way the nurse told them.
  Joan did not like the places that Jim took them to see. She said to John, "You won't let Jim put me in those places will you?" John replied John, even if you have to be fed and clothed I will stay by you and take care of you. We will stay together in our home as long as I am able. Happy ending to that problem.

## Artist
*by Elizabeth Rywelski - age 17*

I am an artist inspired by truth,
strong is what I am,
different is what I seem.

I am an artist drawing over my youth,
strong is what I've become,
different is my truth.

I am an artist living a dream,
strong is what I am,
different is my youth.

I am an artist, I'm not what I seem,
strong is what I've become,
different is what I dream.

*Distinctions of Excellence*

## A Friend
by Hadiva A. Saghir

Is a gift from a blue sky
created to add to life some more butterfly

Like a flower with honey dew
friends service are firm and true

a friend's smiling face
and eyes full of grace

make hearts come to embrace
with beauty and joys just in case

a friend is a box of gold
and a treasure to be hold

a friend and a friend can live in a harmony
and their friendship will be an unforgettable melody

thank God day and night
for a friend makes life more bright.

When all this planet is covered with snow
a friend's face from far will glow

full of memories and a dream
to remember in a tranquil stream

to remember your friendly smile
for you and I had walked awhile

to live never apart
heart within heart

a true friend is a gift
that is really hard to left.

## My Love Will Not Blow Away
by Kalene D. Sanders - age 17

The wind can never change
the pure beauty of a tree
or how the mountains are shaped
Rain can never destroy hopes
or make a house less loved
A gun shall never end pain
or cover up hurt
Therefore,
my love can never grow weak
or be changed by the
wind,
rain,
snow
Nor can it be changed
by the struggles that come
with life
Yet, if I should die alone
Will you weep upon my body?
When they bury me into the soil
of this earth,
Don't let them bury my love
Take it
and grasp it
For love is so limited
Yet so pure
When you find it to be unconditional
Than you've found something good.

## In My Flower Garden
by Marsha Sanders

There's a place I like to wander time and time again
Where flower draped fairies sing angelic hymns
Where all my daily cares and all my earthly woes
Melt into the scented air of herbal flowered rows
It's a place I like to go very early in the day
I remember my days of childhood and the games I used to play
While I wander thru this garden, I hear laughter every where
As though the voices singing had not a single care
Wow..it looks like tiny children!
But then..upon their backs
I see they have wings of gold all trimmed in silver and black
There are fairies in my garden!
Running to and fro..
Giggling and tickling the flowers as they go
As I look about I see them hiding in the leaves
I'll bet I can get in very close if I sneak in on my knees
Oh no..they've seen me coming closer!
So I hold perfectly still
I don't know what to do now or even what to feel
They know that I won't hurt them or want them to go away
So they told me I could sit awhile to watch them work and play
Now..if you see tiny children, in your garden or your yard
Be still and watch them quietly as they work so very hard
They are the tenders of your flowers
The nurses of your fruits
Making magic, singing songs and playing golden flutes
You can hear their music softly floating in the air
As they tend to special gardens with so much love and care
They will always be there, no matter how time marches on
You too can see the fairies, in the garden in the dawn.....

## Marcelino
by Miguel Angel Santiago

The "Jibaro", symbol of our hard work
and sacrifice.
Marcelino is his name, and from sun up
to sun down he paid the price.

He longs to work the sugar plantations,
and its dense fields plow.
But computers and fancy machines do
his work now.

His callused hands are still cracked from
the "machete" he swung all day.
At the end of which he humbly received
his twenty five cent pay.

His sun baked skin tightly wraps his rugged
facial features, which indicate hard times.
In "Vispera de Reyes" his sorrows are known
through traditional song and rhymes.

Endangered species are these fabled unsung
Heroes of old.
For a broken body was the price paid
for the land we passively hold.

## With You
by Jennifer L. Sass - age 19

On a warm winter night
Under the starry sky
We lay together
In each others arms.

As the wind blows
Through our hair
And the dogs bard
At a distance.

It was the end
Of a perfect evening
Just laying there together.

## Agile Warriors Of Poseidon
*by Robert Schafer*

Agile warriors of Poseidon
Crash against weathered concrete barriers,
That protect the city from the angry sea,
   infiltrating wave after wave.

Thick carpets of smoldering black clouds split open
As thunder slowly rolls in.
Lightning blasts Gothic marble structures,
   descending quickly onto asphalt streets.

Shafts of rain sever and spear
Ancient hills of limestone and lilies,
Releasing dead citizens into the populations,
   leaving no body unpossessed.

Tangerine hue of prominent sun becomes crimson.
It explodes vigorously, and stains the Universe with its diseased blood.
Conquering Titans shroud themselves with obscenity,
   plundering and raping on Judgement Day.

## The Child Next Door
*by Carl S. Scheuffele*

Why is the sky blue? There is an answer, but that's just
the way it is, I tell her.

Is God really watching me she asks. Of course, I say yes.

Where do puppies come from? I tell her mommy dogs,
and hope she leaves it at that.

Does Mommy and Daddy really love me? What do I say to that.
I know them, they live next door. I see how they treat her.

Even to me she is just another kid, my little neighbor.
Raggedy clothes, dirty face, hungry eyes.

Just a product from another drunken night.
A Welfare statistic, not a real life.

Food stamp fed, neglected, raising herself in a home where
no one should live.

I think of a song called **Societies Child**, that is,
what she is.

And no one cares.

## Contents of Destiny
*by Barbara Ann Schick*

Today is unwrapping feelings
into tomorrow's attitude.
Trap hope in a pocket --
the future is optional.

Empty the calendar
with chosen interim.
Treasure tall dreams,
protect your balloon,
filling in the almanac.

Hang on for earthquakes;
hold firm to the tempo.
Endure dark history and
wake to promising sunshine.

Stand attention to the
kangaroo fortune.
Walking in a cautious page.
Sighing for fat water.
Ending with what's afterward.

*Distinctions of Excellence*

## The American Farm Animal
*by Justin Schiefelbein - age 16*

Rings shall vanish from our noses
And the harnesses from our backs
Bit and spur shall rust forever
Cruel whips no more shall crack

Riches more than mind can picture
Wheat and Barley, Oats and Hay
Clover, Beans, and Mangel-Wurzels
Shall be ours upon that day

Bright will shine the fields of America
Purer shall its waters be
Sweeter yet shall blow its breezes
On the day that sets us free

For that day we all must labor
Though we die before it breaks
Cows and Horses, Geese and Turkeys
All must toil for freedom's sake

## Appreciate
*by Margaret Scholl*

Hand clasped upon the bosom,
Overwhelming grace of emotion.
Humble heart calm temper full of joy.
Soul soars in expectation and exultation.

Pleasure in happiness closing old wounds.
Asking not gifts but blessings comfort.
Honorable thoughts, deeds, action,
Excite personas humorous forte.

Lift above lifes weight health enjoyed,
Extending beyond self interest crippling sling.
Compassion for suffering, sickness,
Pain, heartache with gentle understanding.

Sharing with our fellow humans,
Drying tears of those who wept.
All leave footprints where they walk,
Culture rises from their doorstep.

## Attack
*by Alissa Schram - age 15*

Silly in his behavior, Like a little rebellious boy,
Plugging his ears when he doesn't want to hear, Obstinately responding to everything he is told,

Laughing at everything, Cognizant of nothing,
Arms around his head, Fingers in tight fists,

No juice, No jelly,
No needles, No medicine,

Sometimes scared, Sometimes mad,
Drowsy then energetic, Childish then commanding,

Worried by his actions, Like a nervous mother duck,
Rushing around to help him, Crying when he won't listen,

First a little worried, Then quite upset,
Pushy, forceful, Frantic, and over-reactive,

Take this tablet, Eat that candy,
Give me your finger, Drop the blood here,

Making him angry, Making him cry,
She threatens him with 911, And begs him not to sleep,

Woken up by mom, Just like a fire drill,
Soothingly talking to him, While mom thinks of what to do,

Asking him questions, Getting stupid responses,
Keeping him awake, By making him talk nonsense,

Recalling the last time, Thinking of the future,
Wondering what will happen, Wishing he was better,

Living in fear, Of what may happen,
I don't want to loose, My diabetic father.

## Aaron Irritating Shakespeare
*by Aaron Schwartz*

Damn the day I was born
Black and somber, gray and dim;
Heaven just ignored it.
Stain it with despair and all the shades of death
Enshroud it, cloud it. Bury it in the darkest night
Alone, silent, bereft of life.

Should have died straight from the womb;
Covered in blood, the life giving tomb
Discards us, longing to see the light.
With no hunger but for crying, no thirst except for dying.
The worlds terrors set against me,
My tears take shape before me

In a storm of words, an eruption of hot air!
How long could he contain it? Or then how long sustain it?
"Take care. That dark and ancient trail
That wise men fear to tread
Offers up to you the haunts of night
Where gutless daylight fled."

I know where I should find it
But when I looked I couldn't spy it.
Listened but didn't hear it.
Picked up the receiver, no one's on the phone.
Peeked 'round the door, and no one's home.
Where's the release that is my birthright?
I expected many things
But not exclusion from the parking lot of stone.

## My Last Day
*by Eva O. Scott*

If this were my last day on earth,
Would I be sorry or glad, of my birth?
Have I shown love to whomever I meet,
And with a smile be inclined to greet?
To be honest, I've not always been my best,
Nor withstood every test.
So God's forgiveness I've often sought;
And done so to others --- as I ought.
If this were my last day on earth
Who would evaluate my worth?
My husband ---- my family?
My friends, who would it be?
Christ Jesus will judge me, I know,
According to the seeds I sow.
Have I worked, His field to till,
In harmony with His Father's will?
I hope, on my last day, I can say
I've been happy, doing things God's way.

## Cosmic Mother
*by Rachel Semancik - age 17*

She sees
She feels
She Is

ever Living
ever Changing
the Void
the Chasm

Her waving
Love flows
reaching All
that is She

ever Mystery
ever Wonder

Giving Force
Red of Life
Birthing All
Cosmic Mother

## Untitled
*by Taryn Seras - age 20*

If the instrument of passion was hot enough,
Could it stir my heart of stone?
Break down the walls that are a result of ceaseless patience?
Met my world of ice?
Wand of fire, druid magic
My being cries out,
The pain is almost too much
But it is necessary
All part of the process to make me
Feel again.

## Only Me
*by Tiffney Serna - age 18*

Completely enraged
At the bleak emptiness standing before me,
I turned to look at the wall;
Dark foreboding corners,
Beckoning softly with tempting whispers,
Seducing my thoughts with vividly agonizing imagery.

The hollow pain,
Coming from the depths of my chest,
Begins to pound stronger, more fierce;
And it trembles my heart,
Shaking it like a withered leaf,
Free falling from the oblivious sky.
My afflicted mind craves consolation and seclusion,
Found only through mediative sedation;
Yet at solitary times, usually most pacified,
I feel burning tears sting my eyes
And I scream my deranged anger.
This outburst frightens even myself
And my emotional weeping
Grows into deep, drowning sobs;
Sinking the feelings that remain
And leaving only me.

## Other Side of the Mirror
*by Dawn Shackelford - age 13*

I killed myself yesterday because the other
guy would have killed me first.
Behind the mirror he stood with finger
on trigger and my heart about to burst.

"Been through and through so much with you!"
I said before my last breath.
Never before had I though of suicide
as my way of death.

At final second's past, a tear left my eye
and at last, the lead it fled from an always open door.
Soon I found myself yearning for more,
but it was too late, the man had opened the gate.

For I had got my revenge,
and I'll never run from him again,
because, yesterday I killed myself when I killed him.

I had to look into my own eyes before there were any other lies,
of who killed who or what the killer might do.

I'm on the other side of the mirror.

## The Call
*by Nicholas E. Schmalz - age 17*

When we look toward tomorrow, do we really see today?
Our lives go by so fast, can we say what we want to say?
When we look towards the past, can it help us find,
the answer we seek forever to find?
So is today gone, the past behind, and the future
only what's in our minds?
Or is there hope for me and you,
Who believe that our lives are whatever we choose,
when the call comes?

## Sis's Gift
*by Shealene Shafer*

In the soft of a straw laid stall,
A silent barn with shadows upon the walls.
A mama's soft nicker, ears perk in delight,
A nudge of a nose in the soft barn light.
From the wisp of the mane, to the tiny tail,
All four legs try with might to get up, but fail.
So she lay on the straw, taking a break,
In the cool, crisp morning starts to shake.
A rooster crows as the sun comes up,
In all the commotion comes a "yelp" from a pup.
With another try, the front is out,
Another nudge and the back comes about.
As hunger hits, the first task down,
All four hooves steady on the ground.
A head bobs here and goes there,
As mom licks the newborn hair.
Within a short time, she finds the right spot,
Starts sucking away, just what was sought.
To a proud mama on a beautiful day,
This could only come on such a May.

## Fear
*by Heather Sharman - age 14*

My days are sad with fear
Not knowing what was coming each day

My life turned around in a second
When he came into view
So small and tiny
Crying with fear of the new world

It sounded like a puppy begging for attention
But now it is asleep,
Thank God, the silence and peace
My fear of a new life is gone
But only of the sweat and caring people
The life is mine.

## A Mothers Broken Heart
*by Joan D. Sharp*

Crying eyes won't let me see,
Broken heart controlling me

Although she looks so much like you,
She's not the same child I once knew.
The happiness that she once brought
Is no longer here, there's only distraught.

Broken heart controlling me.

This can not be a child of mine,
I thought her better, I know that I tried.
Tried to make a life for her,
Filled with dignity, sweetness and pride.

Crying eyes please let me see,
Broken heart stop controlling me.

Maybe I did something! Did I not see?
Did I miss a signal, or not see a sign?

Broken heart controlling me,
Crying eyes won't let me see.

Could I have maybe avoided this terrible crash,
That took her down that losers path?
What turned my daughter, into someone I do not know?
Where is my daughter? Drugs please let her go.

Crying eyes won't let me see,
Broken heart controlling me.

Crying eyes please let me see,
Broken heart stop controlling me.

## I Wish
*by Audrey Shealy - age 18*

I wish I were a bird so I could fly up high,
Up to the clouds and ask they why:
Why do you sway and dance with the wind,
hovering over us again and again?

I wish I were a fish so I could swim down below
To the depths of the ocean and ask the shark so:
How can you keep swimming around all day?
You must get very weary that way!

I wish I were the grass growing tall on a hill,
So when the breeze blows I won't have to be still.
And then I could ask the daffodil:
How do you speak to the whippoorwill?

I wish I were a mountain growing big and tall,
So I could look down and see the world so small.
And ask the snowflakes one and all:
Where do you come from and why do you fall?

I wish I were the earth itself,
To sit in my place on the universe's shelf,
To see a sprightly laughing elf.
Then maybe I'd wish to be myself!

## Path of Destiny
*by Ronni Sherman - age 14*

At dawn I find myself lost. Lost on a path of destiny.
I come to a brilliant meadow of yellow and gold.
My spirit is lifted and without any thought, I walk. I go to the
middle, where I sit and close my eyes. It starts to rain
and the warm rhythmic pitter-patter on my body seems to draw me
down. Without any concentration or second thought I relax my every
muscle and lay down. The rain seems to be trapped on the brilliant
glowing meadow and I reopen my eyes to the world. The water rises
to my chest and my heart is slowed as well as my
thoughts. The water soon rises to my ears and I loose all sound
of the sweet tune of life that once surrounded me.
Soon the water reaches my eyes and I am forced to close them.
As my eyelids reach towards each other tears are mixed with my salty
company for I know that once they are closed they will never open
again. My mouth goes numb as I feel the wetness against my lips. The
sweet kiss of eternal rest that frightens many yet I stay calm
and accept my destiny. For good or bad fait comes only
once in a lifetime and refusal will only make things worse. The water
rises to my nose and as I smell the last sensation of air my breath stops.
With that my heart follows

## A Wish
*by Mike Sherman - age 16*

A wish I made so long ago,
has finally come true.
For very long I have been wishing,
and now I have found you.

Your gentle smile warms my soul,
I treasure your each word.
Without you I am nothing much,
a knight without a sword.

The way your eyes look into mine,
speeds up my lonely heart.
And I can not even imagine,
how much I'll hurt when we're apart.

Now that my wish has come to me,
I hope it never spes.
You are my angel and my sweet,
from your head to your toes.

I want to keep you warm at night,
and kiss away your tears.
For losing you to anyone,
is one of my worst fears.

## The Lady
*by Venus Shipman - age 17*

He watches her with amazed eyes
Fascinated by her beauty
her green gown, that flows in and out
Foamy lace that curves around her edges
She draws him closer
Her sea breeze fingers ruffles his hair
She beckons him to come and he in compelled to go
He cries out as she embraces him
her soothing voice smothers his plea
There is only the sound of the seagull's cry
he is rejoicing in the new arrival
Today the gown is black with death
But a new sea-winged angel learns to fly

## Dimensions
Amanda D. Shumate

Flashing, twinkling lights over a vast expanse
A pale yellow light slowly approaches
   O'er the horizon.
Energy crackles through the air
Nothing is at it seems.
In fact —
   It doesn't really exist at all.
It is an uncharted figment of our
   mysterious imagination
Perhaps, A residual from our subconscious
   Leftover from an exhilarating dream
   long forgotten.
Aurora borealis - like patterns
   Intricately designed
Oh! How our minds long to see them.
The pale yellow light slowly descends
   and is gone.

## Sister Golden Hair So White
*by John Sikora*

Hair white as the new fallen snow,
The tireless Christian soldier
Marching...marching to the beat of her heart
The love she brings to the fold,
Eighty-five years young,
Tiny yet grand in stature,
Heaven can wait another day for the Shepherdess bathed in psalms,
The iridescent glow of a Saint who walks the corridors of the infirmary
Ministering to the needs of the sick,
Lord, please lead this woman by the hand-
   never letting go.
Long hours turn to dusk,
As darkness descends on the translucent figure kneeling humbly in prayer
Before God in the sanctity of the Chapel high on a hill.
A few hours of rest before the first dewdrops of sunshine fall from heaven
Magically touching her soul and launching her feet afresh
For the start of a new day,
Her mission is the message she brings...
   you are not alone!
A faith which transcends the mortal bounds of our imagination.
Her virtue is a pillar to lean on
And her words of comfort give importance and purpose to people's lives...
Lifting their spirits bright and allaying their deepest fears...
Injecting renewed hope into the tattered fabric of their inner being-
On a journey of courage which will lead them to the light of a new dawn.

## Your Love
*by Pamela Simkanich - age 17*

Your love gives me wings
So I can fly.
But it can also bring me tears
To wash away my feelings.

Your love can pick me up
Or knock me down,
But your love frees me
when all else is wrong.

You have always stuck by me,
and baby I'll do the same.
I wasn't sure at first,
But now I know for real,
Our love will last for all eternity.

## Tat
*by Wendy Simms - age 18*

Twirling colors spin incest
words of, denial.
I am me, no matter what
is thought by you.
Pots of gold
found at the end
of a bombing heritage.
Emerald green
four leaf clovers,
no longer offer
good luck
for a nation
torn between
a common belief.
Fire flaming red,
cautious yellow,
tranquil blue
twirl to the
jaded petals of
faded beliefs.
Initialed to be
with me always,
forms far away
but close to touch.
Eternal brand of
the past stays
to keep my feet,
on the ground.

## In Anticipation of Armageddon
*by Mithoo M. Sinha*

Depleting Forests and Poisoning the Lakes with Egotistic Flair,
Choking the Wind with Cost-Effective Vapors,
Scattering Destruction in His Wake, Man Boasts
That He is Master over Fire, Water, Earth and Air...
If One Great Asteroid is All that it Would Take
To Shake this Small Blue Marble Off it's Path,
Or If a Meteoric Shower Could Ultimately Break
The Domination of the Earth by the Dinosaur,
Then What Would it Require to Make Man Cower?
Bailing Out the Ever Rising Tide at Whose Mercy He Resides,
Having Heated Up His Atmosphere at a Monumental Scale,
And Irrevocably Changed the PH Factor of the Rain
That Washes Out His Crops,
He Ponders Now, "What Cause Has Made Them Fail?"
Attempting to Fathom the Glory and Full Scope
Of the Secret that Lay Within the Atom, Man Only Unleashed Fury;
While in Pandora's Box, Though Much Was Gory, Still There Was Hope...
Was It the Wrath of Gods, or Merely Plate Techtonics
That Brought Down Utopia, and Sent Her 'Neath the Surf and Waves?
In Times Gone By, the Dwellers of Atlantis, and Pompeii
Also Fought Battles for their Turf,
And Now They Both Lie Silent in Their Murky Graves...
Precariously Perched Between Two Glacial Ice Ages,
Man Shakes His Puny Fist at Nature,
And Gloats with Off-Repeated Pride,
Upon the Unprecedented Knowledge He Has Acquired,
Built Upon the Backs of Laboratory Rats, and His Sages...

## Growing Up
*by April Skwarcan - age 13*

I play this game called growing up,
And progress in it every day,
At times it's hard, but I believe in myself,
Knowing I can win, despite what others say.

When I'm ready to give it up,
Because I've lost my turn,
I just remember it's only a game,
And that I have much to learn.

When I really, really want to quit,
After I get sent back to start in shame,
I tell myself, "Just try again.
You'll get better at this game."

After a while, I get halfway there,
Then I start to feel good,
I believe that I may win this game,
And have confidence that I could.

Now I'm beating everyone,
I know for sure that I'll win.
Now that I'm an adult, married with kids,
I'll help them and play again.

## Alone
*by Eugenia L. Slagle*

   Silence is deafening to the
ears
   of the soul...Not a voice nor
lyric...
   nor a thought to console...
   All Alone.
   The soundless deaf turns to
a buzz
   as if silence is speaking to
thee...
   Not a bird to chirp...nor a dog
to bark...
   All Alone.
   There are people around but
none
   do I hear... All Alone.
   Is there anyone as deaf as
me...to the
   sounds of the world...the
crash of the sea?
   All Alone.
   Thoughts now come
through the deafness
   but the voice is my own not
another....destined to be
   All Alone
   My voice mine to hear nothing
more...henceforth
   I shall stay...All Alone!

## Untitled
*by Kristyn Smeathers - age 16*

A destined life of confusion laid ahead,
Uncontrollable pain that would have lasted an eternity.
I still feel all of it even though I am dead,
My body consumed by such mutiny.
The soul lives on forever, impassioned by the grief,
The brain continuously rationalizes all of the aches.
I shall never find a relief,
I shall never be given a break.
Resting in Peace will never apprehend the truth,
I will lie remaining in constant awareness.
My whole body consumed by emotional abuse,
I would have lived a prevailed life of carelessness.
No one may ever know what my life had been,
Some may not even understand.
My thoughts had been forever uneven,
Living day to day unplanned.
I hoped to alleviate all of the misery,
and dreamed of living in peace.
If not now, may it endlessly become a mystery,
Why I caused myself to become deceased.

## Fairest Among Thousands
*by B. Pauline Smith*

In Life's Garden there is a rare
and beautiful flower blooming,
with a fragrance
called Heaven Scent

The precious seed from this flower
is taken by the wind,
and the wind finds a place
that is desolate
where no other flower grows

Only the wind knows where
these secret places are,
and gently plants these seeds,
where they will never be forgotten,
because these seeds came
from the heart of this rare flower
in Life's Garden for all to see

This miracle flower's bloom
is immortalized, and knows
no season
No weed or thistle has dared to grow
where this flower grows

Take my hand and let us walk together
and, yes, let us tend this flower
that grows in Life's Garden,
and call it by
the sweetest of names,
and let that name
be called
FRIEND!

*Dedicated to all the victims of domestic violence-and to all battered women-and to all battered children-everywhere*

## The Fall
*by Linda Smith - age 13*

Who you are, who you want to be, who you know
Formerly important factors are irrelevant
You're still susceptible to the fall
Merely one sweet gesture
Perhaps from that breath-stealing male
One step on your part, and you're history
Once you've fallen, don't count on getting back up
You can lose yourself in his eyes
Yet regard yourself more highly with his every word
Fret not, contradiction is the agreement to disagree

As you seek his heart you can
Dive hundreds of feet in the blue, trackless deep
To find the chest which holds his heart
   Covered with moss
Never to be accessible again

Love is a sweet-smelling candle
Ever burning once kindled
Tend it frequently; enjoy the peace
Always be aware of the fall
Which never fails to be bitter-sweet

## Positions of Life
*by Anna Milàn Sole'*

When I saw you behind the cloud of smoke,
the silence broke . . .
You were alone but waiting,
someone forgot you,
someone knew.
And as I tried to get closer,
I didn't dare . . .
You were so perfect, but me . . .
I was nothing
I pleaded on bare knee!
And now that I have no other chance
now, that there is no more Romance . . .
You were always the only one
you always were . . . but now there's none!

## Fly, Swim
*by Tasha Somers - age 16*

Down, down we go
Swim like a dolphin

Up, up we go
Fly like an eagle

Down, down we went
Watch the water sparkle and shine

Up, up we went
Let the wind carry you

Down, down we swam
Look, the wildlife we see!

Up, up we flew
Above the mountains, by the streams!

Onward, onward we go
Navigate through the sea

Fly, fly we must
Through trees and underbrush

Onward, onward we must go
Towards 'land' we see, finally safe in our cove!

Fly, fly we did go on
To find our nest, to land on!

## Listening
*by Katrina Marie Stone - age 16*

Why do people sit
on the grass listening
to the wind in the trees,
the brook rushing by,
the rustling of the tall weeds,
and the soft thud of raindrops
on the hard ground.
Is it just that the sounds of the environment
are so soothing
or that we just need
calm ways to relieve
our tensing stress?

## Christmas Day
*by Patricia White Spikes*

As I walked along the streets in my clothes all tattered and worn
My eyes did behold the most beautiful sight since I was born.
It was a home with an angel - an angel all aglow.
And for some reason, it took my very heart in tow.

I walked a few more blocks till I saw a church door.
Then I parked my wares and entered on the beautiful marble floor.
I wasn't ready nor did I expect the many vicious stares.
Because where else would one go during such a heavenly season?
In my heart, I knew not why they all turned and stared at me
As if I was a man - a man without reason.

As mothers walked past me and pulled their children close to their sides,
Such pain filled my heart - and tears did sting my eyes.
Inside my heart, I cried, I too am God's child.
But, from my mouth, I could only tremble and smile.

I walked back outside into the cold of day
I knew I wasn't welcome here - not even to stay and pray.
As I hastily made my exit, one small child did say
Mister, are you coming to be with us on this Christmas day?
I smiled and thanked her, for I know now it is true -
It WILL be a small child who will lead us all through.

## Man In The Black Trenchcoat
*by Syreeta Springer*

Shuffling through the 34th St. subway station.
Shoulders bent, pants a little too high up, but that still
Serves the purpose.
He is picking in garbage cans looking for something to
Eat while those stand around and watch him
Contemptuously. Not realizing it could easily be one of
Them. Not knowing where their next meal comes from.
Not having adequate clothes for the weather.
Why don't someone help him?
Why don't I?
Can it really be that difficult to take him aside and show
Him a little kindness?
To take him out and buy him something to eat.
It could have been our brother, father, uncle or friend.
Or, Maybe he is?
Man shuffling from garbage can to garbage can.
Some on lookers wondering what he really is like.
Man in the black trenchcoat,
Shuffling from station to station.
Fading into the crowd.
No one pays any attention to his plight.
I wonder how he sees the world?
Maybe like a man in a black trenchcoat
Hungering for his next meal.

## You Called Me Mama
*by Diane E. Staton*

When you were a baby,
I held you gently in my arms.
You looked up and smiled at me.
And you called me Mama

As you grew older, I saw you off to school.
You were a good thinker.
I was very proud of you.
And you called me Mama

Time went by and you turned into an adult.
No matter what the situation was,
I could never find fault.
Because you called me Mama.

Pain was in my heart and tears in my eyes.
Still, I would stick with you.
Through all the many lies,
Because you called me Mama

No matter what situation you were in,
The problems would sometimes multiply.
I would still be your friend.
Because you called me Mama

Now things are not the same,
I've grown tired and old.
This way of life I cannot sustain.
Because you call me Mama

My dear, I have no more to give.
I'm tired of facing all these crisis.
You need to learn how to live.
And not just call on Mama

## Loss of a Loved One
*by Julie Steckler - age 17*

As I awaken from a dream halfway filled with fear.
Trying to forget its contents I wipe away a tear.
Still haunted by its memories, I pray it isn't true.
And there deep within me, I see an image of you.
The image is so lifelike I want to hold it close.
So that it may protect me from what I fear the most.

Now that I'm awake, and you are really gone.
The only question I have for God is, "How can I go on?"
Every song I hear brings back memories of you,
And all the crazy things we had both been through.

As I continue to think of you, I begin to cry once more.
But as the tears fall this time, they are much harder than before.
I try to convince myself that everything's all right,
But I am in a battle in which I cannot fight.

I wish I could go back to the days before,
And fulfill the plans we'd made, and not worry about it anymore.
I guess I'll have to deal with it, my life will just have to go on.
I know that deep within my heart, you will never really be gone.
Because your love and memory, will forever be living on.

## Angel
*by Carrie Marie Stanley - age 15*

Our friendship means more to me,
Than one-thousand singing angels.
I can't picture my life.
Without you here with me.
If something was to happen,
I'd go completely insane.
If I was to die,
I'd ask to be your guardian Angel.
Just to be sure that you'd be fine,
Without me hand and hand.
We've had our days,
We've had our laughs,
But not one day goes by,
When your not thought of by me.
I'm just a call away,
And just a mile or so,
Which seems so far to a friend.
When you get grown,
And have a family,
Remember me,
Cause I could be,
That Angel over you at night.

*Dedicated to my dearest, and best friend,
Jessica Clark*

## In Love Again
*by Dana Stephan - age 17*

I swore to myself it wouldn't happen again.
I vowed to myself that this was the end.
The end of this longing, this yearning so strong.
I said I was over you, but oh, I was wrong.
    Now here it is,
    quite awhile later,
And my love for you, is now even greater.
I spend all my time thinking of you,
All the things you would say and do.
Your warm embrace I long to feel,
I hope one day my heart will heal.
I've fallen in love with you, deep and true,
Each time I see you my heart breaks in two.
The sound of your laughter, the smile on your face,
In my heart, each has a special place.
I think of the days and nights together,
All these memories will last forever.
I don't understand why we said goodbye
My love for you will never die.
I can't believe that this is the end
I pray one day we'll be together again.
All the special things we shared
I gave you my everything because I cared.
Everyday I'm reminded so true,
Of how I fell in love with you.
    I love you always and forever.

## The Climb Up Rakekniven
*by Sheila Sterling - age 20*

I look behind my back and see,
the tracks I left in harmony.
I grit my teeth, and clench my fist,
and gain an inch with every wrist.
I lead my men up to the top,
and for their care I'll only stop.
I'll garb my rope, and all my stuff,
though the trek already rough.
I'll never stop, new land to see,
a place I'd only dream I'd be!
I'll sleep in my hanging tent,
but when I wake I will ascent.
I reached the top and I could see
Antarctica, from sea to sea.
I'm happy to be on this journey,
but I couldn't have done it just by me.
"We've" climbed a place no man has dared—
my friends have helped, I was not scared.
We've won a goal in this breathtaking land,
and here is where our victory stand.
We thank you for letting us come and see—
"Antarctica-this is your story."

## Nightfall
*by Karin Stewart*

I have become the phantom of my dreams,
Speckled ivory face, glassy eyes,
Long, thin fingers.
I am invisible or so it seems,
Vacant stares, focus shifted,
Silence lingers.
I walk alone in the shadows of the night,
Longing, wishing,
Hoping.
I wander in the darkness with labored sight,
Stumbling, reaching,
Groping.
I stare unknowingly at your gorgeous face,
Eased smile, chiseled jaw,
Deep green eyes.
I look to the heavens in this desolate place,
Crescent moon, wispy clouds,
Velvet skies.
Now I come to my time-wearied domicile,
Cracked walls, stained carpet,
Peeling paint.
I lie down and step into a dream, the state of guile,
My escape, my fantasies,
My restraint.

## Leaves
*by W. Forres Stewart*

Pale amethyst bejewels the leaves
of burnished gold and crimson hue,
now fallen from a last reprieve
beneath the unrelenting blue
of autumn sky and autumn chill,
adorning fruitful earth where days
of glade and shade and leafy rill
no longer bask in phoebus' rays;

a whispered sadness tones the chant
of death within the rainbow cloak,
absorbing beams of light aslant
each slender birch, each sturdy oak;

but other leaves in bright lime green
triumphant yet above the strife
of windswept limbs, tho' sparsely seen,
are skybound celebrants of life!

*Distinctions of Excellence*

## My Vanished Blues
*by Yvelette Monique Stines*

The song has been song and the piano played.
The smoke has smoothed in the air and the smell is clear.
The stage is empty and the people have left
My blues have vanished away.

## Compassion
*by Leona Strimple*

To show a little compassion, should not seem like a chore,
To give a bit of attention, when you should give a whole
lot more.
It could be just a kind word, or maybe just a bright smile,
Or a prayer for a stranger to our Lord.
But it seems more will shun and leave the one in need
to go and laugh at the helpless one, while he remains
to plead.
OH!  But for a little compassion.

## Doomed
*by Teresa Sturtevant - age 17*

Fool enough to almost be it
cool enough to not quite see it.
Pick your pockets full of sorrows
and run away with me tomorrow.
We'll try and ease the pain
but somehow we'll feel the same.
Well, no one knows where are secrets go.
I send a heart to all my dearies,
when your life is so, so dreary.
I'm rumored to the straight and narrow.
While the harlots of my perils scream....
and I fail.
Mother weeps the years I'm missing but
all our time can't be given back.
Shut my mouth and strike the demons
that curse you and your reasons.
Out of hand and out of season,
out of love and out of feeling.
Is that so bad...?
Fool enough to almost be it,
cool enough to always feel this.
Always old, I will always feel this.
No more promises, no more sorrows
No longer will I follow.
Can anybody hear me?
I just want to be me!
Try to understand that
when I can, I will.

## Destiny
*by Angela Swereda*

The world shatters
Collapsing all around
The misery engulfs
Decisions  Decisions

All becomes dim and gray
Destroying everything inside
Release me!  Release me!
Let the clouds disappear

Hidden from all eyes
Pretend!  Pretend!
Meanwhile your falling
Into the depths of the unknown

A sudden grasp without warning
Devours the remains
Of a feeble existence
To tired to fight
Surrender to fate

The candle flickers, as you let it burn
It continues to burn
Until the flame fizzles
Out!
Freedom at last!

## Our Tune
*by Sara Tabner - age 12*

We both know the ancient song,
We are right and one is wrong.
Time has given me new hope,
It is now I start a rope.
Feeding me an apple from a pear tree,
Now, sadly, he has to see.
Black is white, white is black,
Colors are confusing to minds that lack.
Together we saw the clouded plane,
Now together we must take the pain.
Dreams are dreams that do come true,
If you do what you're to do.
Hand in hand around the oak,
Only he understands, the ribbon is broke.

## Discovering the Truth
*by Jessica Tanner - age 17*

She's given the signal and walks to the chair

    eyes straight ahead, alert, aware.

She places her fingers and slowly inhales...

    a mistake will be made it never fails.

With a steady clear mind she starts to play—

    this is all that she's hoped for, from the very first day.

As sound fills the air, her music rings clear.

    All is forgotten—the crowd, the fear.

With a final crescendo her performance ends.

    She turns to the audience and then comprehends;

It's not the applause or awards she'll receive,

    but the sense of accomplishment that she's now achieved.

## Break-Up Aftermath
*by Sara Taqi*

Death weaves in and out of our consciousness
reality and in wistful dreams.
Neither controls that pervasive fear.

Different flavors, different forms
death persists in
haunting
through broken hearts, broken relations, broken dreams
shattering reality.

Escape is as elusive as the floating
clouds of serenity.
Acceptance is within the grasp of peace
from living.

But what life to enjoy without facing that
bittersweet foe - Death
my friend.
It will name their heir
and bequeath memories and fleeting moments.

Savoring its fatal blow, recognize...
dead.
And hope blooms, it begins anew
shimmering throughout every existence, every
everything
and then the sun sets.
But the full moon still rises
While the sun waits
to kill the moon
with another
day, only for itself
to die.
Again.

## In the Mist of Twilight
*by Dalian R. Taylor*

Just the other day I saw the sunset. I watched it go down as the darkness started to invade the skies infinite distance and the stars lit up heavens gate. It was as if God had just opened up his eyes and looked down upon me with a twinkling sparkle of light which gleamed from within him. Within an instance the moon glowed as it's brilliant light filled the portal between night and day as it showed us the never ending realm of the universe.

On the wings of the wind a cool breeze blew across the earth; so smooth and quiet it was for, it's serene voice echoed gentle through the trees as it ruffled the leaves and swayed the short blades of grass upon the earth's floor, as it continued on it's way to everywhere else.

Standing there in the twilight I could hear the creatures which are heard and not seen begin to awaken. Their sounds resonated and encompassed the tranquility of the moment. It appeared that they suddenly surrounded me as I stood there gazing at the marvels of our creators work for which I walked beneath.

So sedate was I as I became enticed by the wonders and bewitched by this mist of the twilight.

## Death is Destruction
*by Jennifer Thames - age 15*

Never allowing what has come
   only to say what will be
      forgetting the importance of life.

All of this fighting and why?
   Just to prove who you are
      Can't we all make peace
         like God intended?

We need to learn to love
   to feel, to know what's important
      but if we fight,
         All we do is destroy ourselves!

## Future
*by Brenda M. Thienes - age 19*

I couldn't find the words to say,
That moment when you walked away,
And I was trembling deep down inside,
For I didn't want to say good-bye,
Now the moment I had is gone,
All that's left is me, trying to hold on,
But I won't let him take me,
And I won't let him break me.
For God is in control,
And to this I will always hold,
He keeps me strong,
He will help me move on.
Now it's only my heart that breaks,
For this decision I did make,
I allowed myself to fall in love,
Without the guidance from above,
And left now, with only the memories,
Of what I thought to be my destiny,
But I won't let it take me,
And I won't let it break me.
Maybe I'll never understand,
God's good and perfect plan,
But what I do see,
Is the better life He has in store for me,
Wrong roads I've traveled are now left behind,
I look toward a future much more divine.
And He won't let it take me
And He won't let it break me.

## What Do You See?
*by Michelle Thomas - age 16*

You are so soft-spoken and then your are not.
Because your eyes, they say a lot.
Many people say you are shy.
I know you and wonder why.

You are so sweet and then again no.
Because your eyes they tell me so.
Many people say you are angry.
Could you really be mad at me?

You are so selfish, but yes it's true.
When asked what you think about,
But of course, it's you.
In your eyes that gleam and shimmer
That burn like fire and then icily shimmer
      at me.
Tell me dear friend, what do you see?

## Knight Without Armor
*by Belle Poe*

My knight shed his armor, whilst he lay with me

He set down his sword and shield, did he

And bared the coat of arms, beneath his vest

So to lay his head, upon my breast

His sovereign oath, did he give me

Of loyalty and love, eternally

Wielding his honor in one hand and truth in the other

He then slay all the dragons, hence forth, be my lover

Our colours be mingled, in each other's heart

Curse'd hell be the sword, that wouldst cleave them apart

## Autumn's Spell
*by Shannon Thompson*

Shades of evolving secrets, flutter the whispers, of the legends' journey that kneels soley, in time's honor, walvoring, as if forever burry.

Between it's leaves and roots, it commands, the splashes, of life's sail; heding laws, of this defenseless gilt web, of monist, in nature's dale.

As the Indian summer's encompassing ambrosia, burnishes a chestnut flair; dithering the character, of these shadowed attachments, echoed bare.

Beneath the rainbows, of rustic browns, and the golden treasures, crest; witness, the voyage, of spring's half brother's rustled nest.

Where, the scarecrows embrace, nature's dance, in a rue pardon; that draws, to view the strewn corsage, in fall's fluent garden.

Hearing, the painted leaves' hum; while chasing the whipping wind; in the ever flowing stream, of season's mirth, lavishly pinned.

As clusters, of darkened cedar, slumber, in an interweaved silhouette; environ, to the sun stained ridge's blanket, of the tasseled grass, peiroette.

Unblinding the design, that ensues, night's hidden resurrection brought; on the soft sketches, of the soul, in pride's last view, of birth's thought.

*Distinctions of Excellence*

## Nature's Composition
*by Shannon Thompson*

Say goodbye, to autumn's half brother, when twilights come;
In sketches, that never part, from the warm summer's sung.

With the billows of crimson-gold, that crumble, as time departs;
Silver paled salmon glide, in fluttering sprints, to wayward hearts.

Igniting flight, through a mirror, of a dreamer's drake rhyme.
For the care, of spring blossoms, draws a rose in winter time.

Before God's wrath is unwound, from the eye, of Heaven's door;
Seep the pools, of tears, laced in the tired frosty moor.

Where a snow angel's strife, is lost in the innocence, of ocean rains,
While oaks, hold semblance, to the willow's shagged echo frames.

In spools, of crystal flakes, tattered with cotton swiveled bars;
As moonbeams, ride in a carriage, of Heaven's iridescent stars.

It's Jack Frost, that slumbers, when all seems to be, a lass brought;
For the purpose of life, a thousand faces' colored, in thought.

Buds' bloom the trees, suiting petalled grounds, to it's domes;
Where valley's sway, to the call, of the wind chime's honeycombs.

With strokes, to a fairy dust, that blankets every cloud's opal hue;
As tranquility circles, in the cracks of mystic blue's perfection, due.

These pearled nights grounded, at the journey, in nature's first cast;
While pine breezes, protect sands, from father sky, at last.

But impeding wave's lapse, from the mountain's snow-capped rocks;
To show the curls of sea, beneath summer's steamed sand locks.

Never parting time, between the eyes of dawn, with dusk's mometoes;
As celestial beauty rises, to fall in creation, while it grows.

## Where Have All the Values Gone?
*by D. J. Thorn*

Values learned by youth today often reflect disrespect and anger of adults around them. These values, different from those taught fifty years ago, make the world less pleasant, a more dangerous place in which to live.

From aged eyes I see how values have deteriorated. My bottom was tanned more than once as I learned truth, tenacity, fairness — the Golden Rule and the Ten Commandments.

Along with values we were taught manners, rules for living, like saying "please" and "thank you." Manners were conducting yourself so as to make everyone's life more pleasant. During a dinner at the Royal Palace a guest took a sip from the finger bowl, mistaking it for clear soup. Without hesitation, the Queen picked up her finger bowl and took a sip. Guests in your home were not embarrassed.

Elders were treated with respect. They had lived longer, had more experience, so we respected the wisdom they had acquired.

Two teenagers recently shot a couple who were sitting on the beach awaiting the sunrise, simply because "they wanted to." A teenage girl hits her mother "because she doesn't stop me." An unemployed couple live with his parents, expecting babysitting while they party, without so much as a "please" or "thank you," and then complain when their laundry isn't done.

Battering of elderly is on the rise. It makes me ask, "Has love flown out the window?" Three of my grandparents were cared for and died at home, surrounded by love in their last days.

Where has love gone? As I think about it, love and honor together made values important. Have we lost both?

## Ocean
*by Je'nell Timmons - age 20*

A man can walk along the ocean many times in his life,
And never see anything more than water,
Nor hear anything more than the movement of the sea,
And feel anything more than the ocean's breeze
A man walks along the ocean a million times,
And leaves his footprints in the sand,
But never knows the meaning of what he sees,
Nor what he feels,
And what he hears,
A man can walk along the oceanside forever,
And never understand its importance.
When a man can walk by the ocean and look at what
He sees,
Listen to what he hears,
And touch what he feels,
Then and only then can he see the ocean's true
Beauty.

## Loving You
*by Robin M. Tinay*

As I look into the mirror
I see its tinted red
I cry these scarlet tears
Wishing I were dead

I look for the light; its not there
In the deepest deadly darkness
Into emptiness I stare

I wonder what it is
That has done these things to me
I slowly understand that I am no longer free

I'm in a trap; I can't get out
At least I know what its about
I silently say your name and wonder
If it will always be the same

I try to escape this life of mine
I break the glass; it won't crack
I hit the mirror; it bounces back

I think that this is just a dream
A nightmare; it can't be
I hear myself, my painful screams
I feel the pain inside of me
Is it fear or ecstacy?

I can't hold back anymore
I run, I search for the door
I can't get out, I can't break free
After all, I can't escape what's inside of me

In the story I search my mind
And soon I find that in the end
Loving you was my only sin...

## Sweating Krystals
*by Carlos C. Torres*

Krystal, the jewel, that lights the night,
Make human feelings, come bare its light.
Its burning beauty, can pierce the heart,
The vibrant jewel, most difficult to part!

You wicked smile, adorns the honey tree,
Your twinkling sparkles, we feel and see!
Oh, Queen of Krystal, you're known to be,
The fairest pebble, in frailest Seas,
Our Queen, you rule, our thoughts, our deeds.

Forsake not those, who'll pledge their vows,
Who'll seek to drink, your fountain's fertile flows.
Nor those, who'll need not sleep, for you to hold,
Dreaming of your reflections, in mirror's naked glows.

Your flowing cup teems, with youthful strife.
Your waves, create relentless tides.
Till dawn's new day, it's your domain!
Yes, on you'll grow, and on, you'll reign!

## The Awakening Dream
*by Angela Marciante Toscano*

Down below the deep of a dream,
lay reality and its thorns.
Up, beyond the message of dreams
the meaning is lost, and the dream, is a dream.
The power of Venus is bridged to the sea
for the Earth to embrace, to dream, and be free.

A dream has no light!
It is only seen in the darkness of our sleep.
Yet, light shines on the bridge of a dream
where darkness is in control.

I awake, mesmerized, from a dream that is true.
While still dreaming, I realize
how I'm lost without you!
Now that I'm lost in the crowd of loneliness
listening to the voices of its silence...
    I'm still dreaming...from the awakening dream.

As the Angels caress
the thoughts of my dream,
the demons take charge
of the awakening scream.

## Destiny
*by Renee Valerino - age 20*

Loves destiny may never cease.
That one man's heart may rest in peace,
But yours must sit alone to urn
For that moment once again where passion may burn.
Time can sometimes weaken the flame
They never know exactly who to blame.
Love can be looked for until the end
but never will that flame be lit again.
The heart is a fire that urns for just one
It does not rekindle for just anyone.
A lifelong passion is just a waste,
but it can never be shown on your face.
When the fire dies your soul moves on
to find the love that once was gone.

## Nurture is the Mother of All Beginnings
*by Debbi D. Vasquez - age 19*

You go to your mother
like you go to the heavens. You kneel down
for her like a servant.

When the wish to obey
no longer matters. She lends her shoulder
for you to cry on.

She attends to your wounds
like a nurse
and softens the pain. Every night,

at birth, she crouches at the edge
of the bed allowing
you to suck every ounce

that will please you
and sees your eyes
slowly close under hers.

In the winter, she keeps you close
around the fire.
When in hunger, she feeds you.

When she opens her arms
before you she can't imagine anything
but raising you,

kissing your forehead, praising you.
And when your
away she can see you through

the night shooting
through the sky
in the shape of a shining star.

## The Eternal Being
*by Kathy Veysey*

I cannot understand the depth,
Of this solitary man,
Who can through the eons of time,
Reach and span the gulf,
That touches this heart of mine.
Nor can I fathom the love,
That binds me to him,
To that one I never met.
Why I should be considered of worth,
Among the millions of this earth.
Yet within this being of mine,
is an awakening of the soul,
That testifies to the fact,
Because of him I'm whole.
As long as I am, I will never comprehend,
The eternal being of this single man.

## The Storm
*by Tina Valerius - age 15*

A door slams
I know it's you
a chameleon
once a mild flame
now an icy storm
Your breeze of hate whirls around
intoxicating others with your rain of taunts and jeers
Your bitter remarks will not wound me
I am a shield
decrepit and worn from your abuse
I still survive
watching
waiting
for another storm

## Moist Aroma
*by Bonnie Vincent*

Rumbling thunder

Lightening bolts streak the summer sky

Pouring rain drenches the wide open fields

Rain patted flowers to the ground

The aroma of hot moisture fills the summer

day

The sun is now peeking through the hole in the

cloud

Mud puddles are everywhere

even in children's shoes

## Simplicity
*by Peter C. Vincent*

I cherish idleness; I am humbled only by the
    likes of the busy honeybee in labor.
    If I can avoid worrisome words, I will forge
    along a straight and gentle path; if I
    follow lazy footsteps, I will never waver.

The otiose day is one of splendor;
    these are the moments that I remember:
    I relish the hollow pleasures.
    If my heart is blackened by bodily burdens,
    I will replace the darkness with barren treasures.

I pay homage to the fastidious.
    I dare to reach out and grasp the cue:
    I simplify!
    The arms of the cradle will catch me.
    I rest deeply and rock to the cadence of doing little.
    I wonder if this serene feeling isn't
    something special: an enigmatic riddle!

## Unheard
*by Antonius A. H. Vollenberg*

Night's I cry alone wondering what went wrong

To say I'll make your dream's come true would have been wrong

I thought I could help them along

Once, I could feel your eyes

Now all lies

I would rather feel the hurt inside
than know the emptiness you're heart must hide

Is a dream a lie if it doesn't come true

Night's I cry alone... unheard.

## Last Chance
*by Brad Walker*

That's not true!
I've always cared for you.
I've loved you for years in quiet devotion.
I wept silent tears when tragedy stuck you,
I offered my shoulder when you needed to cry,
I kept you warm while you slept in my arms,
I kept you company when you were so alone.
Don't do this; don't leave me here alone.
I can't go on without my dearest friend.
I'd rather join you in death than leave your side.
I'm begging you,
With tears running down my face,
And my voice quivering in terror:

Please...

Put...
..Down...
...The...
...Gun...

## Terrible Twos
*by Jody L. Wacker*

Two little hands...
clasped together, saying
prayers, reaching for mine.
Patting softly my back
in imitation of my own

Two little feet...
pitter pattering up and down
the hallway, running,
hopping, stomping in
my sandals way too big
for tiny little feet

Two little ears...
hearing your singsong
voice; sweet and soft,
giggling, perfect for tucking
stray blond curls behind

Two little eyes...
sapphire pools, reflections
of my own, twinkling mischief,
drooping closed, fluttering open,
good night

Two short years...
you've grown; not quite big girl
not quite baby.
gone is my princess, so soft and pure...
replaced by flashing tempers,
independence, struggles for control;
all the more endearing for your
emerging self

the best things come in twos...

## Our Heart Beat
*by Sherry M. Wadsworth - age 15*

At night if I am awake I hear one heart beat,
It is mine.
I no longer hear two,
Because you are no longer here.

You left one night,
While I held you in my arms,
I begged you not to leave;
You only replied I love you.

They never found the person,
Who ripped you away from me.
They had several clues,
Yet they did not go very far.

I miss your sweet lips on mine,
The smell of your cologne in the morning.
The way you told me you would never leave me,
That you would always be here for me.

Against your will you left,
One cold, rainy December night.
I held you in my arms in the middle of the street.
While blood poured from the gunshot wounds in your chest.

That night will forever be engraved in my mind,
We couldn't even bring ourselves to say good-bye.
Now I lay alone in our bed,
And listen to my own heart beat.

It hurts me not to hear yours,
For it brings back all of the pain.
Where I hold you for the last time,
And I felt your heart beat the last time with mine.

## Guardian Angels
*by Mary B. Wadzinski*

Enveloping serenely
A teary-eyed small soul.
Comforting the lost and lone
Makes us all feel as whole.

Sent to us as messengers
Of joyful love and peace.
Surrounding us with heartsful
Of hope that will not cease.

Now that life is passing by
And death is at my door,
Let my guardian angels
Take me home evermore.

## The Sanctuary
*by David Wallace*

Amidst a range of silent hills
Descends a vast ravine
Where snowflakes never leave
Lonely evergreens

There a remote hamlet rests
Where candles glow in window panes
Of cottages that wear a fleece
Of downy white and timeless peace

This town of twoscore hears some news
Of a windswept world, erupting and damned
Though the gods of war spare the silent hills
Faraway in the hinterland

## Obsession
*by Tracie Lynn Wambold*

My past is over; CREMATED
Yet, somehow it's still alive
Crawling through tiny crevices,
Haunting me; I can't let go.

Memories crawl about on the
Jungle gym I've created in my mind,
Swinging from vine to vine like Tarzan
And landing knee deep in quick sand.

Candlelight flickers create shadows
That remind me of lost romance
Sweet blueberry smells of burning wax
Dance feverishly though my soul.

The sound of soft music and sensuous touches
Linger about in my mind and do not lessen
My past is still my present clinging to me
Like static cling; OBSESSION.

## Teachers are our life
*by Erika Ward - age 13*

Teachers teach kids large and small,
They work in their rooms to teach them all.
They teach all subjects and teach them well,
And when it is time they ring the bell.
Teachers help kids when they are ill,
And clean up their messes when they spill.
They assist lost children in finding their way,
And always say "Have a nice day!"
They offer you help whenever you need,
A band-aid to cover your scratched up knee.
Teachers will play games with you,
If you ask them politely too.
Teachers teach you all through your life,
So when you grow-up you'll be just right.
A teacher loves kids as you can see,
I already know that's what I want to be!

## Imagination
*by Stevie Ward - age 12*

Imagination is the key to our souls and hearts
without it we are nothing
the imagination is the center of creativity
no matter the age it is important
it tells us what kind of person we are and who it will come to be
the imagination is what creates our dreams both night and day
without our dreams we have no future
without the imagination there would be no color, no life
and the world would be black and white

## My Heart
*by Sherry D. Ware*

My heart is but a young flower,
Waiting to bloom.

Eager to know life's meanings,
But I am slow to groom.

I wish my flower would remain a bud,
But nature calls it away.

Not too far from the nest,
I pray that it will stray.

For my flower so young and brave,
I fight away pain and strife.

The flower so rare and precious to me,
Is always my heart, my daughter, my life.

## Deep River
*by Ruth Warner*

Life calls to mind a deep river
murky, relentless and cold;
poised to entrap the unwary;
only sustaining the bold.

Some are caught in the undertow,
trapped 'neath the surface of fear.
Ships meeting risk in swift currents
can suddenly disappear.

Beware of turbulent waters
that tempt one to enter in,
that murmur of peace and safety,
but lead one only to sin.

Linger beside the still waters,
soothingly peaceful and wide,
that flow beside the green pastures
where Jesus oft would abide.

Follow His paths of righteousness;
let love and mercy be rife;
avoid the murky deep river;
seek the still waters of life.

## Woman of Darkness
*by Holly Warth - age 15*

She lives in the dark, in your soul she leaves her mark.
She is the woman of darkness,
her mind never revealing its sharpness.
She lets out a distinguished cry,
nobody ever letting her try.

She mourns and grieves,
in the end she just leaves.
Her heart is filled with hate, her life in a despicable state.
She wants so much,
but her mind knows it's look but don't touch.

Everyone hear her roar,
woman of darkness no more.
Her mind folds, she fits into their perfect molds.
Now she's like the rest,
always trying to be the best.

She wants nothing more,
not knowing what she has in store.
When she tries to be true it all seems so new.
What she had before,
she can no longer adore.

She wants so much to see, the person she used to be.
She hangs around just to mope,
she explains to her friends she just can't cope.
In the end it seems,
that they all gang up in teams.

They tare you apart from the insides out,
They will soon forget what it was all about.
You will go on living,
no one else seems to be giving.
Now you want more, why can't it be like it was before?

## Daddy's Little Girl
*by Diana Washington*

Little girls are told they are sugar, spice
   and everything that is nice.

Daddy said:

I was always his heart.
And he gave his true Love from his heart.
Many days he rocked me in his arms.
And kept me protected from all harm.

Daddy said:

Baby, you are my little Georgia peach.
But you are out of reach.
You will always be the apple of my eye.
My darling girl you are to be an example.
Let no one use you for a sample.

Daddy's Love for his little girl will last forever!
Because she will always be

  Daddy's little Girl

## Sister Summer
*by Vance Michael Wass*

Smile sister summer
while the dog days creep on
Transform to a woman
the young girl is gone.

Gaze upon you
a mere thousand ways
yet grasp the brother
who invites broken days.

Sing sister summer
dream the white picket fence
Your gift from the heavens
and its name...Patience.

True pride fury
and the casual embrace
Never one flower
alone in the vase.

Cry sister summer
for the autumn it hears
A distant generations
cries and fears.

## Fear
*by Barbara Watford*

I walked along the empty road
And thought about my plight
I knew it would be dark soon
And I would have no light

The trees would move in awesome shapes
And fear would stop me cold
But if I could muster up my courage
This courage would make me bold

I'd move through shadows on the ground
And I'd keep walking on
Until I saw my place ahead
I'd care not, I was alone

The owl would hoot, the gale would call
Yes, I would look around
What ever fear was in the bush
I would stare it down

For fear will paralyze your mind
If it can get a hold
Chase it with your strongest thoughts
Before it take control

## At the Kitchen Table
*by Martha S. Watkins*

Hopelessness

...sitting at the table gazing out the window
over a cold cup of coffee...

What do you want he asked?
She explained.

WHAT DO YOU WANT, HE DEMANDED?
She spoke, but he could not hear.

Weariness

...coping day after day,

How does love die?

## As Aliens Contemplate the Conquer of Earth
*by Nicole Watson - age 19*

The blue waters sing as they flow over the land
blending with the green brown earth below
their feet
which sink in the clay, staining their ankles
the colour of their enemy.

The clear rain pours out of the skies
flooding the valleys, and nourishing the trees
allowing the wealthy to fly
as leftovers are picked out of bins.

The heavens shine down on its creations
and kisses the sweet cheeks of the old and
the young
who reshape their generation by marking their territory
with babies and corpses in the remains of a city.

The lush forests give shelter to the beauty
of the exotic wildlife captured in its essence
lining the soft leaves with the comfort of a home
as it conquers the hostility of the flames
reducing beauty to ashes.

All of earth's greatness controlled by these stupid beings
called humans fighting for the right to take credit
for disasters crated by years of hard work,
so satisfaction to conquer would be meagre and in vain
for death has already come to those who conquer themselves.

## Untitled
*by Desarae Wayne - age 16*

It burns a soul with longing,
  tears up a heart with sorrow.
Like a rose wet with dew,
  it catches the human eye.
Although it has no color,
  it is not black and white.
Soaring higher than an eagle,
  also lower than a sparrow.
What it is,
  is not important.
If you feel the desire to live,
  to fulfill your wildest dreams,
  it is free inside of you.
If you feel no need to live,
  no need to love,
  it is locked in a cage within you.
But you can open the cage,
  with a magic key.
It will be set free,
  with a burning soul as the source.

## Growing Up
*by Krista Weatherspoon - age 17*

I am a little baby,
in my mommy's arms.
She says she'll always love me,
and keep me from all harm.

I am a little girl,
getting bigger everyday.
My mommy prays so hard,
that I won't go too far away.

I am a young teenager,
keeping up with the latest trends.
My mother really worries,
about my choice of friends.

I am a high school graduate,
ready to spread my winds and fly.
My mom doesn't want to let go,
she wants me to stay close by.

I am now a mother,
I have a little girl.
I want to do like my mom did,
and keep her safe from the world.

## Left to Join
*by David Ray Weaver - age 16*

Two hearts left to join as one,
my time for despair is already done.
But I will remain here waiting for you,
when time is old and our souls are new.
Together forever and love to share,
I have to hide my mind not yet aware.
Only to be tortured by the sweetest of pains,
this feeling of love having not yet been tamed.
My heart and yours are beating as one,
together forever until life is gone.
Our souls will always remain intertwined,
down to the very last second of time.
My life and my heart will remain with you,
you have my love and I need yours too.
Nothing to me matters so much,
so I'll keep on trying till your heart I touch.
And on that day when I will get in,
the love of my life will finally begin.
So when the time comes for you to decide,
I will still be right there at your side.

## Fright
*by Kenn Weilacher*

Me, I really don't want to awake
The days troubles are so hard to bear
Sometimes it seems my life's at stake
And I just can't escape anywhere
I wish sometimes, my life I could take
It is so unbearable, I swear
But if I did, I wouldn't go there

I do so very much fear the light
I'm terrified at what I may see
My past life was a blight
I think that it'll always be
In the day, my solitude takes flight
I'm terribly frightened, you see
And I know I'll never be free

I know now, it's the last day of my life
It's so very strange how calm I feel
Funny, I feel cut, as with a knife
Toward death I'll go with zeal
Soon there will be no more strife
No problems which I'll have to deal
And I know now, this is for real

## A Different Place
*by R.M. Welch*

What a kinder world it would be,
If people would let be, be.
If we could see the beautiful flower,
Instead of erecting another tower.
If we took the time to say hello,
Instead of "Hurry up, let's go!"

What a different place it would be,
If we could close our eyes and still see.
For through the darkness, prevails light,
And from the light, we learn - right.

But if we are to live our lives in the night,
Afraid to venture toward the light,
I fear for the existence of the human race,
If we continue to look upon each other as though a disgrace.

## Ike Rosined Up His Bow
*by Sharon Irene Wells*

He was just a lanky, homely boy
When misfortune forced him a blow.
Gunshot to his leg, only to lose it
Ike had to rosin up his bow.

A disappointment it seemed he would be
Not able to follow his forbears in tow,
Farming and ranching were their lead,
But Ike rosined up his bow.

Before manhood had fully set in
He began to create quite a flow
Of musical fans wherever he'd go
As Ike rosined up his bow.

There wasn't any lack of talent
The gypsy bands played Cottoneyed Joe
And symphonies gave concerts of Mozart,
Still Ike rosined up his bow.

It was told many a time
He crossed the frozen Arkansas river flow.
And traveled miles by team and wagon,
Yet Ike rosined up his bow.

Of all the violin players known
Whether the tempo be fast or slow
For hoedown, waltz, prelude, or gospel,
Always Ike rosined up his bow.

In loving memory of the peg-legged man
Aptly described or seemingly so,
In "The touch of The Master's Hand"
And Ike rosined up his bow.

## Burning
*by Jessica M. Wertzler - age 13*

I want to believe,
in what my heart says,
but how's that possible,
in a world where
realities aren't hidden
and they burn,
in our innocent eyes,
burning with them,
hopes and dreams and
wishes.
As the candle leaps
and burns with it,
hopes and dreams,
written on paper,
written through language,
written through music,
written through smiles,
and loves.
But wishes can't burn by candles,
they can only burn by
harsh realities,
and a man-made world.

*Distinctions of Excellence*

## Untitled
*by LaRea Annette Westlake*

My Love, meet me on the beach in the moonlight,
Under the sky filled with stars so bright.
Come and walk with me in the sand,
And we will walk along hand in hand.

We will make wishes of the stars above,
And tell the moon everything we're thinking of,
We will stop now and then to steal a kiss.
And tell each other one thing we wished.

We will make memories for just us two,
Of the moon, the stars, and of me and you.
And in our hearts we'll always be together,
And keep our memories alive forever.

## Diane
*by Rebecca J. Wilde*

She moves cautiously through the night,
With no destination in mind,
Yet each step methodically placed.

Her long raven black fur
Twinkles as the moonlight shines on her
Through the tree limbs.

Her sharp, dark eyes pierce whatever she sees.
Sometimes there is compassion in them,
But tonight they seek nothing.

She has raised several cubs of her own,
And has been a model for others,
But now she is alone, all family gone.

She stops when she sees me. I stop too.
We stare at each other and, with a flick of an ear,
She moves on in silence.

She was a teacher, a mentor to me,
Showing me tricks of the wild,
Now we are just friends.

## Pathways
*by Meghan Orelene West - age 17*

On a camping outing in the mountains,
I find myself, one bright clear morning, taking in all the beauty of this forest home.
I let myself wander to a small path, made by many of the woodland creatures.
Being so at peace in this setting of nature's magic, I find myself daydreaming about paths.
I reflect upon what this path and the many other paths of this world really mean to us all.
We started this path of life as pathfinders, making a way for our futures,
Be it on land, the ocean depths, or out in space.
Throughout life we learn of all the many paths that we can take,
And we are taught to try to stay on the straight and narrow path.
In our day to day lives we are constantly creating paths to take,
Going along a path from one idea to another,
Moving along a path to recovery from an illness,
And living by the paths of the stars, and also the sun and moon.
All of nature travels along paths, moving from stage to stage,
The birds, monarchs, and salmon follow the paths paved by their parents before them,
To live and to create for the next generation.
Blood and air moves through the passages of the bodies of the living,
As does the nutrients of the soil, move through the bodies of plants giving the world life.
I now awaken from my daydreaming,
And find my feet have carried me to the end of this woodland path.
My soul soars as I take in this beholding tranquil sight,
Of a crystal-blue lake and a soft-green meadow.
Is this the way it is at one's life of pathways, the body lays down for its final rest,
And the spirit begins its path to the serenity of the white light,
Where at the end the Creator waits for us?
Yes, all the pathways of the road of life are made and cleared by the Creator,
To help and teach us the lessons of pros and cons,
For us physically, mentally, and spiritually to learn and grow.
And at the very end to return on the pathway
to the crystal-soft white light,
To our loving Pathfinder.

## Polar Storm
*by Ruper H.D. Westmaas*

It was a dream; Intense; Alive;
The meaning of I often strive.
On May the eighth in Ninety-four
'Twas a rounded grey-blue Orb, I'm sure.
Like an eyeball, round, so it seemed,
with intelligence it so teemed.
Then a terrible storm in sky did thrash
and I saw many jagged lightning flash.
It struck a spot on Polar Cap
with very intense and terrible ZAP.
Though cap it was so many feet thick,
it shattered just like blasted brick.
Big chunks were tossed wide here and there
as widening hole each flash did bare;
And sea, though cold, did boil and steam
like devil's cauldron it would seem;
Exposing grey-blue shiny sphere
which then began to gently veer
and it slowly to the right did slide
inside the chasm growing wide;
But strange!; It seemed the globe was nigh
which slowly sank from view of sky.
Anxious then, I wished to see
and wondered where my family be.
With deep concern I suddenly awoke;
A wondering, very sad-heavy bloke.

## Unfulfilled Love
*by James A. Whetzel*

I awake alone in the dark;
For an instant I search for you —
Then I remember it was a dream,
And my dream will have to do.

I am slow to get up —
Rather lay and dream for awhile;
Imagining the beauty of your eyes —
Reliving the magic of your smile.

Finally, I mentally let you go
And arise slowly from the bed;
The house seems nice and warm —
Or is it you lingering inside my head?

I go out on the balcony;
Standing in the new fallen snow,
And watch the full moon shining
Causing the winter sky to glow.

The stars seem to twinkle and dance
Reminding me of the sparkle in your eyes;
Then a snow cloud covers the moon
And the magic of the moment dies.

As if forgotten, the cold surrounds me
and I feel chilled to the bone;
So slowly I go back to bed —
And cuddle under the blanket, all alone.

## Champagne Taste: Beer Budget
*by Dale Wilhelm*

Caviar and fine wines bring me great pleasure.
A taste for grand cheeses and venison doth suit my pallet
    quite nicely.
Expensive linens of kingly designs I would own.
A great castle, built atop the highest mountain, would
    I have.
Of bureaucrats and politicians my friends would be.
Full of refinement and graceful manners, I'd be a
    gentleman to the end.
This I would be all if I was not but a humble man of worth.

## Depression
*by Michelle Wilhelm - age 14*

When you think, but nothing comes out
When you have so much to say, but no courage
When you hide your feelings and your tears speak for you
When you look back, and wonder if it was actually your fault
When the tears on the inside try to find a way to come out, but barely break the surface
When no one understands you because, you don't let them
When you completely change yourself for others, just to find out it's not the real you
And you desperately search for the answer,
Trying to find it,
Searching deep down into the depths of your soul
And all you want to do is scream
Because you know that the answer will not come tomorrow, or the next day
And that alone is hard enough to comprehend...............
So you hide your feelings
You don't let them show
And you can never be the person you should be, because you don't know who that is
And it kills you to think that other people are happy, and your not
And all that you long for is someone who understands you
And you tell yourself that it is OK, even if it's not
Because you don't want to face the truth
And as you look ahead,
You hope that the future will bring you happiness,
For tomorrow is another day, and all you can do is hope.

## The Family Line
*by Martha Diane Wilhelm*

Footsteps of time
   define the family line.
Echoes of silence renew
   the ties of old with fresh blossoms.
The Alpha,
The Omega,
All are part of one.
Don't forget from hence you
   came.
Heredity is not just in a
   name.
Go forth to create good measure.
The family line is much to
   treasure.

## "Free Spirit"
*by Lisa Wilhite*

I feel him in the wind
I feel him in the soft rain
I feel him in the rays heaven does send
I see him on the clouds as he soars
He is the eagle that soars over the fields
That dances over the desert
The eagle that floats over the mountains
The eagle that sails over the seas
The eagle sits atop its throne on the great cliff
He watches, he guards, he guides
the young eagles under its strong wing
He is no longer here
Here to touch
Here to speak
His spirit flies free now
Ever watching over his native land
He is with me always
With me in my heart
With me in my soul
Ever guiding, ever listening
As he did when he walked beside me
My father, my dad, my friend
He is always with me
As an eagle, a father, a dad, a friend
watches over his young eagles
Teaching them to soar
To grow
To learn
To love

## Haiku Seasons
*by Billie A. Williams*

Tiny black-capped songs sung
yet moist with mornings stillness
too early says the snow

Hot desperate days
heated, vibrant drums of youth, strong
cold, winter frozen silent

Corduroy roads wait rain
heat waves vibrate soaring hawks
dust clouds haze blue sky

Oak leaves hang on trees
wrinkles tell of days long gone
winter's come at last

## Help Me
*by Nicole Williams - age 16*

Tender love
Loathsome love
Cradles me
Drops me
Saves my soul
Sells my soul
Oh, hateful stars
Fall upon my broken back
Hate me and I will love thee
Heart of gold, cracks
Death wanders the streets
Life falls between the cracks
I'm alone in the world
With crooked homes
And God-forsaken people
Save me or kill me.

## Time of Forgiveness
*by Kaya Wilson - age 14*

If the world were to come to an end
And the moon would no longer shine
Would it mean I'm not the end of the line?
And the seas dried into a golden ocean
That you've drunken my apology potion?
So have we come to our ends of tears
With no more remarks and sneers
Of painful mercy of all the thorns
So now I'm sorry if we're torn
I hope you can say the same
For the end would be such a shame
So now can we get on with our living
For forgiveness is the start of forgiving.

## Proposal
*by Rachel Winokur - age 14*

Love,

  Your eyes sparkle,
  like a starry night.
    Your olive skin,
    is as soft as a rose I give you
    as a token of my affection.
      The touch of your ebony hair
      reminds me of a dove's wing.
        Everytime I see you,
        my heart melts
        like snow in the spring,
        and is filled with love and happiness.
          And each time I hold you,
          I thank Him
          for I have you.
            When I kiss you, Love,
            you always take my breath away.
              You have possession of my heart
              and there will always be a place
              in my heart for you, Love,
                for eternity.
                  Forever.

*Distinctions of Excellence*

## The Storm
*by Kevin Winstead*

Dark redden sky, surrounds the city like a blanket. A roar of thunder shakes the ground while the light show illuminates the sky. Slowly falling down in seconds tear drops trickle down upon the Earth. In minutes, the drops fall heavier upon the Earth vegetation. Flowers and trees swing in the wind performing a rhythmic beat on cue with the heavy tear drops. Lines and tree limbs snap sending debris rolling down the street. Shutters and windows whistle like an orchestra playing a symphony. Forty-five minutes later, a strange but silent calm encompasses the city. The fallen tear drops begin to evade the soil. Slowly, the sun begins to peak out behind the dark stratus clouds. The nightmare has finally ended.

## A Woebegone Enigma
*by Y.H. Young*

He was a poet, a savior
of a sort. What was past remedy
he had the power to restore
in rhyme. Griefs twice-told already
and ills taken in a triple dose,
all brought back alive by him in live
lyrics to be shared and savored
for real. And he was a soothsayer, too,
with a vision dysphoria-ridden trickling through
the crushed seeds of life ahead to brew
so as to let its original bitterness gather
and accrue, thickening with time,
until it grew acute enough to trigger
off a greater chain of tragedies
fancy-bred.

## I Let Go a Sigh
*by Suzanne J. Winters*

Years go by, life's trailing winds
Dreams of heart, drift by
I reach, though not able to grasp
I let go a sigh
Turmoil stirs, in longing heart
Dreams of youth, sown deep
Eager seeds searching warm rain
Must awaken, from life long sleep
To blossoms bursting, in soulful splendor
Joyfulness radiating
Love, elates my birthing core
Life expresses my dreams
The years of winds go by
I reach, not mine to grasp
it seems
I let go a sigh

## A Darker Shade of Blue
*by Gary Paul Wlodyka*

Babies crying in the Night
Daddy hitting Mommy, again.
Gone fishing!
Catch 'em, throw 'em back. Catch 'em...
I can't hurt anything.

Vietnamese or Viet Cong, Who are Who
Americans' killing Americans, again.
Gone fishing!
Catch 'em, throw 'em back. Catch 'em...
I don't want to hurt anyone.

Protest against the War, Smoking Pot
Bricks through Glass, "Baby Killers", again.
Gone fishing!
Catch 'em, throw 'em back. Catch 'em...
I don't want to hurt anymore.

Prison- Steel Bars and Cold Cement
Screams, Cries, Madness in the Night, again.
Gone fishing!
Catch 'em, throw 'em back. Catch 'em...
Do you hurt now?

## The Power of a Word
*by Tammy Wood - age 20*

Words are a valuable source of information.
They cause pleasure as well as frustration.
Finding the right one is difficult,
But easily done if meant as an insult.

New words are found everyday,
Others change meanings in a drastic way.
Fun words express silly notions,
And serious ones describe deep emotions.

Power is a strong word, but words are power.
Giving orders, you feel like a tower.
But over years, even towers fall.
Then you'll realize you weren't that tall.

Words help us think and communicate.
What will come next, we can only anticipate.
The urge to use words is hard to resist,
For without words, this poem couldn't exist.

## The Old Oak Tree
*by Larry Zimmerman*

I didn't like to roam about, when I was just a tot,
 I'll stay at home till I grow old, at least that's what I thought.
It's safer here in my own room, no harm will come to me.
 The world is kind of big out there. Beyond The Old Oak Tree.

Four tin solider standing tall, in the pale moonlight.
 Keep watch for me while I sleep, and see me through the night.
My days flit by like butterflies, on wings of childish glee.
 I have no fear, no care or woe, with my fiend The Old Oak Tree.

Besides, I said, I can not go, out beyond the hedge.
 Which road to take, north or south? they both drop off the edge.
No, I think that I'll just stay, beside my mother's knee.
 And we will sip a lemonade, in the shade of The Old Oak Tree.

But leave I did, to make my way, and time has passed on by,
 Now one last journey have I left, before I stop to die.
It's homeward bound I have to go, the world is done with me.
 And I shall find my resting place, beneath The Old Oak Tree.

## Ocean of Beauty
*by Tina Xu - age 15*

It is a blue blanket,
Covering the corners of the earth,
Reaching beyond what man's eyes can see.
The waves rolling with the wind,
Traveling in all directions,
Always searching for something,
Or is it someone?

## my friend is dead
*by Jerome Workman*

in this night
beyond hospital doors
and blacktop parking lots,
if one looks into the blackness,
into the starless corridors,
you can see a cold wind
slouching
wounded and alone.

its breathing is
a howling wind,
a mourning sound
in a forgotten place
of pale-white sand,
near a lost sea
of waves in confusion.

you can also see
trees with limbs outstretched,
their grey hands
holding a moon skull.

Where can I go to find my friend?

## Memories Unforgettable
*by Jack V. Wright*

I visited a house not long ago
With cracks through which the wind did blow,
The wood unpainted and weather beaten from time
Nestled amongst the trees, flowers and vines.

Inside, the furnishings drab and gray
Not of the type you would find today,
That had stood the test of thousands of days
Around which, once little ones played

But now, all that could be seen in the dim light
Was one lonely figure, rocking away in the night,
Filled with wisdom, which only life can bring.
Listen; soft and low I could hear her sing...

Time had brought twelve offsprings to be-
Yet now there was not one of them to see,
But knowing that somewhere, in their hearts she stood.
She reasoned with memories, as any mother would.

Beside her chair, lay the family treasure-
A worn black book, that brought her pleasure.
Corners turned down on many a page
To mark the reference to many an age...

Here's not much splendor for the world
Only love for her boys and girls.
I pray that always this house could stand
As a token to the little lady inside so grand.

May God give her a place some day
Among the lilacs, frills and lace
In paradise, where pain is not ---
And she can sit happy in her chair and rock.

## Night after Night
*by Nancy Yang - age 11*

I sit in front of my window night after night
Wondering what you are doing.
Wondering if your tears fall as much as mine tonight.
I picture you sleeping just like the night before.
Watching you breathe so calmly, dreaming of something.
You look so peaceful in your perfect world.
I don't want to wake you, you look so happy.
But you cannot see my pain or hear my cry
I want to be in that perfect world.
But I can't seem to fall asleep.
I can't seem to dream the same thing.
And so I sit in front of my window night after night
Remembering how it was told to you.
Hearing the words I cherish the most.
Ones of which I cannot hear enough.
I scream into the night to see if it will respond.
But it never has anything to say.
I scream louder just for one little noise.
But it still will not respond.
And so I sit in front of my window night after night
Wishing that you were here, beside me.
I close my eyes and feel your breathe on my face.
The chills run down my spine as I sense your sweet smell.
You are saying something but I can't hear it dear.
It sounds like, "I love you."
I open my eyes and turn around
Expecting to see you behind me. But no one is there.
And so I sit in front of my window feeling the wind on my face
And listening to the sound of my heart beating,
"I love you." "I love you." "I love you..."

## Friends
*by Deborah Ann Yeager*

Friends come to your rescue when no one else cares,
They go with you to places where no one else dares.
They are your friends even though you are sad,
And they are there for you when you are mad!

A friend is someone who loves you no matter what others say,
They are people who can brighten any person's day.
They always know the right things to say or do to
make you smile,
And when you're with friends, a long day seems only like a
little while!

Everyone needs at least one friend as you go through life,
They help you especially in your times of worry and strife!
No matter where you go in life, you'll have to make a turn,
And you'll always have a lot of bridges to burn.

So make sure as you live from day to day,
That you have someone you can turn to and say,
"I'm glad I have you as my friend,
I know we'll have fun that'll never end.

Even though we sometimes have our spats,
We'll always have our little chats.
That makes everything a little more lighter,
Because we know how to make dim things brighter."

So put a smile on your face no matter how you feel,
You know that whatever is wrong God can heal.
He can make you better no matter what's wrong,
If you're unhappy, in your heart He can give you a song!
And it will make you happy all day long.

So just remember that it's with God is where you can be strong,
Just go and do your best and know that God will do the rest!

## To Be Above Earth-Level
*by Mimi YIP TONG*

Push them out again
Into their willed and wanted darknesses
So that no indicted stones of judgement will on me rain
But only the clearness of feelings that blesses

Let us kick Subjectivism out
Of our eyeless heads
Lest truth and seriousness it may rout
And lest Oppressiveness on vices only get fed

Down the ruts where insects only crawl
As the basic principles that make their world roll
To struggle out of some generated hell
And listen for whom tolls the bell

It tolls for you and me
For no one is a continent unto himself
That he cannot beyond lowly bounds soar
And to the Universe's edge see the Lord's Light more

## When city sleep tight...
*by Vlad Yudin - age 16*

Shadows of the dark alleys,
Nothing to fear.
Life is long,
But death is near

Running away
From the ruthless reality,
Like a prey
In a jungle of human's mentality.

Rain,
The city is dreaming
Pain,
My cruel hunger for living.

Death, is just around the corner
I can feel it from here.
Feeling shame,
I am walking towards it

Lonely people,
And blood on the sidewalk.
No time for confession,
When city sleeps tight...


## Love Has Flown Away
*by Nancy Ziska*

Love has flown away
away from me today.
Left me all alone to face the day.

Your smile outshines your face
in fragments of my mind.
Eyes sparkling diamonds of the sea
still haunt my memory with thee.

Oh, love why
why have you flown away, away from me?
Shattered dreams left crumbling down before me
in pools of tears
draining, draining me.

Oh, but your spirit still remains
captured here
a prisoner
forever with me.


## Untitled
*by Kristen Zero - age 18*

The atmosphere - black, grey.
No sign of light, no sign of life.
Alone, watching, staring at the wall.
The sudden memories of a moment
passed by, flashing through your mind.
Wondering what has happened to
change everything.
The sudden urge to bash it out of
your skull, not willing to remember.
The talking, laughing of the time
mocking you. Strangling your body
to make you think when you don't want
to.
As you lie in a cold, dark room, alone
listening to the voices heard in your head.
To watch the spirits of the unknown
and hear what they can tell you - is all
you come to know.
Unacceptable, insane thoughts of
tomorrow and days to come. Life
spinning uncontrollably. Surrounding you
with the situations you don't want to
deal with. Alone again with the mind
bottling things of everyday life...
    ALONE


## An Angel
*by Megan Ziesmer - age 17*

The truth be told
An Angel true
With hair of gold
And eyes of blue

In gowns of pearl
And wings unfurled
She hovered near
And shed a tear

For human kind
And human hearts
For love to find
Was not a part

Her lovely face
So pale and white
Shed tears for haste
Shone with light

Her heart did ache
For mortal's sake
As all the earth
Cried for mirth

The song she sang
Sweet as dew
From sunrise rang
In golden hue

A sigh of grace
In a world gone by
A heavenly face
In a celestial sky


## You
*by Rachel Zollinger - Age 18*

You, my bitter love.
Have managed to
change my wandering ways.
You, my intimidator.
Have kept me away with images of
your mirkish eyes and groping hands.
You dominated my mind with words of deceit.
You, keeper of my trust.
Live in my nightmares every night
with your foolish lies and malign smile.
You, my dear boy.
Have managed to keep
my heart in your fist.


## Love
*by Stefania Zilinskas - age 13*

    Love, what does it mean? Is it exhibited in actions toward another being, or measured in wealth? Is it calculated by how many tears drop when one is missed? Is it measured by how far a person will go to be with another? Is it only seen by the eyes of the pure? Or is it hidden from everyone and can never be reached? No matter how high you reach, how quick you jump, how much you crave, you can never reach it. Never.
    Or, is it accessible to everyone? Whether you want it or not, you feel it, have it, see it, smell it, touch it, know it, deep within your soul. Or must you work for it? Sweat and cry and scream for it. Have reached so low, you wish nothing more of life, you want it not within you, dread every second you still breathe- would rather die than live. And suddenly, you are filled with love. Have it flow within your body and spill with every word.
    Perhaps love can be reached by simply feeling strongly for another person- deeply caring. So much, you would die for them? Will you feel love then?
    Is that love?
What........ what if you don't feel love, from anyone? Hollow inside, empty. Can you carry on without love? Or is it a necessity? You must feel this love within you to survive. You must.
    If this is so, I am dead. Because I am hollow-empty, deep inside. I do not possess love, have it not flow within my soul and spill with every word. I don't love anyone, and no one loves me.
    Therefore, you do not need love to survive- you can just live on miserably without it.

# Chapter Two

## The 1999 President's Recognition "About the Authors"

**Distinctions of Excellence**

**Abbott, Kristi** - Born January 11, 1980 in Vincinnes, Indiana to parents Steven Michael and Brenda K. Abbott. She has one younger sister, Lacy. Her family settled in Crossville, Tennessee when she was six years old, and she has made her home there ever since. She was the member of and held leadership positions in several clubs (Beta National Honor Society, Health Occupations Students of America, Fellowship of Christian Athletes, Math Club) while attending Cumberland County High School. She graduated high school in 1998 with high honors. She is currently attending East Tennessee State University as an undeclared major with a concentration in Pre-Med. She is a member of the campus volunteer organization, the University Honors Program, and has made the Dean's list. "Daughter to Mother" was Kristi's first real attempt at poetry. She has received much recognition for the poem, but is most proud of the happiness it has given her mom.

**Allen, Jude M.** - Born and raised in North Vancouver, British Columbia, moving west 15km to West Vancouver six years ago, Jude has always lived on the North Shore, migrating ever so slowly toward the water where she has always felt an affinity. Jude is single, with three Pugs, devoting as much time to them as any loving mother would. After many years working in the field of law, Jude finally went back to university two years ago, majoring in English, with hopes of forging a career in writing. She has been writing poetry most of her life, but only began writing in earnest after the loss of her father (Howard) four years ago to cancer and her mother's (Phyllis) subsequent death from cancer two years ago. Their passing prompted an outpouring of emotional poetry, evolving into other areas. Jude hopes to continue writing poetry, if for no other reason than it helps to heal the worst of wounds. Jude also writes feature film scripts and short stories. She was awarded Honorable Mention for "A Worthy Battlefield" by Iliad Press.

**Anstoetter, Sara** - Born December 15, 1983 in Dubuque, Iowa to the proud parents of Deb and Garry Anstoetter, who reside in Epworth, Iowa. Sara has one sister and is currently attending Western Dubuque High School where she is a freshman. Sara enjoys running in track, skiing, swimming, reading, writing, and most of all, traveling. Sara has received the following awards: The American Legion School Award, President's Education Award, Outstanding Achievement in Math, Science, Social Studies, Language Arts, and English. "I Thought I Knew" is Sara's first publication, which portrays a traumatic time in her life. Sara encourages everyone to strive to achieve all their goals and dreams. To my dearest Aunt Mary and ex Uncle Dick whom I love so dear. When the world came crashing down on me, no one was near. May you understand someday how my life changed with every passing day. With all my love, Sara.

**Ashbeck, Barbara** - Born January 29, 1935 in Spartanburg South Carolina to Edward and Beulah Weathers who were divorced later. Father moved to Ohio and Barbara and her younger brother lived with their mother. Barbara grew up in the "used to be Cotton Mill Town" of Pacolet in South Carolina. She graduated from Pacolet High School in 1953 and from Spartanburg General Hospital School of Nursing as an R.N. in 1956. She married A.R. Ashbeck and moved to florida where she worked in surgery. She had three children and was later divorced in 1990. She returned to Pacolet because of her mother's fight with cancer. Her mother died in February of 1991, her dad died in Ohio two weeks later! Barbara stayed on in the family home in Pacolet and found time in between visiting her children (no grandchildren yet!!) to resume her interest in writing. She could write a book in her mind but on paper it was cold and without feeling. In poetry, she could express that easily. A good example is her poem, "Plastic Flowers" recently published by The Poetry Guild in their *Celebration of Poets* "Show Case Edition." "Plastic Flowers" was a book that she brought to life as a poem. Other of her poems have been published in anthologies by International Society of Poets and in *Poets Review*. Barbara still lives in the family home in Pacolet and is still trying to write "That Book!"

**Auferoth, Jillann** - Born July 22,1975 in Stratford, New Jersey. Has resided in Pennsylvania for seventeen years. Graduated Wissahickon High School in 1993. Attended two and half years of college; is presently employed by Commerce Bank as a Head Teller. Jillann has been writing since she knew how; writing has been her saving grace. Her writings come from her experiences and always from her heart. The biggest accomplishments in her life have all been as a direct result of change. Jillann dreams of someday having a small book of her poetry published.

**Baker, Kari** - Born January 7, 1978 in Louisville, Kentucky. Having moved around a lot she ended up in the South Pacific on an island called Kwajalein. Where she went on to graduate Kwaj High with honors. After graduating she got a job at the post office. She worked there for about a year and soon got her own contract and began working as commodity specialist manager. Her favorite things to do are playing sports, crocheting, and watching the beautiful sunset in the evening on Kwaj. She has been writing poetry most of her life; it was her way of expressing herself. She has had four of her works published in different anthologies. She plans on going to college to become a Dental Hygienist. The craziest thing she has ever done in her life is go bungy jumping in Las Vegas. She says, "It was a total rush, but I will probably never do it again." She says that her poem, "Precious" was inspired by a good friend who got tied up in the ways of this ugly world, and didn't realize it until it was too late. Her advise to everyone is: "Live life to its fullest, but stay out of trouble and be the happiest you can be!"

**Baldwin, Brianna** - (Known as Bre by her friends and family) was born October 3, 1981, in Atlantic City, NJ to the parents of Frank and olleen Baldwin. Bre attends Holy Spirit High School where she will graduate in the year 2000. After high school, she plans on attending college where she will hopefully major in journalism, theatrical arts, or music. Bre was given an award in middle school for her writing talents. "I write because it's the easiest way for me to express myself." She has danced for the majority of her life, and has also performed in a couple of plays. Now she volunteers her time to Oceanville Fire Company. She also enjoys music; she has played guitar for about two years. Bre is also an avid reader and writer. "Thank you mom and dad for pushing me to reach the stars...Smile!"

**Barsic, Joe** - Born naked on May 1, 1981. On this day, I experienced pain for the first time as the doctor slapped my bum. At the age of five, I discovered my ability to fly. At thirteen, I discovered I could write. Writing with all the passion of my soul, I found it good therapy. However, never thinking anyone's eyes but my own would gaze upon them, my poems were always kept as personal as possible. I believe that love is the only emotion that can inspire the words, be it good or bad. Armed only with a few hundred poems, a fistful of short stories, and pieces of a play, I face the world each day knowing it could be my last. I believe that a writer can only write from experience, anything else is pure crap. I've been hailed as "a beat poet, a visionary, a prick," but I don't think its nice to label anyone." I'm engaged to the most beautiful girl in the world, and I like chips and Quesa." Words of wisdom: "Eat your veggies, always double knot your shoe laces, and never, ever be afraid to wear band-aids."

**Bauzo, David** - Born February 11, 1957 in Manhattan, New York to parents, Luis Felipe and Sixta Maria. David has been writing poetry since he was in his early teens. He is medically retired from the United States Army. Having moved many times during his military career, while stationed in Tacoma Washington he met his wife Cathy. They were married in 1995 and have one child. David was a martial arts instructor and a member of the United States Yoshukai Karate. David has had his poetry published by The National Library of Poetry and The International Library of Poetry in *Essence of a Dream, The Lyre's Song and Outstanding Poets of 1998*. David has been elected into the International Poetry Hall of Fame and is a distinguished member of the International Society of Poets. He has received an Honorable Mention award from Cader Publishing, Ltd and the 1999 President's Recognition for Literary Excellence from the National Authors Registry. His poem "The Bum" is published in *Achieving Excellence* by Iliad Press. He has also published one collection of poetry entitled *Poetic Thoughts* which he dedicated to his son Fernando. David says, "Writing poetry helps me heal from within, I hope others who read my poems can also heal from within."

**Baxter, Lilli M.** - (Pen name, Lilli de Chartré). Born: 2/18/1908 in Cols, Ohio. Parents: Pearl and Carolyn Johnson. Married: Herman Baxter. Children: Richard, David, James, Bob, Jack. Has composed 200 songs and 400 poems in the past 50 years. Member of the International Society of Poets.

**Blackwell, Lindsey Nicole** - Born: May 25, 1992 in Jackson County, NC. Parents: Jolyn and Calvin Blackwell. Education: Kindergarten. Awards: 1st Place in Reading Contest, Gold Metal and Certificate. 1st Place Winner in Swimming Contest "Certificate"; Horseback riding. Published Works: "Ever Wonder Why," first written at age 4½ yrs. old, made front page in newspaper, published in *Verses Magazine*; "Reach for Love," "Chips Trixey the Playful Poltergeist," "A Maiden Cherry Ripe Kisses," "Winter Snow's Birthday and Mine," selected by Iliad Press and the National Authors Registry to receive the 1999 President's Recognition of Literary Excellence; Received Editor's Choice Award and inducted into the Hall of Fame, 1997-1999 President's Award, selected Best Poets for 1998 and invited by the International Society of Poets to attend the 1998 Poet of the Year Convention to receive the International Poet of Merit Award Medallion for Outstanding Achievements in Poetry Writing. Grandmother, Elizabeth McCurdy also was chosen. Planned on going and looked forward to the Gala Event but got sick and couldn't attend. Their poems written to compete for the Best Poet of 1998 "Our World Peace Poems." 1999 Present's Recognition of Literary Excellence - chosen by the National Authors Registry and Iliad Press, the youngest person to receive this distinctive honor! Thank all of you.

**Blake, Patricia Payzant** - Born in Shelbourne, Nova Scotia, Patricia Blake received a Bachelor of Science degree in Household Economics from Acadia University (Wolfville, Nova Scotia) before continuing on to a career in Dietetics. She started in a position in Diet Therapy at the New Britain General Hospital in New Britain, Connecticut. Patricia returned to Canada in 1941, married in 1946 and remained in Nova Scotia until 1964. A widow

*Distinctions of Excellence*

with two children, she returned to New Britain and later married Biology teacher John Hodgson Blake. The two retired and moved to Stonington, Connecticut where they enjoyed the view from their Deck House which overlooked Long Island Sound. The beauty of these surroundings inspired Patricia's writings which continued after a move to Naples, Florida. The lovely city of Naples, from its magnificent sunsets to the incredible glow of the Royal Poinciana trees continues to inspire her. Patricia has received three Honorable Mention awards from Cader Publishing, Ltd, and distinctions of being selected for the President's Recognition of Literary Excellence from the National Authors Registry. "Life's Journey" was chosen in 1996 and "Forget-Me-Nots" in 1999.

**Borders, Denise Marie** - Born December 19, 1984 in Berea, Kentucky, to parents Harold and Debbie Borders, is the youngest of four children, having two older brothers and one older sister. Thanks to her sister's marriage in 1998, she also has one brother-in-law. Enrolling in Foley Middle School as a sixth grader, Denise gained new interests as a young teen. She continued to be involved in several extra-curricular activities, including basketball, softball and cheerleading. After having attended a concert by "Bush," a band she was quite fond of, Denise became interested in music. She discovered the band late in 1994, after the release of their first CD, and was inspired to write several selections, including a poem entitled "Gavin." The poem, an entry in Denise's seventh grade portfolio, received critical acclaim by being awarded Honorable Mention in the Iliad Press Literary Awards in fall of 1997. To those who also follow the success of "Bush," it is quite obvious that the poem penned by Denise was inspired by her admiration for Gavin Rossdale, lead vocalist for "Bush." To Denise, Gavin is, in himself, an inspiration. Denise loves to write poetry, and plans to continue in her quest, because as she puts it "I can pour my feelings and dreams into my poetry. I love it!"

**Bradbury, Louise M.** - (nee MacComb) Born in New York City of professional parents. She grew up in Texas where she attended Southern Methodist University. She graduated with a BA in Anthropology and minors in History and Archeology. Her childhood interest in Archeology has firmly connected her with the past and with the land. This has remained a background interest throughout many years in cities working as an environmental planner, lawyer, real estate agent, and artist. The net result of thirty years of work is two MA's and a JD. The last MA is in culture and creation spirituality which has renewed her interest in metaphysics and spiritual things. She now lives in Taos, New Mexico, close to the sacred land, which has been the home of D.H. Lawrence and Georgia O'Keefe. She has won some awards for poetry and is finishing a novel. When she is not writing she is painting the landscapes, stillifes, and portraits that typify the culture here.

**Brooks, Matthew G.** - Born October 6, 1976 in Riverside, California to Gary and Vienna Brooks. I spent my entire youth in the Riverside County area. I attended Jurupa Valley High School until my graduation in 1995. Upon graduating, I entered the United States Army in which I am currently serving now. I am twenty-two years old, and I go by the name "The Phanton." I have one sister that I love dearly, her name is September Brooks. I am in the process of completing a deployment in Bosnia. I started writing poetry in 1989. I have received one Honorable Mention from Cader Publishing in 1997 for my poem "Untitled." I have been a recent recipient of the 1999 President's Recognition of Literary Excellence. For this achievement I owe thanks to my mother Vienna for pushing me to follow my dreams. My grandmother Marra, who passed away in 1996 for giving me the courage to let my feelings show. My great grandmother for always being there for me, family and friends that supported me. But most of all the Lord up above for giving me the gift. It was told to me once, "To achieve any goal in your life you must first try."

**Brown, Mary Cathleen** - I draw my inspiration from my innate desire which is divinely and diligently inspired by significant teachers in my life, and from significant emotional events in the lives of those close to me. My own life situations color my frame of reference and experience. My professional background prior to returning to college, my return to college, my twinhood and a chronic illness are among these influences. I sit still waiting for my Muse to speak to me. My writing then gathers slowly. I love figuring out which words sound truest and best. I love how they fit into a line or sentence. I love to use slant rhymes. Whatever my poems mean in particular, they begin and end in celebration of the world entrusted to me by my life. Poetry, my own and that of others, helps me to understand how things are for me, whether worldly or illusory, and to live more peaceably with what I have. It allows me to express beauty, love, romance, and harmony. It is my common prayer. It helps me to qualify my emotions. Up until recently my writing talents have been limited to poetry; however, I am venturing into the realm of the short story. At least twenty poems under my pen name have been published in various anthologies and periodicals. One, "Autumn Rhythms" has been professionally narrated and produced by The National Library of Poetry on their audio cassette *The Sound of Poetry* in 1996.

**Brown, Chris** - Born August 12, 1972 in Houston, Texas to parents, Gordon and Barbara Brown. Chris has lived his entire life in the Houston area, but hopes to relocate to the west coast eventually. Chris attended and received a B.S. degree in Biology from the University of Houston. He is currently a graduate student in Biology there. In addition to poetry, Chris has many other interests. He enjoys practicing the martial arts, in which he holds a second degree black belt in Tae Kwon Do. He is also a self-taught guitarist, and has been playing since he was fourteen years old. With all of the pursuits he has in life, writing poetry provides a nice change of pace. The poem, "Nothing, Then..." is his first to be published, and hopes it is not the last. Chris believes he has other works that would be just as well received, and hopes that the opportunity to have them published arises in the near future. Chris is currently applying his writing skills towards breaking into the science fiction genre, and is in the process of writing his first novel. So, in the meantime, he plans to spend his time utilizing the two things it takes to be a writer—a pen and a piece of paper!

**Bulluck, Jamie** - Born June 19, 1984 to parents Jay and Janice Bulluck. She has attending Grace Christian School all her life and is currently a sophomore. An A-B honor-roll student, who plays volleyball and basketball for GCS. She received a Woodmen of the World in 1996 and an Honorable Mention from Iliad Press in 1998 for her poem "A Little Chain of Gold." She attends Shenandoah Baptist Church and is the oldest of four children. She will graduate from GCS in 2001 and plans to attend college and major in journalism and creative writing. She is out-going, with a great sense of humor, and has many friends. She has been writing poetry since the age of twelve. Other than sports, her hobbies are reading, writing, and hanging out with her friends. Her personal saying is "Life is short so live it with love."

**Burnside, Wanda Jacqueline** - Born March 9, 1950 in Highland Park, Michigan to parents, Reverend and Mrs. Minor Palm, Jr. She is the oldest of three children: a brother Rodger and a sister Regina. The family moved to Detroit, Michigan in 1952. Wanda graduated from the University of Detroit in 1972 with a B.S. in Humanities/Early Education. Married in November, 1972 to Simmie Lee Burnside, Jr. She has taught in public and private schools in Michigan. She has also attended William Tyndale Bible College and an Honor Student at C.H. Mason Bible College in Michigan. She is certified in several areas in Christian Ministries. She is actively involved in her church and community. She has been employed in the United States Government as an Educational Researcher, Departmental Coordinator at Marygrove College in Michigan and the United States Attorney's Office as NARA Coordinator. She has been an Editor and Office Manager of *Detroit Church World Magazine*; Library Assistant in the Educational Center at the University of Detroit and worked in the Personnel Office of Blue Cross-Blue Shield of Michigan. She has tutored students from primary grades, high school and college. Wanda enjoys writing and reading all of her life. She has written twenty-two plays for children, nearly 100 poems, four short stories, written and won three national recipe contests. She has self published a gospel tract entitled: "Matchless Love" with over 1,200 in print in the United States and Canada. She has received fifteen honors and awards in writing from: The National Library of Poetry, Iliad Press, The Poetry Guild, Famous Poets Society, Byline Magazine and the University of Detroit sponsored by Broadside Press. She has received recognition for Best Poems of 1998 from the National Library of Poetry and Famous Poet for 1998 from the Famous Poets Society. However, she is most honored to received the 1999 President's Recognition for Literary Excellence from The National Authors Registry for her poem "Spring's Wedding" which received Honorable Mention in the 1998 Nature Poetry Competition. Wanda is a member of The National Authors Registry, American Christian Writers, Detroit Black Writers' Guild, The International Women Writer's Guild, and The Academy of American Poets.

**Carlson, Sue Lueck** - Born September 20, 1949 in Glencoe, MN to Roy G. and Anna Lueck. God blessed me with four sisters and only one brother, Dougie, who was killed in 1966 in Vietnam. After graduating from Glencoe High School in 1967, I married and had a daughter, Melissa, and son, Jamie. I have always and continue to be proud of both of them. While they were in school, we owned a ceramic studio where in 1978, I received my certification as a national ceramic teacher. With the business being sold after my divorce, I worked as an Advertising/Marketing Manager and also organized a five county fundraiser to help raise money to build the Vietnam Veterans Memorial in St. Paul. Later I attended Willmar Technical College and transferred to Hennepin Tech where I majored in commercial art. Debt caused me to leave the art world and return to sales for the last seven years. In 1996, I was the "Salesperson of the Year" and have continued to be awarded for my success. I am a member of the American Legion Auxiliary, an Associate Member of 1st Calvary Division Association, The National Association of Female Executives, Hopkins Area Art Association, and A Distinguished Member of the International Society of Poets. In 1998, I received the Editors Choice Award from the National Library of Poetry for my poem "Memories Live Forever" which is published in *Surrounded by Dreams*. Then in January, 1999, I was selected by the National Authors Registry to received the 1999 President's Recognition of Literary Excellence for my literary work "Behind Every Dark Sky" which also received an Honorable Mention in the Spring 1998 Iliad Literary Awards and is published in *Crossroads-Contemporary Verse from Around the World.* "I intend to spend the rest of my life writing and publishing my Christian poetry. That means at least another fifty years, so world 'Look Out' because here I come"!

**Cave, Sheila M.** - Born January 6, 1967 to Keith and Kathy Himmelright. Grew up all her life in the small mining communities of Iron Range of N.E. Minnesota. Married Terence D. Cave in 1993, have five children: Bradley, Gregory, Stephanie, Jared, and Brandon. Sheila graduated from Graphic Arts in 1987 and in 1988 began three years of study in Fine Arts at the University of Minnesota. She is currently enrolled in a Freelance Writers Program and The Childrens Institute of Literature. Sheila has received publication in five different anthologies, a chapbook entitled "Season's of Change," two songwriter's contracts for poetic lyrics entitled "The Change," "A Flip of the Coin," and "If There Are Gardens In Heaven," received Honorable Mention and the Iliad Press 1999 President's Recognition for Excellence. Her book entitled "The Menagerie of The Mind," is currently under review for publication in late 1999. Sheila feels that "writing is the ultimate of expressions for her artistically." Sheila enjoys her quiet country home and gains inspiration from people, nature and life's experiences. Sheila feels "There is never a moment or event that cannot inspire her."

**Cellini, Lottie** - Born October 19, 1963 in San Diego, California to parents, Josephine LoCicero and Lyall Bishop, along with her older sibling. Shortly after Lottie's parents divorced she moved to Florida where she was raised. Years later her mother remarried and gave her another sibling, also very creative. In 1984, after a long battle with cancer, her mother passed away. "Trinkets of Love" was written in dedication to her mother. By then she had already met the man of her dreams. She followed him to Virginia where they now reside along with their three pets. Lottie has been writing for as long as she can remember. She recalls that her very first song was written at age six. She enjoys riding her motorcycle, playing golf and of course, singing, poetry and songwriting. She's received two Honorable Mention Awards from Cader Publishing, Ltd., and the 1999 President's Recognition of Literary Excellence from The National Authors Registry. Her poem "Trinkets of Love" is published in *Distinctions of Excellence* by Iliad Press. Lottie is currently working on making a demo of her songs and is seeking publication for two of her manuscripts "With Love" and "Walking Angel." Lottie attributes most of her inspiration to Mike Donnell, the man of her dreams, her best friend Liz, and her two wonderful sisters, Marshan and Christy.

**Cherepanov, Dasha Gena** - Born November 1, 1980 in Moscow, Russia. Her mother, Elena F. Odintsova, was a movie star and an actress of Chekhov Moscow Art Theatre and her father, Genady P. Cherepanov, a famous professor of mathematics and mechanics. Her grandmother won a USSR car race. Her grandfather, a World War II hero killed at the age 26, was a direct descendant of the famous Russian inventor parallelling British James Watt, and the other grandfather the deputy director of Moscow Avtozavod, the Russian counterpart of General Motors. After having wandered through Russia, Ukraine, and all over the United States, Dasha's family finally settled in South Florida. Graduated from a modeling school in 1996 and SouthWest Miami Senior High School in 1998, Dasha has been writing poetry since very early years starting with "Mommy, Pop, give me a lollipop" and later "Two shells washed up a shore. A kid ran by—I saw them no more." She has a good hundred of unpublished poems in her file and wishes to publish her own book of poetry. She's received Honorable Mention awards from Cader Publishing for poems "Fear" and "Empty Wish" and the 1999 President's Recognition for Literary Excellence from the National Authors Registry. Her poem "Empty Wish" is published in *Distinctions of Excellence* by Iliad Press. She's a distinguished member of The International Society of Poets and was invited to the Famous Poets Convention in California to receive the Diamond Homer Trophy for her poem "Shattered Dreams." Dasha says, "I love the music of words that creates new beautiful worlds. I like the melody of love that makes me feel beloved. I thrill from the whisper of hope, but...what thinks the Pope?"

**Chikezie, Roxana** - Born November 6, 1981 to parents, Desmond and Patricia Chikezie. Father moved to America from Nigeria in 1979, mother and two sisters followed in 1980. Her other sibling (two brothers, two sisters), are currently attending Colleges in Nigeria. She hopes to see them for the first time very soon. She currently lives in Lawrence, Kansas with her parents and attends Lawrence High School, which she will be graduating from in the year 2000. Her interests include: business, law, and world affairs. She is a member of Youth in Local Government, Mock Trail, Youth United Way, Orchestra, and will be inducted as a member of National Honor Society in May of 1999. She has received many awards and compliments regarding her poetry and writing, and hopes to continue to do both in the future for people to read and enjoy. She would like to thank Iliad Press for giving her the opportunity to share her work with the world.

**Cochran, Donald** - Pen name: Roach Singletary. Date of Birth: March 4, 1955 in Manning, SC. Date of Marriage: September 2, 1974 to Elvia Mercedes Griffith Cochran. Children: Keisha Shendell Lesaine. Civilian Education: Manning High School, 1973; Associate's Degree, Interdisciplinary Studies - University of Maryland, 1995; Currently pursuing a major in Elementary Education with a Geography Endorsement, University of Cameron in Lawton, Oklahoma. Military Education: the Primary Noncommissioned Officers Course, Basic Noncommissioned Officers Course, Advanced Noncommissioned Officers Course, and the Jungle Warfare Operations Course. Honors and Awards: elected into The International Poetry Hall of Fame 1996; 1996 and 1997 Poet of the Year Nominee, The International Society of Poets; Legion of Merit Nominee; four Meritorious Service Medals; seven Good Conduct Medals; two National Defense Service Medals; and the Expert Driver's Badge. His poems "Glimmer of Hope," "Outfoxed," and "Songbirds" appear in the Amherst Society's 1997 *American Poetry Annual* and "Beyond Reality" in its 1998 Annual; earning him Honorable Mention in the Iliad Press anthologies, "Glacial Emotionless" in *Collections* and "Daughter" in *Treasures.* Donald has been writing poetry since 1991. He is a US Army Veteran of 24 years currently aspiring to become a teacher as a second career. **Memberships**: The International Society of Poets; Distinguished member, Poets' Guild; Songwriters' Club of America; American Songwriter's Club. Donald's poetry has been published by more than twenty-one different companies in over sixty-six anthologies and annuals. He has written a collection of poetry entitled *Poetic Encounters* and is currently working on volume four of a series. As a songwriter, Donald has three recorded songs - "Songbirds" on the album *Music of America* ©1997 and 1998 released by Columbine Records Corporation; "Daughter" and "Clouds of Joy" on the album *America* ©1997, and "Songbirds" on the album *High Country* ©1998 released by Hilltop Records. **Hobbies**: reading and writing poetry, song-writing, fishing and gardening. Personal Note: Donald says, "Poetry is a refreshing source of entertainment; one of the finer arts bulging with sagacity — recognize, digest, admire and enjoy."

**Cook, Cynthia A.** - Born December 24, 1953 in Columbus, Ohio. Divorced with two children, Rachael and J.R. Graduated in 1971 from Whitehall Yearling High School and Eastland Vocational School where she majored in Chemical Laboratory Assisting. Settled in Lakewood, Ohio, she works as a Pharmacy Technician for CVS Pharmacy and contributes her interest in writing to her first grade teacher, Mrs. Carrie Rarick. She has received three Honorable Mentions for "Mrs. Stevens' Sewing Machine," "Dream Catcher," and "The End Result" from Cader Publishing, Ltd. the 1998 and the 1999 President's Recognition for Literary Excellence from The National Authors Registry, the 1997 and the 1998 Editor's Choice Awards from The National Library of Poetry, and a 1997 Accomplishment of Merit from Creative Arts & Science Enterprises. Her poems have also appeared in anthologies published by Sparrowgrass Poetry Forum and The Poet's Guild. She is currently working on writing her church's history as well as some short stories.

**Cooper, Carolyn Jean** - Born November 4, 1979 in South Bend, Indiana to parents Ed and Donna Cooper. Carolyn is the second of two children; her brother Chris is older by two years. Having had enough of the "big city life," her family decided to go west. They settled in rural Circle, Montana. While living in Circle, Carolyn was hired at the local veterinary clinic. It was there that she found what she wanted to do with her life. She graduated from Circle High School in May of 1998. She ranked first in her class of 28, with a G.P.A of 4.0. Carolyn is currently enrolled at Jamestown College in North Dakota. She is attending school on a Presidential Scholarship. Carolyn is majoring in biology and chemistry with hopes of entering graduate school in Colorado to acquire a degree in Veterinary Medicine. Her passions are God, family, poetry (anything to do with literature), sketching and painting, her best friends, and animals. Her poem "Godsend" received Honorable Mention in the summer 1998 Iliad Press Literary Awards. She has also received the 1999 President's Recognition of Literary Excellence. A fairly new poet, Carolyn believes, "I just get inspired and have to stop and write it down."

**Cooper, Lola Beatrice Baker** - Born July 19, 1912 to the parents of William Coda and Grace M. (Daggy) Baker. She was born and raised in Morgan County, Indiana. Lola had three sisters: Bernice Mae Baker Chapman, Vence Catherine Baker Hacker, and Mary Louise Baker Evans; and four brothers: William Forest, Henry Thurman, George M., and Wallace A. Baker. Lola grew up as a hard worker, milking cows, cutting firewood, gardening and other chores to help take care of her brothers and sisters. Lola married Luther John Cooper on November 16, 1930. They had two girls: Nancy Lou Cooper Chenoweth and Norita Sue Cooper Sheppard; and two boys: Robert Daniel and Huey Luther Cooper. Lola was known as a loving mother and wife, a very giving person, and a great homemaker. She always put herself on the bottom of the totem pole. She was known for her weed-free gardening, cleaning cement forms and lifting blocks onto the trucks when customers purchased them from their family business. She cut weeds, firewood and other hard chores. Lola was well known as a very hard worker and was said to do the work of two men without ever complaining. Her husband, Luther was taken from her to rest on December 15, 1996. Lola was ill for several years and passed away on September 27, 1997 at 5:09 am at Morgan county Memorial Hospital. When she was taken to heaven she left eight grandchildren, sixteen great grandchildren, and eleven great-great grandchildren. Now she is playing the role of our guardian angel. When Lola was taken to rest, she had left the family the treasures of her special talent. Lola had put her feelings into poems instead of keeping them to herself. She left these poems for her family to remember her by, after her departure to a better place with no more pain. Lola was the sweetest person, friend, mother and grandmother anyone could ever dream to have. "May God always be with this special angel until we all meet her at the gate."

**Corona, Ethel Rosemarie** - Born to Earl and Marie Scholander, March 25, 1948 in Brooklyn, New York in a house known as Railroads Flat on Coney Island Avenue. Ethel is the middle of eight children: five brothers and two sisters. She was born poor but otherwise, poetic. She married at 17 and had three daughters by the time she was 21; Paula, Tracy and Dawn. In 1976, her son James arrived. She now has two grandsons, Joshua, age 8 (7-20-90) and just born, Justin (3-11-99). Ethel's lived in Southern California since 1974. In addition to raising a family she attended Barber College in Anaheim and has worked as Ombudsman with the Orange County Council on Aging. Her customers and clients inspired her to write and publish. Her early successes surprised and delighted her. Soon musicians were putting her works to Rock n' Roll beats. She received awards. But mostly, poetry is a challenge that never ends. Her worst set backs became merely the wrappings of new poems. Comments Corona, "Poetry humanizes me -- no longer merely wife and mother, I'm lifted by the good I find in the ugliest of experiences."

**Cote, Jennifer Renae** - Born June 7th, 1979 in Covina, California to parents Victoria Ann and Benjamin Franklin Cote III, along with a younger brother, Benjamin Franklin Cote IV. She attended Northview High School in Covina, California for two years before her family moved to Breckenridge, Minnesota. She graduated from Breckenridge Senior High School in 1997. After her families home was flooded in April of 1997, they relocated to Fergus Falls, Minnesota, where they still live. Her father, Benjamin, is an independent contractor with over twenty years experience in all forms of construction, who is currently working as a press operator at Imation, a factory in Wahpeton, North Dakota. Her mother Victoria, has worked at Imation for four years. Her brother, Benjamin, has won numerous ribbons and awards in the Special Olympics. Jennifer is currently working part-time and attending Fergus Falls Community College where she is looking to attain a Bachelor degree in Liberal Arts. She has been published numerously, most prestigiously from the Iliad Press, who awarded her poem "The Walls" an Honorable Mention. She also has been inducted in several literary anthologies by the National Library of Poetry since 1996. She enjoys writing and never plans to stop. She has gone through several hobbies including: crafting, collection, music, and concludes that reading and writing are the only consistent hobbies she's kept. Jennifer dedicates "The Walls" in particular for Brian, wherever you are, and always to my parents, my brother, my family and Mary. "I love you all!"

**Crossley, Dawn** - Born in Plattsburg, New York, to the parents of Michael and Mary Crossley, along with two brothers and one sister. I lived in Plattsburg until the age of five. My family and I moved to Pittstown, New York after my father had passed away due to a car accident. My mother remarried to Ken Littlefield shortly after we moved to Pittstown. I am currently attending Tamarac High School and I am fifteen years old. Writing poetry is a way I express my feelings. It helps me to deal with the death of my father and other losses and hard times in my life.

**Deaton, Howard A** - Born in El Paso, Texas on January 2, 1917. Father, Enos Deaton. Mother, Alice Atlee. Married, Shelby Janet Minor on October 5, 1943 in Laredo, Texas. Daughter, Durelle Janet, (Mrs. John Steffens,) born October 23, 1944. Son, Howard Atlee Deaton II, born August 14, 1947 (married Mary Valleroy). Attended school in El Paso and San Antonio, Texas. Served in CCC 18 months, Big Bend National Park, 6 months in New Mexico. Enlisted U.S. Army on June 14, 1940, stationed at Fort Bliss, Texas, Fort Sam Houston, Texas; transferred to Air Force, stationed Lackland AFB, Texas; Harlingen AFB, Texas, Laredo AFB, Texas. Served overseas for two months, four days, Saipan. Honorable discharged on November 18, 1945, rank, Sergeant. Worked for M.P.R.R. for 33 years; retired as Review Analyst, St. Louis, Missouri, 1977. Poetry published with National Library Poetry, Poetry Guild, Sparrowgrass, Amherest Society, Iliad Pub; many others. Member South Side Church of Christ, St. Louis, Missouri; member Trans, Comm. Workers, formerly B R C 50 years. Personal Belief: Treat others as you want them to treat you.

**Dumont, Elizabeth M.** - Born September 27, 1960 in Bristol, Connecticut to parents Leo and Leona Dumont. Elizabeth is the youngest of six children, two of whom now reside in Florida. Graduating from St. Paul Catholic High School in Bristol, Connecticut in 1979, she attended Tunxis Community College in Farmington, Connecticut where she majored in Marketing Management: Fashion Merchandising Option and received her A.S. degree in 1982. Currently, Elizabeth devotes her free time between dialysis treatments to her writing which has always been her first love. She is a member of the Academy of American Poets. She received an Honorable Mention Award in 1998 from Cader Publishing, Ltd., and the 1999 President's Recognition for Literary Excellence from the National Authors Registry. Her poem "Denial" is published in *Distinctions of Excellence* by Iliad Press, and her poem, "Guilt" is published in *Feelings*, also by Iliad Press. Her work has also appeared in two other poetry anthologies, magazines and in an internet magazine. She is also working on a first novel. Relatively new to writing poetry, Elizabeth says, "Writing has always been my dream, and I thought it would have to stay that way. If it weren't for my dialysis treatments, I might never have rediscovered myself! Sometimes bad things happen for good reasons."

**Elder, Kathryn (Kathy)** - Owner of Kae Scott Enterprises for eleven years, is a Certified Herbalist, Aromatherapy and Nutritional Counselor. As a hobbyist travel agent, Kathy and her soulmate Scott have traveled the world. Together they share many fascinating interests, one of which is collecting antiques and in Kathy's case, vintage handbags and jewelry. "Life is but a treasure hunt," she so fondly states in one forthcoming article for her journal, *Wholesome Lifestyles*. This she writes through a small subsidiary also of her own devising, *Direct From The Heart Publishing*. She likewise contributes articles to other alternative health journals. Kathy recently integrated into her rewarding lifestyle a temporary position as moderator of the "Art of Successful Living" women's workshop for Barnes and Noble. This new found love gives her an opportunity to utilize her mind and soul, whereas with her challenging vocation she feels committed to use her heart and soul, which many in her international clientele will attest to. "Not a day goes by wherein I do not receive a card, voice or e-mail message thanking me for being who I am." This in itself, she states positively, keeps her inspiration from dying. Kathy firmly believes twenty-five profound years' experience as "Scott's faithful wife" qualifies her to define the makings of (any) satisfying relationship. The couple does not have children but they treasure some of the finest nieces, nephews, grand nieces and nephews, the world over. Kathy has given a voice, through her writing, to "all things wholesome" since Jr. High where she won first prize in an essay contest on "brotherhood." "...Without respect," she stated in her essay, "there can be no real peace, love, in essence...true brotherhood." Her belief in this principle remains firm. Her advice to all: Maintain a healthy self assurance and never cease believing in your own self worth. For when all you have to fall back on is a refined, god given strength of character, your rock solid stature will be there to represent you...beyond your own perceived expectations. Kathy can be reached at kaescott@bellsouth.net, fax 305-552-7441. She warmly welcomes inquiries.

**Emblom, Lindsay** - Born June 4, 1983 daughter to Don and Terrie Emblom in Grand Rapids, Minnesota. Moved to Sauk Centre Minnesota when I was one month old. Now I'm a sophomore at Sauk Centre High School. I wrote my first poem when I was eleven but I started way before that. I had thoughts that most people didn't understand. My freshman year I learned I had a learning disability. A lot of people thought I was just stupid but one person never did. That one person was the one who kept me writing poetry. They may not know it but they did. The poem "Night v.s. Light" received a 1999 President's Recognition of Literary Excellence. Lindsay says, "If I didn't have poetry I would be lost in this world."

**Emerson, Mark S.** - Born in Rockford, Illinois 1963. His education includes: Evergreen, Washington, Belvidere High School, 11th grade. Regular Army Basic training, Honorable Discharge, 1981 veteran. His publications include: "The Olde Bar Scene," *American Poetry Anthology*, 1986, and now a song "Sitting Around A Campfire," a song both pending air play. Other publications include: "The Singing Hills," *Poetic Voices of America* Fall, 1995. "Only With You," *Beyond the Horizon*, 1997. I play the keyboard, piano, organ, I sing, and write songs the way I feel. I am an author of over 100 poems and songs. Recently I have been published in many more anthologies. Also, I won my first award from Iliad Press, Honorable Mention in the Summer of 1998 Iliad Literary Awards Program for my poem "Broken Homes." Recently, I wrote a poem called "At The Landfill Site" and many others. I love the Carpenters, Kenny Rogers, and Dolly Parton that have perhaps been a part in my life.

**Erickson, Sally** - Born February 14, 1944 in Moline, Illinois to Fred and Myrtle Holtschlag. She moved to Tucson, Arizona at the age of four and grew up under southwestern influence. She graduated from Salpointe High School in Tucson in 1962, and from Northern Arizona University with a B.S. degree in Secondary Education/English in 1968. Sally is the mother of a daughter, Carol Ann, and a son, Kenneth Robert. She is also the proud grandmother of one darling grandson and two beautiful granddaughters. Sally retired from a career in correctional programs with the Federal Bureau of Prisons in May 1995. She released the stresses of this calling through her writing and is currently writing a novel based on her experiences in the prison system. She honors herself, her thoughts, and her feelings through her poetry, story writing and song writing. In 1998, Sally's poem "Hell" was published in The Poetry Guild's *Enchanted Dreams* anthology. Also her poem "Get Real" was published in *Treasured Poems of America*, Sparrowgrass Poetry Forum, Inc., 1998. She is extremely proud of her poem "Souls Are Forever" which has received an Honorable Mention and the 1999 President's Recognition of Excellence Award from Iliad Press, in addition to being published in their *Distinctions of Excellence*. Sally says that her poetry and other writings come from her soul. It is heartfelt and expresses her experiences, feelings, and views on life. It is a powerful and invaluable part of her life. Sally does volunteer work with a Writing Life Stories Program for children who have had multiple placements in foster homes who otherwise would not have a record of who they are, what happened to them, or where they have been. She states, "being able to honor the children and helping them understand their own life experiences through writing is the best reward of all." After traveling around the United States and living in several other states throughout her lifetime, Sally has returned to Tucson, Arizona with her husband, Neil, to retire, but keep on writing!

**Favaroth-Peters, Jason J.** - Presently residing in New Canton, VA. Born of Creole descent, on March 15, 1978, in New Orleans, LA; to special parents, William and Donna Peters. Grandson of Ezekiel and Alma Peters, and Robert and Olevkia Williams. My only and favorite brother and sister are August Favaroth III, and Mrs. Youlanda Jimenez. A 1996 graduate of Flucanna County High, and honored with Spanish 5 special award. I'm currently enrolled in the Liberal Arts curriculum at J. Sergeant Reynolds Community College in Richmond, VA, and after completion I hope to pursue a degree in Child Psychology, Linguistics, and Journalism. My hobbies are writing, reading, culinary arts, sports, and music (opera, classical, contemporary gospel, and other secular music of today and yesteryear). Reading and writing have been a first love since the age of three. My poetry has always reflected real-life experiences. Two of my poems, "Lunarity" and "Stucco House" were published in the 1996 *Meditations* anthology (Iliad Press). The latter of Honorable Mention, has also received 1999 President's Recognition for Literary Excellence.

**Ferguson, Jaclyn** - Born January 18, 1986 in Goldendale, Washington to the parents of Noma and Ron with a sister Jolene. Jaclyn has lived in Centerville, Washington all her life. She is presently in seventh grade. Jaclyn, some day wants to travel the world. She owns two registered Quarter Horses, Press and Rosie. Her poem "Wings of a Dove" won Honorable Mention in the Summer 1998 Iliad Literary Awards. "This is my very first big poem, I'm overwhelmed with its success." Jaclyn plans to continue writing poems till the day she dies.

**Fisher, Sharon A.** - I was born on October 10, 1980 in Pittsburgh, Pennsylvania to parents Shawn and Kathleen Fisher. I live in a rural area outside of Hookstown Pennsylvania where I enjoy horseback riding and fishing. I will be graduating this year from South Side Area High School. I am an artist and I have been writing poetry for as long as I can remember. I have been published by Quill Books in their 1998 anthology *Promises to Keep* and by the Poet's Guild in *Best New Poems 1997*.

**Frederick, Adrian** - Born January 16, 1977 in Jacksonville, Florida is the son of Hannah Griffin and his father. He has traveled to many states, attending different schools. Adrian also traveled to Atlanta, there he met his future wife Rashaw Dooley. Staying there for a year, he involved himself in a Job Corp. program, that caused him to move to Earle C. Clement in Morganfield, Kentucky. Graduating within nine months she went back to Atlanta to start his new mission in life. Leaving Job Corp. with him was a Diploma, GED, Drivers License and a new path to see that started in 1995. Currently, Adrian works doing maintenance and is married with no children. His spare time is used for writing and thinking and on top of all that he loves it. He and his wife are members of Avondale Church of Christ. Adrian is the oldest of five children. Earning recognition from Iliad Press and a Honorable Mention Award from the National Authors Registry, Adrian is very proud of himself. Adrian says: "That he will continue to love and write poetry! Adrian has added poetry as a part of his life and hopes you will too."

**Freeman, Christy** - Born June 9, 1974 in Duluth, Georgia to parents Mary and Bobby Barrett. She grew up as the middle child of two other sisters, Amy and Dana. At the age of ten, her mom remarried to Henry Knight which who had three children of his own, Shane, Crystal, and Tonya. She married on December 23, 1996 to her husband Bryan Freeman. They are currently living in the beautiful North East Georgia mountains. She has received two Honorable Mentions from Cader Publishing, Ltd. for her poems, "Children of the Night" and "Family Tree." Her love of writing started at a very young age. She says, "Writing is a powerful tool. With using just words you can touch hearts and souls that could make a difference in life."

**Freeman, Josetta** - Born December 7, 1982 in Lumberton, North Carolina to parents, Ronald and Lori Freeman. Lived there until I was twelve years old then I lived in Fairmont, North Carolina. Then my family and I had to move to Lexington, North Carolina with my mother's job. Both my parents are full-blooded Lumbee American Indian, therefore I, myself, am too a full blooded Indian. I also have a brother fourteen years of age. I am an honor student at West Davidson High School. I have received three awards in English, for works of literature, and excellent grades. I enjoy writing poetry and then trying to add music to them, to see if it fits into a song. I enjoy music, I don't really have a personal statement but, "Without God, I am (we are) nothing!"

**Gallen, Susan** - Born December 4th, 1947 in Budapest, Hungary. I attended a special skill school that is comparable to colleges in the United States, but are not used here. My occupation is a waitress. As a teenager two of my poems were published in a local woman's magazine. I have read some of my poems to an audience of teens at a theater. I've always loved poetry. I started writing poetry again because of so many disappointments in life. Ten of my poems were published and more on the way. My dream is to one day have my own book of poetry. I love to write poetry, listen to music, watch movies, travel and biking. "I actually love life and life's pleasure!"

**Garrett, Deborah** - Born March 13, 1951 in Sylacauga, Alabama to parents Bill and Frances Landers. Graduated in 1969 from Fayetteville High School and attended Jefferson State Junior College. Ms. Garrett has four children and has spent most of her adult life raising her family. Now living in the small town of Columbiana, Alabama, she is the office manager for a therapeutic foster home program in Birmingham, Alabama. Her poem "Lonely" has received Honorable Mention from Carder Publishing, Ltd. Ms. Garrett states that "writing cleanses the soul of all the fears and doubts that one faces in everyday life."

**George, Betty** - Born September 5, 1938 in Harlem, Montana the second of six children to parents, Curtis and Hazel Humphreys. She lived in Montana until she graduated from high school. Upon completion of training at Humbolt Business & Airline School in Minneapolis, Minnesota, Betty moved to Sunnyvale, California in 1957 where she was employed by Westinghouse Corporation. It was during this time that she met her husband Ruben George who was in the United States Navy. They were married in 1958 and have three children, five grandchildren and are expecting to be great-grandparents in July of this year. She retired from United Parcel Service in 1995 and they moved to Nampa, Idaho to be near their children and grandchildren. She is currently employed by the Nampa School District as Educational Assistant in the Title I Reading Program. She has been published in *Season of Change* by JMW Publishing Co., *Pathways* by Iliad Press, *An Eternity of Beauty and Sounds of Poetry* by The National Library of Poetry, *Poetic Voices of America* by Sparrowgrass, *Distinctions of Excellence: The 1999 President's Recognition of Literary Excellence* sponsored by The National Authors Registry. Betty says, "I fell in love with poetry at an early age. My father wrote and quoted poetry to us as we were growing up, but I never seriously attempted to write poetry myself until four years ago. It now absorbs most of my evenings and weekends. My husband is my strongest supporter. If it weren't for his encouragement I would still be writing poetry and hiding it in a drawer."

**Gevargiz, Linda** - Born July 18, 1985 to parents Victor and Angela Gevargiz in St. John's Hospital in Yonkers, New York. She has two siblings, a brother Leon and a sister Victoria. She is currently attending John Burroughs Middle School in Yonkers and will be going to Lincoln High School in year 2000. She is in the National Junior Honor Society and was on the pre-team in gymnastics. She also received an Honorable Mention from Cader Publishing. She's also involved in many sports, she had taken classes for tap dancing, karate, and most recent, gymnastics. "Although I had to quit gymnastics," Linda says. "I know I can achieve my goals with my other talents." Her main goal in life is to be a writer. Linda's favorite hobbies are collecting magazines, working out, and performing plays.

**Gibbons, Stefani** - I am fourteen years old. I was born on October 11, 1984. My hobbies are writing, reading, hanging with my friends, and playing basketball and soccer for fun. My favorite subjects in school are Language, Reading, and Home Ec. My worst subject is Math. I started writing at first because I was always depressed and I found out that writing helped me cope with my feelings and my surroundings. Then it came so naturally to me that I've been writing ever since then.

**Gibbs, Kara Nicole** - Born May 23, 1976 to parents, Martha and Edgar Gibbs. She is the youngest of nine children. She presently resides in Eutawville, South Carolina. She attended Holly Hill-Roberts High School where she graduated near the top of her class in 1994. She currently works at Blu-Bird Medical equipment supply company, as an office assistant. She has been writing poetry since the tenth grade. She aspires to write poetry that will allow people to open their minds and hearts to the beauty of words and their lyrical flow.

**Gilliam, Leon** - (Pen name: Kelly Gilliam). Born in a small town in South Carolina. Attended Union High School then attended a tech school to become a mechanical tech. Married at the age of fourteen, have two children; two grandchildren. Been writing poetry books for several years. I write on all subjects mainly life, faith and love. I have received third place for my poem "Our Love" published in *Passion* by American Poetry Guild. Received numerous Honorable Mentions such as "The Substainer" by Iliad Press; it also received the 1999 President's Recognition of Literary Excellence from the National Authors Registry. I've been published in twenty-three anthologies, local papers, also written two songs that have been recorded. A member of Poets Guild and Honorary Member of Fellowship Counsel. Many editor choice awards. My writing mentor is a published poet with

M.P.D. So I have learned to see thru many different eyes from the young to the aged. To this person I give all the credit for different views on life and to God I give all the glory for the gift. As of now we are writing a book on M.P.D. together. As a poet, I have learned to look in many different ways at the same thing seen every day. Therefore each time I have an expression not seen before. Words are simply words but can be expressed many ways. My wish is to let others see and learn the different expressions of words.

**Golden, Donald Michael** - Author, poet, songwriter, inventor; b. Springfiled, Mass June 5, 1953; s. Donald Leon and Marilyn Ruth (Bush) G; m. Agnes Bozena Meduna, Nov. 13, 1971; children: Steven Frank, Tina Marie Golden Weaver, Tiffany Lynn. Owner, mgr. painting co., Ashford, Conn., 1971-94. Inventor: magic fingers, painter's mate, 1996. Author: (juvenile) "Mulligan Stew Gang," 1996 also various others. Poetry: National Library of Poetry, "Tears of Joy," Editor's Choice Award - also on cassette tape, *Sounds of Poetry*, 1997; "Hand In Hand," cassette tape, 1997, "Gold Dust, Blue Diamonds and Rubies," cassette tape, 1997; "Apple Pie and Cinnamon," cassette tape, 1997; "My Piano," cassette tape, 1998; "Adversity," cassette tape, 1998; Iliad Press: "Hope and Despair," 1998; "Stormy Seas," Honorable Mention, 1998; "What a Great Movie," Honorable Mention, 1998; "My Shoes Fit Just Fine," Honorable Mention and the President's Recognition of Literary Excellence, 1998; "Obstacle Illusion," Honorable Mention, 1998. Songwriting, "Heart-strings and Ivory," The Association of Songwriters and Lyricist, 1998; also various other songs written. Honors: Biography published in *Marquis Who's Who in the West in America*, International Biographical Centre, Cambridge, England, 1998; Smithsonian Archieves. Home: 115 Cemetery Rd., Cordele, GA 31015. "Life can be simplified, simply by reading the directions that are written in the book of life."

**Gordon, Peter** - Born in 1971 in Frederick, Maryland to parents Jack and Joanne. I've always enjoyed creative writing and dabbled in artistry. Professionally, I make a living as a computer programmer. In 1994 I married, but things did not work out well, as my wife was jealous of best friend, Kel, and chose to drive her from my life. This left me something of a Ghost, unable to resolve or even talk about the pain I was going through over this. Eventually, I turned to writing poems and a certain chatroom where I took the name Geist and was able to come to terms with myself. I have my parents, Kel, and God to thank for their unconditional love through it all. My collection of poems and a picture is posted on my home page at http://www.geocities.com/paris/leftbank/7529, and from there, a link to the chatroom, where I can often be found haunting the Graveyard and stealing kisses from the maidens.

**Griffin, Whit** - Born January 16, 1980. Mr. Griffin is an aspiring poet who began to create with words at a young age. He is interested in pursuing a literary career reflecting his diverse influences. Mr. Griffin enjoys the work of Hunter S. Thompson and Kurt Vonnegut, as well as the poetry of Arthur Rimbaud, the Fugitives, and the Beats. Mr. Griffin's poetry is ever evolving; changing its form as a snake changes its skin. He wishes to be known as a gifted poet, yet feels that only death will ameliorate him from obscurity.

**Hall, Brock** - Brock was born on July 2, 1978, in Jacksonville, Florida. He still lives with his mother Brenda and sister Brooke. Brock graduated Cum Laude from Episcopal High School, then attended Jacksonville University. He is currently a student at Jacksonville University, and intends to graduate with two B.S. degrees, and one B.A. degree in Chemistry, Chemical Engineering and English respectively. Though he is only now coming into print, Brock has been a writer his entire life, and fully intends to pursue this interest in the future.

**Hanson, Edward** - Born in Pomona, California on September 28, 1950 to Donald and Joan Hanson. Struck with polio at three, but recovered well. Has two younger sisters: Kristi-Lynn and Kara Lee. Grew up in Chino, California where graduated high school in 1968. Parents divorced in 1961 and lived with mother. Attended Chaffey Community College in Alta Loma, California where received an Associate of Science in 1970. From 1975 to 1998 worked in various Analytical Chemistry Labs, except for five non-consecutive years working in Construction, Horseshoeing, Project Data Management, and computer programming. Married Maureen MacDonald in 1980 and moved to Phelan, California in the Mojave Desert where lived for ten years. Daughter Terra Lowansa was born in 1986. Moved to Denver, Colorado in 1991. Separated from wife in 1992 and divorced in 1995. Left Bench Chemistry in 1998 after five and a half years at Geneva Pharmaceutical to work as a Technical Writer. Realized was always a writer, especially a poet. Began writing seriously in 1993 and submitting to competitions. Have won several awards since.

**Hardy-Winters, Suzanne** - Born November 4, 1949 in Billing, Montana. Has a twin sister Dianne & three other siblings, she graduated from Billings Senior High School in 1968. Has been married for twenty-four years, is a mother at three girls and a grandmother of two. Suzanne began writing poetry in 1997. Creative in many other areas of her life, she had never tried writing poetry. It became a true adventure expressing deep feelings of a life time. She is a member of the National Authors Registry, received two Honorable Mentions from Iliad Press, for her poems "The Mother Image" and "I Let Go A Sigh" also published in *Distinctions of Excellence*. She has received a Diamond Homer Trophy from The Famous Poets Society, her poem is also published in *Pathways, Treasured Poems of America 1999, American Poetry Annual, and A Eternity of Beauty*, and reaching other more anthologies. Suzanne has published her own book of poetry, *Poems from a Multiple Heart* available through Amazon Books or Barnes & Noble. Suzanne is a Mental, Emotional and Physical Therapist. She enjoys helping people find their true selves and express that in their lives.

**Harris, Blaise** - Born January 17, 1980 in Durham, North Carolina to Dorothy M. Johnson and David Perry. I have a younger brother named Linden Harris, and I reside with my grandmother Ora Lee Harris. I attended Bunn High School, and graduated in the class of 1998. I was the class president at Bunn High and I received many awards and honors. I now attend North Carolina State University, and I am a Psychology major. One day I hope to be a guidance counselor. Growing up, I didn't have everything, but I made the best of what I had. In the future, I hope to have enough to support my family so that the younger members can have what I did not. I have been writing poems for about two years now, and I also received the 1999 President's Recognition of Literary Excellence. I write what I feel in my poems. My friends always get me to write for them, and they always seem to find that special person when they use my poems. No matter how many poems I write (please be with me is no exception) I never get the girl!

**Harris, Edyth Valerie** - Born February 7, 1913, to parents Simon and Gisella Wulkan. Lived and educated in Vienna, Austria, received her diploma as Dental Technician in 1932. Interest in the Performing Arts, she toured Italy. Moved to England and married Francis James Harris in 1944. They have one son, Peter John (1946), and two grandchildren, Kendall and Karen. In 1949, they moved to Canada where Edyth continued her education, earning a diploma as Registered Nursing Assistant (Toronto 1954) and Registered Massage Therapist (Toronto 1972). She has taken an interest in herbs since early childhood and studied Herbology with the Dominion Herbal College in B.C. She is the founder of the Natural Nutrition Society of Windsor (1976), and past President of Women Writers of Windsor. Widowed in 1986, she began her fifth career as a writer. Edyth attended courses and workshops at the University of Window and published a book of poetry *Don't Fence Me In* (1994). She wrote a play "The White Gloves" (1994), received the President's Award for Literary Excellence for her poem "Free Fall" (1995), took First Prize in Haiku Competition and several Honorable Mentions. Her work has been published in many anthologies and magazines. Edyth is a member of The National Authors Registry and of the International Society of Poets. Currently, she is enrolled in a course with the Institute of Children's Literature. She believes that "Nothing is as constant—as Change." She is grateful for guidance and support received.

**Hashem, Melinda Sue** - Born May 5, 1984 in Fulda, Germany. I am an American citizen because my father was a soldier stationed in Germany. My birth parents names are Lee Hashem, Jr. and Tina Johns. I have a twelve year old brother Jeff. My parents are no longer married. In 1996, my dad married an awesome lady named Beth, whom I call mom. It was she who encouraged me to submit my poem. I was in the seventh grade when I wrote "One." I thought of it when I was walking home alone from school. "There was a cloud all by itself as I was."

**Haven, Tracy Marie** - Born in San Antonio, Texas on November 22, 1969. Although I have briefly lived elsewhere, San Antonio has always been my home. I have traveled extensively and love the Hawaiian Islands. I earned ny BBA in Accounting in 1992 from the University of Texas at San Antonio, and I am currently working on my MBA there. I have always excelled in both Math and English. In high school, I won numerous awards for creative writing and poetry. I married my high school best friend in 1998 (after a nine year courtship!) and became Tracy Marie Haven Hopkins. My family consists of my loving husband; wonderful, supportive parents, a terrific aunt, and a close circle of friends. I have an extended "cat family" that I care for when needed; I thank them for sharing their cats with us and making us a part of their family. My one addiction is CATS! Everything in my life is cats. I am currently owned by four male felines (my boys). I love all animals and cherish their kind souls and complete devotion. I wrote "Goodbye, Dear Ones" after the death of my two female felines. This poem is dedicated to them, Rusty and Bozo, with love and thanks for bringing so much to my life. I am very proud to have my poem published, and I hope that anyone who has lost a loved one will find some peace and comfort through my words.

**Heiss, Elizabeth Reneé** - Born February 18, 1949 in Princeton, New Jersey to parents Earl and Bernice Marcellious. She graduated in 1967 from Notre Dame High School in Trenton, New Jersey where she was in the Literary Club and on the Yearbook Staff. Four years later, she graduated from Douglas College in New Brunswick, New Jersey with a Bachelor of Science degree in Home Economics Education. She taught Home Economics at Pemberton Township High School for four years, during which time she married Douglas Edward Heiss. In 1976, their first child, Michelle Theresa, was born; she was joined by her identical twin sisters Kimberly Monique and Valerie Nicole in 1980. In 1989, Renée was hired as a teacher of Family and Consumer Sciences at Northern Burlington County Regional High School, Columbus, New Jersey, where she is currently employed as a high school Child Development teacher and a 7th grade Language Arts teacher. She was awarded the 1993 A+ for Kids Disseminator Grant, and twice awarded the NJEA Frederick L. Hipp Foundation Grant for Excellence in Education. She has authored several articles on education, and is a member of the Daughters of the American Revolution. In 1996, Renée was named NJ FACS Teacher of the Year. In 1997, she was included in *Who's Who Among American High School Teachers*. Her poem "Yesterday's Promise" received a 4th place award and is published in *Feelings*, by Cader Publishing, Ltd. This same poem earned her the 1999 President's Recognition of Literary Excellence sponsored by The National Authors Registry. Renée's favorite quote, featured on a sign outside of the gates to the Great Lakes Naval Training Center is, "The only way to predict the future is to create it."

**Henson, Dian F.** - Born November 13, 1945 in Ypsilanti, Michigan has lived most of her life in the Wayne\Westland area. She has been a full time employee of Eastern Michigan University for the last twenty-five years, and is currently a college sophomore majoring in Written Communications, with a minor in Literature. Hobbies are reading, writing, photography, and needlework when there is time between college semesters. She currently lives in Canton, Michigan with her dog Tina. Dian's inspiration for writing comes from growing up loving books. Her favorite author as a child was, and still is, the "Western" writer Zane Grey. His fiction was always pure poetry to read and his books were usually lying about her parent's house. Today she has many fiction favorites, from one extreme of Science Fiction, to the other extreme of Romances and Westerns. Her favorite poets are Walter de la Mare, and Dante. Poetry has always been a part of her life, although she had never read the classics until entering college a few years ago. Learning the different forms for writing poetry, she loves the challenge of making the poetry work, and has tried her hand with all types. Dian's aspirations are to be a full time author in poetry and fiction. She is currently compiling poems for future publishing and working on her first novel.

**Herbert, Charles IV** - Born December 4, 1957 in little section of town called the Iris Channel of New Orleans, LA., to parents, Charles and Lorraine Herbert III. Having moved from school to school as a child, left him paralyzed with fear always wondering, "why am I here surrounded by these people?" Dropping out of high school at age of seventeen, then went back to get my GED at the age of twenty-three from Riverdale High School. From there went to Jefferson Vocational for Structural Drafting. Married his wife Bonnie of seven years, has two great sons Chad and Jeremy. Charles works as a Certified Welding Inspector, inspecting large steel structures. This is his first Honorable Mention award from Cader Publishing, Ltd., and the 1999 Presidents Recognition for Literary Excellence from The National Authors Registry. His poem "Blue Collar Workers" is published in *Achieving Excellence* by Iliad Press. "It makes me proud to say this is my first of many to come," says Charles.

**Hobby, Doreen** - Born June 10, 1968 in New London, Connecticut. I am working full time at a local corporation as a secretary. Recently, I became involved in culture change as chairperson of a communications committee that publishes articles to improve relations between management and employees. As a Gemini, I can be quite the messenger with words and thoughts. I am acquiring credits towards a degree in Liberal Arts and plan to further my education with a Bachelor's Degree. I like being a student part time. Writing poetry has been an emotional release for me since adolescence. Poetry and positive thinking has helped me to deal with various issues in my life. I enjoy listening to most kinds of music, concerts, billiards, travel, rollerblading, biking, reading, and making observations in my daily existence, which inspire me. Published Works: "Invisible," "3 Hearts Loved" in *Pathways* by Iliad Press; "In My Mind" in *Outstanding Poets of 1998* by the National Library of Poetry; "Legends" in *Connections* by Iliad Press; and "By Looking at Me" in *On The Road* by Association of Song Lyrics; and several other poems. "Baby Blue" is dedication to Wes - thanks for the inspiration and chemistry! Practice Random Acts of Kindness.

**Hoover, Tiffany** - Born September 29, 1982. She is a Junior in High School at Fort Zumwalt South High. She lives with her parents, two sisters, two dogs, and pet bird in O'Fallon, Missouri. Her hobbies include: horseback riding, reading, drawing, and socializing with friends. Tiffany plans to go to college to become a Veterinarian.

**Hunsberger, Sidona Marie** - (Pen name: Sidona Marie). Born September 16, 1958 in Kalamazoo, Michigan to parents Russell and Betty Manspeaker. Lived most of her youth in Bangor, Michigan. Graduating from Bangor High School in 1976. Attending Lake Michigan College in Benton Harbor, Michigan from 1977 to 1979 and Western Michigan University in Kalamazoo, Michigan from 1979 to 1983 earning a B.A. majoring in English and minoring Elementary Education. Teaching for four years at St. Mary's Elementary School in Paw Paw, Michigan before marrying Gary Hunsberger and moving to Fennville, Michigan, where she lives at present with her husband and their two children: Justin 8, and Hilary 3. She is for now, a stay home mother. Poetry writing for the most part is a personal and private expression shared with friends and family.

**Ihasz, Oliver Dezsö** - Born June 6, 1946 in Buda-Pest, Hungary to parents, Louis and Carolyne and Brother Nicholas. Oliver and family escaped Hungary during the 1956 revolution, immigrated to the United States and settled in the Bronx, New York. At age twenty he married his childhood sweetheart Ellen. Together they raised two beautiful children to adulthood, son Adam and daughter Tara. Oliver received his higher education in the United States Army wher for six years he attended the JFK Special Warfare School at Ft. Bragg, North Carolina and the First Army Intelligence School at Ft. Mead, Maryland. He graduated as an Intelligence Analyst assigned to the 351st Psychological Operations Group. He continued his studies by taking course work at the New York Institute of Finance and New York State University at Stonybrook. Oliver spent ten years on the trading floor of the New York Stock Exchange as a member and broker/dealer. Today he is employed as a Financial Advisor in an Investment Banking Firm managed by his brother Nick and son Adam in Manchester, Vermont. He is an ordained Minister and in his spare time he offers counseling to anyone in need of spiritual guidance and healing. Oliver began writing in 1995. His poem "We Are That We Are" was highly acclaimed and published in the Third Millennium, a Long Island, New York publication. His book length nonfiction work, "Virtual Reality," a controversial and unpublished philosophical narrative has received the highest praise from scholars and literary experts alike. Oliver's poem, "Today I Am" was selected to receive the 1999 President's Recognition of Literary Excellence by The National Authors Registry and appears in *Distinctions of Excellence* published by Iliad Press. With a passion for writing, Oliver says, "Just give me a pencil and paper, the words will flow."

**Jaeger, Jaclyn** - Born October 7, 1978 in Lynn, Massachusetts to parents, Stephen and June Jaeger. I live in Swampscott, Massachusetts where I graduated from Swampscott High School in 1997. I am the oldest of four with an eighteen year old sister, Kirstin, a fifteen year old brother, Chase, and six year old sister, Shannon. Ever since I learned how to spell in the first grade, writing has always been my favorite hobby. Presently, I am a sophomore attending Saint Joseph's College of Maine double majoring in English and communications. Currently, as news editor for our campus paper, *The Scribe*, I hope to pursue a career in journalism. Last year my poem "The Girl and Her Dad" won first place in our campus poetry literary magazine and this year, is receiving Iliad's Press 1999 President's Recognition of Literary Excellence. My biggest dream is to earn a Pulitzer Prize in journalism.

**Janoski, Maria C.** - Born in Scranton, Pennsylvania on March 1, 1981 to parents Henry and Rita Jnoski. She now lives in Clarks Summit with her parents, sister Elizabeth and grandmother. Maria is currently a senior at Abington Heights High School where she is an active member of several teams and organizations. She plays the clarinet in the marching band and is the current secretary. She was also a two year member of the girls' soccer team and is a three year member of the girls' volleyball team. Maria is also a three year member of Who's Who Among American High School Students, a National Merit Scholar, and a member of the National Honor Society. Maria began writing poetry at the age of fifteen and has published several poems with organizations including Iliad Press, The National Library of Poetry, and the Amherst Society. She is also a current member of the International Society of Poets and a registered author with The National Authors Registry. For her poetic efforts, Maria has received two Honorable Mentions from *Iliad Press* and three Editor's Choice Awards from The National Library of Poetry. Her work has also been featured on four volumes of *Sound of Poetry* from The National Library of Poetry. Maria plans to continue her writing while pursuing an English major at Cornell University.

**Jarvis, Erin** - Born June 4, 1983 in Lorain, Ohio to parents, Krista and Gary Jarvis Jr. Currently attending high school at Lorain Admiral King. Besides her poetry, Erin also enjoys writing short stories. She is incredibly interested in the arts, music, old movies, television and broadway. Her accomplishments include Honorable Mention and the 1999 President's Recognition of Literary Excellence for her poem "The Voice." She is currently taking advanced placement English courses at school. Erin says, "My literary works are my greatest achievements and accomplishments. 'The Voice' has received the most awards though. Being so young with this amazing quality is very astonishing and overwhelming for me."

**Jeetun, Veenaye Kumar** - Born October 5, 1979 at Laventure, Mauritius. Youngest in the family and age nineteen. Never interested in poetry but indeed moved by the difficulties faced by my family and myself while still a kid. Successfully ended my secondary education at Modern College, a school where I lived in like my own house. I'm presently doing my degree in B.A. Joint Humanities at the University of Mauritius and also following a Journalism course from the Writers Bureau College of Journalism in England through Distance Learning. I adore football and play for the Laventure champions, Progressive Youth Club. Besides, I find much interest in poetry, philately, numismatics, collecting newspaper articles, journalism and computing. I had never realized that I've got the artistic talent of writing. I owe this outstanding success to my elder sister, Chandrakanta who's the launch pad of my poetic success. My first poem appeared in *News On Sunday* which helped me publish my works. Yet, I wasn't confident and found my poems childish, but I was encouraged by my close friends Sidhari Preetee and Legrand Christie. I feared my favourite teachers, Anand Rughoobur and Anamika Bunjun would find them too simple, but they shared the same approach and that gave my poetic art a great boost. Presently, I'm secretary of Progressive Youth Club, executive member of Flacq Youth Centre through which I was the laureate of a Prix/Bourse from Confejes and Distinguished Member of the International Society of Poets. I have to my credit two Honorable Mention awards from Iliad Press and two President's Recognition Registry for the 1999 Literary Excellence from The National Authors Registry for my poems "Platonic Love" and "Extinction!(Of the human race: WAR). I got the Editor's Choice Award from The National Library of Poetry for my poem "Tears of the Dead" and besides, selected for *Sounds Of Poetry*. Today, my unique inspiration is my inseparable friend, Manjoo, who's been my sole support. I dedicate all my works to these above-mentioned persons, without forgetting my brother-in-law, Sunil, without whom I wouldn't have been able to write a single line of poetry.

**Johnson, Carole** - Birthplace: Los Angeles, CA; Education: UCLA graduate, Math/Geography major, 1974; Spouse: Geary F. Johnson, 1984; Occupation: Writer, homemaker; Hobbies: Photography, Art decorator, garden; Awards: published in eight anthologies, five Editor's Choice Awards from the National Library of Poetry; published in the Canadian periodical *Tickled by Thunder* under the label-Short Story from Best New Authors of 1998; Distinguished Member of International Society of Poets; Honorable Mention Award from Iliad Press; Member of the National Authors Registry-sponsored by Cader Publishing, Ltd. (Iliad Press). I am a cancer survivor (four years now); I love to read and to write and hopefully I can give people relief and peace to their anguish and happiness through my writing. I love writing—it's a beautiful way to communicate.

**Johnson, Heather LaRae** - Born on January 1, 1983 in Jacksonville, North Carolina to parents, Frank and LaNell Johnson. She attends Citizens' High School and will shortly be a graduate. She has two sisters by the names Amber and Autumn. She is a member of Tarlanding Baptist Church. She has received nine awards for her soccer talent, six awards for softball, one award for All County Chorus, and one Honorable Mention award for her poem "Misery" by Cader Publishing, Ltd. She loves to shop and play soccer. She also loves to spend time with her boyfriend, Stephen. She says that she is very pleased with her writings and awards and that she will continue to write more poetry.

**Johnson, Olivia** - Born November 18, 1943 in Paris, Texas to Douglas and Mettie Hardison. I have lived in Paris all of my life and attended school here. I graduated from B.J. Graves High School and then attended Jarvis Christian College. At the end of my second year in college, I returned home and married Oscar Johnson. I have five children: three boys and two girls. I am now divorced and my children are all grown. I am currently employed with the Campbell Soup Company where I have worked for thirty years. My time is devoted to Christ, my work in the church, and my writing. I attend the Hospitality Church of God in Christ where I am the president of the youth ushers and the Sunshine Band. I also work with the youth choir. Every summer I organize and hold a youth workshop at my church just to give to the children in the area something different to do. My poem "Love" has received Honorable Mention from Cader Publishing, and the 1999 President's Recognition of Literary Excellence. My poems give me a chance to express my feelings for the love of God and life.

**Joseph, Fitzroy Gregory** - Born in Trinidad, West Indies on October 17, 1929. He was educated in Trinidad, USA, England and Europe. He's a medical doctor by profession and has worked as an advisor for the World Heath Organization and Consultant with the United Nations in Africa, Asia and the Pacific; and in recent years, as a Senior Lecturer in Community Health at the Faculty of Medical Sciences, Mt.Hope University of the West Indies, Trinidad Tobago. Apart from health and medical publications, Dr. Joseph has never stopped writing poetry since high school years. Previous publications of poetry and prose have been in magazines in Jamaica, USA, France, Belgium, Solomon Islands, Kenya and in W.H.O.'s journal in, Congo Republic (Brazzaville) over the years. A poem, "The Time When" was chosen and published in the *Anthology of College Poetry* in the USA in 1954, and in the same year a volume of Poetry entitled, "A Living Expression". In 1996 Dr. Joseph put together all his poems published and unpublished since 1954, in a volume entitled *Delayed Spring* which is being published in three volumes (or chapbooks). Volumes I and II are on the market Volume III is expected to be out Spring 1999. The publisher is: The Plowman, Box 414, Whitby, Ontario L1N 5S4, CANADA. Recently, Dr. Joseph has completed another volume of poems about Africa, Africans, and his experiences in Africa, entitled "Oh My Africa," and he's in search of a publisher.

**Kallenbach, Sara** - Born April 6, 1982 in Northern Wisconsin. She now lives on a dairy farm operated by her parents, Russell and Carol Kallenbach. She attends Barron Senior High School in Barron, Wisconsin and will graduate in May, 2000. Some of the possible career options she's considering include teaching and journalism. She had her first poem published at the young age of fourteen. "Blue Moonlight" and "Shades of Gray" are her second and third poems published with "Blue Moonlight" receiving Honorable Mention. Besides her love for writing, Sara enjoys collecting Beanie Babies, antique ruby glass and spending time with the family's fourteen-year-old cat, Moose.

**Kimminau, Joan A.** - Born 1947, youngest of twelve children born to Leo & Elizabeth Sheahan, was raised on a farm near Formoso, Kansas. She has one daughter. Kimminau is a member of the Nebraska State Poetry Society; Nebraska Mothers Association; American Mothers, Inc.; The National Author's Registry, and The International Society of Poets. In 1997, she was elected into The International Poetry Hall of Fame. She has been the honored recipient three times of the President's Recognition of Literary Excellence by The National Author's Registry, a two time winner of the Editor's Choice Award, and a recent 3$^{rd}$ place winner in poetry of the Nebraska Mothers Association. She has total of over twenty awards for poetic achievements on the local, state, national and international levels. Kimminau has been writing poetry for over thirty years, but didn't start releasing them for publication until 1990. Over twenty-five poems have been published in books, newspapers, and magazines such as *The Miraculous Medal* and *Verses*. In addition to the awards and publications, "It Goes Without Saying" and "Anticipate the Moment" were recorded on the Sound of Poetry. "I have recently learned to see more than I ever knew existed. I no longer see the sun slowly sink beyond the horizon. I now see God's creation in the setting sun with all the glory and splendor of His heavenly paints brushing the day into night. It is my hope that you, the reader, get your own messages and never let anyone tell you that you didn't hear what the author was saying. If you feel it in your heart, it's for you and you got the message." Kimminau owns her own company, "Poetry for the Heart", personalizing correspondence, selling greeting cards, bookmarks, etc. You can visit with her on the web at http://www.kdsi.net/poetryfortheheart.

**Kiyono, Mika** - Born July 23, 1977 in Tokyo, Japan. Her mother, Sachiko Kiyono, is author of picture book published in Japan. She moved to the United States in 1991. Started to write poetry in Japanese and English, from 1991. She has private and commercial pilot license. Joined the California National Guard in 1998.

**Kosoff, Flora M.** - Resident of California. My family lives in the area: daughter Linda and husband, their Amy and Michael, and Amy's husband Sam and my great grand child, Sarah Lynn. After nearly 39 years as a nurse, 25 of them with the Federal Government, I fell on duty and was grounded from nursing. After a year of not knowing what to do with my life, the writing bug nipped me in a Michigan blizzard in 1984. I called an editor in Chicago and asked how I could find out if my poetry was any good. He told me to find a writer's magazine and send my poems "over the transom". He said that they will let you know if they are any good. I sent three poems and all three were accepted. Since then, I have written nearly 1700 poems and more than 600 have been published...some of them many times. "Grandma Tells a Ghost Story" was my first money win...about daughter Linda in a Halloween blizzard in 1958. Later that year, I moved back to Idaho where I had nurse training but stayed there only three years before moving to the coast, first, Gold Beach, Oregon...then California. I've written other things too, such as "Little Boris and the Metternicks," about my father coming from Russia in 1914. Marguet du Bois published these before he retired. I've written a nurse's diary, "All The Young Nightingales" that's never been published. I have letters from many famous people: Ted Turner, Bob Hope, Jimmie Stewart, three presidential wives, Katherine Hepburn, Jim Irwin, Milton Berle, and Jane Fonda.

**Ksepko, Irena W.** - Birthplace: June 5, 1951, Poland. Received degree: Technical Economist. Married to Henry K. Ksepko, 27 years and have three children, two sons and a daughter. Immigrated from Poland to the U.S.A. in 1991. Vice Chairman of The New Polish Community Circle, Bayonne, N.J., dedicating my service to the immigrants arriving in U.S.A. Wrote poetry for the last 10 years and shared my poetry with the Polish society. Love to read and write poetry on any subject. My latest themes are dedicated to children, Pope John Paul II, R.C. Church, and environment. I am writing poetry in Polish and they are being translated into English.

**La-Touche, Monique** - Born December 8, 1966 in New York City to Enoch and Edith La-Touche. Monique attended Cathedral High School and graduated valedictorian of her class. An active member of the Community Baptist Church of Christ, she credits her Pastors, Elder Dr. Lester L. Williams and Elder Shirley G. Williams to be at the heart of her inspired creation, *Family and Friends* which attained Honorable Mention in the 1998 Iliad Literary Award Program, as well as having received the 1999 President's Recognition of Literary Excellence from the National Authors Registry. Currently the Executive Assistant to the President of the Association of the Bar of the City of New York, Monique serves on the Executive Committee and the Board of Directors of the New York City Chapter of Legal Secretaries Association. A few of her hobbies (aside from writing poetry) include: sewing, camping, fishing, aerobics, and martial arts. Although her exceptional talent for expression in writing has been obvious since childhood, Monique has finally begun to share her gift with the world. She says, "Through the art of poetry, light burns brightly in hidden places, dust is blown from mental shelves of forgotten clutter, and the revelations found within stimulate inspiration of their own."

**Lofton, Synnikaverse** - Full Pen name: Synnikaverse Alexander Lofton; Age: nineteen. Date of Birth: unknown; Place of Birth: unknown; Parent's names: unknown. Quote: Old realm new realm coalesce, reigning blood of the new breed has been bred.

**Long, Brian** - (Pen name: The Poet) Born February 12, 1975 to Ronald and Jennifer Long in Kokomo, Indiana. His family and he moved to Springfield, Missouri in 1977 and to Fordland, Missouri in 1987. He has an older sister, Tina, who lives in Kokomo, and two younger brothers, Jeremy and Justin, who live in Fordland. Brian graduated from Fordland High in 1993, and attended Southwest Baptist University for one year. He is a member od Seymour First Baptist Church, a distinguished member of The International Society of Poets, and the So Far Gone fan club. His poem "The Thread of Life" received an honorable mention from Iliad Press in the fall of 1997. Brian was inspired to write this poem for his friend Mindy Willis who lost a child shortly after its birth. As a poet he writes about every thing from love to death. About a year ago Brian started writing from the female point of view under the name Sorcha. When asked why he said, "A writer must of many things to open a readers' mind." Spending time on the net and listening to music are places where Brian finds some of his ideas for writing. His favorite band is So Far Gone. His favorite website is sofargone.webjump.com.

**Lotz, Sue** - Born December 18, 1940 in McKeesport PA., to parents Michael and Catherine Abraham. Graduated from McKeesport High School in 1958. Sue has taken some writing courses at Penn State Campus in McKeesport, Writer's Digest Schools, and the Institute of Children's Literature. Recently widowed, Sue ia a self employed owner at Conley's Towing Service located in McKeesport, PA. She also has a small graphic's business called Lotz of Ideas Graphic's Shop. Sue has always loved writing, but until recently has never pursued having her works published. She has written thirteen pieces of poetry which are being published in many anthologies. She has received two Honorable Mentions from Iliad Press on her works "Emptiness" and "Loving Heart." The National Library of Poetry have honored her with two Editor's Choice Awards for "Angel of Mine" and "Guide Me." Two of her poems will be published in the *Distinctions of Excellence: 1999 President's Recognition of Excellence* and *A Celebration of Poet's*, Showcase Edition. Sue says, "It's not how many people you know, it's how many hearts you touch."

**Maddox, Juanita A.** - Born December 8, 1942 in Springfield, Ohio to parents, Floyd and Della Smith. Graduated from Northwestern High School in Springfield, Ohio in 1960, she attended Sinclair Community College in Dayton, Ohio. She married Robert S. Maddox in 1965. Juanita worked at Wright-Patterson AFB, Ohio as a budget analyst, retiring after thirty-six years. Juanita started writing poetry after she retired in 1997. She has been published in *Searching For Soft Voices* and the *Outstanding Poets of 1998* by The National Library of Poetry. Also published in *Poetic Voices of America* by Sparrowgrass Poetry Forum, and "A Time To Be Free" by Quill Books. She received a Certificate of Merit and publication in the *American Poetry Annual* by the Amherst Society. She received Honorable Mention and publication in *Feelings* for her poem "The Cycle of Life" by Iliad Press. She also received the 1999 President's Recognition of Literary Excellence from the National Authors Registry for her poem "The Cycle of Life." She is a member of the International Society of Poets.

**Malon, Diana L.** - Born in 1952 in San Francisco to Richard and Jacqueline Lewis, and now works and lives in Salinas, California. Believing in family and community, she is active in the Auxiliary of the American Legion Post #31 in Salinas. Diana is currently working on the completion of her 14th manuscript of poetry, after having self-published a previous title *Rainbows in the Darkness* in which she reflects upon those experiences in life that she experiences. Her talents are varied. She is an accomplished oil painter, and pays particular attention to landscapes, which reflect an attempt to find that same tranquility in life. She expresses herself in the local newspapers in order to again bring forward her thoughts about life and living in our society. Diana has been published in several anthologies. Among them are *Whispers* and *Inspirations* anthologies by Iliad Press and *Distinctions of Excellence* by Cader Publishing, Ltd.; as well as *Best Poems of 1997* and *Songs on the Wind* by The National Library of Poetry. Diana has also won various Editor's Choice awards in 1995, 1997, and 1998. She was also awarded Honorable Mention by the NAR for the Longfellow Competition as well as Honorable Mention for the Poet of the Year Competition. Most recently she received recognition in the 1999 Spring Issue of *Verses Magazine* and was published in *Who's Who in New Poets* in 1996. She states, "I try to be mindful of the Soul's innate need to soar, and I feel I am blessed by being able to release through writing, not only my own, but other's weight of thought as well." Diana is also known as *The Blupoet* in her locality.

**Markley, Mary Ann** - Born in Annapolis, Maryland May 1, 1969. Nicknamed "Binky" which came from the pacifier she loved. Raised and nurtured by her young mother, Janet. Knowing wealth only in the internal realm, they absorbed life's free and plentiful treasures bestowed from above. Janet instilled great values in Mary Ann's heart; most prominently love kind respect of nature, children, and elders. Her parents divorced when she was five and she was abandoned by her father. An abusive step-father created a home of chaotic turmoil, resulting in her brief marriage to the same type. Through spiritual work, Mary Ann became whole again. She earned a Fine Arts/Art History degree from St. Mary's College of Southern Maryland and was certified at Towson State University to teach Art. She excelled as an Elementary School Art Teacher. Mary Ann sustained a debilitating injury while lifting clay. Mary Ann's kindred spirit enables her to survive the trauma of losing a precious career, the chronic pain of myfacial syndrome and fibromyalgia, her anxieties, and life goals now more challenging to achieve. To cope, she recalls the cherished moments and lessons of childhood. A beautiful new marriage has granted immeasurable happiness. A precious country home adorned with trees, gardens of plenty, adorable pets, and bounty of nature enable her to be strong, hopeful, and gracious. She maintains solace within and is afforded serenity from invaluable rewards given by God, her mother, soul mate and husband, Kieffer, and amazing caretakers. She now recognizes her "gift" and continues to share her message with others. Because of who she has become, Mary Ann never wishes to change life as she's known it and relishes in the promises of how she will live her tomorrows. Mary Ann has been published by Iliad Press, Sparrowgrass Poetry Forum, The National Library of Poetry, The poetry Guild, J. Mark Press, Quill Books Poetry, Chapel Recording Company, Ephimera Publishing, School Arts and True Experiences Magazines, and Charity competitions. Her works have received several awards.

**Martinez, Katrina Francesca Rustia** - Born September 16, 1981 in Maila, Philippines to parents Albert and Maria Martinez. She has two older sisters, Johanna and Clarissa. For elementary school, Katrina attended Beverly Farms in Potomac, Maryland. For middle school and ninth and tenth grades, she went to Stone Ridge in Bethesda, Maryland. In eleventh and twelfth grades, she moved to Tahoma Alternative Program and Bethesda-Chevy Chase High School, both in Bethesda, Maryland. Tentative plans for higher education include majoring in English and attending law school. Katrina's poems, "On Apostrophizing" and "The Eternal Flame" have received Fourth Place awards in the Winter and Spring 1998 Iliad Literary contests, respectively. "On Apostrophizing" is included in *Distinctions of Excellence*, printed by Cader Publishing, Ltd. Two other poems written by Katrina, "Dreams Fulfilled" and "In My Eyes (Before and After)" received Honorable Mentions in the Winter Iliad Literary contest. She has been selected for the 1999 President's Recognition of Literary Excellence. Katrina's personal statement: "I would like to thank my twelfth grade English teacher, Mr. Boswell, for providing me with the incentive to write and write well."

**Martin, Sarah** - Born January 9, 1981 to loving parents John and Loralee Martin. Older sister to Sean and a step sister to Mike and Sable. I enjoy many activities such as highland dancing which I did for twelve years and I played the bagpipes for five years with the Brighton Pipe Band. However, my most consuming hobby is writing poetry, which I have done since I was young. After traveling down a few of life's bumpy roads, I continued to write but I began to express myself through my poems. I used my life experiences as my inspiration and my feelings as my words. I received an Honorable Mention in 1997. My poem "I Know Now" has been published by Iliad Press in their 1997 book *Moments*. My support comes from my family and my boyfriend. They have given me so much strength and they encourage me to do the best that I can achieve. I usually go by the pen name Angel, and when ever I am asked where my creativity comes from, I simply reply, "My heart is my pen."

**McCormack, Dona Lou** - Born December 17, 1980 in Sandusky, Ohio to parents Dr. Lawrence and April McCormack. Dona is the second of four siblings: Lawrence John, Constance Jeanne and Jessica Lynn. Dona's residence is still in Sandusky, however she is a junior at Howe Military School in Howe, Indiana where she is a member of the local chapter of the National Honor Society. She is also active in intense military physical training including Jr. ROTC, martial arts and has lettered in swimming competition and girl's volleyball. In addition to her love of writing, she is also an accomplished pianist, sings in her school choir, as well as the choir in her home church, St. Paul's Episcopal Church, Norwalk, Ohio. She also enjoys painting and sculpting. Upon graduation from Howe Military School, she will be attending college and graduate school.

**McGran-Reber, Maureen** - Born August 12, 1958 in Sommerville, Massachusetts to parents Thomas and Phyliss McGran. At the age of one and a half moved to Dedham, Massachusetts, where she resided for thirty years. At six her parents and she drove across America. She attended the neighborhood Charles J. Capen Elementary School, where she later returned and taught. She attended Dedham Junior and Senior High. There her love for education, history, literature, writing and artistic talents were greatly encouraged, as well as by both her parents. Her first book was a "How To" book, done for a Dedham High, Children's Literature class. She was honored when it was displayed at the Dedham Public Library. At Dedham High she helped develop and implement a Teachers Aide Program. Students interested in teaching went into elementary schools, were paired with seasoned teachers to begin developing their craft of teaching. Growing up in Dedham instilled strong community values and respect for ones roots. Her parents, both from the city of Boston, encouraged and nurtured the wealth of opportunities that Boston offered. History and culture always a shared interest and continuum of family activities. She received her Bachelor of Science in Education from Boston State College and her Master of Education in Special Education from Bridgewater State College. On July 4, 1991, she married her husband Gary Reber, in the historical Kings Chapel, on the Freedom Trail, in downtown Boston. From there group pictures were taken at the swan Boats in Boston's Public Gardens. The reception was held at Dedham's Endicott Estate. As guests arrived the aroma of the traditional 4th of July barbecue greeted them. Now married eight years they reside on Cape Cod. She is an active member of The Cape Cod Writers' Center. For fourteen years she has been teaching Special Education in the peaceful, multicultural, pleasant, seaside community of Wareham, Massachusetts. Her literary work has earned her Honorable Mention in the summer 1998 Iliad Literary Awards and the 1999 President's Recognitions of Literary Excellence, from the National Authors Registry. Recently attending Emerson College her desire to write and develop her voice has been reignited.

**McGuire, Barbara Ann** - Born September 14, 1938 in Salida, Colorado to parents Robert and Viola Jackson. In 1940, my father who worked for the Union Pacific Railroad, was transferred to Green River, Wyoming. I graduated from Green River High School in 1957. I was married March 1, 1957, in Lyman Wyoming; my children are Ernie williams, Jr., Jerry Williams, Barbara White, Evan Williams and Tiffanie Bonella. I have twelve grandchildren, and two great grandchildren. I started writing poetry in 1965, when my children were small. In 1998, I received the President's Recognition for Literary Excellence for the poem "Maybe Skydiving Is For Me." This poem is published in *Commemorating Excellence* from the National Authors Registry. I have received three Honorable Mention Awards from Cader Publishing, Ltd. I write all kinds of things, animals, children, predicaments, you name it. I want my poetry to make people laugh, and make them forget some of their everyday problems.

**McNeely, Robin Renee'** - Born January 30th in Bethesda, Maryland to parents, John and Doris. Being a "Navy Brat," Robin moved several times before the age ten until her parents settled back in suburban Pittsburgh to be closer to their own parents. Robin graduated from Bethel Park Sr. High School and then attended West Virginia University where she majored in Medical Technology receiving her BS degree in 1983. Presently, Robin is working as a Lab Manager for a small hospital in Northern Virginia. Over the years, Iliad Press, JMW publishing, as well as the International Library of Poetry have honored Robin's poetry. Robin has been writing poetry since her teens and has been published in over fifty anthologies since 1978. Poetry is a form of therapy for Robin, her purest form of self-expression. Currently single, she enjoys the outdoors, animals, cross-stitching and singing with a local choir.

**Meehan, Jessie** - Born to the name of Jessica Marie Meehan on January 17, 1984 in Salt Lake City, Utah. She has lived all her life in Park City, Utah, and is now attending Park City High School. She was very blessed to be born to her family of two parents (which are still together), and one brother; and especially blessed to have such a strong relationship with her Grandfather. He taught her morals, and helped her to learn and love. They were two peas plucked from the same pod, they were inseparable. When Jessie was about ten years old, her very loved Grandfather was taken in the night by Cancer. Jessie was devastated, and didn't trust anyone anymore. All of her thoughts were bottled up, until one day she wrote some of those thoughts down onto paper. With the help of her writing and Christ, she has felt joy again. It has been five years since his death, but she will always write about him. A way to mourn for him. Thanks to her savior, Jesus Christ, she would not be as successful with her writing as she is now; being published three different times. This now fifteen-year-old author looks forward to going to college and hopefully taking up a career in writing. "All her thanks goes to her grandfather for inspiration, and her heavenly father, God."

**Miller, Ken** - Born July 30, 1949 in Morgantown, West Virginia. His mother divorced his father when Ken was one year old. Ken's mother took him to live with her parents in Washington, D.C. and Ken's grandmother raised him until he was eight years old. He then lived with his mother and her third husband in Lanham, Maryland until another divorce eight years later. After graduating from high school, Ken attended Prince George's Community College in Largo, Maryland. He transferred to The American University in Washington, D.C. in 1972, and earned a B.A. degree in Communications. Ken worked as a U.S. Congressional caseworker from 1970 through 1992. He now works for Safeway in Dunkirk, Maryland as a dairy stocker and checker. Ken first wrote poetry when he was a teenager. He thought of his poetry as song lyrics. He wanted to be a singer songwriter like Bob Dylan or have a band like The Doors. Ken wrote love poems to Sheryl Blanchett while they were dating and then stopped writing poetry. They got married on February 12, 1972, and have a daughter. In 1995, Ken's mother inspired him to again write poetry. Ken is now a member of the International Society of Poets. Their National Library of Poetry has published twelve of his poems and six of his poems have been recorded for their *Sound of Poetry* series. He received a third prize in The National Library of Poetry's North American Open Poetry Contest in 1998. He received an Honorable Mention Award from Cader Publishing, Ltd., and the 1999 President's Recognition for Literary Excellence from The National Authors Registry. His poem "Doomed Children" is published in *Moments* by Iliad Press. A member of The National Authors Registry, Ken says, "My poems can be pretty intense. However, by writing them I have gotten something out of my system, which seems to be a positive release. I hope anyone who reads something I have written will find the work helpful or cathartic. To have someone relate to what I am saying would be truly rewarding."

**Mosten, Jordana Lynne** - Born September 10, 1984 at St. John's Hospital in Santa Monica, California. She is an only child to parents Claudia Parodi and Forrest Mosten. As a child of divorce from the age of one, she has lived in both the Valley and West side of Los Angeles. Jordana currently attends Marlborough High School as an honor roll student in the ninth grade. She spends her free time writing poetry, swimming, practicing speech and debate, acting, and managing props for various school productions. Jordana is an avid reader, which has inspired her written work. Her preferred authors range from John Steinbeck, Robert Graves, and Mark Twain. Jordana's interest in poetry began in the seventh grade when doing a report on poetry. "The Path" is her first published work expressing her fears of the future. Jordana is strongly influenced and encouraged by her mother. Jordana writes poetry because, "I have so many intense emotions erupting inside myself, that poetry is my creative outlet."

**Mourashkin, Boris** - prolific composer, performer, and poet, Bio-Sensor Sound Therapist was born in Kemerovo, Siberia, February 27, 1949. He is a Russian pioneer and founder of the *Healing Power of Music* and a world renowned expert in the field of Music Therapy. He graduated from the Novosibirsk Musical College and studied theory and composition at the M.I. Glinka Conservatory. In 1998, Mr. Mourashkin was elected as an *Academician - Member of the International Informatization Academy* (*IIA*). The *IIA* is sponsored by the United Nations and is part of the *Worlddidac with UNESCO*. The *IIA* concerns itself with the acquisition, crediting, and taxonomy of all new information in all fields of human endeavor. Mr. Mourashkin discovered his special *Bio-Energetic Psychotropic Music*™ after suffering sever injuries in an automobile accident in 1982. While working in the recording studio, he discovered that certain frequencies, tones and vibrations found in his music seemed to relieve his pain, so he began his research on *sound psycho-neuroreflect therapy*. Since 1983, he has been creating *"Healing Music"* that soothes the entire human system. Mr. Mourashkin writes music in various styles: choir music, piano composition, compositions for string orchestras, incidental music and music scores for films and plays. Sine 1979, he has been working on his poetry and prose. Mr. Mourashkin has also performed in various films and has been audio director for Novosibirsk-Telefilm. He has traveled extensively—having been in the Arctic Circle at least nine times — and has performed across the USA. Awards: *Volunteer of the Year Award*, St. Christopher-Ottilie Home, Sea Cliff, New York, Volunteer Service: Manhattan Psychiatric Center, Wards Island, New York,(1997 to present); Gift of Life, Inc.,(1993 to present); Siberian Prison, (1976-1989); Siberian Orphanage (1972-1989). Memberships: International Informatization Academy (1998); Cinematographer's Union of Russian Federation (1989); Distinguished member of The International Society of Poets, and member of The National Authors Registry, 1999 President's Recognition for Literary Excellence. Mr. Mourashkin is a Scientific Consultant of Research Laboratory (Bio-Energetic Music) for Bio-Energetics and Ecology of Consciousness, at the Russian Federation Institute of Human Ecology, Academy of Technological Sciences, since 1993 to present. Credits and Publication: several music recordings, conferences, radio interviews, TV interview, and articles. Discography: (Published by The Relaxation Company, Roslyn, NY): CD - "Points of Light" (1994), "Healing Music;" (Four Pioneers Explore the Healing Powers of Music) - (Acoustic Research Series, 1998). Bio-Energetic Psychotropic Music; Disk One - "Touching the Mystical of Outer Space;" Disk Two - "Night of Open Doors" (1995).

**Nagelberg, Barbara** - Born on October 27, 1949, daughter of Bernard and Eleanor Kramer. I grew up in Freeport, New York. I graduated from Freeport High School as a member of the National Honors Society. I attended Hofstra University graduating with honors and obtaining a BA degree in Elementary Education and a minor in Psychology. I have been married to my college sweetheart, Marc, for 28 years. My husband is a Special Education teacher, as well as my biggest supporter and fan of my writing. We have two sons who are attending college, who also are proud of my writing accomplishments. We lived in the hamlet of Copiague, New

York for twenty-three years. When my children were in school full time, I attended Long island University and received my MA in Special Education, graduating with a 4.0 cum. Awards received are: Nominated for the Poet of the Year for 1998 and 1999; First Place, "On Becoming a Man," *Ages and Stages, The Wonder Years*, (Poetry Unlimited, 1997); Poet of the Year and Editor's Choice Awards, "The World At My Feet," *The Helping Hand* and "Searching," *Notable American Poets* (J.Mark Press, 1998); 1999 President's Recognition for Literary Excellence by The National Authors Registry; Editor's Choice (National Library of Poetry, 1997); Honorable Mention, "Dream Of Love," Iliad Press; Third Place, "World Poet," *Word Weaver*. Memberships included are: Distinguished Member of The International Society of Poets; member of several writing clubs and newsletters. I also belong to several gardening clubs. While teaching severely brain injured children, I received a severely debilitating back injury. Yet, after losing my life long goal of teaching, I received an unusual gift. Writing poetry is a magnificent way of expressing feelings and observations that have evolved from life's continuous struggles and joys. Adaptive gardening has also inspired me to see the beauty of flowers and life, not the weeds that get in the way.

**Nations, Lynn** - (Pen name: L.E. Nations) Born April 18, 1943 in Darnestown, Maryland to parents, Rev. William L. and Norma Everhart with one sister and two brothers. Being a minister's family meant moving several times before they settled in Jeffersonville, Pennsylvania when Lynn was six years old. At age sixteen, the family then moved to a church in Engelwood, Florida where she graduated from Venice Senior High School in 1961. It was there she met her husband, Jimmy E. Nations and they were married in 1962 and have two sons. After living in Los Angeles, California and Washington, D.C. for thirteen years, Lynn and the boys moved to Winter Haven, Florida where they now reside. She is employed at the Red Lobster as a server and has been there for ten years now. Lynn has been writing poetry for only a year and a half, but believes she has always been a poet in her soul, even as a child. She has received Honorable Mention Award from Cader Publishing, Ltd. in the spring 1998 for her poem "Solitude" which also is published in *Crossroads* by Iliad Press. Also in that same year Lynn's poem "My Little Dove" is published in *Of Time and Tide* by The National Library of Poetry, her poem "Treasures of My Heart" is published in *Best New Poems* by Poet's Guild and her poem "The Hand of God" is published in *The Helping Hand* by J. Mark Press. Lynn says, "I have always had a passion for words and now have found a way to use that passion to express my feelings and thoughts. I truly love to write and hope my poetry may in some way give someone else just a portion of the enjoyment it has given me in its creation."

**Nielsen, Dana** - born on February 2, 1982 in Saskatoon, Saskatchewan, Canada to parents Lloyd and Margaret Nielsen. Have only one brother named William. Lived in Buffalo Narrows, Saskatchewan for 14 years. Then moved to Norway House, Manitoba in 1996, now living there for three years. Attending grade 11 at Norway House High School. I've been writing poetry steadily since the age of 13. Also, a few more poems have been published and hope to keep writing poetry in the future.

**O'Bryant, Cathy** - Born January 5, 1941 in Camden, New Jersey to parents, James and Ruth Jackson. Seventh of nine children born to that union. Married and separated with five children while earning an Associates in Arts from Camden County College and a Bachelors in Psychology from Glassboro State (Rowan) College both with honors. Currently divorced, retired, and have five grandchildren ages 2-10 years. Affiliations have included: Allegheny East Conference Women's Ministries, National Alliance of Black Social Workers, Phila. Chapter Black Women's Health Project, National Women's Conference Committee, Former Director D.C. National Congress of Neighborhood Women, and Assistant State Chairperson of New Jersey Welfare Rights Organization. Conducted awareness workshop at IWY conference in Narobi, Kenya in 1985. Continue work-shops, speaking engagements and poetry recitals at various conferences, churches and community forums throughout the United States. Has self-published a book of poems and short stories entitled "If My People." Recipient of The Bronze Star Award for Outstanding Achievement in creative writing by the Cherry Hill, New Jersey Chapter of the National Hook Up of Black Women. Founder and Director of Poetic Skits n Sketches, Inc. [Geared to fledgling young poets (still in planning stages)]. Other published poems each received Honorable Mention and appeared in the following 1998 anthologies: "Take Power" the 1999 President's Award of Literary Excellence by the National Authors Registry; "Give Them Oil in Their Lamp" Poetic Voice of America by Sparrowgrass; "Gone Fishing" The Promise of Dawn by the National Library of Poetry; "Where Is God" Great Poems of Today by the Poetry Guild. As a Christian writer my theme remains: "My heart is overflowing with a beautiful thought! I will write a lovely poem to the king, for I am as full of words as the speediest writer pouring out his story." Psalms 45:1 (TLB)

**Oldham, Paige** - Born July 31, 1982 in Adana, Turkey on Incirlik Air Force Base, to Carolyn Darling and David Oldham. When Paige moved from overseas with her parents and her older brother, they moved to South Carolina for about a year, and then moved to Rhode Island. There, Paige was blessed with a younger sister named Ashley. After Ashley was born, Paige's family went on long vacations to Colebrook, New Hampshire. The family decided they liked it so much, they wanted to move to the North Country. Paige started school at Colebrook Junior High where she participated in many school activities. Paige was president of the school newspaper and had one of her poems published in *A Celebration of Young Poets* in her eighth grade year. She said her seventh and eighth grade English teacher encouraged her to keep writing, and told her if she put her mind to it, she could achieve just about anything. After graduating from junior high, she moved on the Colebrook Academy. Now in her junior year, she has been having great success with her poetry. "Dad, I Still..." has received an Honorable Mention award from Cader Publishing, Ltd., and the 1999 President's Recognition for Literary Excellence award from The National Authors Registry. As a new member to The National Authors Registry, Paige says, "Writing poetry comes with many dreams and challenges that she's not afraid to tackle and is looking forward to pursuing."

**O'Neal, Lillian M** - Born August 29, 1939 in Boston, Massachusetts to Arthur and Olive Morgan. I was one of six children. My father worked two jobs to put food on our table, while my mother worked as a homemaker. I am a graduate of the Jerimiah Burke High School. I am the mother of ten children: Danita (forty-two), Arthur (forty), Cynthia (thirty-eight), Kendra (thirty-six), Anthony (thirty-four), Rosalea (twenty-seven), Tamara (twenty-five), Melissa (twenty-three), Roosevelt (twenty), and Eddie (sixteen). I am also proud and blessed grandmother of twenty-five grandchildren and the great grandmother of five great grandchildren. To this date, I have authored and published a total of twenty-one poems. My credits include five Editor Choice Awards from the National Library of Poetry; eight Honorable Mention Awards from Iliad Press; and now two President Awards from the National Authors Registry. I have been inducted into the National Library Hall of Fame, the International Poet's Society and have been published on the web. I am Supervisor with the United States Postal Service and presently serve at the Boston, Massachusetts Post Office. During my employment with the Post Office I have written poems dedicated to: Aids Awareness Day, Multicultural Day; Veteran's Day; and the unveiling of the new Malcom X stamp. During the unveiling ceremony, my poem "I believe This" was also read to Malcolm X's family. The subject poem was also read at the Black Achievements Awards ceremony hosted by Boston Mayor Thomas Menino. I have also written a poem titled "Corridor Of Their Minds" in recognition of Mr. Robert Winfrey a music teacher who taught at the Rollin Hayes School of Music. This poem was also read at the Black Achievement Awards Ceremony. Mayor Menino praised both poems and personally thanked me for "a wonderful, wonderful job." In addition to the previously mentioned poetry, I have written for Sparrowgrass and the Poetry Guild. Another poem I authored titled "Unselfish Sacrifices" and dedicated to firefighters was published by the Boston Fire Department Newsletter. I have also shared my poem "In The Line Of Duty" dedicated to Police Officers with the Boston Police Department. I am presently in the process of writing five short stories at the request of an individual. Hopefully they will be in print shortly. "Dare to dream----------Then write it down!"

**Otegui, Jorge** - Born June 30, 1948, in Buenos Aires, Argentina, to parents Jorge and Elsa. In 1974 he married Cristina Otamendi and they have three children: Soledad, Rafael, and Martin. In 1984 the family moved to Neuquen, a main city in Patagonia, the southernmost extreme in South America. His poetical works are published in Spanish, his mother tongue, but he loves to write poetry in English, too. His work "Pieces" received an Honorable Mention in the Summer 1998 Iliad Literary Awards and has recently been selected for the 1999 President's Recognition of Literary Excellence.

**Paterson, Gloria** - (Pen name: Mrs. Brian Paterson, Ms. Gloria Paterson). Author of "Wave Lengths." Born December 1946 in Detroit, Michigan to Millard and Irene Lutz. Studied SE, Pe, Rec. Eng. Occupations: Songwriter, Poet, Cashier, Secretary, Pharmacy Clerk, Post Office, McDonald's, Hostess. Family: four sisters, one brother, three children, three grand children.

**Pederson, Tamara** - Born April 1, 1982 in Saskatchewan, Canada to parents, Wendy and Lewis. Moved to Alberta in 1991. Tamara has always enjoyed reading and writing and is currently enrolled in high school. At seventeen years old she is an aspiring singer/songwriter and someday hopes to pursue a career in the fine arts. Tamara says her inspiration not only is derivative of her friends and family, but her appreciation of nature. She has received honorable mention from Cader Publishing, and one from the National Library of Poetry. Published in numerous books Tamara hopes to continue her already successful literary career.

**Peets, Erica** - Born May 10, 1953 in St. Kitts (Caribbean) to Arlington and Winifred Peets. Her family settled in St. Thomas during her teen years where she stayed until she migrated to Augusta, Georgia. Having a love for reading and writing, Erica decided to further her education. Graduating from Charlotte Amalie High School in St. Thomas, she attended the University of the Virgin Islands. There she earned a Bachelor of Arts in Social Sciences and Secondary Education. Erica is currently a veteran teacher of over twenty-two years and has also earned a Master of Arts in Counseling and Psychology from Laharoi Bible College and a Master of Arts in Counseling from Friends International Christian University. She's received two honorable mentions awards from Cader Publishing, Ltd and the 1999 President's Recognition for Literary Excellence from the National Authors Registry. Her short story "Raging Inferno" is published by Iliad Press. Erica has two children and is devoted to studying and writing.

**Pegg, Mary Christina** - Poetess and Catholic, born October 28, 1960 in Los Angeles, California. The daughter of William Joseph Pegg, a sales Engineer of Mexican descent who was president at one time of his own Management Consulting Firm, and Gertrud Anna Speis, a West German. Her early childhood was spent in Mexico City, Mexico attending school. During the summer at age fifteen, she began to teach English as a second language to Mexican businessmen and others. She graduated from Wichita State University, Wichita, Kansas, with honors and she received a fellowship to study Economics at the University of Wisconsin-Madison in 1985. She entered the United States Air Force in 1987 as an enlisted woman for two years and seven months; she was a Commissary Accounting Technician on Andrews Air Force Base. She became severely disabled in May of 1990 and was awarded Social Security at a later date. She also received service-connected disability payments from the Department of Veterans Affairs in October of 1993. She has been trying to cope with her disability and she is dedicating her time to reciting, reading and writing poetry; because of her disability, her progress in poetry writing is extremely slow. Some of her great poems are: "God Wakes Me Up," "God's Love," "Love, America!," "The American Flag Anthem," "Ode To A Robin," "Holy Spirit," and "Our Letter to God."

**Peterson, Marion M.** - Born Vernadine M. Lyons on March 25, 1921 in Lansing, Michigan, to parents Ward and Nina Lyons. Attending school in Lansing, she lived in or near the Lansing area until 1986. Married to Clifford Peterson in 1943, they had two children. She has been a cook, worked in nursing homes, and worked at the Michigan School For The Blind when she retired in 1984. She started writing poetry at the age of seventy-one. She has received six Honorable Mentions awards from Cader Publishing, Ltd., and three Editor's Choice awards from the National Library of Poetry. She has also been a member of the VFW Auxiliary Post 4090 in Portland, Michigan, for twenty-two years. In 1986, she moved to Lake City, Michigan, to be closer to her daughter, six grandchildren, and her four great-grandchildren. Her hobbies include: crocheting, quilting, card games, reading, and writing poetry. She had her name legally changed to Marion M. Peterson in 1982. She is also a distinguished member of International Society of Poets.

**Petrilli, Ryan** - Born in Wilmington, Delaware. He began writing poetry when he was fourteen. He currently resides in Charlotte, North Carolina and continues to write when work doesn't consume the majority of his day. He attended High Point University and moved south to join his older brother. When he has some spare time he enjoys the outdoors: hiking, running, traveling, skiing, and landscaping, as well as doing volunteer work within the city. Ryan is an avid songwriter and has had over twenty songs recorded, plus he has received recognition for his achievement in both songwriting and poetry, with numerous poems published in various anthologies. He has three Honorable Mentions from The Iliad Press, 1998 Poet of the Year Award with J. Mark Press, Editor's Choice Award in 1997, 1998, and 1999 with The National Library of Poetry; plus he has received the 1998 President's Recognition for Literary Excellence from The National Authors Registry. He has received a first place and third place award in two separate songwriting contests and a Trailblazer Award for independent songwriters in 1997 and 1998. Ryan draws the majority of his inspiration from people and nature. He is captivated by the growth and changes that take place in each season, and all the facets of wonder within them. People move him in every way possible to the closeness he shares with his family and friends to simple observation of fascinating strangers. Marriages, births, special occasions, and special times are some of the topics that have inked his journal, along with the many ups and downs of life's experiences through happiness and sorrow with triumph and heartaches always seeming to have his page turning. The future ahead is filled with a lot of excitement with different opportunities as he is working with The Institute of Children's Literature, continually writing poems and songs, and now he has begun writing screenplays. Ryan follows his heart in life, thankful for the blessings within each day. Ryan says, "I write from my heart, for it will see and feel more than my eyes and hands ever will."

**Phillips, Heather** - Born on July 25, 1985 in Newhall, California to her parents Susan and John Phillips. She has three brothers younger than herself. At age thirteen she received an Honorable Mentions award from Cader Publishing, Ltd. and the 1999 President's Recognition for Literary Excellence from the National Authors Registry. She has also received many language awards from school and awards in sports. She enjoys writing in her journal during her summer vacation, and she plans on doing so for many years to come. Her poem "Candles in the Sky" is published in *Distinctions of Excellence* by Iliad Press. Heather says, "I just hope to be successful in achieving all of my goals in life."

**Plunkett, Joseph "C.J."** - was born in Centerville, Tennessee on December 3, 1933. He received the Ph.D. Degree from Texas A&M University, MSEE from Georgia Institute of Technology, BSEE from the University of Tennessee, and a B.S. from Middle Tennessee State University. After several years as an Engineer-Scientist in the field of Radar and Communications, he spent approximately 20 years in the university teaching. He has published numerous technical articles and book chapters. He has been biographed in numerous international publications, including: Marquis' *Who's Who in the World, International Book of Honor, The International Who's Who of Intellectuals* (Cambridge, England), and *The First Five Hundred* (Cambridge, England). He served as an Army Reserve Officer through the rank of Captain. Since retirement, he has pursued creative writing as a hobby, and often uses the pen name, "Bo Tandy Margruder".

**Pritchett, Michael T.** - I've always disliked writing my own biography. To me it seemed self aggrandizing. But here is my meager offering. I am a sixty-year-old retired professor of English and speech living in Sylva, North Carolina. I have held many jobs: Race Relations Specialist, Career Guidance Counselor, newspaper reporter, carpenter, professional diver, and was once a *talking house*. I was selected for *Who's Who Among America's Teachers'* and am currently a Distinguished Member of the International Society of Poets, and inducted into the International Poetry Hall of Fame in 1997. I have published over thirty poems, eight of which have won awards and recognition and six which have been translated into five languages. These are things that I have accomplished, but it is not who I am. Here is who I probably am. (I am Bipolar I). In my anthology there isn't just one me. There is the suicidal me, the romantic me, the angry me, the reflective me, the sardonic me, the loving me, the lonely me, and the observant me, and I am sure other me's I've yet to realize. My Manic Depressive disorder has allowed me to let my imagination soar into the realms of the unknown and inspired me to soaring heights, and demonic lows. I wistfully think of those times that I could flit like a butterfly and suck all the nectar of the sweet earth, and I dreaded the days looking through barred windows and feeling as if I was terribly alone in dark turbulent sea. This is who I am!

**Pustaver, Cory E.** - Cory E. Pustaver, a.k.a. Thunder Wolf. Born October 18, 1974 in Concord, Massachusetts. Growing up in Sudbury, Massachusetts, Cory found out at an early age that she really loved arts, especially theatre and writing. Upon graduating from Lincoln-Sudbury Regional High School, she left home to start college, as an oceanography major, at the Florida Institute of Technology. Finding that this was not for her she returned to New England and her first love, the arts.3fai Cory is currently working on her B.A. at Franklin Pierce College. She is majoring in theatre arts with a technical concentration, and will be graduating in May of this year. Cory has also studied photography, stained glass and creative writing. In her free time she loves to write poetry and the occasional short story. The surrounding environment of woods, lakes, and mountains, provides plenty of inspiration for her writing. Much of her writing focuses on the natural world as well as her own private world and emotions. Cory feels a very close connection to the planet and all of its inhabitants. Animals especially have been a great source of inspiration, helping her to grow and learn. Often her work will be set in the Medieval or Renaissance times. These two periods have been a source of fascination for her and she loves to attended the local Renaissance fairs whenever she can. As a big fan of science fiction and fantasy, Cory loves to write dragon stories, space odysseys, and the like. She is also a Nationally Registered Emergency Medical Technician, and has plans to enter the field of emergency medicine and eventually go into search and rescue. Eventually, she hopes to be able to be retire to a beautiful log cabin surrounded by woods and mountains, but until then she plans to make the most of her life. "If you're not having fun, you're not really living!"

**Radula, Natalia** - The daughter of Thomas and Mia Grandin (both gifted radio broadcasters during World War II). Natalia has been writing since she was capable of holding a pencil, and is blessed with a nurturing family who encourage her to find words for all things she holds most precious, particularly her husband of thirty-five years, Rod, and their four pawed "child" Alice Rose. Natalia feels that life itself is her best education and valued profession: ever attempting to be good Christian, loving wife and mommy, caring sister, niece, and honest friend. She is a member on The Authors Registry, Distinguished Member of The International Society of Poets, and in 1996 was elected into The International Poetry Hall of Fame, being awarded her own site of the World Wide Web (html//www.poets.com/Natalia Radula.htm). Her work has appeared in both domestic and foreign publications, including *The Poets Corner Magazine*, and anthologies published by The National Library of Poetry (she received the Editor's Choice Award 1996, 1997, and 1998) The Poetry Guild, Iliad Press, Sparrowgrass Poetry Forum, and Horizon Poetry Press. Her personal favorites are her short stories about Alice Rose which have been featured in *The Yorkshire Terrier* Magazine.

**Ramick, Ricky** - Born on Veterans Day, November 11, 1960 in Heidelberg, Germany to James William Ramick and Now, Jeanne Cleveland. After his tour of duty, Ricky's father moved the family to San Francisco, California. In 1973, the family of two sons, Ricky, and Mark; three daughters, Terry,

Kimberly and Georgina moved to San Jose, California. Ricky was a student at Overfelt High School, but in 1978 chose to take a GED, rather than continue in school. At that time he went to work for a Computer Circuit Board Plating Company in Santa Clara, California. In 1979, Ricky's family decided to move back to Lawton, Oklahoma, his mothers hometown. In 1980, Ricky began an intimate seven year relationship with Dana Spencer. On December 18, 1983 a son was born to this couple. Ricky named his son Todd Eric, but his mother chose to give him her maiden name rather than Ramick. Ricky is very proud of his son, Todd Eric Spencer and they enjoy a loving relationship, although living apart, Ricky in Tulsa, Oklahoma and Todd with his mother in Lawton, Oklahoma. Ricky has worked several occupations. He has four years experience as a pressman and three years in oil field construction. In August of 1988 he moved to Sebring, Florida to build boats with Wellcraft Marine. Ricky is now working for C & S Insulation of Tulsa, Oklahoma. The National Authors Registry selected Ricky to receive the 1999 President's Recognition of Literary Excellence for his literary work, "Dad" which received Honorable Mention in the Summer 1998 Iliad Literary Awards. He also received an official invitation to The Best of Quill Poetry competition for his poem "Feel Me?". Ricky began writing in July of 1998 with no formal training other than high school. He writes of family, friends, and his feelings for them. His poems are from times in his life when emotion was a strong influence. At age thirty-eight and never married, Ricky says, "When inspired, I write down my thoughts, put the lines together later, if I can sit still long enough. On the go too much I guess."

**Read, Crystal** - Born June 15, 1983 in Hanover, NH to parents Tammy Richardson Read and George Read Jr. She is an only child, but looks forward to coming home after a tiring day of working at the local cinema, or school, and being by herself for a while after having to deal with rude, judgmental people. She lives in a large farmhouse in Gilford, NH. Being a junior at Gilford Middle High School, she loves to keep herself busy. Her hobbies are piano, singing, figure skating, swing dancing, music, movies, acting, reading Anne Rice's vampire books, and collecting angel figurines. Contradicting? Maybe. But interesting. She also likes art, to workout, and obviously, writing. Besides that, she sings in her church choir. In the summer of '99, Crystal will be traveling to England, Ireland, and Wales as a member of the People to People Student Ambassadors Program. She's received one Honorable Mention award from Cader Publishing, Ltd., and the 1999 President's Recognition of Literary Excellence from the National Authors Registry. Her poem, "A Poem for the Abandoned" is published in *Distinctions of Excellence* by Iliad Press. And she'd like to say, "For entering a contest for poetry for the first time and actually receiving recognition, I am very grateful and hope that I can keep coming up with better work. It's great."

**Rea, Julie** - As her verse so aptly demonstrates, Julie has always shown a flair for the poetic and never once feared the consequence of wearing her heart on her sleeve. Throughout a colorful (if not always amiable) life, her career has been varied, versatile and very interesting. In the throes of housewifery and motherhood, dappled with sundry jobs of waitressing, receptioning, secretarying, title searching and black jack dealing, she has managed to keep pen in hand and create a special poetry that never fails to tug at the heart. Married nineteen years, and uncommonly young mother of two adult sons and grandmother to her precious Joslyn, she daily struggles and wins a most admirable battle with Multiple Sclerosis. Although we make her sound unique and undaunted here, it is the stuff of these very things that cause other people to know and understand her words when they read them-allow her readers to love these things they read. Julie's gift is her perception of what goes on before her eyes, and unfolds itself upon the paper she sets before her.

**Renate, Ursula** - Born and raised in Wygryny, Poland. She lived in Germany for a short time before moving to the United States in 1973. Now residing in Virginia, Ursula is the Vice President of a home service company and is an aspiring actress with one of the leading ad agencies on the East Coast. Ursula loves meeting new people and visiting new places. She enjoys nature, deep-sea fishing, and learning new tongues. She is fluent in four different languages. Ms. Renate writes poetry because she feels that it is one of the best ways to express her feelings and opinions. In writing, Ursula feels she can reach the highest expression in thinking with a deeper sense of life's meanings and values. By using poetry, Ursula hopes to draw more light into her readers' lives.

**Roberts, Heather** - Born March 7, 1980 in Lee's Summitt, MO., to parents Harvey and Jennifer Roberts. The third of four children, her family includes brother Jason Parker and wife Paula, sister Mary Parker and her son Blake, and brother Eric Roberts. Her family, including grandparents Lee and Mary Owen, make their homes in the small town of Bates City, MO. Heather attended Odessa High School until receiving her GED in August 1997. She is currently in her second semester at Blue River Community College, Blue Springs, MO., with hopes to transfer to the University of Missouri-Columbia School of Journalism, where she plans to earn a bachelor's degree in broadcast news. She has a goal of being a sports broadcaster/NFL analyst. During her first semester she has earned a 3.5 GPA and a spot on the Dean's List. She feels she owes a lot of her writing abilities to her sixth grade teacher Monica Baird and English Professor Paul Skidmore along with her family. Heather has enjoyed writing most of her life, but didn't open up to poetry until the age of fifteen. In the four years she has been writing poetry, she has received an Honorable Mention award from Iliad Press. Her proudest accomplishment as a writer, however, was writing a poem in memory of her great grandmother Mary Whiteside, who passed away on December 14, 1998, and having her cousin Bryan Hyatt read it as part of the eulogy. Heather says, "I write from my heart and soul, about my life and those who have touched it. I hope everyone who reads my writing can gain something from it, weather it be happiness or sadness, I hope they can relate."

**Rogers, Rozanne** - The only daughter of Ethel Nemer Rogers and John Reid Rogers, Jr. Born in Bonham, Texas on August 13, 1955. She and her family moved to Waco, Texas in 1959, where she currently resides with her three dogs and four cats. Rozanne graduated from Robinson High School in 1973. After attending McLennan Community College and Tarleton State University, she worked in Building/Construction for ten years. She then became Associate Executive Director of the Y.W.C.A in 1988. Now a self employed entrepreneur, Rozanne is an avid photographer and a skilled carpenter. She enjoys fishing, antiquing, and collecting. She is a big fan of "The X-Files" and "Xena: Warrior Princess." Rozanne says of poetry, "Poetry has given me a voice - a vessel through which I can communicate my innermost thoughts, needs and desires." She has had a number of poems and song lyrics published and has several scheduled for publication including: "Twenty-Two Years Today," "The Voice Within Me," "For A Friend," "The Carousel," "The Last Fairy Princess," "All Is Well," "Obsession," "Will You Dance With Me?," "A Legend In His Time," and "Oceans Of Blue."

**Rutherford, Ronald** - Born September 27, 1963 at Harper Hospital in Detroit, Michigan to parents, Earnest and Erma Rutherford. Which remarried to Arlie Stamper at the age of eight years old. During my teen years, settled in Michigan. Graduating from Roseville High School in 1981, also Enterprise High School. I began singing in bands since I was sixteen years old, I quit, began to learn how to play guitar. Then I met my wife Barbara Moore, we were married in 1992 and had a daughter Ashley Marie. Leaving Roseville after high school, I moved to Mt. Clemens, Michigan where I took courses in heating and cooling. While working at several different machine shops, I decided to become a machinist. I began writing poetry and lyrics for fourteen years off and on. I received a New York Pro/Am Song Jubilee Certificate of Achievement, two Award's of Merit Achievement, two Silver Poet Award's, Golden Poet Award and a Trophy. Lately I won an Honorable Mention and the 1999 President's Recognition of Literary Excellence. My personal statement, "My afflatus are the seeds, inspired from my heart, brandish into meaning the experiences of life and love. Fabulize especially to those who are, the closest moments to my thoughts, manifested through the realm of my memories, I love to express for all the world to read.

**Sanders, Kalene Denise** - I would like to first give honor and praise to God. Born January 10, 1981 in Montclair, California. I have been writing poetry and short stories since elementary school. I attended Fontana High School and was involved in the following: Christian Club, Indian Education Club, Colorguard Flag Team, Classroom Aide, Spanish Dancer, Ballet Student, "Church of God in Christ" Model and Usher. I also received certificates and was honored for: student member of the San Bernardino County Superintendent of Schools Regional Occupational Program, member of the International Poets Society, Awarded Who's Who Among American High School students, received Honorable Mention for three poems and awarded the 1999 President's Recognition of Excellence for one of my many poetic works. Working since the age of fifteen, I was involved in secretarial work, disabled student note taker, teachers aide, bilingual tutor, and a cashier. I graduated from high school in 1998 at age seventeen. Presently, I am attending San Jose State University, majoring in Occupational Therapy. Total, I have one hundred and fifty poems and am currently writing more. I thank God for this special gift and pray that my poetic words will touch the heart of at least one soul.

**Santiago, Miguel Angel** - Born on March 14, 1968 in Chicago, Illinois to parents Maria Julia Santiago and Miguel Rosado. My grandparents: Hilda Gonzalez and Jose A. Alvarado, nurtured me since my infancy. We lived in New York for a time, then in 1973 settled down in Boston, Massachusetts. I attended Brighton High School and then completed an Associate Degree in Liberal Arts. In 1993 I moved to Coamo, Puerto Rico, were I began to pursue a BA in Secondary Education, at the Pontifical Catholic University of Puerto Rico. It was there that I met my wife Martha J. Burgos. We got married September 16, 1995. We have three children: Miguel Angel, Michael Angelo and Marc Anthony (deceased six days after birth). I received an Honorable Mention and the 1999 President's Recognition for Literary Excellence for my poem "Marcelino." Writing is a liberation of the soul, thus inspiration is the birth pang of a creation yearning for freedom.

**Schick, Barbara** - Born: August 25, 1936 in Bakersfield, CA (Native

Californian). Parents: Adolph and Flora Schwartz. Married: Doyle Preston Schick (deceased) in Hollywood, CA. Children: Christy, Donna, Leila, Shem, Brian, and Nobi. 10 Grandchildren. Education: B.S., California State University, San Bernardino. Graduate Courses: Long Beach State University and Loma Linda University. Occupation: (Retired) Medical Record Analyst for Loma Linda University Medical Center. Membership: The National Authors Registry. Poetry Awards: Write for local newsletters. Personal Statement: "You don't find happiness. You cause it!"

**Schiefelbein, Justin** - Born November 10, 1982 in Pittsburgh, Pennsylvania to parents, Lee and Marilyn Schiefelbein. He has two older siblings, Lee Jr. and Hiedi Schiefelbein. He goes to school at West Allegheny Senior High School in Imperial, Pennsylvania. Justin began writing when he was fifteen and is still writing. He plans on going into the field of Technical Writing. He gets his ideas and motivation from the support of his family, friends, and teachers. Justin also plays soccer all year round. The awards that Justin has received are Honorable Mention in the Spring 1998 Iliad Literary Awards Program and he was also selected to receive the 1999 President's Recognition of Literary Excellence. Justin is now working on getting the children's book he wrote published. His favorite quote is "If you never try, you won't succeed."

**Schmalz, Nicholas** - Born May 26, 1980 in Sacramento, California to the parents of Kenneth and Linda Schmalz. Within eighteen hours of his birth, Nick was fighting for his life in surgery. He was born with a congenital heart defect which severely compromised his circulatory system. Over the period of seventeen years he fought for normalcy in his life. He was in and out of the hospital for tests, blood transfusions and three major open heart surgeries. Throughout it all, Nick kept his extraordinary sense of humor and love for life. He enjoyed the outdoors and loved to help kids. He volunteered as a Junior Safety Instructor for the DNR, as well as, a volunteer at the Children's museum. He was unable to participate in any strenuous physical activity but he was able to express his thoughts and feelings in writing. He completed a science fiction novelette for his writing class in school and received credit for two full English classes. His poem, "The Call" received Honorable Mention in the Winter 1998 Iliad Literary Awards. Nick would have been so proud to know his work was published, as are we, his parents. Nick died February 7, 1998 from complications while awaiting a heart-lung transplant, just a few months short of his eighteenth birthday.

**Schwartz, Aaron** - Born June 15th in Roswell, New Mexico to relatively average parents. Having lived as far west as Guam and as far east as Korea, he had a some what jaded view of the world. By the age of seventeen he has attended more than twenty-one schools from the Pacific to Europe, coming away with a deep love of learning and great loathing of education. Aaron has worked as a newspaper writer/photographer, cook, administrative clerk, security policeman, heavy equipment operator, electronics technician, and even as a career advisor. He is also an ordained minister, and sometimes teaches theology in his spare time. Aaron has been previously published in several anthologies, a few magazines and once even on a web site. He plans to slow down a bit when he's closer to middle-age.

**Spikes, Patricia White** - Born November 30, 1951 in Houston, Texas to parents Albert Carr and Willie Mae White. After graduating from the E.E. Worthing High School in 1969, she attended Texas Christian University in Fort Worth Texas and graduated in 1974 with a Bachelor of Science Degree in Biology and Medical Technology. She has two children, Sheatri and John II. She is married to John Ray Spikes. She is employed as a Senior Medical Technologist for the Harris County Hospital District and is a Community Relations Specialist for the City of Houston Health Department. A member of the Blueridge Baptist Church, Pat is involved in numerous community organizations and has been writing most of her life. Only recently has she started to published any of her writings. Of her writing, Pat says, "I love writing prose and poetry and I hope it will make a difference in someone's life."

**Staton, Diane Elizabeth** - Born in Baltimore, Maryland on March 27, 1941. Her parents were the late Eugene Woolford, Sr. and Minnie Elizabeth Woolford. She had one brother, the late Eugene Woolford, Jr. She married at an early age to James H. Staton, Sr. and had five children: James H. Staton Jr., Tyrone Staton, Darlene Staton-Brown, Kimberly Staton and Michele Watts. She left high school before completion, then later returned to Dunbar Senior Evening High School, in Baltimore, Maryland and received her high school diploma. Later, she attended the Community College of Baltimore and graduated with an Associates Degree. She was employed as an Income Maintenance Specialist with the Department of Human Resources for twenty-six years until she became ill and had to retire. At that time, her aging parents were also ill, which caused a very difficult time in her life. She wrote poems and stories as a child and during these difficult times in her life, found herself writing again. Her poetry, while therapeutic and personal to her, also made her realize that God was making a difference in her life. She received two awards from the National Library of Poetry and earned an Honorable Mention from Iliad Press for "You Called Me Mama." She believes that you don't miss anything you've never had. You must learn to count your blessings and anything that God wants for you, nothing will take it away. "I have been blessed with loving parents and a brother, five beautiful children and five delightful grandchildren. We've had our ups and downs, but we've remained a family who supports, respects and loves one another. This for me, has been my gift from God and what I'll always cherish."

**Sterling, Sheila (Shots)** - I grew up in the Fox River Valley all my life. As I entered my teen age years my mother and I moved out of my grandparent's house. It was tough getting around town now. We didn't own a car, so I had to adjust to the city bus. I started to meet more and more people, and making more friends. At the time, I was enjoying my summer vacations reading "Perry Mason" mysteries. I met a bookstore owner who ran his own newsletter with poetry. It was he who inspired me to write. I started writing songs for the spy shows I enjoyed watching. I wrote songs about criminals and homeless children. This was when I was in 8th grade. I continued writing poems/songs for friends, and other various ideas. As I entered high school I found my true love - Geography. I was inspired the most by Mr. Bock, my geography teacher. Now I continue to write songs about countries. I dedicate my life to him. He passed away on April 20, 1996. As of now, I write my own 30 poem song books (about 10 so far), my own illustrated high school year books, and I love photography. In my future I hope to be a flight attendant, and to continue writing. I'll be attending F.V. Tech, and taking Hospitality, Tourism and Management. I dream of writing a world culture song book and having it published. I am publishing in *Musings, Remembrances,* and *Voices.*

**Stone, Katrina Marie** - Born August 6, 1982 in Pomona, California to William and Catherine Stone. She has one brother, Christian, and one sister, Colleen. She is currently a Senior at Weber High School. She is a member of the Warrior Marching Band and Symphonic Band. In her spare time she enjoys playing the clarinet.

**Sturtevant, Teresa** - Born February 28, 19981 in Harrisburg, Pennsylvania. She is the youngest of five children, one boy and a total of four girls. Teresa's fiancee and her have been really close for the past five years and hoping to be married in the fall of 1999. Their first baby was born on September 3, 1998. Her name is Tiaonna. Along with writing she enjoys ceramics, art, reading and other crafts. She is currently pursuing Veterinary career. With a cat, two dogs, and a horse; taking care of animals is her second passion. Her poem "Shades of Morning" was published in 1997 by Iliad Press. In 1998 she won two President's Recognition for Literary Excellence. The poems were "Skimming the Seas" and "Manhood." She also received an Honorable Mention for "Doomed" in the 1998 summer competition. As a member of the National Authors Registry, she now knows she has the gift of writing.

**Tabner, Sara** - Born November 1, 1985 in Toledo, Ohio to parents, Scott Tabner and Amanda Cross. Sara moved to Goshen , Indiana as a baby after her parents divorced. Living half her childhood in Goshen, Sara grew up with older brother and mom. Sara started reading poetry at a very young age. Reading works of her favorite poet, W.B. Yeats, made her realize she needed to write. W.B. Yeats poems touched her so much, Sara knew she wanted to be able to touch people in the same way. A lot of Sara's poetry comes from her own life experiences and dreams. Recently, at the age of thirteen, Sara has moved back to Ohio with her father Scott, to "Start all over" after having a difficult time living in Indiana. Now, living in the country, Sara has more time to write!

**Thienes, Brenda Marie** - Born November 25, 1978 in Indianapolis, Indiana to parents, Larry and Margarita Thienes. I have lived in Indiana all of my life. I have an older sister Michelle who is twenty-three years old and an older brother David who is twenty-two years old. I have attended a Christian school all of my life. I graduated from Heritage Christian School in 1997. I currently attend Liberty University in Lynchburg, Virginia where I am a sophomore studying public relations. I am also a part of the Liberty University Division I Women's Soccer Team. Things I enjoy are writing, painting, drawing singing, sports of all kinds, and dancing. Hoping to graduate from Liberty University in the year 2001, I have set a lot of goals and dreams for myself. I love helping people and being around people, so a career in that area would suit me. My main hope through is to one day be a wife, a mother and a charity coordinator. But if all else fails, I hope to go where ever my Lord leads me. I have been writing for many years, though this is the first award I have received from the Iliad Press and I hope there will be more to follow.

**Poe, Belle** - Born 1958 in Kansas City, Missouri to parents, Ronald D. and Laura B. Schroll. She graduated high school in 1982 and attended writing and literature classes at Morningside College in Sioux City, Iowa. She married her husband Terry A. Thompson in 1987 and has three daughters. Belle is a member of the SIGB organization and a distinguished member of The International Society of Poets. She has received five Editor's Choice Awards and one Merit Award. In addition to being published in local newspapers, her work has been published by: World of Poetry, The American Poetry Association, The Poetry Guild, The National Library of

Poetry, Sparrowgrass Poetry Forum, and most recently, Iliad Press. She also has an exhibit in The International Poetry Hall of Fame on the web @www.poet.com under Belle Poe. Belle says, "My writings bear future witness to my life."

**Timmons, Je'nell** - Born November 5, 1977 in Los Angeles, California, born in the middle of four children, Je'nell was raised by her mother Julia Vernon, and grandmother Dora Vernon. Je'nell was the winner of the 1996 Art Instruction School Contest. Traveling to many places through out North America, Je'nell graduated from James Madison High School in Atlanta, Georgia in 1996. Currently Je'nell is an aspiring singer/songwriter. Je'nell has been writing songs since age thirteen, She also enjoys writing poetry and short stories. She's received an Honorable Mention Award in the 1998 Summer Iliad Press Literary Awards program, and the 1999 President's Recognition of Literary Excellence from the National Authors Registry for her poem "Ocean".

**Vasquez, Debbi Denette** - Born August 10, 1979 in Laredo, Texas to Thelma Ramirez. Her siblings are her older brother Darren and younger brother Duane. Debbi has lived in Florida, Virginia, and Mississippi and came back to Laredo in 1994. She graduated from J.W. Nixon High School with honors in Laredo. She is in her third year of college and plans to get a degree in Business Administration. Debbi has been writing poetry since she was thirteen. She likes writing about experiences in her life, dealing with true emotions. One of her poems was published in a small book at her college called "La Frontera." She wrote the poem "Narture Is The Mother Of All Beginnings," for her mother who has been the greatest inspiration for her, "without my mother's love, my life would be empty."

**Vincent, Peter C.** - Born June 6, 1936 in Watertown, New York to Elizabeth (living) and Charles (past). Moved via train to Portland, Oregon in 1943. In June 1946, relocated and settled in Anchorage, Alaska. Lived in Alaska since 1946, and obtained B.S.C.E. from U. of A. in Fairbanks in 1959. Married to Donna Lee, 1961; two boys, Lance and Thor; Pamela Lee, 1966; two girls, Kim and Molly. Worked as registered civil engineer until 1980, retiring with disability. Now divorced and writing full-time with publication in anthologies of Pablo Lennis, Famous Poets Society, Sparrowgrass Poetry Forum, Creative Arts & Science Enterprises, and The National Library of Poetry. Contract with Vantage Press, Inc. to publish forty poems, *A Journey Through Time*. Novella of 30,500 words, *The Year of the Dragon*; agent Daniel King to find publisher for the novel. Given Voices of the New Century Award, poem "The Unknown Soldier," fourth place, Sparrowgrass Poetry Forum. Given Editor's Choice by the National Library of Poetry, *A Starlit Night*, *The Promise of Tomorrow*, *Embrace the Morning*, *The Drifting Sands*, *Of Summer's Passing*, *An Eternal Flame*, *Thoughts By Candlelight*, *Outstanding Poets of 1998*, *Boundless Journey*, *Captured Moments*, *Guided by Voices*, *Hearts of Glass*, *Return to Forever*, *The Lyre's Song*, and poem, "Pandora's Box," *A Celebration of Poets*; Iliad Press/The National Authors Registry gave Honorable Mentions for "Yearning," "Tempest in a Teapot," and Tranquility," 1998 Nature Awards Program. Honorable Mention and fourth place for "Bendeth Thy Olive Branch" and "Simplicity," (1999 President's Recognition) published in anthology. Poem "In A Mother's Eyes," *Reaching Other Worlds* by Creative Arts & Science Enterprises. Past hobbies include: hunting and fishing with brothers, David, Lynn, sister Risa; rapping, flying, training dog obedience, oil painting, sketching, and sculpturing soapstone, and skiing. Currently, I consider writing my poems and stories as a non-profit hobby and am interested in current events. In college, American Literature, Advanced Exposition, Magazine Article Writing, and Photography were my initial stimuli; Thoreau was my final afflatus. Past member National Society Professional Engineers, Toastmasters, Dog Obedience Training Club of Anchorage, U. of A. Fairbanks Alumni Association.

**Wadsworth, Sherry** - I am fifteen years old and attending my Sophomore year at Southland High School. I live in the South Plains area of Texas. I am a cheerleader, student council secretary, and an active Junior member of my American Legion Auxiliary Unit. I have written a total of 48 poems since May of 1997. I have had five of them published so far. They include: "Mourning," "A Broken Heart," "The Condemsion," "Never Again," and "One Heart Beat." I thank my father, Bruce Wadsworth who is now deceased and my best friend Stephen Cavanaugh for inspiring my writings.

**Wallace, David** - Born July 26, 1953 in Rockville Centre, New York to parents, Edward and Nancy Wallace. David has three older brothers and two younger sisters, Eddie, Tony, Danny, Trish and Annie. He has lived most of his life on Long Island. He graduated in 1971 from Garden City High School and four years later graduated (Cum laude) from Adelph University, where he was a member of the history and French honor societies. Since 1986 he has worked for Catholic Charities. Most of that time he has been involved with the Food and Nutrition Program, which has assisted many of Long Island's hungry people. David is an avid sports fan, and his favorite team is the New York Rangers. He started writing a few years ago. He has received eight Honorable Mention awards from Cader Publishing, Ltd., and the 1997, 1998 and 1999 President's Recognition for Literary Excellence from The National Authors Registry. He belongs to The First Presbyterian Church of Mineola (his hometown), and he believes that a writer's job is to tell the truth.

**Wambold, Tracie** - Born December 14, 1974 in Waterloo, New York to parents William and Deborah Johnson. Graduating from Waterloo Senior High School in 1993, she attended Cayuga Community College where she earned an Associates degree in early childhood education in 1996. In June of 1997, Tracie married her "childhood crush," Shawn Wambold. Tracie and Shawn have a daughter. Currently Tracie is training for a jewelry department manger position. Tracie has been writing poetry since 1990. She's received a Certificate of Literary Merit in 1993; a high school award, an honorable mention award from World of Poetry in 1990, a Golden Poet 1990 award from World of Poetry, a Golden Poet 1991 award from World of Poetry an honorable mention 1997 award from Iliad Press. "Having many dreams, Tracie hopes to return to college for Journalism."

**Warner, Ruth** - Born October 6, 1923 in Toledo, Ohio to parents David and Pearl Edwards. She graduated from Woodward High School in 1941 and attended Stautzenberger Secretarial School. She married Neal E. Warner of Pontiac, Michigan on October 27, 1945 and has a son, Craig A. Warner. She is a housewife and former secretary retiring in 1954. She is a member of the International Society of Poets, National Authors Registry and International Society of Authors & Artists. Her latest awards are two 1998 Editors Choice Awards from the National Library of Poetry; a 1998 Honorable Mention Award from the National Authors Registry; a 1998 President's Award for Literary Excellence from the National Authors Registry. Her poem, "Capriccio" was published in *Outstanding Poets of 1998* by the National Library of Poetry; "Like An Old Pair Shoes" was published in *The Fabric of Life* by the National Library of Poetry; "A Shadow of Oneself" was published in *Sensations* by Cader Publishing in 1998; "The Gift" was published in *Crossroads* by Cader Publishing in 1998. Some of her hobbies include: collecting sports memorabilia, postcards and figurines.

**Washington, Diana** - Born and raised in St. Louis, Missouri. She was also educated in St. Louis Public School System. She is the oldest child of fourteen children and her parents were the late Mr. and Mrs. Theodore R. Lucas. She is a family oriented person and a devoted Christian who believes and trust in God. She also loves mankind and enjoys working with people. One of her many pleasures are working with children in her church, community school, and other social settings. Another enjoyment for her is helping adults, family and friends to achieve goals they have set and to be all that they can be. Her hobbies are reading, writing, crocheting and volunteering at the Inglis House. She is an active Missionary in her church The Victory Deliverance Temple, Inc. and other community activities with children and adults. She is a widow, the mother of four beautiful children: Bettye, Oliver, Diane and Nikki; six grandchildren: Theodore, DeYanna, Stephen, Kecia, Christine and Alonzo of whom she loves very dearly. Her motivation for her writing is to help, encourage others and herself to be the best you can be. To let your inter beauty shine from within to without! Her mother often wrote speeches for her to read at church on special occasions. She has plans in the future to do a complete book of poetry and also a couple of books.

**Wass, Vance M.** - Born December 12, 1961 in Chamberlain, South Dakota to parents Leland and Marlis Wass. Having moved to Hot Springs, South Dakota during his teen years, he excelled in sports and learned the ethics of hard work. Graduating from Hot Springs High School in 1980, he moved to Douglas, Wyoming where he met is soul mate and wife of eighteen years at the Wyoming State Fair. They married in 1989. Leaving Wyoming after spending seven years in the oil fields, he pursued coaching college basketball in Georgia and Alabama. He then went overseas to coach professional basketball for three years. In 1993 he returned to South Dakota and worked for the railroad and built log homes. In 1995, Vance and his wife ventured north to Alaska. Currently he is on the North Slope, "roughnecking" for an oil company. Vance has been writing poetry since 1995. His poem "Sister Summer" received the 1999 President's Recognition of Literary Excellence, Honorable Mention Award from the Iliad Press. Vance says, "I write what I can't say, says his heart."

**Wayne, Desarae Lynn** - Born August 29, 1982 in Gatesville, Texas. She moved to different states, but settled in Richmond, Virginia at age three. At age six she was adopted by Douglas and Carol Wayne. Desarae is also known by most as Daisy, a nickname she received as a counselor. Desarae is a junior at St. Gertrude High School in Richmond. She is an avid reader and enthusiastic writer. Some favorite physical activities are repelling, white water rafting, and horse back riding. In eighth grade, Desarae received an award titled "Poet Laureate." She excels in English, due to her skills in creative writing. She started collecting her works in the eighth grade. Her collections not only contain poems and short stories, but also sketches and paintings. Desarae has been published in school magazines since sixth grade. She's received an honorable mention from the Iliad Press and the 1999 President's Recognition for Literary Excellence form the National Authors Registry. Her poem "Untitled" has been published in another Iliad Press book. Desarae says, "Writing is my way of escaping the stress and issues of everyday life. I fully intend to keep writing, even if it's just for me."

**West, Meghan Orelene** - Was born in the country of Spain at Torrejon AFB, near Madrid, on October 16, 1981, so this makes the author dual-nationality, Spanish/American. Her father just retiring from the United States Air Force has, over the years, toured much of the world with Meghan and the rest of the family; Spain, Utah, England, New Mexico, Washington state, Florida, plus other countries and states besides those where they had been stationed. At eleven, Meghan whose writing ability is inherited from grandmother and namesake, Orelene Inez Golay Petersen, began writing poetry in school and entered into and won her first poetry competition. Meghan has won publication honors on over fifteen poems in anthology books: *Anthology of Poetry by Young Americans, Whispers, Interludes, A Celebration of Florida's Young Poets, American Poetry Annual, Beginnings, Sensations, Moments, Outstanding Achievements, Pathways,* and *Distinctions of Excellence.* 1998 found Meghan with Honorable Mentions on four poems, and by 1999 three awards of the *President's Award for Literary Excellence.* Meghan has written for her high school newspaper and has had other works in different publications. With Meghan's father being a professional artist, she has formed an interest in arts and has won different recognitions and awards for her art. At the moment, she is finishing an art course that will provide her with an Associates Degree in art. At seventeen, and a senior in high school, Meghan is in the Running Start Program, and so is completing her senior year while also doing her freshman year of college. Since the age of four, Meghan has taken ballet and played the piano. She has added to her music learning the guitar, harmonica, and drums. Between school, music, art, dancing, and writing, Meghan stays very busy. She also loves to fish, swim, ice-skate, bowl, golf, cross-stitch, and tour with her family. Meghan dreams of someday becoming a marine biologist and helping out the environment. She also hopes to be able to use her writing knowledge to write to the public to help them become more aware of problems concerning any of God's creations.

**Westmaas, Rupert Harvy Desmond** - Born British Guiana, South America, now the Republic of Guyana on 4th May 1920. The 5th of 8 boys (No sister, my second wife said that's why I don't understand women), I attended public schools and college. Retired Guyana Public Service. Emigrated to Canada November 1977. Canadian Citizen 1981. With my first wife we begat three boys and two girls. Two of my children and my wife each died under separate tragic circumstances. Fifteen years after her death, I remarried and begat a son and a daughter (now in their thirties). In all, 7 children, 9 grands and 5 great grands with whom I romp happily. Membership Brotherhood of Man. Hobbies, Reading, Riting but not Rithmetic, but of course, Lyric Poetry. My book is titled *130 - Lyric Poems - On Controversial Subjects - Philosophy, Love and Humour.* Have a few Literary Excellence Awards. Have successfully dodged the twinges of the hinges by Rollerblading. Retired December 1996 after eleven years at Switchboard/Reception Desk of "The" Private Club of Ottawa.

**Whetzel, James Allan** - Born November 1, 1946 in Mariemont, Ohio to the parents of William and Edith. James is an Investigator for the Commissioner of the Revenue for the City of Norfolk, Virginia. He is a member of the International Society of Poets and recently had six poems published. James' fiancee is compiling his many writings into a book, while James continues to write poetry and has started a novel.

**Wilhelm, Dale** - Born January 28, 1970. After graduating from George Washington High School, I entered th United States Army in 1988. I served in Desert Storm and Desert Shield, returning home in March 1992. I lived in Houston, Texas from August 1999 until November 1994 when I returned back to my home city of Indianapolis. I am employed by Sears National Tire and Battery. I have put together the poetry books, *The Boys in Black: From the Shadows to the Light* for fellow co-authors, Alice Deque, James Hambrick and Martha Diane Wilhelm. The book is being presented for publication. My co-author's and I share the pen name: U.R. Best. Together we are writing a novel *The Snake Charmer*, which will be completed by December 1999.

**Wilhelm, Martha Diane** - Born April 23, 1951. I went to work for Indiana Bell upon graduating from George Washington High School in June 1969. I attended Ivy Technical State College before retiring from Ameritech in January 1992. I have four children: Monica, Michelle, Dale and Benjamin. I currently share the pen name: U.R. Best, with my son Dale, my nephew James and my friend Alicia. Together, the four of us have written poems for the poetry book *The Boys in Black: From the Shadows to the Light*, in which Dale has presented for publication. I am presently co-ordinating a novel, *The Snake Charmer* which will be completed by December 1999. My co-authors and I hope to intrigue readers with our work.

**Wright, Jack V.** I came here, born or hatched, I know not which, in November, Nineteen Hundred and Twenty Eight. During the peaceful age of the switch, when respect for elders was accepted, not for children to debate. I was given the hard to pronounce name of Jack Wright. From the cradle I was really dumb, to think I was very bright. My honest hard working father died when I was two. Leaving six children with mother, to remain forever true, not a sad life for children growing up on the farm. A struggling mother remarried, to have six more true to form. Growing up with the wish to put everything on paper, never forgetting my childhood teachings, from them I could never taper. Fighting my country's battles, not because I was brave, but the right thing to do, if it led to my grave. Never understood contemporary poetry or modern art, old fashion in character, loving the past, probably still riding the cart. One thing I have learnt without much education, is to honor all human beings with full dedication. At the golden age of seventy how far am I from the throne. "Please tell me young educators are my deep thoughts so wrong."

**Yang, Nancy** - Born on November 19, 1986 in Manhattan, New York to parents Zi Jiang Yang and Judy Zheng who are now divorced. Being the one with the most fashion sense and wearing the most stylish clothes, she has been pretty popular in school. She went to elementary school, P.S. 64 and currently going to Junior High School 210. She lives with her grandparents in Queens, New York. Her best friend is Maria Deleon, she means a lot to her. Wanting to be a fashion designer and a part time writer, she spends a lot of time drawing and writing. She also spends time on America Online and listening to music. She loves R & B and rap. Her favorite singers and role models are Madonna and Mariah Carey. Her poem "Night after Night" is published in *Distinctions of Excellence* by Iliad Press. Nancy says, "Being asian doesn't mean that I'm not as good looking and popular as other girls you just have to work hard for what you want!" Her address is (if you want to write to her): 97-36 75th St., Ozone Park, New York 11416.

**Yeager, Deborah Ann** - I am from Nashville, Tennessee. I was born and raised in Nashville. I have been reading poetry all of my life, but I've only been writing poetry since December, 1994. I've had several poems published. I love to write poems for other people's birthdays and anniversaries, I love to make people smile. In my hobbies that I like to do include: tennis, bowling, movies, goint out to dinner, travel, I like to learn everything I can about computers, love to go to gatherings with single people, I love children, singing, writing, going riding, and writing down church signs and putting them in my books of sayings. I also love to enter poetry contests and seeing my poetry in print. I hope it helps people when they read it, it helps me to express in words how I feel; and I'm very thankful when someone understands and gets something out of it. It makes me feel good, I hope I can write more poetry in the future that will help others.

**Ziska, Nancy** - Born October 31, 1952 in Cleveland, Ohio to parents Albert and Lucille Ziska. Single, and currently residing in Parma Heights, Ohio. Graduated from West Tech High, and attended Community College. Employed at United Way Services-Payroll Clerk for twenty-nine years. Have been writing poetry for only one and a half years, and received several Editor's Choice Awards from the National Library of Poetry; the 1999 President's Recognition of Literary Excellence for "Love Has Flown Away" by the National Authors Registry. Member of American Business Women's Associations; received Woman of the Year Award for 1998. Hope to publish my first book of poetry before the year 2000. "I enjoy writing poetry, I like to envision what can be. Reach out to capture your dream for others to see, now close your eyes, and relax with me."

# Alphabetical Index by Author

## A

Abbott, Kristi DeShannon 1, 109
Adam, Monique 2
Adams, Janet M. 1
Akus, Laura Anna 1
Alexander, Kate 1
Allen, Amanda Christine 1
Allen, Jude M. 1, 109
Allen, Opal 2
Allen, Sindy 2
Alluri, Sri 2
Alvarez, Monica 2
Amerise, Charles Patrick 3
Amnotte, Sherry L. 3
Anderson, Rachel 3
Andren, Delores A. 3
Andrzejewski, Jennifer 3
Annarino, Amanda M. 4
Anstoetter, Sara 4, 109
Aritonovich, Dana 4
Ashbeck, Barbara 4, 109
Auferoth, Jillann 4, 109

## B

Baase, Jorden M. 4
Bachhuber, Lynn E. 5
Baer, Stephanie 5
Bagley, Renee 5
Baker, Kari 5, 109
Baldwin, Brianna K. 5, 109
Banks R.A., Hope 5
Barraza, Nancy Eseberre 6
Barrett, Graceann 6
Barsic, Joe 6, 109
Baugh, Mandy 6
Bauzo, David 6, 109
Bavington, Bette A. 7
Baxter, Lilli M. 7, 109
Bayer, Frank 7
Beauregard, Jennifer 7
Beck, Danielle M. 7
Belle Poe 97, 124
Beltz, Nikole E. 7
Berezkin, Gala 8
Berggren, Shelly 8
Berrard, Krystal A. 8
Blackmon, Shelby Y. 8
Blackwell, Lindsey Nicole 8, 109
Blaine, Jesse 8
Blake, Patricia Payzant 9, 110
Blanks, Amanda 9
Bodley, Antonie M. 9
Boileau-Labrie, Louise 9
Borders, Denise 10, 110
Borquist, Luan 10
Boverhof, Jennifer 10
Bowden, Virginia Ann 10
Boyle, Mary Frances 10
Boyza, Dave 11
Bradbury, Louise M. 11, 110
Brandenburg, Kandi 11
Brandt, Rachel 11
Braun, Jessica 11
Brenciforte, Gene R. 11
Brickman, Sarah 12
Bridges, Shelly 12
Brigham, Elladean 12
Briguglio, Jr., Basil 12
Brooke, Crystal 12
Brooks, Matthew G. 12, 110
Brown, Chris 13, 110
Brown, Jackie 13
Brown, Mary Cathleen 13, 110
Bryant, Terrea 13
Buccigross, Nikki 14
Buckley, Keith 14
Bulluck, Jamie Lynn 14, 110
Burnazaki, Katie 13
Burns, Liza 14
Burnside, Wanda J. 14, 110

## C

Capuano, Susan 15
Carlson, Sue Lueck 15, 111
Carney, John T. 15
Carpenter, Kaye 15
Carver, Barbara 15
Case, Gregory Andrew 16
Cave, Sheila M. 16, 111
Cellini, Lottie 16, 111
Chapman, Debra Anne 16
Chen, Melanie Anne 16
Cherepanov, Dasha 16, 111
Chesham, Jean E. 17
Chikezie, Roxy 17, 111
Childers, Chris 17
Chilkotowsky, Mary 17
Chilson, Carol 17
Christenson, Jessica 17
Chung, Sophia 18
Cibbarelli, Bill 18
Clark, Christine 18
Clark, Jesse D. 18
Cleaveland, Burt 18
Clemens, Sabrena 18
Clontz, Stephenie 18
Cochran, Donald 19, 111
Coghlan, Shae 19
Colao, Sarah Marie 19
Collins, Jessie 19
Collins, Jolene 19
Collins, Robert E. 19
Colombo, Beverly 20
Conrad, Danielle M. 20
Cook, Cynthia A. 20, 111
Cook, Lisa 20
Cooper, Carolyn Jean 20, 112
Cooper, Lola 21, 112
Cooper, Neva 21
Cope, Holly 21
Corona, Ethel R. 21, 112
Cote, Jennifer Renae 21, 112
Coulter, Kimberlee 21
Cox, Angela 22
Coyle, Amanda 22
Craig, Robert 22
Craig Jr., Bennie G. 22
Cranor, Larry W. 23
Crichlow, Eleanor L. 23
Crossley, Dawn 23, 112
Crow, Dawn 23
Curtis, Pamela J. 23

## D

Dalrymple, Crystal 23
Daly, Desiree B. 24
Dancy, Brandy 24
Dane, Angela 24
Daniels, Vernon 24
Davis, John Clifton 24
Dawson, Ronald K. 25
DeLarre, Linnette 25
DeMeno, Maura 25
Deaton, Howard A. 25, 112
DeForest, J.D. 53
Dehlinger, Barbara W. 25
Delgado, Andrea Lee 25
Dembroski, Lauren 25
Deschenes, Bryanna 26
Dickerson, Brandy 26
Donovan, Kathleen 26
Doty, Jalleh 26
Dovie, Victoria C. 26
Drummond, Vanessa 26
Drye, Erica 27
Dumont, Elizabeth M. 27, 112
Dunlap, Eva Marie Ann 27
Dunn, Michael P. 28
Dutcher, Christine S. 27

## E

Earthchild, Feather 27
Eckman, Lisa 28
Elder, Kathryn Ann 28, 112
Ellingson, Rick 28
Ellis, Rick 28
Emblom, Lindsay 29, 113
Emerson, Mark S. 28, 113
English, Monica 29
Erickson, Sally 29, 113
Erney, Kristin 29
Estelle, Doris S. 29
Evans, Lynda 29

## F

Fabiaschi, Mara 29
Fahnestock, Amber 30
Failla, M.J. 30
Favaroth-Peters, Jason 30, 113
Feith, Donalda 30
Felmet, Rachelle 31
Ferguson, Jaclyn 31
Fernandez, Jenna 30
Fields, Melody L. 30
Fischer, Danielle 31
Fisher, Sharon A. 32, 113
Fleming, Bruce A. 32
Fox, Alanna F. 32
Fox, Jennifer 32
Franzen, Linda M. 33
Frazee, Kira D. 33
Frederick, Adrian 33, 113
Freeman, Christy 33, 113
Freeman, Josetta 33, 113
Fritz, Karen K. 33

## G

Galati, Jacqueline Ann 34
Gallardo, Corinne M. 34
Gallen, Susan 34, 114
Garayua, Melissa 34
Garcia, Celeste Perez 34
Garcia Jr., Joseph 35
Garges Jr., Philip R. 34
Garner, Jaime B. 35
Garrett, Deborah 35
Gartshleyn, Jenny 35
Gaskins, Jennifer L. 35
Gemmill, Krista 36
George, Betty J. 36, 114
Gevargiz, Linda 36, 114
Gibbons, Lara 36
Gibbons, Stefani 36, 114
Gibbs, Kara Nicole 36, 114
Gibson, Jennifer 37
Gideon, Dru 37
Gilliam, Leon 37, 114
Goede, Heather Jyll 37
Gohn, Becky 37
Golden, Donald M. 37, 114
Goldsberry, Michael N. 37
Gonzales, Gretchen Cameros 38
Gordon, Peter 38, 114
Grattan, Ruth M. 38
Green, Sabrina Melissa 38
Griffin, Whit 38, 114
Grumbling, Carol Ann 38
Gurney, Mary Ann 39
Gusler, Anne 39

## H

Hagerlin, Jan 39
Haigler, Elizabeth K. 39
Hairston, Geneva 39
Hall, Brock 40, 114
Hall, Sabrina 40
Hamlin, Lana 40
Hammel, Erin 40
Haney, Elizabeth 40
Hansen, Anna 40
Hanson, Ed 41, 115
Harnett, C. Cornelius 41
Harris, Blaise 41, 115
Harris, Edyth V. 41, 115
Harrison, Karen Ann 42
Hartle III, Thomas J. 41
Hartzell, Crystal Lynne 42
Hashem, Melinda 42, 115
Hatch, Kristen 42
Hauser, Christy 42
Hawkinson, Patricia Lynn 42
Haywood, Phillip W. 42
Hazel, Rebecca K. 43
Headman, Rachel 43
Headrick, Carolyn M. 43
Hehn, Danielle 43
Heiskanen, Matt 43
Heiss, E. Renee 43, 115
Hemmingfeld, Karen 44
Henson, Dian F. 44, 115
Herbert IV, Charles 44, 115
Herzing, Krista 44
Hettrick, Sarah 44
Hiddleson, Heather 45
Hirsch, Mary E. 45
Hobby, Doreen 45, 116
Hodgdon, Liz 45
Holcomb, Denise M. 45
Hoover, Melissa Elena 45
Hoover, Tiffany 46, 116
Hopkins, Tracy Marie Haven 46
Howell, Gerry L. 46
Huffman, Kenneth 46
Humphries, Liz 46
Hunsberger, Sidona Marie 46, 116
Hutson, Linda P. 47

## I

Ihasz, Oliver D. 47, 116
Irwin, Sarah 47

## J

Jackson, Alicia 47
Jackson, Marva Olivia 47
Jackson, Rhonda 48
Jacobsen, Debbie 48
Jaeger, Jaclyn M. 48, 116
Janoski, Maria C. 48, 116
Janson, Jessie 49
Jarvis, Erin M. 49, 116
Jeetun, Veenaye Kumar 49, 116
Jim, Melanie 49
Jimenez, Tony 49
Johnson, Carole 50, 116
Johnson, Heather 50, 117
Johnson, Heather N. 50
Johnson, Jill Fahey 50
Johnson, John D. 50
Johnson, Olivia 51, 117
Johnson, Victoria 51
Jones, Annie M. 51

Jones, Shirley A. 51
Joseph, Fitzroy G. 51, 117

# K

Kai, Cyrus 60
Kallenbach, Sara 52, 117
Kaminski, Dorothy 52
Karnes, Kathy 52
Keen-Smith, B. Pauline 93
Keller, Megan C. 52
Kelly, Brian 52
Keown, Theresa L. 53
Khakoo, Salza 53
Kimminau, Joan A. 53, 117
Kinley, Jolene 53
Kitt, Tom 53
Kiwanuka, Ba 54
Kiyono, Mika 54, 117
Klann, Ryan-Iver T. 54
Knutson, John 54
Kordalchuk, Crystal 54
Koski, Donna Kay 54
Koslucher, Katie 54
Kosoff, Flora M. 55, 117
Kostyra, Charles Ken 56
Kozuchowsky, Heather 55
Ksepko, Irena 55, 117
Kuntz, Amy 55
Kurylo, Sota 10

# L

LaPre, Sandra Kay 56
La-Touche, Monique 57, 117
Lademora, Mira 56
Land, Julie 56
Larsen, Barbara Ann 56
Larsen, Meghan 56
Lashier, Susan M. 56
Lazarovich, Regina 57
Lee, Jennifer So-Young 57
Leong, Christine 57
Leshley, Ami 57
Lewis, Louise 58
Lewis, Michelle 58
Lewis, Stewart 58
Li, Stacy 59
Light, Lindsey A. 58
Liliane, Li-Cho 58
Lipson, Danielle 59
Lockman, Margaret 59
Lofton, Synnikaverse 59, 118
Lombardi, Patricia 61
Lomen, Alice Rundell 59
Lorenzen, Jade Marie 60
Lotz, Sue 60, 118
Loveland, Jenny 60
Lowery, Amee 60
Luna, Yashira 61

# M

MacAllister II, Alicia C. 61
MacLennan, Ian 61
Maddox, Juanita A. 61, 118
Madruga, Lourdes 61
Malon, Diana L. 62, 118
Mandrillo, Germano 62
Mannis, Casey 62
Marano, Michelle 62
Marchand, Kelly J. 63
Markert, Cory 63
Marshall, Austin 63
Marshall, B. Lynette 63
Martens, Sunny 63
Martin, Sarah 64, 118
Martinez, Katrina 63
Massengill, Robert D. 64
Matthews, Mark 64
Matyasik, Christiana Angelique 64
Mays, Jon 65
McCague, Mandy 65
McCormack, Dona L. 65, 119

McCormick, Jessica 65
McGaw-Sullivan, Margaret 66
McGran-Reber, Maureen Ellen 66, 119
McGuire, Barbara 66, 119
McKay, Darlene 66
McLemore, Don S. 66
McMickle, Maria H. 66
McMillen, Marieta L. 67
McNeely, Robin Renee' 67, 119
Meehan, Jessie 67, 119
Miles, Kyla 67
Milkes, A.R. 67
Miller, Ken 68, 119
Millison, Marjorie 68
Misoyianis, Shelli 68
Montgomery, Amanda 68
Monticelli, Joseph S. 68
Moon, Crystal R. 68
Moore, Amy M. 69
Moore, Sarah Anne 69
Moore, Sheila 69
Morgan, LaDonna 69
Morris, Margaret E. 69
Moss, Tanya 70
Mosten, Jordana 70, 119
Mourashkin, Boris 70, 119
Mrozek, Erin Kathryn 70
Mula, Suzanne Marie 70
Munson, Ruie 71
Murphy, Joan 70
Myers, Alice G. 71
Myers, Melissa 71
Myles, Jacqueline S. 71

# N

Nagelberg, Barbara 71
Nations, Lynn E. 72, 120
Nelson, Teri 72
Nibley, Spence 72
Nielsen, Dana L. 72, 120
Nonnast, Elizabeth Anne 72
Novozilova, Sofia 72

# O

O'Bryan, Lauren 73
O'Bryant, Cathy 73, 120
O'Neal, Lillian M. 73, 120
Oakes, Jennifer M. 73
Oldham, Paige Marie 73, 120
Oquendo, James 74
Orendorff, Rachel L. 74
Osho, Idayat A. 74
Osunsan, Olutayo 74
Otegui, Jorge 74, 121

# P

Pamin, Diana Dolhancyk 75
Panzek, Ann Marie 75
Patchen, Dale R. 75
Patel, Rachana 75
Paterson, Gloria 4, 121
Patterson, Amy 75
Patterson, Holly Sue 75
Patterson, Patricia E. 76
Paul, Bonita Arlene 76
Pearson, Erika 75
Pederson, Tamara 76, 121
Peets, Erica I. 76, 121
Pegg, Mary Christina 76, 121
Peirce, James Walter 77
Peoples, Helen M. 77
Perea, Elaina C. 77
Perez, Diane 77
Perez, Michelle Y. 77
Pering, Melanie 76
Perry, Holly Michele 77
Perry, Tamara 78
Peters, Andrea 78
Peterson, Jenny 78
Peterson, Marion M. 78, 121

Peterson, S. Doreen 78
Petrilli, Ryan 78, 121
Phillips, Heather 78, 121
Phillips, Steve 79
Phounsavath, Chinetana 79
Pickel, Juanita 79
Pickens, Rebecca 79
Pierce, Jennifer A. 79
Pierce, Laura 79
Pierce, Mysti 80
Plourde, Anne 80
Plunkett, Joseph "C.J." 80, 121
Poirrier, Annette M. 80
Pollard, Linnie L. 80
Poskriakov, Sergei 81
Poulsen, Cherie 81
Pratt, Alma K. 81
Presley, Robyn 81
Price, Mary D. 81
Pritchett, Michael T. 82, 121
Przechocki, Julie 82
Purdie, Aretia 82
Putman, Marie 82

# R

Rader, Cheryl 83
Radula, Natalia 83, 122
Ramick, Ricky 83, 122
Ray, Brenda 83
Rea, Julie 83, 122
Read, Crystal 83, 122
Reid, Rose 84
Renate, Ursula 84, 122
Rentschler, Clare Chandler 84
Richard, Jeremy 84
Richter, Amanda 85
Rider, Georgette 84
Rizzo, Lisa 85
Roan, Robert 85
Roberts, Angela 85
Roberts, Heather 85, 122
Robinson, Mireille 85
Robles, Violeta E. 86
Rodriguez, Anita G. 86
Rogers, Raymond 86
Rogers, Rozanne 86, 122
Romano, Melissa M. 86
Romanoff, Kent E. 86
Rose, Lisa 87
Rosenberg, Michelle J. 87
Ross, Nicki Lynn 87
Rutherford, Ronald 87, 123
Rutter, Marilyn B. 87
Rywelski, Elizabeth L. 87

# S

Saghir, Hadiya A. 88
Sanders, Kalene Denise 88, 123
Sanders, Marsha 88
Santiago, Miguel A. 88, 123
Sass, Jennifer 88
Schafer, Robert 89
Scheuffele, Carl S. 89
Schick, Barbara 89, 123
Schiefelbein, Justin 89, 123
Schmalz, Nicholas 90, 123
Scholl, Margaret 89
Schram, Alissa 89
Schwartz, Aaron 90, 123
Scott, Eva O. 90
Semancik, Rachel 90
Seras, Taryn K. 90
Serna, Tiffney 90
Shackelford, Dawn Marie 90
Shafer, Shealene 91
Sharman, Heather 91
Sharp, Joan D. 91
Shealy, Audrey 91
Sherman, Mike 91
Sherman, Ronni 91
Shipman, Venus 92
Shumate, Amanda 92

Sikora, John R. 92
Simkanich, Pamela Jean 92
Simms, Wendy Ann 92
Sinha, M. M. 92
Skwarcan, April 93
Slagle, Eugenia L. 93
Smeathers, Kristyn 93
Smith, Linda 93
Sole, Anna Milan 93
Somers, Tasha Anne 94
Spikes, Patricia White 94, 123
Springer, Syreeta 94
Stanley, Carrie Marie 95
Staton, Diane E. 94, 123
Steckler, Julie 95
Stephan, Dana 95
Sterling, Sheila 95, 124
Stewart, Karin 95
Stewart, W. Forres 95
Stines, Yvelette Monique 96
Stone, Katrina 94, 124
Strimple, Leona 96
Sturtevant, Teresa 96, 124
Swereda, Angela Leah 96

# T

Tabner, Sara 96, 124
Tanner, Jessica 96
Taqi, Sara 96
Taylor, Dalian R. 97
Thames, Jennifer 97
The Poet 60, 118
The Raven 65
Thienes, Brenda M. 97, 124
Thomas, Michelle 97
Thompson, Shannon 97, 98
Thorn, D. J. 98
Timmons, Je'Nell 98, 124
Tinay, Robin M. 98
Torlen, Carrol 57
Torres, Carlos C. 98
Toscano, Angela A. 99

# V

Valerino, Renee 99
Valerius, Tina 99
Vasquez, Debbi Denette 99, 124
Veysey, Kathleen 99
Vincent, Bonnie 99
Vincent, Peter C. 99, 124
Vollenberg, Antonius A.H. 100

# W

Wacker, Jody L. 100
Wadsworth, Sherry M. 100, 124
Wadzinski, Mary B. 100
Walker, Brad 100
Wallace, David 100, 125
Wambold, Tracie L. 101, 125
Ward, Erika 101
Ward, Stevie Nicole 101
Ware, Sherry D. 101
Warner, Ruth 101, 125
Warth, Holly 101
Washington, Diana 102, 125
Wass, Vance M. 102, 125
Watford, Barbara 102
Watkins, Martha S. 102
Watson, Nicole 102
Wayne, Desarae Lynn 102, 125
Weatherspoon, Krista 103
Weaver, David Ray 103
Weilacher, Kenn 103
Welch, Robert M. 103
Wells, Sharon Irene 103
Wertzler, Jessica 103
West, Meghan Orelene 104, 125
Westlake, LaRea Annette 104
Westmaas, Rupert H.D. 104, 125
Whetzel, James A. 104, 126
Wilde, Rebecca J. 104

Wilhelm, Dale 104, 126
Wilhelm, Martha Diane 105, 126
Wilhelm, Michelle 105
Wilhite, Lisa 105
Williams, Billie A. 105
Williams, Nicole 105
Wilson, Kaya 105
Winokur, Rachel 105
Winstead, Kevin 106
Winters, Suzanne J. 106, 115
Wlodyka, Gary Paul 106
Wolf, Thunder 82, 122
Wood, Tammy 106
Workman, Jerome 106
Wright, Jack V. 107, 126

# X

Xu, Tina 106

# Y

Yang, Nancy 107, 126
Yeager, Deborah Ann 107, 126
YipTong, Mimi 107
Young, Y. H. 106
Yudin, Vlad 108

# Z

Zero, Kristen 108
Ziesmer, Megan 108
Zilinskas, Stefania 108
Zimmerman, Larry P. 106
Ziska, Nancy 108, 126
Zollinger, Rachel A. 108